A

BARTÓK

AND HIS WORLD

BARTÓK
AND HIS WORLD

EDITED BY
PETER LAKI

•

PRINCETON UNIVERSITY PRESS

Copyright © 1995 by Princeton University Press

Published by Princeton University Press, 41 William Street,
Princeton, New Jersey 08540
In the United Kingdom: Princeton University Press,
Chichester, West Sussex

Library of Congress Cataloging-in-Publication Data

Bartók and his world / edited by Peter Laki.
p.   cm. — (Bard Music Festival series)
Includes bibliographical references and index.
ISBN 0-691-00634-2 (cl : alk. paper). — ISBN 0-691-00633-4 (pbk. : alk. paper)
1. Bartók, Béla, 1881–1945. I. Laki, Peter. II. Series.
ML410.B26B272 1995
780'.92—dc20   95-13368

This book has been composed in Baskerville
by The Composing Room of Michigan, Inc.

Music typeset by Don Giller

Princeton University Press books are printed on acid-free paper and meet the
guidelines for permanence and durability of the Committee on Production
Guidelines for Book Longevity of the Council on Library Resources

Printed in the United States of America
by Princeton Academic Press

3 5 7 9 10 8 6 4 2

Designed by Laury A. Egan

Contents

Preface vii

Acknowledgments ix

PART I

ESSAYS

Out of Hungary: Bartók, Modernism, and
the Cultural Politics of Twentieth-Century Music 3
LEON BOTSTEIN

Why Is a Bartók Thematic Catalog Sorely Needed? 64
LÁSZLÓ SOMFAI

The Gallows and the Altar: Poetic Criticism and
Critical Poetry about Bartók in Hungary 79
PETER LAKI

Bartók's Reception in America, 1940–1945 101
TIBOR TALLIÁN
TRANSLATED BY PETER LAKI

Bluebeard as Theater: The Influence of Maeterlinck
and Hebbel on Balázs's Bluebeard Drama 119
CARL LEAFSTEDT

The Miraculous Mandarin: Melchior Lengyel, His Pantomime,
and His Connections to Béla Bartók 149
VERA LAMPERT

Bartók and Stravinsky: Respect, Competition, Influence,
and the Hungarian Reaction to Modernism in the 1920s 172
DAVID E. SCHNEIDER

· v ·

Contents

PART II

WRITINGS BY BARTÓK

Travel Reports from Three Continents: A Selection
of Letters from Béla Bartók   203
TRANSLATED BY PETER LAKI

Béla Bartók: An Interview by Dezső Kosztolányi   228
TRANSLATED BY DAVID E. SCHNEIDER

A Conversation with Béla Bartók   235
TRANSLATED BY DAVID E. SCHNEIDER
AND KLÁRA MÓRICZ

PART III

WRITINGS ABOUT BARTÓK

Recollections of Béla Bartók   243
TRANSLATED BY PETER LAKI AND BALÁZS DIBUZ

A Change in Style   276
EDWIN VON DER NÜLL
TRANSLATED BY SUSAN GILLESPIE

Bartók's Third String Quartet   278
THEODOR ADORNO
TRANSLATED BY SUSAN GILLESPIE

Bartók's Foreign Tour   282
ALADÁR TÓTH
TRANSLATED BY DAVID E. SCHNEIDER
AND KLÁRA MÓRICZ

Two Bartók Obituaries   290
BENCE SZABOLCSI
TRANSLATED BY PETER LAKI

A Selection of Poems Inspired by Béla Bartók   296
TRANSLATED BY PETER LAKI
AND CLAIRE LASHLEY

Index of Names and Compositions   307

List of Contributors   313

Preface

Fifty years have passed since the death of Béla Bartók. Many of Bartók's works have earned a firm place in the standard repertoire, and consensus places him among this century's greatest composers, along with Igor Stravinsky and the three masters of the New Viennese School. Yet it seems that on the whole he has proven a more elusive figure than his great contemporaries. In the introduction to his recent *Bartók Companion*, Malcolm Gillies observes how separate the historical and analytical approaches to Bartók's music have been and notes that Hungarian scholars have tended to favor the former and Westerners the latter.[1] It appears as though different people saw different aspects of the man and his oeuvre; there has arguably been insufficient communication between the various approaches. Much important work has been done in recent years in several different areas of detail (biography, cultural history, analysis, ethnomusicology), and a new overall picture is waiting to be put together. A book that will play the same role in the 1990s as Halsey Stevens's classic life-and-works did in the 1950s is badly needed.

The present volume is obviously not that book. By definition it cannot be, for it is a collection of more detailed studies and of selected documents. But it may contribute to a future synthesis in that these studies attempt to familiarize readers of English with a Bartók usually hidden from them by the language barrier. That barrier, I am convinced, explains at least in part why the Western scholars have often focused on the analytical aspects: many historical sources have been available only in Hungarian. Therefore, the sociocultural context, which in the case of other major composers has been much more easily integrated into the musicological discourse, has often been left to specialists working in Hungary. The books of József Ujfalussy, Tibor Tallián, and János Kárpáti have all now been published in English translation, but they were originally written primarily with a Hungarian audience in mind—an audience that had long been exposed not only to Bartók's music but also to the folk songs that are so central to his style. In addition, viewed from a Hungarian standpoint, these excellent scholarly works are only the tip of an iceberg whose lower layers are formed by literally millions of words of secondary literature ranging from countless newspaper articles for nonspecialized readers to such items as Júlia Székely's often-reprinted biography for young people, *Elindultam szép hazámból* ("I departed my beautiful fatherland"— the first line of a folk song made famous by Bartók, here applied to his own emigration, dramatized and sentimentalized in the book).[2] Although its scholarly and literary value may be limited, this book provided generations of young readers with an early introduction to Bartók's life and works that readers outside Hungary never had.

On the international scene, Bartók is only one of the century's greatest composers, not the center of the musical universe as he is in Hungary. For this reason, much that can be taken for granted in the composer's native country must be spelled out, or presented differently, to an international audience. In particular, such topics as Bartók's connections to Hungarian literary figures and his reception in his homeland must receive more attention in the West than they have in the past if Bartók and his world are to be properly understood by Western readers and listeners.

Therefore, large parts of the present volume concentrate on aspects of Bartók that are intimately connected to Hungary and the Hungarian language. Carl Leafstedt's essay deals with Béla Balázs, the librettist of the first two of Bartók's stage works, while Vera Lampert discusses Menyhért Lengyel, the author of *The Miraculous Mandarin*. Parts II and III contain translations of letters and documents previously available only in Hungarian.

The two essays mentioned explore some of Bartók's most important literary interactions. Further intellectual and musical links with his contemporaries are addressed in David Schneider's study and in the three essays on Bartók's reception history, by Leon Botstein, Tibor Tallián, and myself, each dealing with different times and places during Bartók's lifetime and afterward. Finally, the essay by László Somfai presents the Bartók thematic catalog currently in progress and surveys some of the most significant accomplishments and lacunae in current Bartók scholarship.

Peter Laki

NOTES

1. Malcolm Gillies, *The Bartók Companion* (London, 1993), pp. xi–xiii.
2. Júlia Székely, *Elindultam szép hazámból* (Budapest, 1968).

Acknowledgments

Many people—more than I can acknowledge within the space of a single page—have helped with this book in ways large and small. First of all, I wish to thank Leon Botstein for devoting the 1995 Bard Festival to Bartók and providing the initial impulse for this volume. I am grateful to the authors of the essays, who brought the project to fruition through their insights and scholarship. The translators' efforts were a real sine qua non in a book whose main objective was effectively to transcend the language barrier.

During my stay in Hungary in September 1994 I received valuable help from László Somfai of the Budapest Bartók Archives, and his colleagues, especially Dorrit Révész, Adrienne Gombocz, and László Vikárius; Katalin Szerző, head of the Music Department at the National Széchenyi Library; Ágnes Gádor of the Library of the Franz Liszt Conservatory; and Ilona Prunyi, pianist and professor at the Conservatory. My mother, Mária Laki, secured books and other materials for me that I was unable to obtain during my short visit.

In the United States I would like to thank Denis Sinor of Indiana University for important advice; David Schneider for his kindness; and Ivan Waldbauer for sharing with me his memories of Bartók and his many insights gained from decades spent in Bartók research.

At Princeton University Press the book was in the best of hands with Lauren Oppenheim, always efficient and calm even when the going got rough. Elizabeth Powers lent considerable support and remained closely involved during each of the project's numerous stages.

Finally, I would like to thank my wife, Adrienne Elisha, who was with me every step of the way, helping with research, reading drafts of essays and translations, and offering encouragement when it was most needed.

PART 1
ESSAYS

·

Out of Hungary: Bartók, Modernism, and the Cultural Politics of Twentieth-Century Music

LEON BOTSTEIN

In those circumstances where the evolutionary direction of Western music failed to be realized fully, as in some of the rural regions of southeastern Europe, tonal material could be used, until quite recently, without shame. One thinks of the magnificent art of Janáček: all its folkloristic tendencies clearly must be counted part of the most progressive dimension of European art music. The legitimation of such music from the periphery is based ultimately on the fact that a coherent and selective technical canon emerges. In opposition to a "Blut und Boden" [blood and soil] ideology, true extraterritorial music . . . possesses a power of alienation that makes it compatible with the avant-garde.
    —Theodor W. Adorno, *Philosophie der neuen Musik*

There is great activity on the part of American composers, la Boulanger's pupils, the imitators of Stravinsky, Hindemith and now Bartók as well.
    —Letter from Arnold Schoenberg to Rudolf Kolisch,
    12 April 1949

This Leverkühn shares certain characteristics not only with Schoenberg but with Stravinsky and Bartók. Thomas Mann, in a grand manner, understood how to characterize all the maladies and difficulties of modern music and musical life . . . and put them on two feet in the person of Leverkühn.
    —Hanns Eisler, *Materialien zu einer Dialektik der Musik*[1]

Bartók is a composer . . . whose style cannot be described . . . by means of standard generally accepted terms or "isms." He propounded no systems as did Schoenberg and Hindemith, established no clear cut direction as did Stravinsky. . . . The direct influence of his music on younger composers . . . has been correspondingly small. . . . The evolution of his style, never so radical as Schoenberg's, was accomplished . . . with no revolutionary "breaks" such as we find in the works of Stravinsky and Schoenberg.
    —Everett Helm, "The Music of Béla Bartók"

· 3 ·

Bartók and the Politics of Modernism

Of all the leading figures in twentieth-century music—those whom Pierre Boulez in 1961 termed the "Great Five" of contemporary music, Stravinsky, Schoenberg, Berg, Webern, and Bartók—only Bartók, from the start of his career to this day, has remained closely identified with a single national group.[2] Despite revisionist research on the link between Stravinsky's music and Russian folk sources, within the canon of twentieth-century music Stravinsky's oeuvre retains its cosmopolitan aura, in part owing to the duration and significance of his career in France and America.[3] Bartók as a Hungarian is the only one of the five to experience continued reception as being, in terms of his music and politics, "from the periphery," as Adorno put it in 1949.

Questions about the meaning of notions such as "periphery" and, by inference, the "center" in the context of aesthetic judgments—particularly for the twentieth century—have taken on singular importance during the last several decades. The claims of modernism—the "progressive" art and music of the first half of the century—have been under siege (especially as contemporary music has become ever more eclectic since the mid-1970s). Likewise, the critical and historical assessment exemplified by the four epigraphs at the head of this essay has been subjected to skeptical reflection.

Terry Eagleton's 1990 tract *The Ideology of the Aesthetic* is an example of the trends in current analysis. It seeks to strip the modern Western tradition of critical theorizing about art of its claims to authenticity and universality. The conceits of the philosophical and historical defense of modernism, including those of Adorno, are put forward as part of an ambitious project, dating from the eighteenth century, to create an ideology, at once insidious and subtle, designed to justify the hegemony of one class and group. A "specious form of universalism" drawn from evidently "exhausted" discourses of "reason, truth, freedom, and subjectivity" was propounded, which helped to sustain a form of cultural domination.[4]

In this revisionist context, long after the heyday of modernism when Schoenberg's vision of the modern held sway, how might our understanding of Bartók and his music change? In our "postmodern" era, in the face of a powerful movement that celebrates the art from what otherwise might have been regarded the "periphery" (e.g., women, disadvantaged racial ethnic and national groups, and homosexuals), what is the significance of Bartók's example, of his way of resolving the competing pressures to be decisively Hungarian and yet European and cosmopolitan?

The fashions of æsthetic and cultural theory notwithstanding, a reconsideration of Bartók seems timely, if for no other reason than the reemergence of a pervasive cultural and political nationalism throughout Eastern Europe, including Hungary, in the postcommunist world of the 1990s. This essay argues that Bartók offers an important alternative model. Throughout his career, in his music he engaged the politics of national identity and attempted a novel representation of a distinctive ethnicity, which he connected to the great European tradition of the early twentieth-century avant-garde. Bartók, in part because of the special character of Hungarian cultural politics at the fin de siècle, forged an alternative route for cultural nationalism and modernism and challenged the dominant ideological premises of music history in ways that were prescient.[5]

If this view is right, then a rethinking of the standard critical assessment of Bartók's music, particularly the early work, might be in order. Writing in 1992, the distinguished Bartók scholar Malcolm Gillies noted, "I personally do not hear in his output a truly great work—at least not one that brings him close to Schoenberg's and Stravinsky's achievement—until his pantomime *The Miraculous Mandarin*, written in 1918–19, when he was in his late thirties."[6] In a similar vein, the very late music from the 1940s still suffers from critical condescension, despite its popularity with audiences. With the exception of a few often-played works, Bartók's music is less well known outside Hungary than is implied by his reputation. Two extremes in the Bartók catalog have been favored by non-Hungarian audiences and critics: those that seem most accessibly and charmingly Hungarian, and the "least" ethnic and most modernist-sounding works.

The central dilemma within Eisler's "maladies and difficulties of modern music and musical life" faced by Bartók's generation was the clash between the apparently "logical" consequences of the historical evolution in musical styles and the tastes of the public. The "progressive" directions taken by composers in the name of modernism—those original aesthetic and technical innovations seemingly adequate to modern life—unleashed a sustained negative response on the part of the audience. Listeners remained attached to the vocabulary of late romanticism and turned instead to the aural blandishments of modern popular vocal and dance music, ranging from the operetta to jazz. The music that turned out to be most compatible with modern life and mass society as exemplified by the film, the radio, modern sports, commerce, and technology was composed, in terms of the ideology of progressive modernism, in a regressive manner. By the mid-twentieth century, art music was experiencing an extreme isolation from the public that set it apart not only from modernism in painting and literature but from the pattern of musical life in the nineteenth century.[7]

Bartók's strategy and ambition as a composer, teacher, and scholar were influenced decisively by the politics, society, and culture of fin-de-siècle Hungary. Conversely, Bartók never lost his desire to influence the course of politics and culture in his native land. The sources of his unique contribution to modernism lie in the special circumstances of the early twentieth-century Hungarian context.

A comparable claim of contextual cultural influence can be adduced for Schoenberg (and, for that matter, Berg and Webern). The key reference point within the same large political unit, the Habsburg Empire, was quite different. Vienna was a center of German language and culture. In contrast to the case of Budapest, the international appropriation of the modernist achievements dating from the first half of the century emanating from Vienna (and also for Paris) in music and the visual arts was achieved with a significant loss of identification with any "local" national historical context of origin.

Outside of music and painting the work of many of Bartók's Hungarian contemporaries, particularly that of György Lukács, Karl Mannheim, Arnold Hauser, and even Menyhért Lengyel, the *Miraculous Mandarin* librettist who went on to a successful career in Hollywood, also has ceased to betray its origins.[8] But Bartók has remained steadfastly a Hungarian figure. The absence of any pretense to having transcended a "local" identity is partly responsible for the more limited acceptance of Bartók's music and influence, vis-à-vis Stravinsky and Schoenberg. The illusion of universalism and nonparticularity put forward by Schoenberg about his own music remains with us.

Of Boulez's five twentieth-century masters, Bartók alone has continued to play, posthumously, a significant role as a symbol of politics and culture within his native country. When Bartók's remains, which had been in New York since 1945, were reburied in Hungary in the summer of 1988, the then-disintegrating communist regime exploited the occasion. As Susan Gál has observed, the crass official and commercial celebration only proved to reproduce the many contradictory meanings that have been associated with Bartók within twentieth-century Hungarian politics. He was the nation's greatest nationalist scholar and artist. Yet he was a true European, who had transcended any remnant of Hungarian provincialism. A Budapest newspaper, *Magyar Nemzet*, proclaimed in its headline on 8 July 1988 that Bartók "showed the way that Hungarians can truly become Europeans."[9] At the same time, Bartók represented a viable patriotism distinct from rabid reactionary nationalism. He had been an advocate of multinational harmony, particularly with respect to Romania (as a result of his researches into Romanian folk music). Even though the chauvinism inherent in the reburial celebration was unmistakable, Bartók was hailed as an antifascist, as a victim of Stalinism, and, last, as the "uncompromising pure, universalist humanitarian."[10]

The history of the posthumous Bartók reception suggests the extent to which modernist aesthetics in this century has continuously displayed a political subtext. The categorization and censorship of musical modernism by the Nazis in the 1930s as "degenerate" (and part of the presumed decadence of democratic Weimar Germany) lent the aesthetic claims of Schoenberg and his followers an unmistakable aura and moral edge lasting well into the 1950s. Radical modernists became at once crusaders and victims in the struggle against the central political evil of modern times.

The cold war after the end of World War II secured the link between musical modernism and progressive politics. After 1945 Hitler and National Socialism were recast as part of a larger phenomenon in modern politics defined as totalitarianism.[11] From the perspective of the theory of totalitarianism, which experienced its heyday in the early 1950s, Stalinism and National Socialism were parallel historical phenomena. A pre–World War II "left-right" model could not be applied easily to the politics of musical aesthetics.

The antimodernist agitation in the Soviet Union of the 1930s and the Zhdanov decrees of 1948 therefore enhanced the idea that the radical musical modernism of the Second Viennese School was the legitimate aesthetic strategy by which to challenge twentieth-century terror, oppression, and exploitation. Musical modernism could unmask false consciousness and express genuine freedom and individuality. Dmitry Shostakovich's music, particularly the Seventh Symphony, caricatured by Bartók in the Concerto for Orchestra, had been popular in the 1940s in America as emblematic of the Soviet-American alliance against Hitler. But by the 1950s Helm could write that Bartók's satirical use "may, in fact, constitute the only reason for remembering the Shostakovich *Seventh Symphony* in the future."[12]

Adorno's 1949 tract, *Philosophy of New Music*, offered the most sophisticated justification of a progressive theory of music history constructed around the work of Schoenberg. Tonality and neoromanticism were outdated and seductive falsifications of the realities of modernity. They were the logical tools of economic and political domination. A narcotic illusionism and an aesthetic inducement to collaboration with real evil in the world were fostered by Richard Strauss (and other comparable composers, such as Hans Pfitzner, Friedrich

Klose, Siegmund von Hausegger, and Max von Schillings) and by the continued use of the rhetoric and clichés of late romanticism in the popular and commercial music favored by capitalist societies. Equally important and possibly more dangerous, owing to its deceptively progressive surface, was the false modernism and corrupt neoclassicism of Stravinsky and his followers.

The overt hostility to the music of the Second Viennese School on the part of the bourgeois audience was taken as a partial validation. It was evidence of how the urban cosmopolitan audience maintained a misleading sense of art and culture. The educated middle-class audience of modern industrial capitalist societies resisted the liberating potential of true modern art.[13] Negation (i.e., Adorno's "alienation") in audience response was a necessary stage in the process of restoring the ethical power of music.

At the core of Adorno's view was a reformulation of Schoenberg's neo-Wagnerian conceits concerning his own place in history. Schoenberg's compositional achievement was the logical and true twentieth-century response to the nineteenth century. Thomas Mann, with Adorno's help, recognized in Schoenberg the perfect model for the modern artist in *Dr. Faustus*. Schoenberg had realized, in a normative manner, the motto inscribed on Joseph Maria Olbrich's 1897 Secession building in Vienna: "To each age its art; to art, its freedom."

In this view, the arts were part of an objective evolutionary historical process. New dominant paradigms displaced obsolete predecessors. To write music in 1945 in a style that came of age in 1880 (e.g., as in the case of emulators of Richard Strauss) was clearly regressive. The use of tonality, as Adorno argued in 1949, was "shameful." Historical logic legitimated the twelve-tone system and lent it its ethical as well as aesthetic prestige.

Given the corruptions of modern life, art adequate to history could function as an instrument of critique. Modernism realized the immanent metaphysical power of art to sustain freedom against contemporary civilization. As Schoenberg wrote in 1951, he wished that he might serve as "a counterblast to this world that is in so many respects giving itself up to amoral, success-ridden materialism; to a materialism in the face of which all the ethical preconditions of our art are steadily disappearing." Musicians in the modern world needed to be "priests of art, approaching art in the same spirit of consecration as the priest approaches God's altar."[14] For Schoenberg the task of radical modernism was to help ensure that musicians "of the old kind" will exist so that music "can make our souls function again as they must if mankind is to evolve any higher."[15]

In Schoenberg's view as well as Adorno's the history of high art in music was, without contradiction, at once universal and a continuation of a Western European—but mostly German—tradition dating from the seventeenth century in which Beethoven was the pivotal figure. Bohemia, Moravia, Slovakia, Hungary, and America were "extraterritorial" and "peripheral." They suffered, as cultures, from what mid-twentieth-century students of the history of economic modernization termed "backwardness."[16] The ideology of twentieth-century musical modernism—for all its vocabulary of objectivity and universalism—was ultimately nationalist. The claims to legitimacy of the avant-garde associated with Schoenberg were extensions of late nineteenth-century German conceits regarding cultural "readiness," the proper cultural context for the "musical genius," and the German nation's superiority.[17]

In his effort to chart the future of music in the wake of the collapse of Nazism, Adorno was careful to identify Stravinsky and not Bartók as representing the false path. The reason was that Stravinsky, through the popularity of his works and the successful proselytizing by Nadia Boulanger among young composers, was the central rival of Schoenberg. Bartók, as Adorno had observed in 1925, was "poorer" and "more sheltered." He revealed a "self-limitation." He avoided an "open struggle with problematic forms." Bartók had integrity but retreated "into himself." Yet he belonged "to the same generation as Schoenberg and Stravinsky" and grew out of the same musical conditions. The central question facing that generation was "how music could grope its way home to the core of the full truth on the fragile terrain of a romanticism detached from human existence."[18]

To Adorno, the progressive element in Bartók seemed remarkable, despite shortcomings. Bartók's limitations, of course, derived from his "folkloristic tendencies," his sustained identification with folk music, particularly Eastern European materials. Provincialism both insulated Bartók and rendered him marginal. In his 1929 review of Bartók's Third Quartet—which in Adorno's view was the best of Bartók's works to date—Adorno noted that Bartók "does not move forward, like Schoenberg, with dialectical steadiness, does not advance by leaps around the unconstructable middle, like Stravinsky." Rather, Bartók's music "moves as a spiral in faithful repetition of the tasks of its origin . . . the only danger that threatens it is aberration." In Bartók the "still glowing embers of Hungarian folklore" were ignited by "the blast of European musical consciousness."[19] In 1965 Adorno explicitly distanced himself from too severe a criticism of Bartók. Indeed, in Adorno's reviews from the 1920s, even when he was less taken with a single work, as with the Dance Suite, his admiration and enthusiasm for Bartók's talent (consistently marked by condescension regarding the idea of using the exotic to achieve parity with "European" art) remain evident.[20]

Postwar Bartók critics who shared Adorno's basic outlook avoided the embarrassingly Germanocentric notions of periphery and extra-territoriality. René Leibowitz set the non-German terms of the debate in 1947. Bartók's failure was understood in terms of a "compromise," which limited his importance in music history. In his last works Bartók failed to realize the immanent, "objective," formalist possibilities evident in his own most progressive works.[21] Independent of Schoenberg, Bartók ventured close to realizing a valid modernist solution but then retreated.

The notion of a compromise seemed plausible, given a normative account of the history of music, which chronicled the dissolution of tonality at the end of the nineteenth century, the subsequent "emancipation of the dissonance," the abandonment of tonality, and the creation of new modes of pitch organization and forms deriving from novel pitch usages. When Leibowitz first used the term "compromise" with respect to Bartók in the immediate postwar years, the political overtones associated with his formalist argument were not far from the surface. Bartók's retreat was in a regressive direction reminiscent of fascism.[22]

Bartók, Leibowitz argued, had reached his most progressive moment in the Fourth Quartet. But then, inexplicably—perhaps as a result of his final years in America—he faltered. The last works display, as Pierre Boulez, following Leibowitz's lead, wrote in 1961, a "smoothing down." Boulez regarded the Concerto for Orchestra as "far from being good." He wrote, "Often the pieces most applauded are the least good." Bartók failed to surmount the "contradictions" of an "older world." In general his works were "pathetic" and "lacking" in unity, novelty, rigor, complexity, acuity, and dynamism when compared to the other great twentieth-century figures.[23] Adorno, like Leibowitz, described the late Bartók as exhibiting "compromised structures in the purely musical sense."[24]

In the 1950s, therefore, the Bartók works that received the greatest critical attention were the supposedly most modern—the Third and Fourth Quartets, and the piano music from the 1920s. The early Bartók was ignored entirely. The alleged superficiality of the Concerto for Orchestra proved the authenticity and dialectical necessity of a post-tonal modernism. During the late 1950s the Princeton Seminar in Advanced Musical Studies, supported by the Fromm Foundation, represented the avant-garde in America. Among its contributions was Allen Forte's seminal essay on the Bartók Fourth Quartet entitled "Bartók's 'Serial' Composition." Forte concluded that the "refined techniques demonstrated by every measure of the work" testify to Bartók's "perspicacity." Independent of Schoenberg, Bartók found the valid solution to the aesthetic challenge of modernity.[25] As in the history of science, two men reached the same conclusion at the same moment of history. If Schoenberg was cast as Newton, Bartók, judging from the Fourth Quartet, might have earned to right to play Leibniz.[26]

Yet, to most postwar critics in the West, Bartók seemed to have, as Everett Helm put it, no system.[27] Contrary to Schoenberg's assertion to his brother-in-law, Rudolf Kolisch (whose quartet premiered the Bartók Fifth Quartet in 1935 in Washington, D.C.), Bartók had few imitators in postwar America. In his Norton Lectures from 1951 entitled "Music and the Imagination," Aaron Copland barely mentioned Bartók. Stravinsky, Schoenberg, and Webern dominated as models. Paul Hindemith was also a force, perhaps owing to his teaching at Yale. A few Bartók works, particularly the mature quartets, the Sonata for Two Pianos and Percussion (1937), *Contrasts* (1938), and the Music for Strings, Percussion, and Celesta (1936), seemed significant.[28]

Bartók's reception behind the Iron Curtain in the 1950s took a somewhat different direction.[29] Using Thomas Mann's fictional character Leverkühn, Eisler argued that Bartók merited close inspection. For political reasons, Eisler had his doubts about the conceits of modernist composers in the 1940s and 1950s. It was not sufficient to use the audience rejection of modernist works, in a manner reminiscent of psychoanalysis, as evidence of discomfort with the truth. Bartók achieved, as Eisler put it, a synthesis between rigorous aesthetic criteria—including originality, modern musical means, and refined techniques—and the necessity to communicate with humanity—the audience—in one's own time. Bartók, Eisler argued, "overcame and transcended" the influence of Stravinsky and Schoenberg. Bartók's works, precisely because they consistently derived their modernity and originality from folk-musical sources, became a central model for the future.[30]

Within socialist countries an alternative to Schoenberg's austere modernism was sought. Likewise, the reactionary aspects of American commercial film music and popular music needed to be avoided. The "official" socialist music of the sort advocated in the Soviet Union offered limited possibilities. Bartók came to represent a distinct alternative, not only in stylistic terms, to the seemingly inflexible and restrictive logic of modern music history. In Bartók, populism and modernism merged effectively.

Using the very same metaphor as Eisler—Thomas Mann's Leverkühn—Bartók's contemporary György Lukács, in his *Aesthetik* from the early 1960s, challenged Adorno and his imitators. Bartók's music uniquely integrated the demands of modern aesthetic formalism with progressive politics. Citing the *Cantata profana*, Lukács wrote, "The battle of the humane against the overwhelming powers of the antihumane, which—in the era of the evolution and rise of power of fascism—is the basic content of his objectivity . . . the antipower living in Bartók is exactly his connection with the people."[31] For Lukács, Bartók's modernism was not abstract (as Schoenberg's might be viewed) but an appeal to the people and to nature. Precisely Bartók's "peripheral" quality, his tie to folk music, rendered him the central model of musical modernism: adequate to its time, consistent with the inherent demands of music as an art, and communicative to its audience. He resisted the "capitulation" of the avant-garde in the twentieth century in the face of the spiritual and religious need of human beings—the ways in which people functioned in everyday life.[32]

Bartók overcame the paradox of the clash between the legitimate claims of modernist aesthetics and the audience. As if to anticipate the rage for musical minimalism nearly half a century later, in his 1943 Harvard Lectures Bartók himself noted, "You will probably agree that a material reduced . . . to almost nothing represents a rather scanty approach in the creation of a musical work of value . . . it is not very interesting to have a theme played over and over again twelve times without change . . . reduction of means seems to be a rather poor device for satisfactory artistic communication." Not "monotonous oversimplification" or abstract theorizing (as in the case of Alois Hába) but rather the transformation of overlooked historical materials was the source of originality and modernity.[33] Because "artistic communication" as a critical and not merely affirmative exchange was essential, Bartók's strategy was to reinterpret history, to bypass the nineteenth century and assert a premodern populist source for contemporary musical communication: rural folk music. The reinterpretation of history, the reformulation of national identity, and the critique of modernity (defined not in terms of industrial capitalism but rather as the domination of cosmopolitan urbanism) were roots of a new aesthetic.

The ironic dimension of Bartók's achievement was that the instrument on which his ethnomusicological work was dependent—the phonograph—was entirely novel and the product of the urban industrial culture he rejected. Bartók appreciated the phonograph as an essential part of modern musical culture. Part of his ability to understand, distill, reconfigure, and transform the folk materials he collected was dependent on the capacity to hear mechanically the same musical event over and over again.

Bartók's enthusiasm for the phonograph is metaphorical for the dualism to which he clung throughout his career. He placed an idealized preindustrial notion of nature against a conception of modernity understood as artificial, inauthentic, and urban. Bartók sought a synthesis between the self-consciously radical aspirations of aesthetic modernism and a sentimental preindustrial construct of the world and the humane, embodied by the simple Hungarian peasant, untainted by the ravages of modern history.[34]

From his earliest years Bartók, by virtue of his membership in a "peripheral" nation—not unlike his contemporary Karol Szymanowski—was forced to confront the assumption that German and French civilizations were superior in art precisely because they were more advanced economically and technologically. What lent the Western European artistic movements particular prestige in turn-of-the-century Hungary and Poland was that they came from more modern societies, measured in terms of literacy rates and quality of diet, transportation, lighting, sanitation, medical care, and commerce. Preference for Western art and culture among the educated classes of Budapest and Warsaw mirrored a contempt for the local residues of backwardness and an admiration for a foreign but more civilized way of life.

The artistic models of Bartók's youth were German—primarily Brahms and Wagner—as communicated by their regional disciples, Hans Koessler and Ödön von Mihalovich. Bartók's first independent object of enthusiasm was Richard Strauss. Later Kodály and Bartók found in Debussy a route to an emancipation from German cultural hegemony, an objective as compelling in terms of politics as it was in music. Ultimately Bartók and Kodály sought ways around German and French examples and the ideological baggage of objective merit that came with musical models from the West.

Likewise, Szymanowski—who came from Poland, a distinctly Francophile culture when compared to Hungary—realized that exchanging one Western European model, even if it was French, for another was not sufficient. For Bartók, Strauss and Debussy became way stations with dual musical and political significance. Both Bartók and

Szymanowski sought to develop a musical construct of national identity that displayed a serious resistance to the Western European monopoly on cultural superiority.

In the 1920s these two composers, independently, became interested in Eastern, so-called oriental sources. They flirted with distancing themselves from their well-educated fellow countrymen who saw in the culture of the "West" the clearest path to parity with France and Germany. The representation of one's own culture as not only indebted to the West but partly "Eastern" and therefore distinctive and original appeared historically plausible. In terms of Western European critical discourse, assertion of an autonomous "oriental" dimension in local and national folk culture helped to circumvent the trivialization of the Polish and Hungarian as merely exotic or alluringly primitive.[35]

It is easy to underestimate the legacy of the camouflage of bias evident in the criteria applied in the historical and critical judgment of modernism and twentieth-century music. Adolf Weissmann, the distinguished Berlin critic, writing in 1928 defined Bartók's place in modern music as "tragic." A great talent (who "stands between Stravinsky and Schoenberg"), Bartók had drifted away—as evidenced by the works written after the Dance Suite—from idealism, purity, and the spiritual in music. The effort to elevate the folkloric to a "higher humanism" had led Bartók to embrace the modern as mechanistic; to exploit the exotic, to deny the piano's human qualities, and to empty music of its soul.[36]

Malcolm Gillies's 1992 analysis of Bartók's "borrowings" from other composers—his shifting models of influence, from Strauss in the early years to Reger, Debussy, Stravinsky, Schoenberg, and Szymanowski—sustains this deceptively normative tradition of analysis. Gillies's discussion of originality and stylistic "security" (like Weissmann's account of purity and spirituality in music) does not take into account the historically contingent differences between the ambitions of Bartók (and, curiously, Szymanowski) on the one hand and contemporary composers in France and Germany on the other.[37] The task facing composers in Eastern Europe at the turn of the century involved the seemingly contradictory challenge of writing music that was on a par with the dominant cultures and yet representative, in a novel and not subordinate manner, of national identity. National representation vis-à-vis a dominant neighboring foreign culture and the task of redefinition, through musical culture, of collective identity within a nation—given the near-monopoly on the rhetoric of historical centrality and aesthetic objectivity by the German tradition—did not trouble

Strauss, Schoenberg, or Reger. In the cases of Debussy and Stravinsky the issue of German music as seen against French and Russian was, for obvious historical and political reasons, more a matter of rivalry than one of subordination.

From the start, Bartók undertook a synthetic approach. Stylistic appropriation facilitated national assertion through a "modern" style that could be respected by dominant foreign cultures. The search for an adequate stylistic medium and language in the wake of the late romanticism of the fin de siècle became more than the quest for individual artistic originality. The seemingly neutral terminology about "stylistic integrity," "influence," and "insecurity" and its attendant language of critical condescension and disapproval ("[Bartók] was ever looking over his shoulder, always susceptible to the latest trends and to the influence of novel ideas he observed in the work of others, whether alive or dead"[38]) demands reconsideration.

At stake for Bartók was not merely greatness in some amorphous universalist aestheticized context. The metaphor of "looking over one's shoulder" is indeed apt for the Hungarian nationalist in search of a leading place in European culture as a Hungarian. Looking over one's shoulder, historically considered, may reveal genius and not insecurity or weakness. As Bartók observed relatively early in his career, in 1911, should a new generation of Hungarian composers achieve a synthesis between individuality and a common style "under the influence of genuine Hungarian folk music," that style "will show also the influence of twentieth-century music." Success, using the distinctly Hungarian, in the work of art, would carry with it a fundamental assertion—from the periphery of Europe against its center—of cultural parity. Ironically, the root of this parity stemmed from the "backwardness" of the periphery in terms of modernization.

With uncanny prescience, Bartók anticipated the prejudices inherent in the critical vocabulary of Western European observers: "Those who have a faulty ear will call such influence as being the Strauss, Reger, or Debussy type, for they will not be able to sense the subtle nuances."[39] About the rural Hungarian music to which he turned after 1905, Bartók wrote that it "attains an unsurpassable degree of perfection and beauty to be found nowhere else except in the great works of the classics."[40] His ambition was to use the folk primitive to create great modernist works that, by rivaling the "classics" of the West, delivered a blow to the belief that the cities, industries, and culture of the West were superior to the unique source of modern Hungarian culture: the endangered way of life of rural Hungary.

The Roots of Bartók's Modernism: Politics and Literature in Budapest, 1899–1911

All Bartók's biographers agree that the young Bartók did not take well to Budapest when he arrived there to study at the Conservatory in 1899. From the start, he felt repelled by the culture of the city, particularly its elite, which was made up of the cosmopolitan and Magyarized Jewish population, the German community, and the urbanized Hungarian gentry and middle class. Fin-de-siècle Budapest was dramatically different from the smaller environments of Bartók's childhood. The composer's fragile and retiring personality was ill-suited to city life. Judit Frigyesi has brought to light evidence of extensive prejudice on the part of the young Bartók toward the Jewish community of Budapest.[41] Her explanation of his anti-Semitism rests in part on a contrast between the role of the Jews in Pozsony (Pressburg) and in Budapest. Bartók presumably never encountered the sort of Magyarized assimilated Jew that predominated in Budapest and played a decisive role in the city's cultural and therefore musical life. Pozsony's Jews were, by comparison, more segregated and traditional.

The level and extent of Jewish assimilation and influence in Budapest at the turn of the century would have been shocking to any Hungarian for whom the Jewish question was already an issue, which was the case for most Hungarians of Bartók's generation. Bartók's prejudice—even its virulence—was unexceptional and had little to do with the contrast between Pozsony and Budapest. Pozsony (with a population in 1900 of approximately 70,000, half of whom were German-speaking and 7,000 of whom were Jews) had a much more influential middle-class Jewish population than Frigyesi suggests.[42]

The key difference was that in Budapest (with a population of approximately 750,000 in 1900, of whom slightly more than 100,000 spoke German, and 170,000 were Jews) the Jewish population had grown dramatically since 1870, when Jews accounted for 17 percent of the population. By 1920 they constituted nearly one-quarter of the population and most likely, judging from social class distributions, around half the active urban intelligentsia.[43] In contrast to Budapest Jews, the assimilated Jews of Pozsony retained more of an allegiance to German culture and were not as Magyarized. Pozsony (i.e., Bratislava), which was also one-third Slovak, was linked to Vienna rather than to Budapest, as Bartók's mother realized when she was searching for a conservatory for Béla.[44]

In Budapest the concert audience and the patrons of art and literature could be seen as "dominated" by Jews. Insofar as Budapest gained in influence in Hungarian politics, questions about the role of the Jews were not far behind.[45] Many of Bartók's friends, patrons, and teachers—including Emma Gruber, István Thomán, and David Popper—were Jewish by birth. But as Frigyesi has pointed out, the key factor for Bartók was that the Budapest Jews considered themselves legitimate bearers of modern Hungarian nationalism. However, from the point of view of the Hungarian countryside, the assimilation of Jews and their acceptance within late nineteenth-century Hungarian urban culture represented a dangerous corruption of national identity by foreign cosmopolitan elements. A distortion of the "true" Hungarian character, carrying with it the ills of modernization and urbanization, could be ascribed to the undue influence of Jews.[46] Not only were Jews, no matter how Magyarized, not real Hungarians; they represented a falsification of cultural identity.

The focus of the young Bartók's resentment in his first years in Budapest was not by any means limited to the Jews. Bartók held the Hungarian gentry responsible for the sorry state of Hungarian affairs. His political critique dating from the fin de siècle had a psychological as well as an ideological dimension. He harbored—as did Beethoven—a mix of ambivalence, resentment, and illusion regarding his own status with respect to the aristocracy.[47] At the same time, he recognized the pitfalls and futility of maintaining any pretense of membership in the gentry class. Rather, his position was that gentry had betrayed the Hungarian nation by exploiting and abandoning its people: the peasants.[48] The true roots of Hungary were to be found in the rural life. The enemies of the true Hungarian spirit seemed to have taken refuge in the cities and urban culture.

The rapid development of Budapest and Hungarian nobles' support of its growth were linked to the political accommodation with the Habsburg Empire after the Compromise of 1867. The gentry's economic alliance with Jews and its tolerance of them as Hungarians ran parallel with a self-interested acceptance of Hungary's subordinate status relative to Vienna and, ironically, the too-limited place assigned to the Hungarian language in the affairs of the Empire.[49]

Bartók's idealized view of the peasant and rural Hungarian culture was in part motivated by a need to compensate for the feelings of insecurity he felt when he arrived in Budapest. As part of a Hungarian middle class, he was caught in an amorphous middle ground between the gentry and the Jews. Traditional nineteenth-century Hungarian nationalism was an ideology of and for aristocrats. Furthermore, his mother was German and spoke German to her sister.

Bartók had lost his true link to the Hungarian nation, his father, who died when he was seven years old.

Without drifting too far into the imprecise world of psychobiography, it can be said that parallels exist between Bartók's youthful anti-aristocratic, anti-cosmopolitan, and anti-Semitic nationalist ardor and his lifelong adherence to an idealized vision of peasants and rural life on the one hand and Richard Wagner's polemical engagements with German nationalism and anti-Semitism on the other. The significance of the loss of the father in the lives of both composers and the attendant uncertainties about origins and the legitimacy of group membership suggest an interplay among politics, aesthetics, and psychology.

In Bartók's case, his first effort at an autobiographical sketch from the crucial year 1905 places the death of his father and the resultant hardships at the forefront. As the correspondence with Othmar Jurkovics from 1903 indicates, it was very important to Bartók, who recently had graduated, to return to his hometown to perform, which he did in April 1903. His hostility to the tastes of Hungarian aristocrats, particularly their attachment to gypsy music, his distrust of the city, and his appropriation of the peasant as the alternative can be linked to an idealization of his father and his early childhood.[50]

The consequence in terms of Bartók's evolution as a composer was that his search for the modern and the authentically Hungarian became cast as opposition to late nineteenth-century modernity. A linkage was sought between the present and future on the one hand and a premodern past on the other. Bartók sought an alliance between old and new that in effect delegitimated the culture and politics—including Jewish assimilation—exemplified by fin-de-siècle Budapest. As Bartók recalled in 1931, at the beginning of the century a "complete break with the nineteenth century" seemed the only solution.[51]

The persistence of Bartók's mistrust of Jewish urban cosmopolitanism and its attendant Magyarization as unauthentic and deleterious can be inferred from an offhand remark he made in a letter to his Romanian friend János Buşiţia in December 1931. Bartók was poking fun at having received the French Legion of Honor. He noted that in addition to Joseph Szigeti, the composer and pianist Tivadar Szántó (for whom Bartók had little respect) had also received this honor. Bartók put in parentheses, after writing down Szántó's name, "used to be Smulevic!"—a contemptuous reference to the clearly Jewish and Slavic original version of Szántó's family name.[52] The extensive Magyarization of Jewish names from 1880 on in Budapest was ultimately seen as a mirror of a corrupt urban definition of national identity, not as a welcome gesture of solidarity in the task of creating the modern Hungarian nation.

Bartók's first son, Béla, Jr., observed that Zsigmond Móricz (1879–1942) was his father's favorite author. Bartók visited Móricz and "bought every book" by him.[53] Writing to Buşiţia in 1918, Bartók, who was sending him a Móricz book, wrote, "One is of course reminded, in more ways than one, of the greatest novelists (Flaubert, Dostoevsky), which is a pity in so far as this makes it seem less original. . . . The author is a master of style and characterization. There is a quality of feverish excitement."[54] Móricz, like Bartók, collected folk materials, traveling to northeastern Hungary for the purpose. As a novelist, Móricz, whose father had been a farmer, became known as the "Émile Zola" of Hungary.[55] His penchant was for a self-consciously nonsentimental naturalism. He focused on the peasantry as a subject (although Bartók thought his best book, ironically, was not about rural life). What appealed to Bartók was Móricz's candor about the destructive economic and social injustices to which the peasant class was subjected.

The explicit and unvarnished rural realism Móricz cultivated was itself an affectation, a naturalist distortion designed to shock the reader, whom Móricz knew would most likely be a member of the urban middle class in Budapest. Violence, cruelty, sexuality, vitality, and above all oppression were sharply drawn. In the 1918 novel *The Torch* the rich aristocrat and the smaller landowning gentry (and their allies, the civil servants of the Empire) are subjected to severe rebuke for twisting Hungarian patriotism for their own narrow political and economic gain. In contrast to Bartók, Móricz's peasant was not sentimentalized. Peasants were not pure and benignly natural but were depicted as psychically disfigured, cynical, and violent. Little hope was held out for a civilizing process as exemplified by cosmopolitan Budapest. Like Bartók, Móricz saw in rural life the authentic Hungarian character. He was the "first Hungarian writer who wrote about the psychic depths of their peasant race."[56]

The parallels between Bartók and Móricz, despite Bartók's far more generous and romantic view of rural life and the peasant, include the use of the raw material of rural life as the source for modernist innovations in the work of art. The striking placement and language of graphic description in Móricz's work mirror Bartók's concern for structural symmetry as well as his use of tonalities derived from folk materials. In a manner comparable to Bartók's process of compositional transformation, Móricz used fragments of authentic detail to blur the distinctions between inner subjective perception and external reality.

At the end of *The Torch* the protagonist, a young Calvinist clergyman who has been exploited and abused by his village parishioners and by the ruling gentry, fantasizes about a massive conflagration. The symbol of the torch first appears at the start of the novel. The hero appropriates that image as a metaphor for his ministry. A real fire occurs at the end, killing hundreds of peasants trapped in a barn set up for a village dance. The pastor survives for a few days and then dies, transfigured but not redeemed. The backdrop of premodernity, in terms of landscape and psyche, as in Bartók's mature use of the folk materials, becomes Móricz's platform for an unusual juxtaposition of dialogue, radical skepticism, characterization, description, and narrative.

To the non-Hungarian reader, Móricz's originality—his form of realism—was obscured (as Bartók realized) by the particularity of his subject matter. Likewise, Bartók's persistent fundamental adherence to rhythmic patterns and forms of tonality derived from the archaic logic of folk material inadvertently diminished, for the outsider, his originality.[57] Apart from shared political sentiments, what drew Bartók to Móricz was the idea that a candid portrayal of the Hungarian peasant character and rural life could contribute to a distinct Hungarian modernist aesthetic. Through art Móricz furthered the cause of a better and more just society without conceding the definition of social progress to the corrupt legacy of nineteenth-century politics and cosmopolitan culture.[58]

Despite Bartók's striking sophistication as an ethnomusicologist, he never accepted urban popular music of the nineteenth century—the gypsy café tradition and the popular song—as a valid "folk" or populist expression worthy of sympathetic scholarly consideration. The idea that urban street music, particularly among the poorer classes, was susceptible to a political interpretation outside of its questionable association with Hungarian gentry nationalism remained foreign to Bartók.[59] He used the *verbunkos* and csárdás in the first period of his composition, thinking it was genuine folk music. After the 1905 turn to peasant music, he abandoned it explicitly until 1928. They reappear, often ironically, in the last phase of his creative work.[60] But from 1905 on, between the grand concert tradition of Europe, from the Renaissance to modern times, and a preserved ancient folk music "unaffected by city culture" or "unspoiled by urban civilization," there was nothing in musical culture that interested Bartók.[61] In fact, "perfection" in art existed only at the extremes, in the work of the "greatest masters" and in the primitive "very beginnings of art."[62]

Bartók was unable to reach a point of self-criticism adequate to question the premise that what he and Kodály recorded and transcribed was "spontaneous" and the result of "a natural force whose operation is unconscious in men who are not influenced by urban culture." The recourse to scholarship to argue that rural peasant music was a natural phenomenon and a pure unconscious cultural expression devalued all urban culture as being somehow artificial and contrived. Urban "folk music" was really "popular art music" by "dilettante authors from the upper class and propagated by that class." Urban music reached the peasantry only indirectly through the gentry, whom Bartók in 1911 called "supercilious Hungarian squires."[63]

A remarkable anecdote reported by Antal Doráti—in which Bartók in 1944 displayed little or no recognition of the name of Franz Lehár and *The Merry Widow*—gives a clue to the depth of Bartók's self-distancing from the urban culture of his own time.[64] His nearly puritanical disdain for street and commercial urban music, particularly dance music of the 1920s and the operetta (the work of Imre [Emmerich] Kálmán and others was extraordinarily popular in Budapest until the late 1930s), set Bartók apart from all his better-known contemporaries. Schoenberg, Berg, and Webern each engaged the traditions of urban popular music, including the cabaret and operetta. They reserved their disdain primarily for operetta's weakest examples and its commercial exploitation. In contrast to Stravinsky, Milhaud, Hindemith, and Křenek, comtemporary urban populist materials—particularly jazz—offered no attraction to Bartók. It was as if they did not exist.[65]

This aversion to cosmopolitan culture—particularly the operetta, a hybrid outgrowth of Parisian and Viennese popular theater—was part of Bartók's self-definition as a Hungarian artist serving a task of national cultural renewal. Urban culture was little more than a compensation for the uprooting of peoples achieved through a facile and commercially lucrative urban culture. That urban Jews were specifically skilled at urban popular music was a fact probably not lost on Bartók. Yet he realized that the city's domination of Hungarian life and politics was irreversible, that in practical terms the future of the Hungarian nation did not rest with the rural areas whose way of life was threatened by modern politics and economics.

Bartók therefore sought to reform and renew Hungarian urban culture by converting it away from the stylized imitation of the urban cultures of Vienna, Berlin, Paris, and London. If the authenticity of peasant culture could be preserved and communicated through a modern aesthetic strategy derived from folk materials free of the practices of the nineteenth century, an alternative modern construct of Hungarian national culture could be developed. As Bartók recalled in 1944, "As modern Hungarians . . . we felt the mighty power of the rural music in its most undisturbed forms: a power . . . from which to develop a musical style imbued . . . with emanations from this virgin source."[66]

Bartók formulated this project during the years between his arrival in Budapest in 1899 and his first extended folk music–collecting expedition in 1906. He did not develop his ideas in a vacuum. He drew from parallel developments in literature, art, architecture, and philosophy in Budapest. Bartók's contribution is compared most frequently to that of Endre Ady (1877–1919), five of whose poems he set in 1916. Móricz (whose first book appeared in 1910) may have been Bartók's favorite writer, but it was Ady who became the symbol and focus of a new Hungarian artistic generation.[67] Ady's 1906 poems, *New Verses*, represented an overt and inspiring break with the past. Even though he met him only briefly in 1915, Bartók owned seven of Ady's books, each of which he read closely.[68] Ady, like Bartók, invested old traditional Hungarian forms with a new poetic aesthetic. Central to the idea of aesthetic modernism was more than a break, as Ady put it, with "academic pedantry." Rather, novel aesthetic means were weapons for the regeneration of Hungary, for the construction of a new Hungarian nationalism.

Unlike Bartók, Ady did come from gentry. His view of the future of Hungary, unlike Bartók's, focused on the urban worker as well as on the peasant. Not unlike Bartók, whose neo-Straussian 1903 *Kossuth* catapulted him to notoriety in Budapest as a nationalist composer, Ady's first great stylistic achievement in poetry grew out of an encounter with Western European models.[69] In Ady's case the Western European framework was French symbolism. In contrast to Bartók, however, Ady was far more committed to the identification of the political and cultural reform of Hungary in terms of the introduction of "civilization" and progressive ideas from the West.

What distinguished the sense of the historical moment in Budapest among young artists and intellectuals from comparable sensibilities in Vienna, Berlin, or Paris at the turn of the century was the close, substantive connection between the impetus for aesthetic rebellion and that behind radical political change. The political change that Bartók sought—as did Ady and Móricz—was an emancipation from the self-deceptions of late-romantic Hungarian nationalism. The political critique of the Compromise of 1867—and the Habsburg Monarchy— was understood as part of a more general epistemological skepticism regarding aesthetic tastes and cultural habits, particularly the conceits of realism.

The late nineteenth-century glorification of the Hungarian nobility, its role in 1848, and the merger between a feudal tradition and modern capitalism represented by the absorption of the urban middle classes—including Jews—into the cadres representing the Hungarian nation were understood by Bartók's generation as mirrored in culture. Realism in art, historicism in architecture, and emulation of the music of Brahms and Wagner, modern science, and positivism all appeared objective and rational. Yet they were in harmony with a cosmopolitan way of life, a liberal but moderately nationalist politics, and an industrial economy. The essence of Hungarian culture would be little more than a synthesis of modern English, French, and German elements led by an aristocratic elite.

Ady's embrace of art nouveau and symbolism and his defense of French and Viennese fin-de-siècle avant-garde aesthetics were direct attacks on this version of the Hungarian future. Using the weapons of modern art fashioned by the generational rebellion in the very centers of Western culture emulated by the Budapest ruling classes, a new Hungarian generation sought to pierce the illusionism masquerading in the Hungarian adaptations of Western forms of nineteenth-century historicism. The normative aesthetic realism that supported the mix of liberalism and chauvinism prevalent in the salons of turn-of-the-century Budapest had to be supplanted.

The appropriation of Western European aesthetic modernism turned out to be a powerful strategy in light of the social and political power structure of Budapest. Bartók's interpolation of Hungarian materials (even though he rejected them later) into the framework of what in 1903 was regarded as a radical modernist model, Richard Strauss, and the effect it had in Budapest reflected this. Nineteenth-century literary practice, pictorial realism, historicism in architecture, and the compositional standards of Hans Koessler possessed legitimacy in the eyes of the public by reason of analogy to an epistemology validated by modern science, which in turn lent prestige to the political status quo. The confident assertion of the coincidence between object and subject in perception and in the evaluation of evidence through science and history demanded a concession to universalist criteria of judgment that included, but went well beyond, the realm of art.

A radical departure from the nineteenth-century notion of the "real" and its linkage to culture seemed essential if, as Bartók put it somewhat ironically, "to use the German technical term . . . a new *Weltanschauung*"[70] was to emerge. Impressionism, for example, became the object of severe criticism after 1906 in fin-de-siècle Budapest as a further extension of realist conceits. The young Hungarians of Bartók's generation used the Western avant-garde to challenge through art the imitation by the older generation in Budapest of nineteenth-century cultural and political practice.

Modernism, in its symbolist and expressionist phases and later in the use of abstraction, represented the idea that the "real" in life—the human truth—was not a matter of historically validated styles or the depiction of representative correspondences. Both in the work of art and in its engagement with the audience, a more penetrating and spiritual sense of the real needed to emerge. The expression of subjectivity or surface distortion generated new norms of representation.[71] Nineteenth-century techniques of realism and naturalism, particularly in the treatment of historical subjects such as *Kossuth*, masked a bias toward a socially unjust feudal nation of Hungarian nobles that entitled the aristocracy to define and represent Hungarianness. Bartók's 1903 *Kossuth* can be seen as the first stage in his critique of the official visual and historical tradition of representation. Although the work adopts the rhetoric of late romanticism and remains in this sense conventional, it was radical in its concept of nationalism. *Kossuth* was at odds with the official pro-Habsburg national history presented in the great millennial celebrations in Budapest of 1896, whose residues were visible for decades after.[72]

The aesthetics of modernism in fin-de-siècle Budapest transcended the limitations of art for art's sake—the aestheticism that mirrored the value vacuum so sharply pilloried by Hermann Broch as the central characteristic of fin-de-siècle Viennese modernism.[73] The integration of politics and aesthetics—the sense of urgency within a generation to define a new Hungarian nation through modernist art—lent Bartók's compositional output, from *Kossuth* on, its coherence. Even though Bartók, after his Straussian period, continued to appropriate an eclectic array of Western modernist strategies—those of Reger, Debussy, Stravinsky, and Schoenberg—each phase was measured in terms of its utility to the national cultural political project. As Aladár Tóth, one of Bartók's Hungarian admirers, put it in the late 1920s, Bartók, first through Debussy, "emancipated his art entirely from the hegemony of German music." The real goal, however, was to develop "the ultimate national and individual cast of his style."[74]

Leon Botstein

Bartók's ambition was fully conceptualized by the end of his first ten years in Budapest. By 1909 he had completed the Fourteen Bagatelles and the String Quartet No. 1, both of which were realizations of the synthesis between the task of unearthing a "real" Hungarian spirit and finding a postrealist modernist stylistic analogue. In 1911 he and Kodály founded the short-lived New Hungarian Musical Society. That year Bartók wrote *Bluebeard's Castle* and the *Allegro barbaro*. Having defined and refined his fundamental artistic outlook within the repugnant crucible of Budapest, in 1912 Bartók distanced himself from the cultural and concert life of the city.

Early Models: Fin-de-Siècle Hungarian Art and Architecture

In the Budapest of 1899 the potential of a novel aesthetic critique of realism and historicism and its relevance to a new politics and national sensibility would have been more evident to Bartók in art and architecture than in literature. Ady's dramatic appearance on the cultural scene, like that of Móricz, came after Bartók had completed his first phase as composer (exemplified by *Kossuth*) and had already formulated the outlines of his project to turn to peasant music. Of the cultural developments in Budapest Bartók would have encountered in the years 1899–1906, the modern art and architecture of the city were most suggestive of the link between aesthetic issues and the renewal of Hungarian culture and politics. Bartók's rejection of the city and celebration of the rural world and the peasant, and his search for a means to articulate the uniquely Hungarian through modernism, were already evident in contemporary painting and architecture.

Three years before Bartók arrived in Budapest, in the summer of 1896, a group of Hungarian painters revolving around two leading figures, Simon Hollósy (1857–1918) and Károly Ferenczy (1862–1917), moved to Nagybánya, a small town 340 kilometers east of Budapest. They returned from Munich and the West explicitly to find fresh inspiration in the Hungarian landscape.[75] That same year, the first of Ödön Lechner's (1845–1914) distinctive Hungarian modernist buildings, the Museum of Applied Art, was built in Budapest. Even more striking was Lechner's Hungarian Institute of Geology, completed in 1899, the year Bartók first arrived. During Bartók's years as a student in Budapest, Lechner's most important building, the 1901 Postal Savings Bank, was under construction.[76]

Lechner's break with the historicist style of Budapest architecture is perhaps best understood when his early buildings are contrasted with

· 25 ·

Detail of the historicist mural *Conquest*, by Mihály Munkácsy, in the Upper House of the Hungarian Parliament Building, depicting Arpad's ninth-century conquest of Hungary. Reproduced in *A Golden Age: Art and Society in Hungary, 1896–1914*, ed. Gyöngyi Éri and Zsuzsa Jobbágyi (Budapest, London, and Miami, 1990).

the Hungarian Parliament Building, designed by Imre Steindl and begun in 1884, and the neo-Renaissance Budapest Opera House, designed by Miklós Ybl, finished in 1884.[77] The massive Parliament on the Danube drew from English and Continental medieval models. The neo-Gothic framework of these buildings was intended to evoke a romantic connection between Hungary and the West, a linkage between the Hungarian gentry and aristocratic traditions and monuments of London, Paris, and Vienna. The Upper House was graced by the historicist mural by Mihály Munkácsy (1844–1900), depicting the conquest of Hungary by Árpád (d. 907), who, leading the seven Magyar tribes, occupied Hungary in the ninth century. His dynasty included St. Stephen, whose crown was sent by the pope in the year 1000. Arpad symbolized the Hungarian nobility, including its tradition of bravery on behalf of the nation and Western Christendom.

The aesthetics of Steindl and Munkácsy exemplified and celebrated the realistic illusionism of Hungarian nationalism. The historicism of nineteenth-century Hungarian painting was directly imitative of Western models. Munkácsy, Viktor Madarász (1830–1917), Mihály Zichy (1827–1906), and Pál Szinyei Merse (1845–1920) were among the leading exponents. Their works centered on romantic landscapes, the glorification of aristocratic traditions of patriotism, and daily life. Many of these artists worked and lived abroad. Even the most famous and perhaps greatest of fin-de-siècle Hungarian artists, József Rippl-Rónai (1867–1927), despite flashes of Hungarian elements in his designs, remained wedded in his canvases to Western European realist strategies, including impressionism.[78]

In contrast, Ödön Lechner responded by overtly and systematically integrating folk Hungarian elements into his designs. While the massing of the Museum of Applied Arts pays surface homage to nineteenth-century historicism, the fenestration and exterior decoration lend the building a distinctive oriental character. Inside, in the entrance and the main hall, this peculiarly Hungarian fin-de-siècle evocation of Eastern influences is unmistakable. The Geological Institute is more radical in that a departure from the monumental style of the West is discernible. The model and materials for the structure were taken from northern Hungary. An intentionally provincial coloration is employed, and the lines of the building offer organic shapes directly at odds with Western historicist models. More to the point, the influence of modernism, particularly of the Vienna Secession architects Joseph Maria Olbrich and Otto Wagner, is evident in the integration of detail with structure and in use of the ornament. Bartók could not have failed to notice Lechner's dramatic fusion of modernism with rural, non-Western Hungarian elements.

The Postal Savings Bank reflects Lechner's originality and design approach most clearly. The provincial Hungarian elements are no longer decorative additions but structural variations of Viennese Secessionist design patterns. The Hungarian elements Lechner used had little in common with the traditions of the Parliament and Munkácsy. The Postal Savings Bank featured a narrow vertical alignment of windows, which departed radically from the conventions of how the facades of public buildings were framed. The ornamental elements, particularly on and near the roof line, are sufficiently bold as to become part of the structure. The building is distinctly "foreign-looking" in terms of the surrounding nineteenth-century historicist structures that characterized Pest and the building's immediate neighborhood. The foreign and exotic aspect is, ironically, Hungarian. In the center of Budapest, Lechner challenged the reigning aesthetic and cultural symbolism of Hungarian identity. His evident debt to Jugendstil was transformed by his emphasis on native Hungarian motifs.

It would have been clear to the young Bartók that Lechner's Hungarian design elements were taken from the countryside. Two other Hungarian architects, István Medgyaszay (1877–1959) and later Károly Kós (1883–1977), both of whom began working in Budapest during the period before 1914, concentrated on a synthesis between architectural modernism and rural Hungarian motifs. Given the range of their projects, particularly in the arena of private houses, it is unlikely that Bartók would not have seen their work. Kós discovered the beauties of rural architecture in Transylvania in 1900. He formed a circle of architects, the "Young Architects," who explicitly declared a program that identified Hungarian folk architecture in the rural districts of the country as the essential source for modern Hungarian architecture. In 1909 Kós wrote, "The architecture of the Hungarian people is the direct descendant of the middle ages. . . . Our architecture rests on these Medieval foundations, which must be the foundations of our national art."79

The first decade of the twentieth century also witnessed a revival of interest in Hungarian folk art among painters and artisans. Although the group of painters at Nagybánya were more tied to the impressionist open-air tradition, Ferenczy (who later in 1905 moved to Budapest to teach), particularly in his canvas *Ruthenian Peasant Boy* from 1898, showed a particular attraction for rural and peasant subject matter (the figure in this painting holds a violin) and the unique formal pos-

Ödön Lechner's 1901 Postal Savings Bank in Budapest. Reproduced in *Lechner Ödön: Late Nineteenth-Century Hungarian Architecture*, ed. Akachi Tsuneo (Tokyo, 1990).

Design for a Manor House, by Károly Kós. Reproduced in *A Golden Age: Art and Society in Hungary, 1896–1914*, ed. Gyöngyi Éri and Zsuzsa Jobbágyi (Budapest, London, and Miami, 1990).

sibilities in terms of color and composition located in the non-urban Hungarian landscape and its culture.[80]

The most significant sign of the nationalist folk renewal during Bartók's student years in Budapest was the creation of an artists' colony, which included craftspeople, designers, and architects, in 1902 at Gödöllő, a small town 30 kilometers northwest of Budapest. Its aesthetic philosophy was based on the later writings of Leo Tolstoy and on the ideas of William Morris and John Ruskin. Bartók's awareness of the Gödöllő experiment can be inferred from the influence exerted by the colony's celebration of Tolstoyan virtues. The display of allegiance to a credo of anticapitalist, antimodern spiritual simplicity among the Gödöllő circle, particularly in the case of the main ideologist of the Gödöllő group, the painter Aladár Körösfői Kriesch (1863–1920), was later emulated by Bartók.[81] In 1907 Bartók exchanged the traditional nineteenth century–style Hungarian national outfit to which he had become attached (which he wore at his final recital at the Conservatory, despite the strenuous objections of his teacher, Thomán, who was understandably uncomfortable with its chauvinist and implicitly anti-Semitic symbolism) for a distinctly Tolstoyan outfit, characteristic of Gödöllő.

Beyond the search for a simpler rural life as an alternative to the corruptions of urban industrialization and an allegiance to preindustrial artisan modes of production, the Gödöllő group was committed to documenting and emulating a "true" Hungarian folk art that predated 1848. This group of artists participated in a major study of rural peasant folk art, which ran parallel to Bartók's and Kodály's researches. A five-volume study was published, of which two focused on Transylvania. Bartók's affinity for Hungarian folk furniture mirrored a fashion among Budapest intellectuals and artists dating from before 1905.

The notion that the rediscovery of a vital rural folk tradition could function as a critical opposition to established Hungarian national ideology emerged in the visual arts before Bartók and Kodály began their work. Even the crafts done at the Zsolnay factory at the turn of the century, which Bartók certainly saw, reflect the ideal of a fusion between the folk Hungarian and the modern.[82] Members of the Gödöllő circle and the Nagybánya group, particularly the painters Sándor Nagy (1869–1950) and István Csók (1865–1961), shared the conviction that in the synthesis between the rediscovery of a Hungarian rural folk tradition and Western aesthetic modernism a distinctly modern Hungarian art and culture would develop.[83]

Gödöllő's leading figure, Kriesch, was commissioned to paint the main mural for the new home of the Budapest Conservatory. The 1907 building, designed by Kálmán Giergl and Flóris Korb, showed the influence of Lechner. The building was begun in 1903, the year of Bartók's *Kossuth*. Unlike Lechner's work, the frame of the building was more directly evocative of Western European historicism. Nevertheless, Jugendstil elements were evident in the exterior, particularly in the design of the facade, around the windows, and the entrance. The exterior statuary of the Conservatory was done by Géza Maróti (1875–1941), Hungary's leading Jugendstil sculptor and architect, whose designs for the Milan Exposition of 1906 celebrated folk, rural, and native Hungarian motifs.

The interior of the new Conservatory building was more radical. The decoration, particularly along the staircase, evoked the styles of distinctly Hungarian crafts. Kriesch's mural presented a symbolist allegory in which the embodiment of innocence, simplicity, devotion,

Detail of the mural *The Fountain of Art*, in the Budapest Academy of Music, by Aladár Körösfői Kriesch, leading figure of the artists' colony at Gödöllő. Reproduced in *A Golden Age: Art and Society in Hungary, 1896–1914*, ed. Gyöngyi Éri and Zsuzsa Jobbágyi (Budapest, London, and Miami, 1990).

and nature becomes a metaphor for the true source of art. The aspiration to a state of premodern purity evident in Kriesch's renderings mirrored the anti-urban and anti-cosmopolitan direction of Hungarian aesthetic visual modernism during the first decade of the twentieth century. Kriesch wrote, "We cannot bring art worthy of the name into modern life until we consciously restore the social conditions . . . in their more primitive and unconscious manifestations."[84] Few statements were as reminiscent of and congruent with Bartók's own rhetoric about folk music than Kriesch's 1908 view concerning folk art: "The art of the Hungarian people, like all true art, is a fully organic part of the life of the people. It is called primitive because it is innocent of falsehood and opportunism. . . . Our responsibility is to preserve its individual and ancient forms before they disappear and to adapt them so that they might benefit a new, more modern stage of cultural development."[85]

The irony of this turn to the countryside and to folk art among Budapest artists was that Budapest, Hungary's key link to Western European civilization, provided the negative inspiration, and yet the crucial audience and the source of patronage. In Vienna, the private and public patronage of Secession painters and designers was comparatively devoid of political content. In Budapest, a political radicalism directed against the patrons and culture of the city existed beneath the benign surface of new aesthetic trends. This had its echo in Bartók's hostile relationship to the Budapest concert audience. From the start, aesthetic modernism in music and the visual arts in Budapest possessed a nativist anti-cosmopolitan dimension ignored by the assimilated Jewish community.[86]

In the years 1906–9 a second wave of change occurred in Budapest. In painting and literature a new movement was discernible. In the visual arts it was spearheaded by the painter Károly Kernstok (1873–1940), who came to head a group of painters called "The Eight."[87] Their first exhibitions in Budapest in 1909, 1911, and 1912 were significant events. Kernstok's hero was Cézanne. In place of the decorative extension of realism that impressionism and Nagybánya represented, Kernstok argued for a more radical departure, and with it a more pointed agenda of social change. Kernstok sought to go beyond the work of Lechner and Kriesch. An overt generational break with the past was called for.

Kernstok's group did not share an aesthetic per se, but rather a political and cultural attitude toward the social role of art. By linking themselves to radical Western European painterly strategies, particularly Cubism, their notion of the Hungarian element went beyond the appropriation of folk materials or the celebration of the rural landscape. Modernism, in formalist terms, had to become an integral medium of a new cultural and national consciousness. The poet and artist Anna Lesznai (who was a friend of Ady and Lukács and designed covers for Ady and Béla Balázs and for Bartók's Four Dirges, Op. 9a) directly reflected this effort to subordinate the folk Hungarian element to a new modernist reconceptualization of form.[88]

Yet, as Éva Forgács has argued, this new direction taken by "The Eight" in painting did not lead to a reconsideration of the urban landscape. Budapest "played no role in their art"; it was not a Muse for this phase of modernism. In fact, the countryside was "imported . . . into the city on canvases."[89] The images used by the Budapest Eight were either abstracted landscapes or portraits and private subject matter. Kernstok's major work, including his designs for stained glass, was about figures and nature. Róbert Berény (1887–1953), a self-taught member of "The Eight" who painted Bartók's portrait in 1913, dealt with figurative subjects. Béla Czóbel (1883–1976), perhaps the most gifted of the group, concentrated on landscapes.[90]

What made Cézanne compelling to "The Eight" and their adherents was the idea that by breaking the surface link of correspondence between the ordinary experience of the viewer and the work of art, the artist and viewer were forced to penetrate beyond external forms. This in turn liberated the power of the work of art to reveal and communicate hidden spiritual truths—to plumb metaphysical depths otherwise inaccessible. The reemergence of a taste for the metaphysical also strengthened the link between the primitive (i.e., the rural peasant tradition) and the modern. This attitude demanded a heightened emphasis on autonomous formal rigor in the work of art itself. The mere identification with an image—whether idealized as symbols or as subjective vision, as in impressionism—no longer sufficed. The integration of formalism and modernism heightened the power of aesthetic devices in a work to reach beyond the remaining vestiges of realist illusionism evident in the work of the Gödöllő and Nagybánya artists. Kernstok stressed raw brushstrokes, stark, "unreal" colors, and abstraction in his paintings.

In contrast to parallel artistic movements in Berlin, New York, and Paris, modernity—as represented by industry, the city street, the railroad, the skyscraper, the tenement, and the skyline—did not figure as an inspiration for modernist aesthetics. Despite their more outspoken advocacy of political and social reform, Hungarian modernists after 1906—inspired by Ady, Kernstok, and eventually Bartók and Kodály—adopted the anti-industrial, anti-urban, anti-cosmopolitan and anti-bourgeois perspectives of their immediate predecessors, the adherents of Nagybánya and Gödöllő.

Endre Ady's decisive moment of influence in 1906 preceded Kernstok's and set the stage for the new phase. In 1908 Ady recalled the

Stained glass window from the Schiffer
Villa in Budapest, by Károly Kernstok,
member of the "Budapest Eight."
Reproduced in *Lélek és forma. Magyar
művészet 1896–1914* (Soul and form:
Hungarian art, 1896–1914), ed. Gyöngyi
Éri and Zsuzsa Jobbágyi (Budapest,
1990).

moment in the following manner: "I was useful, indeed very useful, as a battering ram at the beginning of my career in this Budapest that is united only by its lack of culture, in this sassy city that is false although filled with zeal. I had a good hard head that possessed the *passe-partout* of a somber and (to the unsuspecting) harmless Magyar who by accident was also of the right religion."[91] There was in Budapest no analogue to Adolf Loos in Vienna who, inspired by Louis Sullivan, formulated a credo of modernism that confronted and absorbed the facts of modernity: the technology and materials of industry. Budapest possessed no equivalents of Alfred Stieglitz and the group of artists he supported in New York for whom the modern city, as symbol and reality, was an aesthetic inspiration.

The period 1899–1909 in Budapest, therefore, can be divided into two phases. The first, 1899–1906, can be considered the years in which Secession and Jugendstil influences from abroad—primarily from Vienna and Paris—were altered by the inclusion of anti-urban national elements, particularly from Hungarian folk art and architecture. The politics of this period involved a critique of academicism in art and architecture, but also what one Bartók biographer called the "chauvinist, reactionary pseudo-patriotism" of the aristocracy, the gentry, and the upper middle classes of Budapest.[92] The work done before 1905 by Tivadar Csontváry Kosztka (e.g., *Storm on the Great Hortobágy* [1903]) and Károly Ferenczy (e.g., *Fellers Returning Home* [1899]) represented an adaptation of Western trends—in these cases impressionism, symbolism, and the example of Gauguin—which consciously idealized and celebrated the simplicity and spirituality of the Hungarian rural landscape, its people, and its folk traditions.[93]

In the second phase, from 1906 to 1909—which evolved and characterized the Hungarian scene until 1919, the year of the brief Béla Kun regime and its collapse, and the year in which *The Miraculous Mandarin* was written—a more radical aesthetic modernism came to the fore. The earlier effort to integrate the folk Hungarian into the aesthetic framework of Jugendstil seemed unsatisfactory. The distinctively Hungarian was rendered subordinate or was used in a decorative manner. A new framework was called for in which the Hungarian was not grafted on but evolved organically out of a strategy that concentrated on criteria of aesthetic transformation. Political and cultural reform could be inspired by an aesthetic vocabulary that represented a sharper break with the immediate past. For Bartók and his contemporaries Ady and Béla Balázs, this route seemed appropriate to their aspirations for Hungary. But it was Bartók who, in music, uniquely demonstrated how a truly novel, formal, modernist aesthetic strategy could be developed from the Hungarian folk sources whose use had become commonplace in the arts during the first years of the century.

The Sojourn Abroad, 1904–1905

The two phases in the evolution of the arts in Budapest in the years 1899–1911 are mirrored nearly exactly in Bartók's career. As more than one scholar has noted, 1905 was "the decisive year" in the composer's life.[94] Bartók, in his autobiography, dates the start of his folk song collecting in 1905. He wanted to "study Hungarian peasant music unknown until then." Bartók wrote that in 1905 he "felt an urge to go deeper into this question." The "question" stemmed from his observation that what passed for Hungarian folk music—including the materials he had used in earlier compositions, particularly *Kossuth* and the Suite No. 1—were in actuality "more or less trivial songs by popular composers" without much value. They did not qualify as "folk" because at best they were cosmopolitan adaptations and were not spontaneous, innocent, and traditional materials uncorrupted by town life and the nineteenth century. What passed for authentic peasant folk tunes had been urbanized material, or was even of urban origin.

Bartók's encounter with the dramatic wealth of new material in the countryside and the development of rigorous techniques of observation, interviewing, recording, relistening, and transcription preceded the writing of the two significantly more modernist works—the first representatives of a so-called mature Bartók style—the Bagatelles and the Quartet No. 1. The impact of the patterns of ethnomusicological research—the scholarly procedures of analysis and close and constant rehearings—on Bartók's compositional command of form and detail should not be underestimated.[95] The question remains, however, as to what led Bartók to the "urge," and what influenced his mistrust of existing notions of the definition of Hungarian music.[96]

Kossuth had its closest analogue in Lechner's early architecture. One can hear the application of Hungarian materials and use of Hungarian motifs throughout a work defined by a close adaptation of a Western European model (in this case Strauss, whose *Also sprach Zarathustra* and especially *Ein Heldenleben* were studied and admired by Bartók). As an attempt at a national Hungarian style, *Kossuth* had been preceded by the 1902 settings of four texts by Lajos Pósa for voice and piano, which used both *verbunkos* and csárdás elements.[97] Likewise, in the Piano Quintet written in Berlin in October 1903 and premiered in 1904 in Vienna, a csárdás motif appears in various guises. The Suite No. 1 represented an advance away from these illustrative uses of the Hungarian. A comparison between the Suite No. 1 and the Postal Savings Bank is more apt, as is the link to the work of Kriesch and the Gödöllő artists. In the Suite a more novel and original use of Hungarian elements can be heard. The emphasis is no longer on the declarative use of Hungarian elements but rather on their aesthetic transformation.[98]

Bartók's shift from the Straussian model and a late-romantic conception of Hungarian music has been linked to some disappointment on the composer's part with the success abroad of his earlier compositions, *Kossuth*, the Piano Quintet, and the Suite, in the years 1903–5. However, from a critical vantage point the trip was not a total loss. For example, the premiere in Vienna of four movements from the Suite No. 1 on a program with music by Hans Pfitzner and Siegfried Wagner on 29 November 1905 was on the surface a triumph. The respected, tough-minded, and influential critic Robert Hirschfeld wrote:

> The most appealing gift was an orchestral suite by Béla Bartók, a still very young composer of Hungarian origin. Here one encounters a fresh and vigorous talent that not only fully uses all modern orchestral means but also puts them into the service of expressing comprehensible and lively musical thoughts. One basic theme governs the four movements of the suite. This theme is transformed rhythmically and harmonically in interesting ways and appears in ever new and surprising ways, enveloped by motifs of national coloring and with supple technique put in forever changing combinations. The themes given in the program notes tell, even on superficial inspection, that Bartók's ideas developed from popular folk song. However, a still-fresh creative art idealizes those popular motifs. The charming cadenza on the basic theme in the intermezzo brings forth the most beautiful of effects. The frolicsome scherzo comes through gracefully and easily; in the finale the entire thematic material is summed up. The instrumentation is masterfully executed. Without disavowing the individual instruments' character, the work shows many bold and original facets. If the talents of the young artist, who is also

lauded as a pianist, deepen and grow more assured and do not—
as the virtuoso orchestral technique makes us fear—get out of
hand, then there is much to look forward to in the work of Béla
Bartók. The audience confirmed the success of the Suite with
vigorous applause.[99]

Bartók did meet with profound disappointment at the Rubinstein
Competition in Paris during the summer of 1905. He accepted rejection as a pianist (Wilhelm Backhaus won), but it was difficult to bear
the fact that his compositions, including the Four Hungarian Folk
Songs for piano and voice, were passed over.[100] Indeed, it is during
his trip to Paris that Bartók wrote one of the most revealing letters of
his life, to Irma Jurkovics, in which much of his life's ambition first
was articulated. As the letter reveals, beyond the competition, the encounter with Paris (more than the earlier trip to England) placed in
stark relief the dominance of German models in the evolution of
nineteenth-century Hungarian constructs of national identity. Coinci-
dentally, Paris also was crucial in the aesthetic evolution of Ady.[101]

Firsthand contact with the capitals of Western Europe forced Bartók to realize that outside of Hungary his compositions would not be
deemed as original as or equal to those coming from the main national traditions of composition. Rather, they would be regarded as
either derivative of the non-Hungarian or dependent on the charmingly exotic. Insofar as the Hungarian dimension was concerned, it
was inevitably trivialized. The overwhelming impression would be
that Bartók was a young composer from a marginal context seeking to
civilize his native culture using defined, recognizable, mainstream
Western historical models. The use of the Hungarian in *Kossuth* and
the Suite, as mediated through the critical perception of the West,
despite overt praise for the talent of the composer, appeared demean-
ing to Bartók in that it was understood as special pleading so that the
Hungarian might appear equal to the European.[102]

Bartók's dissatisfaction with his own definition of the Hungarian
was fueled by the offhand ease and condescension with which the
Hungarian elements he himself had employed were noticed and acknowledged abroad. If he was talented, as Hirschfeld suggested, the
character of the talent had little to do with his Hungarian identity. He
was writing in Strauss's manner, using Hungarian decorative elements
in a way not dissimilar from the way Brahms had done. Strauss had
used folk materials in a similar fashion in *Aus Italien*.[103] Bartók admired Ernő Dohnányi's D-minor Symphony. But Dohnányi's alle-

giance to Western models was so complete that Bartók's respect for his older contemporary's music focused from the start on the qualities of compositional craft. It was clear to Bartók before 1905 that Dohnányi's neo-Brahmsian example (which might be compared to fin-de-siècle Hungarian historicist painting) was not the route to a new national music. Furthermore, as Bartók acknowledged, that was not Dohnányi's ambition.[104]

Bartók was convinced by his reception by critics and audiences abroad that the example of Lechner and Kriesch—the strategy taken in his first attempt at an encounter between modernism and the Hungarian—was not sufficient. The audience and context for architecture remained Hungarian and ultimately local. Likewise in literature, because Hungarian was not an international language like French or German, the move to "Westernize" Hungary, as with the powerful journal *Nyugat* (West), remained imprisoned as part of a localized intra-national, intra-ethnic debate. But even in Hungary, particularly in Budapest, the strategy of integrating the Hungarian with a European, modern, late-romantic style—even in the Piano Quintet and the Suite—was doomed as a counterweight to the cultural habits of the dominant classes of Budapest. In 1905 Bartók sent to Lajos Dietl with contempt a clipping from the paper *Az Újság* filled with seemingly vacuous phrases about Bartók's warm Hungarian heart and his "ardent patriotism."[105]

In his sojourn abroad Bartók recognized the paradox peculiar to music as an art inherent in any explicit effort to reconcile the Western European tradition and the Hungarian. As a performing art and as a printed form of communication whose readership was international, music generated a different context for finding a proper Hungarian language of expression that could work across national boundaries. In 1903 Bartók became particularly partisan in the political crisis surrounding the use of Hungarian in the Habsburg military. He announced himself as virulently anti-Habsburg and forbade his mother to speak German or call his sister by her German name.

The linkage of language and national identity around the period of his experiences abroad forced Bartók to question the paradoxical circumstances of his career as a musician. His admiration for Strauss—expressed as late as 17 March 1904, in a letter to Dietl—ultimately was the moral equivalent of the German language. Yet such styles masqueraded as the "logical" internationally valid modern consequence of the history of Western music since the death of Beethoven. In August of 1904 Bartók went to Bayreuth and once again was deeply impressed by the Wagnerian achievement.

Between 1904 and 1907, the year he discovered the pentatonic foundation of authentic folk music (which he used in the bassoon line at the opening of the fourth movement of the Second Suite, written in 1907), Bartók retained some ambivalence about continuing to proceed along lines comparable to Lechner, to adapt an expressive Western framework in which to use Hungarian materials. A multi-movement structure without a program (in the Suite No. 1) was the first step away from Strauss.[106] The Suite No. 1 was completed in the spring of 1905. Yet its strategy failed in part because the non-Hungarian audience aestheticized the Hungarian elements. As Bartók commented a week after the premiere of the Suite, for all its "Hungarianness" the Suite caused a sensation in Vienna.[107] Polite condescension such as Hans Richter's response to the Scherzo, Op. 2, or Richard von Perger's 1905 article in a Viennese daily paper did not go unnoticed.[108] Furthermore, Hirschfeld's very warm review made it clear that from the Western perspective, the Hungarian element had a conservative function, in effect minimizing the modernity of the music. Bartók's failure to be recognized as a composer in Paris in 1905 only underscored the dilemma. In the West the assertion of Hungarianness was depoliticized at the expense of the original or modern character of the work of art. In Budapest the Hungarian elements alone in the early work were sufficient to mark him as "new" and modern. The conservative philistinism of the Budapest public remained equally aesthetic and political in character.

The evidence that Bartók, fresh from his Manchester and Berlin experiences, reflected on the special dilemmas facing the Hungarian musician of his generation lies in a letter he wrote his sister in December 1904.[109] The purpose of the letter was to hammer home the difference between music and literature and painting. In all fields, the history of art could be learned through books by the well-intentioned, intelligent individual. Not so for music. To really know the history of music, or individual works on a respectable amateur basis, was nearly impossible. Bartók opened with his plea that his sister not try to obtain in music the kind of book learning or follow a "golden middle way" of knowledge characteristic of the cosmopolitan urban middle class. Music was different. More was required to understand it.[110] This was not the case, Bartók argued, for art and literature.

Bartók went on to a long discussion of Maksim Gorky and his work. His analysis revealed a crucial observation that linked literature and music: that every work of literature worth reading and admiring and that used its power of language to communicate was motivated by a desire to "take a position with respect to some kind of social, artistic, or similar question (to be 'tendentious'); ultimately to explain some sort of philosophical theory." In the last analysis, a work of art was meaningful within some political context with a point of view. That point of view was contingent on both the artist's aesthetic perspective and his political convictions. Bartók lauded Gorky's technical "between-the-lines" ability to communicate the idea that the simple "pariahs" of society—the oppressed—were "in the exact same manner as good or as bad as members of the elevated ruling class." Bartók lamented his lack of knowledge of Gorky's life.

Not surprisingly, it is in this letter that Bartók, *directly* from the Gorky discussion, asserted his desire to "collect the most beautiful folk songs and elevate them to the level of the art song by providing them with the very best possible piano accompaniments." Bartók proceeds to the reason for this project: "so that abroad," with such a collection, the public will "get to know Hungarian folk music." Bartók noted that the Hungarian elite would oppose such a project, preferring the corrupt gypsy tradition so popular among "educated foreigners."[111]

Bartók's first efforts to deal with folk music were tied to language. Only later did he detach the musical possibilities from their link to text. Between the end of 1904 and the 1906 publication of the Ten Hungarian Folk Songs with Kodály (the first public presentation of the new material), Bartók wrote the Székely Folk Song and the Five Slovak Songs for voice and piano while he was in Vienna in 1905.[112]

Bartók's formulation of the novel project of representing the Hungarian nation drew directly from the analogy of literature in the sense that music could not be without its political purpose. The letter to his sister preceded his 1905 trip to Paris and Vienna. Earlier, in the spring of 1904, Bartók, recently returned from abroad, went to northern Hungary, to Gerlicepuszta. That summer he encountered folk songs "with which we urban dwellers are not familiar," sung by the Transylvanian servant girl, Lidi Dósa. Bartók was already looking for something. He admitted to being "weary of too familiar material"—that is, of what passed conventionally as Hungarian folk music. He was searching for a new source for compositional and stylistic originality within the rural Hungarian landscape.[113] The assertion of the existence of an undiscovered, pristine tradition of folk music was an additional triumph over the German alternatives. As Ernst Křenek observed in the mid-1920s, Germany, by virtue of its extensive industrial modernization and urbanization, had no true "folk melody" source left.[114]

Aesthetics and politics merged in Bartók's 1904–5 turn to the peasant class. The unique possibilities that opened up in Gerlicepuszta were confirmed in an unexpected manner by his experiences in Paris. In letters from Paris to his mother and his aunt Irma in August 1905 Bartók expressed his astonishment at the city: at the Louvre, at the fact that of all the newspapers of Eastern Europe only the Hungarian ones could be bought on the street, and at the noise of the Metro and the height of the Eiffel Tower. Paris seemed far more impressive than Berlin or Vienna. But of all the things that struck him, one item stood out. Bartók compared the impression of the paintings by Bartolomé Esteban Murillo in the Louvre to his hearing *Tristan* for the first time, and *Zarathustra*. It was a "magic blow." The Louvre in 1905 had on exhibit Murillo's *The Immaculate Conception, The Birth of the Virgin, The Beggar Boy,* and *The Holy Family.*[115]

Why, of all the treasures of the Louvre, Murillo?[116] Bartók apparently knew some paintings in reproduction. The scale of the paintings and the realization of the compositional form impressed him, as did the "harmony of the colors." His focus on the formal qualities of the large compositions—the more abstract criteria of aesthetic discourse—is all the more interesting since the subject matter, the imagery of Murillo, offers the most obvious clue. Bartók mentioned *The Beggar Boy.* Here the heartbreaking portrayal of poverty is idealized by Murillo's command of the aesthetic means at his disposal. The colors are dominated by tan and golden tones.

In Murillo's larger religious compositions the studied sympathy for the rough, rural surroundings and the peasant faces is striking. The figures transcend their economic and social class. Art elevates their status from objects of pity to ones of admiration. The furnishings—the beds, plates, and clothes—evoke simplicity and piety. Murillo's penchant for depicting children and the poor in biblical narratives and for genre scenes of ordinary life displayed neither a patronizing attitude nor overt sentimentalizing. That made him close to Gorky in spirit.

It was the translation of the explicitly nonaristocratic figures into a classical formal composition of a striking scale and complexity, however, that in turn forced Bartók to consider Murillo's paintings beyond any surface "message." Aesthetic and formalist means—the integration of complex elements, the use of color and motion—transfigured the subjective and the particular into the universal without denying its specificity. *The Birth of the Virgin,* in which the Christ child is at the center, is replete with symbolism of rurality and simplicity, including the hearth on the left, the midwives at the center, and the exhausted and realistically portrayed Mary in bed on the left.

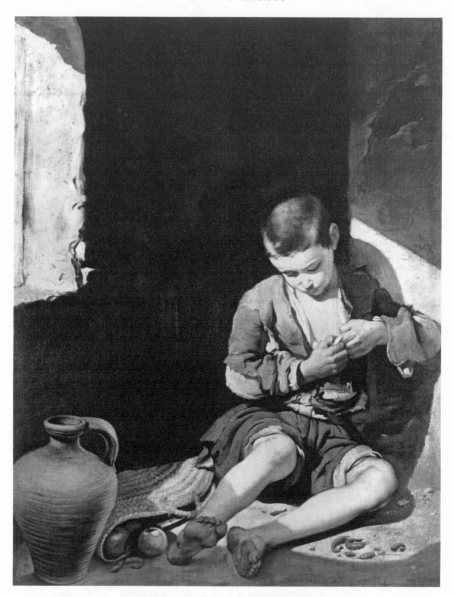

The Beggar Boy, by Bartolomé Esteban Murillo, which Bartók saw in the Louvre in 1905. Reproduced in *Tout l'oeuvre peint de Murillo*, ed. Claude Esteban and Juan Antonio Gaya Nuno, trans. Simone Darses (Paris, 1980).

In Murillo's work the peasant became for Bartók an icon for humanity without denying the peasant's specific character.[117]

The encounter with Murillo helped to convince Bartók that the peasant and the mundane worked as subjects for large-scale, ambitious, intricate, formal compositions. Murillo set an example of the use of aesthetic means, not to falsify the particular "tendency" of a work but rather to transform it so that it might be communicated beyond the limits of time and country as art. Yet the specific meaning, such as the cultural significance of the peasant tradition, was not falsified. In the letter to Irma Jurkovics in which Bartók described his reaction to Murillo, he mused on Liszt as a model despite Liszt's failure to be truly Hungarian.[118] Bartók then made the crucial claim: "Unfortunately the Hungarian peasant who decides to take on a scholarly career is a rarity. Our intelligentsia is almost exclusively of foreign origin . . . and only the intelligentsia can engage art on a higher plane. . . . Let us rather educate the Hungarian provinces." Bartók expressed his political ambition in the context of a reiteration of his disgust at the ruling classes of Hungary and the public for culture in Budapest, particularly its Jews and Germans ("It's a waste of time trying to educate them in a national spirit").[119]

A year and a half later, after his first major collecting tour, in a letter he never sent (probably intended for Emma Gruber, Kodály's future wife), Bartók's sentiments became even more strident. The actual encounter with the rural experience convinced him further of the need for cultural political reform. The rural world offered the contemporary artist an original, modernist path to the future on a par with the great Western cultural tradition. In anger Bartók wrote:

> This time from your letter there comes a too highly urban odor. The odor of urban people! A despised thing! . . . I went to a village wedding. Those perfect young figures full of life, those faces radiant with joy, this naiveté and naturalness! . . . When I come to Pest the next time I will make a comparison between the peasants and the average Hungarian intelligentsia. For the latter I have increasingly developed an almost pathological hate. . . . The gentry in the provinces who does not understand the peasant . . . talks such nonsense when speaking of the peasant that I would like to jump out the window.[120]

Bartók originally sought to label the research he and Kodály embarked on in March 1906 as dealing with "peasant" music, in order to separate it all the more clearly from any urban popular music. Although Bartók retained his prejudice, he gave in to Kodály's view that the term "folk" was ultimately more appropriate than "peasant."[121] The culmination of this period in Bartók's career came with the publication in 1908 and 1909 of the set entitled *For Children*. The eighty-five solo piano pieces were, like the *Mikrokosmos* from twenty years later, a pedagogical-political act. Balázs translated the Slovak songs into Hungarian. Here, for a new generation, was the essence of a new antiromantic modernist Hungarian culture and the basis for a radical departure from the destructive legacy of late nineteenth-century Hungarian nationalism.[122]

Bartók and the Philosophers: The Aesthetic Discourse in Budapest, 1909–1918

In the years immediately following 1905, when modernist aesthetics and radical politics worked hand in hand, Bartók came closest to the ideas and issues that concerned the leading figures of the young Hungarian intellectual elite of Budapest, which included György Lukács, Lukács's close friend Leo Popper (the cellist David Popper's son), Béla Balázs, and Karl Mannheim. There were a few personal ties between Bartók and these figures. He had taught Lukács piano, but briefly. Balázs and Lukács were close, but despite the fact that Balázs wrote the texts for two of Bartók's largest and most successful works, he and Bartók were not as friendly as the collaboration on two major works might imply.[123]

Bartók either subscribed to or was aware of the leading radical journals of the time, including *Nyugat* and *Ma*, but how closely he read them is not clear. In contrast, Kodály, who had been Balázs's roommate, and his wife, Emma Gruber, who figured centrally in Bartók's first years in Budapest, remained more closely tied to the intellectual circles of Budapest. That Bartók was sympathetic to the intellectual ferment is clear from his observation in 1917 that if the new young people got a chance, the future would hold promise.[124]

A group centered around Lukács eventually formed the so-called Sunday Circle in 1915. The members included Arnold Hauser, Anna Lesznai, Charles de Tolnay, Frigyes Antal, Lajos Fülep, Balázs, and Mannheim. At one gathering Bartók played *The Wooden Prince* on the piano for the group.[125] In 1917 Mannheim started the "Free School for the Human Sciences," at which in February 1918 Bartók lectured in a series that included Balázs, Hauser, and Kodály.[126]

Central to Lukács and Mannheim was the development of what Mannheim termed "a philosophy of culture" for the new generation that could make them conscious of how things created by individuals and events in the world came to assume coherent meaning. For the members of this Budapest group the question of the nature of art as a dimension of modern culture was central, if somewhat romanticized. It is significant that Mannheim, for one, stressed the question of the relationship of constructs of "nature" with those of "culture," as well as the dynamic between "civilization" and "soul" and "culture."

The tradition of art for art's sake, in which art was viewed as a privileged and autonomous phenomenon, was rejected. So too was the use of art as objects of display and consumption by the patrons and audiences of the wealthy middle classes, as symbols of civility and *Bildung.* The Lukács group shared with Bartók contempt for such urban popular forms as the operetta. The political and social function of art, at the same time, needed to be reconciled with some valid formulation of the autonomy of artistic expression and the link between art and, for lack of a better phrase, a philosophy of life.[127]

Members of the circle embraced Kernstok and "The Eight." Much earlier, in 1904, Lukács launched his own theater company, the *Thalia.* In 1911 he started a short-lived journal. In its search for some overarching common ground for art and culture within their own highly abstracted discourse—something that could "triumph over subjectivity" —before World War I members of the group turned to fairy tales, folk material, and peasant art. For all the differences in philosophies within the group this was "the most generally shared enthusiasm . . . in the prewar years." Lukács supported Balázs's effort to find an aesthetic adequate to modernity in the simple and primitive sources of folk traditions. These materials could help in the formulation of a metaphysics, which, Anna Lesznai wrote, "is the art of experiencing things in all their relatedness and yet individually. It is the lifting of the subject-object opposition to such a plane where they cease to be antithetical but become different aspects of one fundamental reality."[128]

In 1910 Lukács wrote a talk entitled "The Parting of the Roads," which was explicitly designed to support the work of Kernstok. The new postimpressionist art of the day—including the poetry of Ady— was designed to "express the essence of things"; to fulfill a "yearning" and realize a "revolution." Lukács wrote, "We long for our daily affairs to acquire meaning and consequence . . . for profundity and seriousness." One route was through modernist works of art. This justified Lukács's idealized assertion in his 1911 book *Die Seele und die Formen* that "the form is the highest judge of life. . . . The form is the only honest revelation of the purest experience, and therefore it must and will collapse in the face of unclear or depressing realizations."[129]

In the winter of 1918, at the start of the Free School semester in which Bartók would lecture, Karl Mannheim, who like Lukács had been influenced by Georg Simmel's conception of art as part of the "objective" culture of an era, cited Ady and Bartók as "pathbreaking figures" who were helping to show the direction toward the discovery of a "unity" between life and thought in the modern age. Mannheim viewed the age as possessed of parallel developments in German, French, and Hungarian cultural forces. The work of art had to reach the inner soul of the individual. It also had to communicate between two individuals, as a cultural object. The central question of the age was how the subjective individual engages the "objective" culture in and around oneself.

After analyzing the complex process of cultural apperception by the individual and the relationship of society to the single object of culture, Mannheim turned to the work of art itself. The form of a work of art represents on the one hand a distancing from the creator and on the other hand the common ground for becoming a future part of a larger objective culture. It stands in between the soul of the creator and the soul of the perceiver.

Mannheim expressed the hope for a "cultural renaissance" in Hungary whose precondition was a critical understanding of the dynamic and the links between the objective culture of society and the subjective sensibility of the individual. The utility of folk art for this project, for Mannheim, was that despite its being "culturally foreign" from the tradition of high art, the search for a new modern art could benefit from the folk sources. The "sentimental longing" for folk art was now replaced, Mannheim argued, in the work of Bartók and Kodály by an awareness of the different sociological context. This was accompanied therefore by an acute interest in the "formal structures" of folk art. The distance integral to cosmopolitanism—an undeniable characteristic of both Bartók and Kodály (despite any affectations, they were not peasants)—Mannheim claimed, would help them to discern otherwise hidden possibilities for modern culture contained in folk art.

What could be learned from folk art was twofold: the processes of how subjective culture became objectified, and formal qualities of an effective modernism. An aesthetic modernism that drew on these two potential qualities might function in the regeneration of art and culture. Creator and public might be linked in a manner more directed to progressive social change. Indeed, for Mannheim, it was the precise way in which Bartók sustained the "sentimental longing" for folk art derivative of the romantic era (a perception Bartók might have resisted) that helped him identify the "strangeness of forms" in folk art that might serve as the source for a unique modernist aesthetic.[130]

When one considers the enormous emphasis that the leading young Hungarian thinkers and artists in Budapest placed on the task of finding a place for art in the task of social reform, and on the discovery of personal meaning and truth in art and culture as well as in political renewal, it comes as no surprise that Bartók was flattered and felt sympathetic to this group of intellectuals, even though they, by origin, were precisely the sort of cosmopolitan people he distrusted. What made Bartók so appealing to his contemporaries, despite his social distance from them, was the unique power of the synthesis he achieved.

Mannheim's appreciation of Bartók had its ironies. Mannheim situates Bartók's treatment of folk music in the context of the *Bildungskultur*, a heterogeneous urban cultural formation capable of lending stylistic perfection to cultural impulses from primary culture but always in danger of "frivolity" and a "rapid consumption of substance."[131] Mannheim co-opted Bartók into the cosmopolitan social milieu he most despised and yet could never wholly escape.

Between 1908, when Bartók published his first written essay on folk music, and 1911, Budapest was made aware of his music and work. His integration of the folk and the modern seemed to achieve a contemporary art at once all-encompassing, adequate to inner and external reality, pure, and possessed of the seeds for a new modern Hungarian culture. In February 1909 Bartók articulated the very themes later struck by Lukács, Lesznai, and Mannheim:

> I firmly believe and admit that all true art manifests itself through the impressions taken from the outer world—under the influence of the "experience." If someone paints a landscape in order just to paint a landscape, if someone composes a symphony just to compose a symphony, then he is merely an artisan, in the best of cases. I can conceive of a work of art solely as a medium in which unlimited enthusiasm, despair, sorrow, anger, revenge, burning scorn, and sarcasm of its creator finds expression. I used not to believe that until I found out myself that the works of an individual imparted more precisely than his biography the most portentous events and the defining passions of his life. . . . The musical world of revenge, of caricature and sarcasm, . . . is coming to life only in our times. Therefore, one could call the art music of the present—in contrast to the idealizations of earlier

periods—genuinely realistic. It seeks to give expression to all human emotions, randomly and honestly. In the last century we only find a few individual examples of this dimension—Berlioz's *Symphonie fantastique*, Liszt's *Faust*, Wagner's *Meistersinger*, and Strauss's *Heldenleben*. However, an entirely different factor lends today's music, in the twentieth century, its realist dimension. That is that this music collects—at times from an almost unconscious search—impressions from the greater reality, from an all-encompassing folk art.[132]

This statement suggests the link between Bartók's folk music–collecting experience in the years before 1911 and the sequence of large works, particularly *Bluebeard*, *The Wooden Prince*, and *The Miraculous Mandarin*. Bartók sought to realize a coherent worldview based on his idealization of the peasant and the rural life. In that worldview the authentic detail—the folk basis of the musical elements—remained perceptible. Yet artistic individuality, formal innovation, a modernist construction of reality and meaning, and the creation of a bridge between the individual and society based on a progressive political and ethical agenda were sustained. For this reason Bartók emerged a hero by 1912, despite the distance he kept from his literary, philosophical, and artistic contemporaries in prewar Budapest.

Bartók's lifelong project was to represent, through music, a Hungarian identity at odds with the nineteenth-century construct and adequate to modernity. A new art could function within Hungary in a cultural renaissance that could influence political change against the alliance between the gentry and the urban middle class. A modernist solution that drew on Western European developments but was based on genuine Hungarian sources could communicate the power and character of the Hungarian abroad and establish the Hungarian as equal and not peripheral. A modernist synthesis between the Hungarian and the European could demonstrate how the preindustrial world and its protagonist, the peasant, particularly the Hungarian peasant, functioned as a source of modernism independent of the nineteenth century. Last but not least, the classical traditions of music dating from before the nineteenth century could merge with the folk tradition to form the basis of an art that was at one and the same time particular and universal.

That Bartók succeeded—perhaps exclusively as a result of his own genius—was observed in 1925 by Adolf Weissmann:

Hungarian music has entered a new phase as a reflection of race through Béla Bartók, and to some degree Zoltán Kodály. One does not want to contest the fact that Bartók, the well-schooled researcher in folklore, utilizes the folk repositories of South Europe in a fruitful manner. Insofar as he is an innovator, song and dance are used again and again without loss to their special character. . . . This is a unique case; the man is also an intellectual. One cannot regard "Magyarness" as having been rescued by Bartók, who looks far beyond any borders, takes part in the culture of Europe, and even with others helps determine its course.[133]

Bartók traveled through five distinct phases in his pursuit of these objectives. The first involved his use of the neoromantic direction from the West as a framework. This phase came to an end with the Suite No. 1. The second phase began in 1905–6 with the folk song–collecting project and the collaboration with Kodály. It ended in 1919 with *The Miraculous Mandarin*. This phase was characterized by his use of modern French and German expressionist models altered by a formal emphasis on local folk materials. The techniques of aesthetic modernism achieved a balance with the intent to present folk materials. Bartók made his first unique contributions to European modernism.

The third phase began after World War I. The Trianon Treaty and the disbandment of old Hungary changed the political context. The collapse of the Béla Kun regime in 1919 and the advent of Horthy further recast the political overtones of Bartók's allegiance to folk music. In this period the emphasis on the abstract and dissonant formal transformation of musical materials was strengthened, diminishing the evidently "realistic" use of the folk material. Bartók's sympathy for internationalism as opposed to the contemporary Hungarian chauvinism of the 1920s only led to his music becoming more in line with Western European developments exemplified by Schoenberg. The integration of modernism and the folk element achieved its most cloaked and original surface.

The period between 1930 (*Cantata profana*) and the *Mikrokosmos*, completed in 1939, mirrors Bartók's return to a balance between modernist aesthetic and local cultural issues. The *Mikrokosmos* was the fullest realization of the ideal of contemporary art as a force in the creation of new cultural values. It was a folk-based modernist analogue to Bach's *Well-Tempered Clavier*—an artistic bridge between the rapidly vanishing, preindustrial rural world and progressive modernity. Bartók's distance from the fascist appropriation of the folk heritage and nationalism widened further.

The last period covered the American years. The folk material was used in its most populist and democratic manner. The surface of modernism was modified. As if to combat the reduced role of high art music in modern life Bartók cultivated a direct analogue to the original surface simplicity of the folk material. The elegant structure and accessibility of the last works are evidence of his success.

In all phases, from *Kossuth* to the Third Piano Concerto, Bartók uniquely managed to reconcile the claims of formal musical aesthetics and the ideology of a progressive musical modernism with the cultural politics of identity and subjective particularity. His significance for Hungarian and non-Hungarian audiences has never been greater. His revisionist engagement with Hungarian history led him to appropriate the universalist tradition in the arts. A fundamental commitment to what otherwise might have been an exclusionary construct of national identity and ethnic individuality was transformed by modernism. But, as Weissmann observed, it may ultimately have been the extraordinary flexibility and originality of Bartók's musical imagination that made his reconciliation not only possible but compelling for audiences—past, present, and future.

NOTES

1. The habit of using the image of Leverkühn to characterize Bartók continues. See, e.g., Tibor Tallián, *Béla Bartók: The Man and His Work* (Budapest, 1981), p. 91.

2. Pierre Boulez, "Bartók," in "Items for a Musical Encyclopedia," in *Notes of an Apprenticeship*, trans. Herbert Weinstock (New York, 1968), p. 311.

3. On Stravinsky, see Richard Taruskin's two-volume *Stravinsky and the Russian Traditions: A Biography of the Works through "Mavra,"* forthcoming from the University of California Press. Bartók was keenly aware of Stravinsky's debt to folk music and repeatedly reiterated the connection as late as his Harvard Lectures of 1943.

4. Terry Eagleton, *The Ideology of the Aesthetic* (Oxford, 1990), pp. 3–9, 413–15. In this discussion the question of periphery and centrality is understood historically. I am clearly skeptical of the positions taken by Schoenberg and Adorno and think that the German claim to have developed a supranational musical tradition is suspect. At the same time, finding links between music and historical culture in no way diminishes the capacity for any music to communicate across historical and temporal boundaries in unpredictable ways having little to do with any given cultural context of origin. In these patterns of reception lies the privileged claim of music as a language of communication that is more susceptible to universality than painting or literature.

5. A caveat is in order here: I do not read Hungarian. Therefore the anal-

ysis is hampered by a crucial dimension of expertise. However, it is hoped that as an analysis explicitly "from the outside" this essay will have utility. I want to thank David Kettler, Peter Laki, Todd Crow, Judit Frigyesi, Irene Zeldacher, and Michele Dominy for their assistance.

6. Malcolm Gillies, "Bartók and His Music in the 1990s," in *The Bartók Companion*, ed. Malcolm Gillies (London, 1993), p. 10.

7. Two texts, one by a moderate advocate of modernism, the Berlin critic Adolf Weissmann, *Die Weltkrise in der Musik* (Berlin, 1922), and one by the conservative composer and theorist Erhart Ermatinger, *Zerfall und Krise des nachklassischen Musiklebens* (Bern, 1939), are notable articulations of these issues as they were understood before World War II. The present essay does not deal with the question of Bartók's reception in England, which has its own distinct history, beginning in 1903. See Malcolm Gillies, *Bartók in Britain: A Guided Tour* (Oxford, 1989).

8. See the essay by Vera Lampert in this volume. Lengyel's career might be compared to that of the composer Erich Wolfgang Korngold.

9. Susan Gal, "Bartók's Funeral: Representations of Europe in Hungarian Political Rhetoric," *American Ethnologist* 28, no. 3 (1991): 442.

10. Ibid., pp. 440–58.

11. See, e.g., Hannah Arendt, *The Origins of Totalitarianism* (New York, 1951; enlarged ed., 1958); and *Totalitarian Dictatorship and Autocracy*, ed. Carl J. Friedrich and Zbigniew Brzezinski (New York, 1961).

12. Everett Helm, "The Music of Béla Bartók," in *European Music in the Twentieth Century*, ed. Howard Hartog (New York, 1957), p. 32.

13. The comparison in attitudes between Schoenberg and Bartók vis-à-vis audiences would be instructive. I suspect that Bartók's attitude was more generous—particularly considering his career as a pianist. His hostility may have been confined to the Budapest audience.

14. Letter to Frank Pelleg, 26 April 1951, in Arnold Schoenberg, *Letters*, ed. Erwin Stein (Berkeley and Los Angeles, 1984), p. 286.

15. Ibid., p. 287.

16. See particularly Alexander Gerschenkron, *Economic Backwardness in Historical Perspective* (Cambridge, Mass., 1962) and *An Economic Spurt that Failed: Four Lectures in Austrian History* (Princeton, 1977).

17. Consider, e.g., Schoenberg's statements from 1919 (regarding the task to "ensure the German nation's superiority in the field of music") and the claims from 1931 regarding Germany's historical centrality and from 1947 regarding "readiness," folk music, and the cultural conditions of "genius," in Arnold Schoenberg, *Style and Idea*, ed. Leonard Stein (London, 1975), pp. 161, 165–66, 172–73, 369–70.

18. Theodor W. Adorno, "Über einige Werke von Béla Bartók," in *Gesammelte Schriften*, vol. 18 (Frankfurt, 1984), pp. 282–83.

19. See the translation of this 1929 review in this volume. Theodor W. Adorno, "Béla Bartóks Drittes Streichquartett," in ibid., p. 287.

20. Theodor W. Adorno, "Béla Bartóks Tanzsuite," in ibid., pp. 279–81.

For an excellent analysis of Adorno's view of Bartók and its consequences, see Dénes Zoltai, "Bartók in Sicht der Frankfurter Schule," in *International Musicological Conference in Commemoration of Béla Bartók 1971*, ed. József Ujfalussy and János Breuer (Budapest, 1972), pp. 13–17.

21. The original essay appeared in French in Jean Paul Sartre's journal *Les Temps Modernes* in October 1947. This discussion is based on the German translation. See Rene Leibowitz, "Béla Bartók oder die Möglichkeit des Kompromisses in der zeitgenössischen Musik," in *Béla Bartók*, ed. Heinz Klaus Metzger; and Rainer Riehn in *Musik Konzepte Nr. 22* (Munich, 1981).

22. This view, however, was not shared by American left-wing critics, who saw in Bartók an ideal, antifascist solution to the dilemma of the alienation between mass audiences and concert music. They took a position more akin to Hanns Eisler's. See n. 29.

23. Pierre Boulez, "Bartók," pp. 310–12.

24. Theodor W. Adorno, "Zuschrift über Bartók," in *Gesammelte Schriften*, vol. 18, p. 295.

25. Allen Forte, "Bartók's 'Serial' Composition," in *Problems of Modern Music*, ed. Paul Henry Lang (New York, 1960), pp. 95–107.

26. This reference to the twin developers of calculus is intentional. The significance of a nearly mathematical formal complexity as a precondition for acceptance into the canon of modernism in the discourse of post–World War II American musical criticism is reflected in the major leading formal studies of Bartók's music—by Elliott Antokoletz (1984) and Paul Wilson (1992). Antokoletz lays great stress on Bartók's intricate compositional logic, his systematic use of pitch relations, and the creation of coherence through symmetries. Wilson, invoking the science of hermeneutics, adopts a strategy tied more to individual works. But he is no less intent on revealing functional structures and hierarchies that validate the innovative modernity of Bartók. See Elliott Antokoletz, *The Music of Béla Bartók: A Study of Tonality and Progression in Twentieth Century Music* (Berkeley and Los Angeles, 1984); and Paul Wilson, *The Music of Béla Bartók* (New Haven, 1992). It is important to remember that Antokoletz was trained by George Perle, whose magisterial work on Alban Berg served as a model, and that Wilson was trained by Forte.

27. This seems ironic, considering the work of Ernő Lendvai in the late 1950s and 1960s, which argued systematic parallels to the "golden section" and proportional symmetries in Bartók's music. For a quick summary see Wilson, *The Music of Béla Bartók*, pp. 6–8.

28. Copland's interest seems to have been limited to instrumental innovations in Bartók. See Aaron Copland, *Music and Imagination* (Cambridge, Mass., 1952), p. 30. It should be noted that Paul Hindemith, like Schoenberg, had a system extensively documented in his textbooks.

29. However, within the West there were assessments that ran parallel to Eisler's, with similar politics. An American example of this can be found in the sympathetic discussion of Bartók in Sidney Finkelstein, *Composer and Nation: The Folk Heritage in Music* (New York, 1960), pp. 271–79.

30. Hanns Eisler, "Über das Volkslied," in Eisler, *Materialien zu einer Dialektik der Musik* (Leipzig, 1976), pp. 248–49.

31. György Lukács, *Aesthetik* (Neuwied, 1963; reprint, 1972), vol. 3, pp. 136–37. It is ironic that Thomas Mann met Bartók while the composer lived, during the 1920s, in the home of Lukács's father in Budapest. For Mann's recollection and other documents on their encounters, see Yolana Hatvany, "An Evening with Thomas Mann and Béla Bartók in Budapest" and "Thomas Mann and Bartók," in *Bartók Studies*, ed. Todd Crow (Detroit, 1976), pp. 173–78.

32. Lukács, *Aesthetik*, vol. 4, p. 209. The later Lukács essays on Bartók rework the same ideas, each using the *Cantata profana* as the main example. See György Lukács, "Béla Bartók (On the Twenty-Fifth Anniversary of His Death)," in Crow, *Bartók Studies*, pp. 203–16.

33. Béla Bartók, "Harvard Lectures," in Béla Bartók, *Essays*, ed. Benjamin Suchoff (New York, 1976), pp. 358–61, 374. This is, as Peter Laki has pointed out, an oblique criticism of the Shostakovich Seventh Symphony.

34. As many biographers have noted, Bartók was an enthusiast for the natural world and the outdoors. He was concerned with diet and fitness. His affection for his Cambridge Avenue apartment in Riverdale was in part the result of its proximity to Ewen Park, which reminded him of the open and green areas of Budapest. This aspect of Bartók's view of nature and the human body might be studied in light of the suggestive historical interpretation concerning these issues for Kafka's and Bartók's generation in the Habsburg Empire. See Mark M. Anderson, *Kafka's Clothes: Ornament and Aestheticism in the Habsburg Fin de Siècle* (Oxford, 1992), pp. 74–97.

35. It should be noted that Schoenberg included many Bartók works in his Society for Private Music Performances programs from 1918 to 1922. See Walter Szmolyan, "Die Konzerte der Wiener Schoenberg-Vereins," in *Schoenbergs Verein für musikalische Privataufführungen*, ed. Heinz-Klaus Metzger and Rainer Riehn (Munich, 1984), p. 111. On Szymanowski, see Christopher Palmer, *Szymanowski* (London, 1983); and Jim Samson, *The Music of Szymanowski* (London, 1990). Szymanowski was fascinated with Islam and Persian culture. Szymanowski, like Bartók, maintained an interest in the Orient, which was linked to the deepening of his attraction to an original national folk tradition. Bartók, in search of common roots to recurrent patterns in diverse folk musics as well as the non-Western roots of Hungarian peasant music, was drawn to Turkish and Arabic materials. Furthermore, both Bartók's and Szymanowski's turn to peasant folk music was in part motivated by the desire to find an authentic alternative to the eighteenth- and nineteenth-century mythic formulations of a proud nation of "nobles," which dominated nationalist sentiment in their respective cultures before World War I.

36. Adolf Weissmann, *Die Entgötterung der Musik* (Berlin, 1928), p. 93.

37. Malcolm Gillies, "Stylistic Integrity and Influence in Bartók's Works: The Case of Szymanowski," *International Journal of Musicology* 1 (1992): 139–60.

38. Ibid., p. 145. For a discussion of the stylistic innovation and national consciousness in the beginnings of modernism, see Helga de la Motte-Haber, "Nationalstil und nationale Haltung," in *Nationaler Stil und Europäische Dimension in der Musik der Jahrhundertwende*, ed. Helga de la Motte-Haber (Darmstadt, 1991), pp. 45–53.

39. Béla Bartók, "On Hungarian Music" (1911), in Bartók, *Essays*, p. 302.

40. Tallián, *Béla Bartók*, p. 95.

41. Judit Frigyesi, "Béla Bartók and Hungarian Nationalism: The Development of Bartók's Social and Political Ideas at the Turn of the Century (1899–1903)" (Ph.D. dissertation, University of Pennsylvania, 1989). It must be noted that despite the prejudice displayed by Bartok in his youth, he never associated himself at any time in his life and career with the political movements tied to anti-Semitism. In this respect his conduct was exceptional and honorable when compared to that of others who shared similar attitudes.

42. Despite the relatively smaller numbers of Jews in Pozsony, it may be that Bartók and his mother had more contact already in Pozsony—particularly in school, domestic music making, and concert life—with assimilated Jews of the kind found in large numbers in Budapest.

43. For a brief summary see the entries "Budapest" and "Bratislava" in the *Encylopaedia Judaica* (Jerusalem, 1971), vol. 4, pp. 1448, 1309.

44. Ibid., pp. 25–61. On Pozsony, see p. 58. Also see László Katus, "Die Magyaren," L'udovit Holotik, "Die Slowaken," and Wolfdieter Bihl, "Die Juden," in *Die Habsburgermonarchie, 1848–1918*, vol. 3: *Die Völker des Reiches*, ed. Adam Wandruszka and Peter Urbanitsch (Vienna, 1980), pp. 431–36, 796–99, 885–902. See also Kodály's childhood recollections of Pressburg's cultural life, cited in *Bartóks Briefe in die Slowakei*, ed. Vladimir Cizik (Bratislava, 1971), p. 147.

45. See, e.g., Géza Buzinkay, "The Budapest Joke and Comic Weeklies as Mirrors of Cultural Assimilation," in *Budapest and New York: Studies in Metropolitan Transformation, 1870–1930*, ed. Thomas Bender and Carl E. Schorske (New York, 1994), pp. 224–47, especially pp. 230–42.

46. See Judit Frigyesi, "Jews and Hungarians in Modern Hungarian Musical Culture," in *Modern Jews and Their Musical Agendas: Studies in Contemporary Jewry*, vol. 9, ed. Ezra Mendelsohn (Oxford, 1993), pp. 40–60.

47. On Bartók, see Tallián, *Béla Bartók*, pp. 9–11; on Beethoven, see Maynard Solomon, "The Nobility Pretense," in *Beethoven Essays* (Cambridge, Mass., 1988), pp. 43–55. Bartok's nobility pretense was reflected in his use of the nobility name qualifier "Szuhafő."

48. Judit Frigyesi, "Béla Bartók and the Concept of Nation and *Volk* in Modern Hungary," *Musical Quarterly* 78, no. 2 (Summer 1994): 255–87.

49. For the most recent accessible English-language description of Hungarian Jewry at the turn of the century, see William O. McCagg, Jr., *A History of Habsburg Jewry, 1670–1919* (Bloomington, Ind., 1989), especially pp. 123–39, 187–95. The tragic consequences of the resentment of Jewish assimilation and the denial of the significance of anti-Semitism among Hungarian Jews in

the 1930s and 1940s are clearly analyzed in Ezra Mendelsohn, *The Jews of Central Europe between the World Wars* (Bloomington, 1983), pp. 85–130.

50. *Documenta Bartókiana*, ed. Denijs Dille and László Somfai (Budapest, 1964–81), vol. 3, pp. 22–25.

51. Bartók, *Essays*, p. 340.

52. *Béla Bartók Briefe*, ed. János Demény (Budapest, 1973), vol. 2, p. 94. Szántó was actually born in Vienna but studied in Hungary. He lived abroad in the 1920s and died in Budapest in 1934. On Szántó and Bartók, see Dille and Somfai, *Documenta Bartókiana*, vol. 3, p. 83.

53. From an interview with László Somfai, cited in Malcolm Gillies, *Bartók Remembered* (New York, 1991), p. 31. The great musicologist Bence Szabolcsi, in an essay analyzing Bartók's idealization of the peasant and rural life (expressed by Bartók as late as 1943)—his "fantasy of a golden age" and the "happy village"—noted that Bartók "failed to notice what . . . Zsigmond Móricz had perceived long before." See Bence Szabolcsi, "Man and Nature in Bartók's World," in Crow, *Bartók Studies*, p. 69.

54. *Béla Bartók Letters*, ed. János Demény, trans. Peter Balabán, István Farkas, Elisabeth West, and Colin Mason (London, 1971), p. 136. Bartók comments here on the paradox that faced him and other Hungarian artists and writers of his generation. The models of Western Europe were sources of inspiration, comparison, and also devaluation and distortion, particularly in the effort to gain equal recognition for one's aesthetic achievement outside of Hungary.

55. See the biographical material on Móricz in *The Columbia Dictionary of Modern European Literature*, 2d ed., ed. J. A. Bede and W. B. Edgerton (New York, 1980), pp. 549–50; and in *The New Guide to World Literature*, ed. Martin Seymour Smith (New York, 1985), pp. 704–5. Of Móricz's major work only *The Torch* and *Be Faithful unto Death* were translated into English.

56. John Lukács, *Budapest, 1900: A Historical Portrait of a City and Its Culture* (New York, 1988), p. 168.

57. Bartók predicted this phenomenon in 1911. See Bartók, *Essays*, p. 302.

58. Zsigmond Móricz, *The Torch*, trans. Emil Lengyel (New York, 1931). The novel was published in Hungarian in 1918. The other connection to Bartók may have been Móricz's theology, to which Bartók may have been sympathetic. See, for example, the extensive discussion of God and faith in the letters to Stefi Geyer from 1907, and the end of Móricz's novel, where the "eternal laws of nature" are invoked over traditional theology.

59. Compare this position with that taken in Bálint Sárosi, *Volksmusik. Das ungarische Erbe* (Budapest, 1990), p. 13. It might be argued that the interest in urban popular music as a dimension of ethnomusicology developed later in the century. This would make Bartók's oversight understandable.

60. See Ferenc Bónis, "Bartók und der Verbunkos," in Ujfalussy and Breuer, *International Musicological Conference in Commemoration of Béla Bartók 1971*, pp. 145–53.

61. Bartók's phrases are in Bartók, *Essays*, pp. 316 (1920) and 394 (1944).

62. Tallián, *Béla Bartók*, p. 95.

63. See Béla Bartók, "What Is Folk Music?" from 1931, in Bartók, *Essays*, pp. 5–6, and "On Hungarian Music," in ibid., p. 302.

64. Gillies, *Bartók Remembered*, p. 187.

65. For an account of the popularity of the operetta in Budapest from the turn of the century, see Andras Batta, *Träume sind Schäume. Die Operetta in der Donaumonarchie* (Budapest, 1992); Bernhard Grun, *Kulturgeschichte der Operetta* (Munich, 1961), pp. 373–89; and Péter Hanák, "The Cultural Role of the Vienna-Budapest Operetta," in Bender and Schorske, *Budapest and New York*, pp. 209–23. It might be suggested that Bartók found the popular music of the 1920s and 1930s in Hungary neither interesting nor very good. But these so-called purely musical judgments demand critical scrutiny.

66. Bartók, *Essays*, p. 393. It should be remembered that when Bartók referred disparagingly to the nineteenth century he excluded Beethoven, who obviously represented a compelling model as a composer.

67. See Péter Hanák, "Endre Ady: Poet und Prophet," in *Kultur und Politik in Österreich und Ungarn*, ed. Péter Hanák, Waltraud Heindl, Stefan Malfer and Eva Somogyi (Vienna, 1994), pp. 78–83; and Péter Hanák, "Der Aufbruch Endre Adys," in *Der Garten und die Werkstatt. Ein kulturgeschichtlicher Vergleich Wien und Budapest um 1900* (Vienna, 1992).

68. Vera Lampert, "Works for Solo Voice and Piano," in Gillies, *The Bartók Companion*, p. 408.

69. On the Budapest reception of the *Kossuth Symphony*, see Frigyesi, "Béla Bartók and Hungarian Nationalism"; and János Demény's annotated collection of documents in Dille and Somfai, *Documenta Bartókiana*, vol. 1, pp. 30–65.

70. In Béla Bartók's article "Hungarian Music" (1944), in Bartók, *Essays*, p. 393.

71. One thinks, of course, of the work of Béla Balázs and the interplay of narrative, symbol, and meaning in *The Wooden Prince* and *Bluebeard's Castle*.

72. On the millennial celebrations, see *A Golden Age: Art and Society in Hungary, 1896–1914*, ed. Gyöngyi Éri and Zsuzsa Jobbágyi (Budapest, London, and Miami, 1990), pp. 47–55; also John Lukács, *Budapest, 1900*, pp. 71–72.

73. See Hermann Broch, "Hugo von Hofmannsthal und seine Zeit," in *Schriften zur Literatur*, vol. 1: *Kritik*, ed. Paul Michael Lützeler (Frankfurt, 1977), pp. 111–75.

74. Aladár von Tóth, "Béla Bartók," in *Ungarischer Künstler Almanach. Das Kunstleben Ungarns in Wort und Bild. Musik*, ed. Béla Diósy (Budapest, 1929), p. 99.

75. For a contemporary English-language description of Nagybánya and Gödöllő, see Karl Baedecker, *Austria-Hungary, including Dalmatia and Bosnia: Handbook for Travelers* (Leipzig and New York, 1905), pp. 372, 347.

76. See the excellent discussion and plates in Éri and Jobbágyi, *A Golden*

Age, pp. 72–81. On Lechner, see the plates in *Lechner Ödön: Late Nineteenth-Century Hungarian Architecture*, ed. Akachi Tsuneo (Tokyo, 1990).

77. See the reproductions of historicist fin-de-siècle Budapest buildings, including the Opera and Parliament, in *A Thousand Years of Hungarian Masterpieces* (Budapest, 1988), plate nos. 368–89. For the prehistory of historicist architecture in Hungary, especially neoclassic and gothic revival before 1870, see Anna Zádor, *Revival Architecture in Hungary: Classicism and Romanticism* (Budapest, 1981).

78. The best source for nineteenth-century Hungarian painting, including reproductions of work by Simon Hollósy, the founder of Nagybánya, is Júlia Szabó, *Painting in Nineteenth-Century Hungary* (Budapest, 1988). A reproduction of the Munkácsy is found on p. 288.

79. Cited in Judit Szabadi, *Art Nouveau in Hungary: Painting, Sculpture, and the Graphic Arts* (Budapest, 1989), p. 121; see also Éri and Jobbágyi, *A Golden Age*, p. 75. In this essay the terms "art nouveau" and "Jugendstil" are used interchangeably for the movement that dominated Europe around 1900, except when direct references to the Viennese or German origins of influence are made; then "Jugendstil" is preferred.

80. See Éva Hárs's text in *Modern Hungarian Gallery Pécs*, ed. Éva Hárs and Ferenc Romváry (Budapest, 1981), pp. 44–46.

81. Tallián, *Béla Bartók*, p. 57; on Gödöllő, see Szabadi, *Art Nouveau in Hungary*, pp. 81–94, 119–20.

82. See *Lélek és forma. Magyar művészet 1896–1914*, ed. Gyöngyi Éri and Zsuzsa Jobbágyi, pp. 58–59, 90–95 (this is the Hungarian version of Éri and Jobbágyi, *A Golden Age*).

83. On Csók and Nagy, see Szabadi, *Art Nouveau in Hungary*, pp. 41–44, 90–92. Like Ady, Csók spent a crucial period abroad in Paris.

84. Ibid., pp. 83–84.

85. Quoted in Éri and Jobbágyi, *A Golden Age*, p. 179. The close similarity to Bartók's 1911 essay, which appeared in the Budapest journal *Aurora*, is striking; see Bartók, *Essays*, p. 301. See also József Ujfalussy, *Béla Bartók*, trans. Sophie and Robert Bohati (into German) (Budapest, 1973), p. 456.

86. See, e.g., the pseudo-provincialist and Hungarian folk-inspired modernist design of the Jewish Charity Home (1910–11) in Budapest by Béla Lajta (1870–1920), in Éri and Jobbágyi, *A Golden Age*, p. 83.

87. Szabadi, *Art Nouveau in Hungary*, pp. 47–52.

88. See Hárs and Romváry, *Modern Hungarian Gallery Pécs*, p. 78; Lesznai's beautiful Ady pillow from 1912 in Éri and Jobbágyi, *Lélek és forma*, p. 85; and Szabadi, *Art Nouveau in Hungary*, plate nos. 81–87.

89. Éva Forgács, "Avant-Garde and Conservatism in the Budapest Art World, 1910–1923," in Bender and Schorske, *Budapest and New York*, pp. 309–31, especially pp. 314–18. It is ironic that in this otherwise first-rate essay, the author entirely misunderstands Bartók and his project. Her one reference states, "His metropolitan rhythms and sounds . . . evoke fast-paced twentieth-

century city life. . . . Bartók distilled the kernel of urban experience into his music" (p. 317). This is characteristic of the methodological barrier that exists between the "readings" of music and art. An unfortunate notion of the parallels between music and life is imposed on Bartók without regard to biographical intent, the constituent materials, compositional processes, formal structures, and historical references.

90. Bartók liked the painting and sought to send a photograph of it to his friend János Buşiţia in 1918; see *Béla Bartók Letters*, p. 139.

91. Quoted (with a few minor modifications in the translation) in Anton N. Nyerges, "Endre Ady: The World of Gog and God," in *The Poems of Endre Ady*, trans. and ed. Anton N. Nyerges (Buffalo, N.Y., 1969).

92. Ujfalussy, *Béla Bartók*, p. 47.

93. See *A Thousand Years of Hungarian Masterpieces*, plate nos. 400 and 411. On Károly Ferenczy (1862–1917) and Tivadar Csontváry Kosztka (1853–1919), see Szabadi, *Art Nouveau in Hungary*, pp. 32–35, 69–72.

94. Ferenc Bónis, *Béla Bartók: His Life in Pictures and Documents* (New York, 1972), p. 62; and Tallián, *Béla Bartók*, pp. 48–58.

95. For a modern summary of the results of the tradition of Bartók's research, continued by the composer László Lajtha among others, see Iván Balassa and Gyula Ortutay, *Ungarische Volkskunde* (Budapest and Munich, 1982), pp. 468–75. For a later interpretation of Bartók's work in folk music research, see Oskar Elschek, "Bartók's Beziehung zur Volksmusik und Volksmusikforschung," in Ujfalussy and Breuer, *International Musicological Conference in Commemoration of Béla Bartók 1971*, pp. 197–207.

96. For an excellent summary of the phases of Bartók's scholarly engagement with folk music research—collection and documentation (1906–18), analysis and systematic ordering (1918–28), comparative study (1929–40), and critical style analysis and the investigation of common origins (1940–45)—see Oskar Elschek, "Einleitung," in *Béla Bartók, Slovenske L'udove Piesne*, vol. 1 (Bratislava, 1959), pp. 17–28.

97. See Vera Lampert, "Works for Solo Voice with Piano," pp. 388–89.

98. For descriptions of the Suite No. 1 and the Piano Quintet, see Gillies, *The Bartók Companion*, pp. 454–62, 223–24.

99. Robert Hirschfeld, "Feuilleton. Orchesterkonzerte," *Wiener Abendpost*, 2 December 1905, pp. 1–2.

100. Halsey Stevens, *The Life and Music of Béla Bartók* (Oxford, 1993), p. 326.

101. On the relation between Paris and Bartók's interest in folk music, see Denijs Dille's brief gloss on a phrase about the yelling in the street markets of Paris in Dille and Somfai, *Documenta Bartókiana*, vol. 4, p. 41. French poetry was the most proximate model for Ady's pathbreaking *New Verses* of 1906.

102. See Frigyesi's work on *Kossuth* in "Béla Bartók and Hungarian Nationalism"; and János Demény's short comment on the Suite in *Béla Bartók Letters*, p. 14.

103. See Dille and Somfai, *Documenta Bartókiana*, vol. 1, pp. 30–62, especially the English reviews on pp. 60–62.

104. *Béla Bartók Letters*, pp. 20, 27–28.

105. Ibid., p. 44.

106. For the detailed English-language program for *Kossuth*, similar in format and intent to Bartók's own program explanation from 1905 for Strauss's *Sinfonia domestica*, see Dille and Somfai, *Documenta Bartókiana*, vol. 1, pp. 70–73; and Bartók, *Essays*, pp. 437–45.

107. *Béla Bartók Letters*, p. 54.

108. Ibid., pp. 42–43, 53.

109. Dille and Somfai, *Documenta Bartókiana*, vol. 4, pp. 39–40.

110. As Bartók wrote to Stefi Geyer in September 1907, "People who do not understand serious music show in other spheres, too, that compared with those who can appreciate serious music, their intellects are not so well developed," in *Béla Bartók Letters*, p. 85.

111. *Béla Bartók Ausgewählte Briefe*, ed. János Demény (Budapest, 1960), pp. 60–64.

112. Stevens, *The Life and Music of Béla Bartók*, pp. 326–27; Ujfalussy, *Béla Bartók*, pp. 414–15; and Lampert, "Works for Solo Voice and Piano," pp. 390–91. Bartók did publish the Székely song in February 1905. Bartók's passionate interest in and monumental research achievement on Slovak folk music had an autobiographical basis in his years in Pozsony.

113. Tallián, *Béla Bartók*, pp. 46–49. Dille, in his 1970 analysis of the Gerlicepuszta period, took a different view, which argued that although "fate knocked" at his door, Bartók was still some distance from realizing the role the new "old" folk material would play, or its potential as a creative source (Dille and Somfai, *Documenta Bartókiana*, vol. 4, pp. 15–28). But he agreed that the experience, given the subsequent events, would prove decisive.

114. Ernst Křenek, "Musik in der Gegenwart," in Hans Heinsheimer and Paul Stefan, *25 Jahre Neue Musik. Jahrbuch 1926 der Universal Edition* (Vienna, 1926).

115. Karl Baedecker, *Paris and Environs: Handbook for Travelers* (Leipzig and New York, 1910), p. 134.

116. There is some possibility also that Bartók might have seen the five Murillos in the old National Gallery, later in the Museum of Fine Arts, in Budapest. See Karl Baedecker, *Österreich-Ungarn, Handbuch für Reisende* (Leipzig, 1903), p. 394.

117. See the reproductions in *Tout l'oeuvre peint de Murillo*, ed. Claude Esteban and Juan Antonio Gaya Nuno, trans. Simone Darses (Paris, 1980). Bartók was also impressed by the statuary in Paris, particularly of composers; see the plate opposite p. 48 in *Béla Bartók Letters*.

118. The question of Liszt and his role as a model in Bartók's development is a key one. Ironically, both Bartók and Schoenberg wrote short essays in 1911 on Liszt and his significance. Szabolcsi wrote a brief introduction to Bartók's 1911 talk. A close comparison of the two would be instructive. They both are sympathetic, although Schoenberg is more reserved. Both see Liszt as misunderstood and underrated, as an inspiration for those dedicated to

the task of finding a genuine "modern" voice and model for the artist. In 1944 Bartók claimed for Liszt's music an absolutely "non-German transparency." See Arnold Schoenberg, "Franz Liszt's Work and Being," in *Style and Idea*, pp. 442–46, and the Bartók 1911 essay in Crow, *Bartók Studies*, pp. 119–24; see also Bartók, *Essays*, p. 362. On the use of gypsy and so-called Hungarian elements—the kind Bartók turned against—in Western music, including by Liszt, see Jonathan Bellman, *The "Style Hongrois" in the Music of Western Europe* (Boston, 1993).

119. Demény, *Béla Bartók Briefe*, vol. 1, pp. 75–76; *Béla Bartók Letters*, p. 50.

120. Dille and Somfai, *Documenta Bartókiana*, vol. 4, p. 73.

121. See the text of Bartók's and Kodály's 1906 "Manifesto to the Hungarian Public," with critical notes by Dille and Somfai, in ibid., pp. 85–88.

122. Ujfalussy, *Béla Bartók*, pp. 420–23.

123. Bartók sent a Balázs poem to Stefi Geyer in 1907 along with the score of the Quartet No. 1. See Tallián, *Béla Bartók*, p. 66; for Balázs on Bartók, see Gillies, *Bartók Remembered*, pp. 36–41.

124. *Béla Bartók Letters*, p. 135.

125. See Mary Gluck, *Georg Lukács and His Generation, 1900–1918* (Cambridge, Mass., 1985), pp. 14–16; also David Kettler, "Culture and Revolution: Lukács in the Hungarian Revolutions of 1918/1919," *Telos* 10 (1971): 35–92, and "The Romance of Modernism," *Canadian Journal of Sociology* (Winter 1986–87): 443–55.

126. Bartók's lecture was most likely some version of what is published as "The Relation of Folk Song to the Development of the Art Music of Our Time," in Bartók, *Essays*, pp. 320–30.

127. Anna Wessely, "Der Diskurs über die Kunst im Sonntagskreis" (typescript, n.d., courtesy of David Kettler); and "Simmel's Influence on Lukács's Conception of the Sociology of Art," in *Georg Simmel and Contemporary Sociology*, ed. Michael Kaern et al. (Norwell, Mass., 1990), pp. 357–73.

128. For Lesznai's work and her relationship to the Gödöllő group, see Éri and Jobbágyi, *A Golden Age*, p. 179; cited in Gluck, *Georg Lukács and His Generation*, p. 152 (see also pp. 153–60).

129. György Lukács, *Die Seele und die Formen* (Neuwied, 1971), p. 248. See also Lee Congdon, *The Young Lukács* (Chapel Hill, N.C., 1983), pp. 118–44; and Arpad Kadarkay, *György Lukács: Life, Thought, and Politics* (Oxford, 1991), pp. 89–172.

130. Karl Mannheim, "Seele und Kultur," in Karl Mannheim, *Wissenssoziologie. Auswahl aus dem Werk*, ed. Kurt H. Wolff (Berlin, 1964), pp. 66–84, especially pp. 81–82. See also the 1918 review of Mannheim's talk by Julia Lang, "Karl Mannheim: Seele und Kultur," in *Georg Lukács, Karl Mannheim und der Sonntagskreis*, ed. Éva Karádi and Erzsébet Vezér (Frankfurt, 1985), pp. 160–61.

131. See Karl Mannheim, *Structures of Thinking*, ed. David Kettler, Volker Meja, and Nic Stehr (New York, 1982), pp. 265–68. Mannheim, whose text dates from 1921, writes: "While the style of a folk song changes only with

infinite slowness, because every anonymous poet and modifier of the song revises it only imperceptibly in the direction of the new stylistic and global volition, the composer of art songs [*Kunstdichter*] is already focused . . . on the stylistic tendency of the song and, . . . without awaiting any alteration in its basis in life, forces the development in the direction of carrying the style to its culmination" (p. 266). The participants in *Bildungskultur*, Mannheim asserts, "come from various existential communities and introduce the tendencies that originate in those communities into the common stream of cultivation, which is why that stream is not uniform but polyphonic and dialectical in constitution" (p. 267). I am indebted to David Kettler for this observation.

132. Dille and Somfai, *Documenta Bartókiana*, vol. 4, pp. 78–79.

133. Adolf Weissmann, "Rasse und Nation in der Musik," in Heinsheimer and Stefan, 25 *Jahre Neue Musik*, pp. 98–99.

Why Is a Bartók Thematic
Catalog Sorely Needed?

LÁSZLÓ SOMFAI

Béla Bartók's oeuvre seems to be neither extremely large nor unknown. Nonetheless, the orientation for both the interested music
lover and the professional—the performer, the music librarian, the
musicologist—is severely hindered. Every Bartók biography contains
some kind of work list, and the general information about the major
works' year of composition and premiere is established. But ask a
pianist which version of the Two Rumanian Dances he or she plays,
for example, and watch the confusion. Most pianists do not even
know that different "versions" exist, that different editions are sold
in the United States, Hungary, Western Europe, and that all these
various copyrighted editions may be available in only a few Bartók
collections and major libraries. The pianist might play from the Schir-
mer Bartók Album, which supposedly restored the authentic original
form but in fact only reproduced the first edition, which Bartók later
revised several times. Or that pianist might proudly show you an edition with the annotation *rev. par Frédéric Delius* on the title page, a
bargain at a sale—a nice document, but unfortunately without any
source value. Or perhaps he or she plays from the Archive Edition,
edited by Benjamin Suchoff (New York: Dover Publications, 1981),
which may be the best choice, since it contains the rewritten sections
of the Second Dance. But this in itself is not good enough, for the
most detailed Bartók revision of the First Dance is to be found in
Rózsavölgyi's Bartók Album and the later editions by Editio Musica
Budapest. Our pianist, then, should combine two editions in his or
her study. And let our friend not forget that there are two recordings
of the First Dance played by Bartók himself, which may entirely revise
his or her concept of the proper tempo, character, and style!

Is the case of the Two Rumanian Dances specifically confusing, an exceptional example? Perhaps it is, but every Bartók work has its problems, and one might not even be aware that they exist. In connection with a large group of works, mostly those first printed by Hungarian publishers in Budapest before 1918 (some of which are already in the public domain in the United States, according to copyright law), there is indeed a chaos of versions similar to that surrounding the Two Rumanian Dances: originals and reprints, first and revised editions, those issued by the original publisher and those issued by other publishers, outdated versions from the composer's life and corrected versions in unauthorized, posthumous edition—all exist alike. In most cases only an expert knows what is what, and not even the catalogs of the largest music libraries can offer reliable assistance. Why such chaos? According to the twentieth-century philosophy of music publishing, the maintenance and the necessary correction of the text of a copyright-protected work in collaboration with the composer is the mutual interest of the author and the publisher. Therefore, announcing a "corrected" reprint is considered unnecessary. Moreover, from a business standpoint it might even be hazardous—think of the buyer of an older copy, who for the price would be entitled to the later, "correct" edition.

In 1939 Bartók changed publishers, switching from Nazi-governed Universal Edition to Boosey & Hawkes, where a few trusted men, who had been forced to emigrate from Vienna to London, looked after his work. This switch involved further complications. When Bartók left Hungary in 1940, he left the major part of his library behind. After his move to New York, the first reprints of Universal Edition scores began to appear under the imprint of Boosey & Hawkes. These were mostly photo reproductions of the Universal Edition version, based on a copy, any copy, available in London or New York—often the Universal Edition first edition, containing misprints and incorrect metronome markings. Several such reprints in the American estate attest that Bartók exploded when he first saw them: he nervously corrected the typography of the metronome indications but not the obviously wrong numerical metronome markings, and so forth. Then he cooled off and began to revise these scores, without, however, having access to or remembering his latest corrections made in Europe. As a result of this practice, in many cases we have two versions of the "corrected" score: the Universal Edition version (carefully maintained by publisher and composer) and an American revision that, in spite of its later date, does not necessarily override the other one (either because of the improvised nature of the correction or because Bartók could not finalize the revision, including the proofreading and so on). For the time being, then, the issue of the final authentic musical text of Bartók's works, the so-called *Fassung letzter Hand* containing the correct tempos and metronome markings, what musicians are so eagerly hunting for, is terra incognita.

Why, then, one might ask, is a complete critical edition of Bartók's oeuvre, which would automatically solve all these problems, still missing fifty years after the composer's death? After all, volumes of the Schoenberg (d. 1951) and Hindemith (d. 1963) *Gesamtausgaben* are growing nicely on library shelves. Of course, we also know that only recently has work on Berg and Webern editions been started, and a Stravinsky critical edition is not even on the horizon yet.

The plans for a Bartók *Gesamtausgabe* go back to the late 1960s, when the bulk of the manuscripts of Bartók's music had already been accumulated but was confined to estates and archives in New York and Budapest. Without access to the primary sources, Bartók studies in general were limited, and performers of his music had to be satisfied with commercial editions, obviously not without misprints and problems. Yet in the midst of litigations and rivalry on the Bartók scene, in spite of the systematic preparatory work that was done in the Budapest Bartók Archives in the 1970s, the planning had to be interrupted. The death of Ditta Pásztory-Bartók in 1982 then changed the scene. In 1988 Peter Bartók, the composer's younger son, owner of the holdings of the one-time New York estate and archive, forwarded photocopies of the American sources to the Budapest Bartók Archives for research and preparation of the complete critical edition. Béla Bartók, Jr., the elder son (who died in July 1994), the owner of a considerable number of the original sources in Budapest, also backed these studies.

The scholarly preparation of a forty-eight-volume Béla Bartók Complete Critical Edition (hereafter abbreviated BBCCE) is already at an advanced stage. In the Budapest Bartók Archives I myself have examined the sources extensively with a reliable small team of dedicated musicologists. In addition to the large collection of originals in our archive, photocopies of most of the other sources have been obtained. The copyists as well as the music papers are cataloged. New aspects of Bartók's habits in sketching ideas, working on his drafts, and correcting and editing his works have been explored.[1] We believe that the BBCCE, although it is intended to be directly useful to the performer as well, must be a scholarly edition. It will follow the best traditions of other such monumental undertakings in music but with a partially modified philosophy. With Bartók it must be recognized, first, that successive forms in the creative and editing processes do not automatically represent straight maturation with a single authentic version at the end of the source chain; and second, that the musical notation of a composer, in the absence of sufficient knowledge of his particular conventions in writing and reading music, can be ambiguous, and therefore the author's own performances—specifically, Bartók's gramophone recordings—must also be considered as primary sources. With dedicated work on the scholarly and editorial aspects of the project, the printer's copy or camera-ready form of all forty-eight volumes might be accomplished in ten to fifteen years. (The actual production and distribution may take considerably longer. These days, libraries can hardly afford to subscribe to series that publish more than two volumes yearly.)

But initiating the actual production of the BBCCE must still wait at this point. On the one hand, given the financial support currently available in Budapest, the anticipated intensity of the scholarly work, including the preparation of volumes by outside volume editors, is hardly possible. On the other hand, Peter Bartók, the legal heir and owner of the largest collection of primary sources, contends that, first of all, the functional, commercial editions should be made available free from misprints. Since 1991 several new editions by Universal Edition, with red paperback covers and designated "Revision: Peter Bartók," as well as a few Boosey & Hawkes revised reprints containing Peter Bartók's foreword, belong to this project.

·

Until the BBCCE volumes are on the shelf, a reliable guide to the compositions remains badly needed for the praxis and scholarship as well as for music lovers and contributors to secondary Bartók literature. Traditionally, the best such guide is a thematic catalog. It may contain an immense amount of yet-unpublished primary material in well-organized form, which in the case of the quite extensive but disorganized Bartók literature is vitally important. In fact, a thematic catalog is to be the "house manual" of the editors of the BBCCE, as well. After all, without the collected and critically surveyed complete data on each composition both individually and in relation to its neighboring works in chronology and genre, the volumes of the critical edition cannot be prepared.

The forthcoming Béla Bartók thematic catalog naturally includes thematic incipits, but that is the least important aspect of it. The organization of the catalog, however, is crucial. That the catalog of Bartók's oeuvre should list the compositions in chronological order has never been questioned. His output is not a vast one, and he consistently dated his compositions or otherwise provided basic information by assigning opus numbers or making lists, checking the dates in printed work lists, and so on. But a chronological organization means numbering, and in this respect Bartók's output is already confusing.

Bartók himself began to assign opus numbers at three separate periods (as a child, as a young man, and as an established composer), but the third series of opus numbers suddenly ended in 1920 with the Improvisations, Op. 20, because—to make a long story short—he himself became less certain about distinguishing between important works (with opus numbers) and lesser works (without opus numbers). In 1948, a few years after Bartók's death, composer-philologist András Szőllősy made a chronological list containing numbers 1–121 (these are the "Sz" numbers), which in subsequent decades he amended with (a)'s and (b)'s, adding and withdrawing titles, as new works and versions came to light.[2] In 1974 a new numbering appeared in Denijs Dille's magisterial *Thematisches Verzeichnis der Jugendwerke Béla Bartóks, 1890–1904* (Budapest: Akadémiai Kiadó, 1974), a thematic index of the juvenile output and more: a compendium of everything worth knowing about Bartók's life and work up to the beginning of his mature style. This catalog contained the "DD" numbers 1–77, incorporating Sz 1–25. These DD numbers, in conjunction with the remaining Sz numbers, were a temporary solution but impractical, although they were adopted in the Bartók entry of the *New Grove Dictionary of Music and Musicians*. Moreover, for the really important part of Bartók's output the sorely needed information was still not publicly available. A third, unpublished, numbering exists as well, made by Iván Waldbauer, who worked in the New York Béla Bartók Archives. It was planned as a thematic index, whose numbers were (and still are) included in the call numbers of the primary sources in the American estate. These "W" numbers 1–85 correspond to neither the Sz nor the DD numbers.

The Béla Bartók thematic catalog will be organized chronologically, according to the new "BB" numbers 1–129, which I assigned after reexamining the complete source material of the whole oeuvre. The decisions about the strict chronological order and the designation of compositional units to be numbered separately was not without problems. In a preliminary report I discussed some of the problems:[3] assembling works under one number (e.g., DD 1–77 is now condensed in BB 1–33); numbering versions and transcriptions; positioning of the revised versions as well as of fragments and discarded pieces; handling planned works; and the chronological identification of works with "from–to" dates.

The catalog is still in progress; only the smaller portion of the individual BB items has been undertaken so far. Needless to say, in a book some six hundred pages in length, lack of the introductory and supplementary chapters, part of the quoted text seems to be in something of a lingua franca: the abbreviations, the formalized description of manuscripts and paper structures, the references to other BB work numbers, and other items. Furthermore, without the context, it is not always clear to the nonspecialist why contradictory data (e.g., concerning duration) have been given, or why contemporary work lists are referred to while seemingly more relevant recent ones are not.

BB 63, the *Allegro barbaro*, not only is a famous work but may serve as a typical example of the content, style, and format of the entries in the forthcoming Bartók catalog. The structure and elaboration of the headings or subheadings, depending on the genre, might be different, either more or less detailed, in another case. (As a matter of fact, the *Allegro barbaro* is *not* a typical case in certain respects: the documentation of the compositional process of this piece is surprisingly poor, for example; there are no linguistic variants of the title, so the heading "original titles" does not apply.[4]) The editorial principles guiding the decisions in the most problematic aspects of the cataloging can, however, be seen here. These include, among others, matters of proportions, languages, and handling hypotheses.

PROPORTIONS. The history of the composition and the primary sources will be discussed in detail, because in this respect the Bartók literature is traditionally poor. An adequately detailed identification of the printed editions and their variant forms is crucially important as a much-needed practical aid for performers and librarians. On the other hand, for early performances after the premiere, only selective information will be given, because extensive documentation has already been published by János Demény, Béla Bartók, Jr., Tibor Tallián, and others—though for the full reception history an immense amount of additional data would have to be obtained. The heading "Literature" will be developed up to the publication of the catalog, but references to secondary literature (biographies, analyses, etc.) will be selective.

LANGUAGES. Unpublished German and French texts by Bartók are quoted without English translation. Unpublished Hungarian texts from Bartók's letters or from his autograph manuscripts appear in the original plus English translation (though already-printed letters and so forth usually appear only in English). Original titles in Hungarian, Rumanian, Slovak, and other languages will be given with a translation only if their meaning is different from that of the established English titles.

HYPOTHESES. Instead of restricting itself to indisputable facts and concealing still-unsolved research problems, the catalog intends to open up significant questions to further study.

Abbreviations (in addition to those for names of instruments and such conventional abbreviations as p. or pp. for pages) are as follows in the sample entry:

BB = Béla Bartók thematic catalog number
BBA = Budapest Bartók Archives (Bartók Archívum)
BBCCE = Béla Bartók Complete Critical Edition (in progress)
BBjr = Béla Bartók, Jr.
BBjr/Apám = Béla Bartók, Jr., *Apám életének krónikája* [The chronicle of my father's life] (Budapest: Zeneműkiadó, 1981)
BBjr/Műhelyében = Béla Bartók, Jr., *Bartók Béla műhelyében* [In Béla Bartók's workshop] (Budapest: Szépirodalmi, 1982)
B&H = Boosey & Hawkes
Bónis/Quotations = Ferenc Bónis, "Quotations in Bartók's Music," *Studia Musicologica Academiae Scientiarium Hungaricae* 5 (1963): 298ff.
BRS = Bartók Recording Studio; Bartók Records
Családi = Béla Bartók, Jr., and Adrienne Gombocz-Konkoly, eds., *Bartók Béla családi levelei* [Béla Bartók's family correspondence] (Budapest: Zeneműkiadó, 1981)
Dictionary-1924 = Bartók work list in the "Bartók" entry in A. Eaglefield-Hull, ed., *A Dictionary of Modern Music and Musicians* (London: Dent, 1924)
Dille-1939 = Bartók work list in D. Dille, *Béla Bartók* (Antwerp: Standard-Boekhandel, 1939)
Dille/Regard = Denijs Dille, *Béla Bartók. Regard sur le passé*, ed. Y. Lenoir (Louvain-le-Neuve: Institut Supérieur d'Archéologie et l'Histoire de l'Art, 1990)
DocB = *Documenta Bartókiana* (Budapest: Akadémiai Kiadó, 1964–81)

Essays = Béla Bartók, *Essays*, ed. B. Suchoff (London: Faber & Faber, 1976)

Gillies/Remembered = M. Gillies, *Bartók Remembered* (London and Boston: Faber & Faber, 1990)

HMV = His Master's Voice

Hungaroton/Centenary Edition = L. Somfai, Z. Kocsis, and L. Sebestyén, eds., *Complete Centenary Edition of Bartók's Records*, 2 vols., LPX 12326-38 (Budapest: Hungaroton, 1981)

Hungaroton/CD-1991 = L. Somfai and Z. Kocsis, eds., *Bartók at the Piano, 1920–1945*, HCD 12326-31 (Budapest: Hungaroton, 1991)

J.E.&Co. = Joseph Eberle (Vienna) music paper

Letters-1971 = J. Demény, ed., *Béla Bartók Letters* (Budapest: Corvina, 1971)

Letters-1995 = M. Gillies and A. Gombocz, *Bartók Letters: The Musical Mind* (Oxford: Oxford University Press, 1995)

Levelei = J. Demény, ed., *Bartók Béla levelei* (Béla Bartók's letters) (Budapest: Zeneműkiadó, 1976)

Mácsai = J. Mácsai, "Törölhető kérdőjelek?" [Superfluous question marks?], *Muzsika* 37, no. 1 (January 1994): 14ff.

Mf = Die Musikforschung

MS = manuscript

MZSz = Bartók work list in *Magyar Zenei Szemle* 1, no. 1 (March–December 1941)

PB = Peter Bartók's collection (Homosassa, Fla.)

ReM-1921 = Bartók work list ("Table analytique des oeuvres de Béla Bartok") in *La Revue Musicale* 2, no. 1 (March 1921)

SM = Studia Musicologica Academiae Scientiarium Hungaricae

Somfai/Tizennyolc = L. Somfai, *Tizennyolc Bartók-tanulmány* [Eighteen Bartók studies] (Budapest: Zeneműkiadó, 1981)

Somfai-1995 = L. Somfai, *Béla Bartók: Composition, Concepts, and Autograph Sources* (Berkeley and Los Angeles: University of California Press, 1995)

st. = staff

Stevens-1993 = H. Stevens, *The Life and Music of Béla Bartók*, 3d ed., prepared by M. Gillies (Oxford: Clarendon Press, 1993)

Sz = Szőllősy work list number according to the list in B. Szabolcsi, ed., *Bartók. Sa vie et son oeuvre*, rev. ed. (Budapest: Corvina, 1968), pp. 283–313, with few corrections as reprinted in J. Ujfalussy, *Béla Bartók* (Budapest: Corvina, 1971), pp. 400–430

Székely/Tanár = J. Székely, *Bartók tanár úr* [Professor Bartók], rev. ed. (Budapest: Dunántúli Magvető, 1978)

UE = Universal Edition

W = Waldbauer work list number (in MS; used in the call numbers of sources in the American Bartók estate, now in Peter Bartók's collection)

ZT/X = *Zenetudományi tanulmányok*, vol. 10, ed. B. Szabolcsi and D. Bartha (Budapest: Akadémiai Kiadó, 1962)

BB 63
Allegro barbaro for piano, 1911 (or 1910), BBCCE Vol. 36

Duration   *Aufführungsdauer/Durée d'exécution: cca 2'35"* (cf. letter to UE of 30 May 1930, but not identified as the duration of Allegro barbaro; see printed edition [b]); *Zeitdauer des Stückes ca. 2'30"* (Bartók to UE, 8 Jan. 1937; cf. printed edition [c]; no revised UE edition issued in Bartók's lifetime indicated the duration); 2'35" (measured by Bartók in America and entered ca. 1943 in a B&H print; first published in the UE "new edition" in 1992). (In connection with concert programs, as a simplified reference, Bartók usually gave "2 mins.") Measured durations of Bartók's recordings: (1) HMV gramophone record, 1929: 2'22"; (2) Hilversum Radio studio recording, 1935: 2'27".

Composition   No year in the manuscript, no authorized date in the printed editions. The first recorded date of the composition is *1910*, printed in a 1917 concert program, which seems to go back to Bartók.[5] Unless it is a misprint, this is chronologically the closest evidence. On the next program (1921),[6] however, *1911* was printed. The ReM-1921 work list, also based on data from Bartók, gave *comp. 1911* (the Dictionary-1924 work list contained no date), and 1911 was confirmed by the latest contemporary work list, which Bartók personally revised (Dille-1939).—The circumstances of the composition are unknown. Had the Allegro barbaro been written in 1910 or early 1911, it did not fit into Bartók's concepts of any of the thematic sets of solo piano music finalized and contracted with Rozsnyai and Rózsavölgyi between June 1910 and June 1911, either because of its character (cf. the collections of Rumanian dances, dirges, burlesques, elegies) or because of its size (cf. the Seven

Sketches). The motivic resemblance between the Allegro barbaro theme and a motive in Ravel's Scarbo (cf. Bónis/Quotations, p. 372), played by Bartók in recital 12 December 1911, may offer the latest possible date of the composition (end of 1911?) for speculation.—**Title.** The autograph draft was not titled. "*Allegro barbaro,*" in quotation marks, appears in the preliminary edition (*Nyugat*, 1 January 1913); the form *Allegro barbato*, printed in the program of the premiere (1 February 1913), could have been a misprint. It has been pointed out (Reinhold Sietz, "Ein Vorläufer von Bartóks 'Allegro barbaro,' " *Mf* 5 [1952]: 370–72) that Charles Valentin Alkan titled a piano piece "Allegro barbaro" (Douze études, Op. 35) and another "Allegretto alla barbaresca" (Douze études, Op. 39); Bartók owned a copy of the latter. After Dille's close study of the relevant sources and his interviews with Bartók's first wife, Márta, and with Kodály (Dille/Regard, pp. 205–12), the most probable explanation seems to be the one given by Kodály: the adjective *barbaro* is a somewhat ironic reflection to the expression "jeunes barbares hongrois" of a Paris review about the 12 March 1910 concert (Bartók played Bagatelles, and No. 1 of the Two Rumanian Dances).

Premiere 1 February 1913, Kecskemét (Casino), in the course of a "Kuruc Evening" of the Kecskeméti Dalárda (Kecskemét Choral Society), played by Bartók as the closing number of his solo, including a group of piano pieces: "(a) Bear Dance, (b) Evening in Transylvania, (c) Two Burlesques, (d) Ten Bagatelles, (e) Allegro barbato [*sic*] (manuscript)."—The next known Bartók performance: 10 March 1919, Budapest (Vigadó), an encore after BB 36b, the Rhapsody for piano and orchestra. From 1920 to 1941 Bartók regularly played Allegro barbaro, mostly as the final piece of mixed groups. Although he occasionally seemed to tire of the hits of his repertoire (cf. Családi, p. 381: he related how happy he was in June 1926 to have written new pieces to replace "the constant Allegro barbaro, A bit drunk, and the [first] Rumanian Dance"), but he kept Allegro barbaro as one of the most important items on his programs until the end of his career.

Primary Sources

(a) **autograph**, the original draft: BBA 176 (in 1925 Bartók presented it to pediatrician Ignác Péteri; until 1961 in the collection of Magyar Zene-művészek Szövetsége Budapest [Association of Hungarian Musicians]). 2 bifolia (= one binio), the second bifolium turned over as a cover sheet; J.E.&Co./No.4/16-li. paper. No original pagination. Music on fol. 2^r–4^r; fol. 1^v and 4^v blank. Fol. 1^r subsequently became the title page: *Allegro barbaro* (written by Bartók, not at the time of the composition, in pencil); *A szerző kézirata. 1925.* [The composer's manuscript. 1925] (in blue pencil, unidentified hand). No date, no title on the first page of the music, no signature, no metronome marking. Draft notation in ink, only scattered performing instructions (but accents occasionally differ from those in the final form; cf. Peter Bartók's notes in the UE "new edition" of 1992). On fol. 3^r one natural added in red pencil.

(b) MS copy, missing. A collation of the text of the draft and the *Nyugat* facsimile edition proves the existence of an intermediate stage. This missing copy of the autograph was presumably made by Márta and furnished with performance instructions by Bartók, and served as the printer's copy for the facsimile edition in *Nyugat*.

Printed editions

(a) preliminary editions (1) Facsimile edition in the literary biweekly *Nyugat* 6, no. 1 (1 January 1913): [57], 58–69, reproducing the fair copy of a professional copyist (Copyist "X"; his initials given above and below the double bar at the end of the facsimile edition as M.I.): "*Allegro barbaro*["] / *szerz:* [composed by:] *Bartók Béla*. No initial Italian tempo indication; ♩ = 96–84. (According to a note on p. 80, with this issue the periodical started publishing original musical compositions, and Allegro barbaro was "written for *Nyugat*," an overstatement not corroborated by other data.)—A corrected copy of this facsimile edition (pp. 49–80 torn out from the issue) served as the **printer's copy** of the UE 5904 first edition: Wiener Stadt- und Landesbibliothek MH 14293c. Bartók corrected in ink (mostly accents, dynamics, tempo indications, and the insertion of m. 114), UE's senior editor, W[öss], in pencil. *Tempo giusto* added by Bartók. Dated *Zum Stich / 6.7.[19]18*.—**(2)** Publicity edition: *Allegro barbaro* as *Notenbeilage* in the 1 November 1919 issue of *Musikblätter des Anbruch* (published by UE), marked "copyright 1919 [*sic*] by Universal-Edition," plate no. M.A.1.; probably engraved from the same printer's copy as the UE first edition but with an eight-page layout instead of six. Distinctive features: on p. 1, ♩ = 96–84; ending on p. 8, *pp*.

(b) first edition UE 5904 (copyright 1918, actually published January 1919; engraving [see p. 2]: Breitkopf & Härtel, Leipzig). Green cover: *BÉLA BARTÓK / ALLEGRO BARBARO / PIANO SOLO*. Title page: *Allegro barbaro / für Klavier zu zwei Händen von . . . / zongorára 2 kézre írta. . . .* Distinctive features: on p. 2, ♩ = 96–84; ending on p. 7, *pp*. First printed in 500 copies. (Reprints: 500 in 1921; cf. UE 18 August 1922. 1000 in 1923; cf. UE 9 December 1923.) Publication history (i.e., Bartók-UE correspondence): on 20 June 1918 Bartók offered Allegro barbaro for publication; on 25 June UE accepted; on 3 July Bartók mailed printer's copy to Vienna; on 5 July UE received it and inquired about the prospective opus number; on 15 August Bartók sent the corrected proofs and stated that Allegro barbaro *hat keine Opuszahl*; on 31 January 1919 Bartók received five copies of the printed music; on 24 November 1920 review in Revue Musicale was sent to UE; on 30 May 1930 Bartók's letter:

. . . ich habe die Absicht von nun an bei jedem veröffentlichten Werk auch die Aufführungsdauer anzugeben, am Schluss jedes Stückes bzw. der einzelnen Sätze; ungefähr so:
Aufführungsdauer/Durée d'exécution: cca 2'35"
Ich glaube dies trägt bei um Missverständnisse vorzubeugen (wie z. B. dies bei der Militär-Orch. Aufnahme des "Allegro barbaro" der Fall ist, aus welchem Stücke—wahrscheinlich in Folge eines fatalen Druckfehlers der 1. Ausgabe bei der M.M.-Bezeichnung—ein "Adagio barbaro" geworden ist!)

But there was no reprint in 1930, and the timing (not identified in the letter as the timing of Allegro barbaro, incidentally) was not introduced in UE prints.

(c) corrected reprint End of 1927. On 16 September 1927 UE sent the proofs, based on Bartók's *Korrekturexemplar* (this corrected copy is missing); on 24 April 1928 Bartók asked for a copy of the reprint. Distinctive features: on p. 2, $\d = 76–84$; on p. 5, m. 143, left hand added; ending on p. 7, *f*. Printed in 500 copies.—Further reprints referred to in the Bartók-UE correspondence, (1) 1936: correction requested 5 and 16 June; unchanged version went to print 10 July; Bartók, 13 July, recognizing that he was late, wrote, "*Ich hätte übrigens nur die Zeitdauer und die Gram.platten-Nummer der authentischen Aufnahme hinzugefügt*"; on 16 July UE still asked for these data; in connection with David Grey's planned instrumentation in 1936–37 (see Arrangements), on 8 January 1937 Bartók added, "*Nur muss er das Tempo unverändert beibehalten: Zeitdauer des Stückes ca 2'30". (In der 1. Ausgabe ist als Druckfehler bei der M.M. Zahl ♩ statt ♩ !!).*" (2) 1938: corrections requested 11 November and 2 December, which Bartók, for lack of time, waived on 11 December, but added, "*Allᵒ barbaro wurde übrigens schon mehrmals (gelegentlich der bisherigen Neudrucke) überprüft, so dass es eigentlich als fehlerfrei betrachtet werden kann.*" About the silent revision of this "faultless" printed text in Bartók's performance cf. Recordings.

(d) Boosey & Hawkes reprint edition Copyright assigned 1939 to Hawkes & Son (plate no. H. 15180). Printed in U.S.A. On p. 7, marked "10.41.W." (i.e., October 1941). Reproduction of the UE corrected print (with $\d = 76–84$). The New York office of B&H sent two copies of the reprint to Bartók 18 February 1943, without cover, which was criticized by Bartók (cf. missing letter, 28 April, and B&H, 1 May).—A **corrected copy**: PB 29PFC1. Beyond Bartók's minor typographical and other changes, the only significant correction is the addition of timing in parentheses at the end.

(e) new edition UE Neuausgabe 1992. Revision: Peter Bartók (with notes; contains no information about the textual changes on Bartók's record).

Recordings Two Bartók recordings are extant; a third one is missing. According to Bartók's letter (Családi, p. 331), he played Allegro barbaro for a Pleyela roll in Paris, 12 April 1922 (UE's letter of 2 June 1922 acknowledged that Bartók recorded the First Rumanian Dance and the Allegro barbaro for Pleyela). No copy of the original paper roll seems to exist; the Hilversum Radio recording was mistakenly designated as a Pleyela piano roll in the Hungaroton/Centenary Edition.—(1) His Master's Voice gramophone record HMV AM 2622 (1930), recorded in Budapest in November 1929 (matrix number BV 727[II]). Reissued after a disk: Bartók BRS 003, etc.; from the matrix: Hungaroton/Centenary Edition 1, 1/4; Hungaroton/CD-1991, 1/8. Significant textual changes include Bartók playing a six-bar ostinato instead of the printed eight bars from m. 50; twelve instead of thirteen from m. 88; and eight instead of seven from m. 144. Furthermore, he plays accents and slurs in mm. 13–14, 29–31, 67–68, 84–86, 113, 181, and 192–93 considerably differently from the printed copy (cf. Somfai/Tizennyolc, pp. 135–41; DocB/6, pp. 261–67; and Somfai-1995 [. . .]). This is a version of the Allegro barbaro habitually played by Bartók not from the score but from memory, which might be called the "final revision" although the alterations are missing from the printed edition. As quoted earlier (see the corrected reprint), Bartók intended to let a reference to this HMV record as the "authentic recording" be printed in the UE edition.—(2) Undated, unidentified recording in the Hilversum Radio archive (formerly identified as the 1922 Pleyela roll, which Mácsai, pp. 15–16, rightly disputed), now believed to be the recording of Bartók's concert performance in the Hilversum Radio studio, 31 January 1935:[7] Hungaroton/Centenary Edition 2, 1/9. Bartók plays a six-bar ostinato instead of the printed five bars from m. 62; twelve instead of thirteen from m. 88; eight instead of seven from m. 144; and seven instead of eight from m. 213 (cf. Somfai/Tizennyolc, pp. 135–40).—N.B.: A short silent film, made by Tibor Serly in September 1942 in New York (Serly's estate; copy in BBA) contains two cuts showing Bartók playing the piano, which have been identified (video reconstruction of Hungarian Television 1987, assisted by Ernő Lendvai and Erzsébet Tusa) as the beginning and perhaps the middle part of the Allegro barbaro performance.

Arrangements Instrumentation for band (1929) by Arthur Prévost (1888–1967), conductor of the Orchestre des Guides (Brussels), which was recorded at the wrong "*Adagio barbaro*" tempo (HMV [Belgian] H 16); cf. Dille/Regard, pp. 210–12. Gaston Verhuyck-Coulon, manager of Prévost, mediated the permission with Universal Edition (letters in BBA of 2 and 14 May 1929). Cf. also Bartók to UE, 7 and 25 May and 6 June 1929, and 14 January and 30 May 1930 (after 8 January, in Brussels, Bartók heard a concert performance of the arrangement—"*sie klingt sehr gut*"—but this time the tempo was not mentioned; 16 January Bartók asked: "*Wie steht es mit der Herausgabe dieser Transkription?*" which UE could not publish; see also the interview with Bartók about the concert in ZT/X, p. 370), and 30 May 1930 (the previously quoted criticism, after Bartók received a copy of the disk).—Plans for an orchestration: David Grey, director of an English dance group, asked permission to orchestrate Allegro barbaro (UE 22 December 1936), which Bartók granted in principle (8 January 1937).

Dedication   None.

Correspondence   Bartók to UE: 25 September 1920 (according to a letter from Prunières, Cortot was enthusiastic about the Allegro barbaro); and 10 May 1921 (Bartók sent his autograph copy of a review in *New York American*, 14 March 1921, by Max Smith, about Dohnányi's performance in New York).—Családi, pp. 291, 304, 306, 310, and 330; Levelei, pp. 259, 272–73, 290, 358, 567, 599, 708 (considering gramophone recording in 1944); DocB/2, p. 51; DocB/3, p. 142; DocB/5, p. 79; DocB/6, pp. 187, 191; Letters-1971, pp. 159, 186, 339; Letters-1995, [. . .].

Literature   DocB/5, p. 79; DocB/6, pp. 154, 156, 158, 259–72; Essays, p. 493;—BBjr/Műhelyében, pp. 124, 126–131, 132–33, 136, 138, 142–43, 145–47, 154, 156, 158–60, 162, 165–66, 168, 170, 172–73, 175, 178–79, 181, 183–89, 193, 195–96, 198–99, 203, 205, 209, 211, 214–15, 221, 224, 226, 229, 245, 247–48, 251, 330; BBjr/Apám, pp. 131, 184–442;—Gillies/Remembered, pp. 59, 93, 128, 144; Székely/Tanár, pp. 53–55 and facsimile after p. 142 (with music examples of the correction of the first edition); Stevens-1993, pp. 117, 120.

Work list numbers   Sz 49, W 29.—**Contemporary work lists**: ReM-1921: *Allegro barbaro, comp. 1911, publ. . . . 1918*; Dictionary-1924: *Allegro barbaro*; Dille-1939: *1911 Allegro barbaro*; . . . MZSz-1941: *1911 Allegro barbaro*.

NOTES

1. In a book to be published later this year, I summarize the essentials. See L. Somfai, *Béla Bartók: Composition, Concepts, and Autograph Sources* (Berkeley and Los Angeles, 1995).

2. The first elaborated form appeared eight years later. See A. Szőllősy, "Bibliographie des ouevres musicales et écrits musicologiques de Béla Bartók," in B. Szabolcsi, ed., *Bartók. Sa vie et son oeuvre* (Budapest, 1956), pp. 299–345, or, in the rev. ed. (1968), pp. 283–313. The revised and authorized Sz numbers can be quoted from J. Ujfalussy, *Béla Bartók* (Budapest, 1971), pp. 395–430.

3. L. Somfai, "Problems of the Chronological Organization of the Béla Bartók Thematic Index in Preparation," *Studia Musicologica Academiae Scientiarum Hungaricae* 34 (1992): 345–66.

4. I recently presented the planned entry on BB 64, Four Orchestral Pieces,

as another typical example: see Somfai, "Béla Bartók Thematic Catalog: Sample of Work in Progress," ibid., vol. 35, nos. 1–3 (1993–94): 229–41.

5. On Dohnányi's program (17 October 1917, Liszt Academy, Budapest), his first famous public espousal of Bartók's music, the well-designed Bartók block included ten items. Each was dated correctly on the printed program, and the controversial "Op. 8" numbers of the printed editions were also revised: BB 27/1, Study for the Left Hand (1903); BB 51/5 and 51/10, "Evening in Transylvania" and "Bear Dance" (1908); BB 49/2, Two Elegies, Op. 8/b, no. 2 (1909); BB 63, *Allegro barbaro* (1910); BB 58/1 and 58/2, Four Dirges, Nos. 1–2 (1910); BB 55/1 and 55/2, Three Burlesques, Op. 8/c, Nos. 1 (1908) and 2 (1911); BB 27/4, Scherzo (1903). Only Bartók himself could furnish the date of *Allegro barbaro*. (For an enthusiastic review of this concert, see Béla Bartók, Jr., ed., *Bartók Béla családi levelei* [Béla Bartók's family correspondence] [Budapest, 1981], p. 273.)

6. 7 January 1921, Liszt Academy, Budapest. An all-Bartók program, including a block of solo piano pieces presented by Dohnányi—one Burlesque, the first Dirge, the Bear Dance, Evening in Transylvania, and the "Allegro barbaro (1911)"—and BB 33, the Piano Quintet, played by Bartók.

7. The program included (1) BB 79, Fifteen Hungarian Peasant Songs, Nos. 6 and 7–15; (2) BB 63, Allegro barbaro; (3) BB 51/5, Evening in Transylvania; (4) BB 51/10, Bear Dance; (5) BB 56/1, first Rumanian Dance. (2) and (4) were recorded in their entirety, (3) and (5) fragmentarily (see Hungaroton/Centenary Edition II/1/6–9).

The Gallows and the Altar:

Poetic Criticism and Critical Poetry

about Bartók in Hungary

PETER LAKI

"Ah, presso del patibolo bisogna ben l'altare!" ("Oh, next to the gallows there has to be an altar!"), exclaims Rigoletto in act 2 of Verdi's opera. The phrase seems strangely appropriate to the history of Bartók's reception in Hungary, a history traditionally characterized by two extreme positions. Bartók was placed on a pedestal as not only a composer of genius but also as an embodiment of an intellectual and moral stance—a model for the entire country. On the other hand, his music was, for a long time, a frequent target of criticism for what was seen as radical modernism and incomprehensibility.

The goal of this essay is to show the evolution and the interdependence of these two positions. Bartók's reception in Hungary had, from the start, transcended the purely musical domain and taken on a more general significance, with aspects ranging from the social and political to the moral and ethical. The wide swings of the "reactive pendulum" between enthusiastic praise and violent rejection attest to the magnitude of the issues involved. In the process, Bartók's public image was strongly idealized, and his music became an arena in which a whole gamut of nonmusical questions were fought out.

Great composers have always had their champions as well as their detractors; Bartók's case, however, differs somewhat from those of his contemporaries. From the earliest days, discourse about Bartók's music was often characterized by a degree of personal involvement rarely seen in reviews of Schoenberg and Stravinsky, although the latter were just as hotly debated in the musical centers of Europe. Bartók's early, overtly nationalistic works were greeted in the press as the words of a new musical genius, who raised Hungarian music to new artistic heights.[1] Some critics—Aurél Kern, for instance—praised Bartók from a standpoint of extreme Hungarian nationalism and turned against him when faced with the increasing radicalism of Bartók's music.[2] The exceptional range of responses to Bartók's music is partly due to the fact that he was both a cultural icon of national importance and a controversial modern composer. Even those who admired him for his iconic status often had to struggle to comprehend his musical thought.

In his fascinating psychological study of the composer, Bertalan Pethő made a brief statement only four words long in Hungarian; yet its proper translation in English requires considerably more space: "Bartókot követni feladatot jelent," wrote Pethő—or, literally translated, "To follow Bartók is a task."[3] This sentence sums up a whole chapter dealing with forms of artistic understanding and has broad implications expressed by the special connotations of two of its four words. First, "to follow" is not merely to understand but also to become a follower, a disciple in the spiritual sense. Second, "task" is not merely something one has to do but also a challenge and a moral imperative. In a word, there seems to be a consensus that Bartók's music makes special claims on its audience, whom it challenges to become not only listeners but committed followers. This case differs from that of Schoenberg, for example, in that it is inseparably linked to issues of nationalism: Bartók was considered a spiritual guide for the entire Hungarian nation.

The origins of this consensus reach back to the very beginning of Bartók's career. As early as 1911, musicologist and critic Sándor Kovács was haranguing against those who rejected Bartók, and the passionate tone of his writing was motivated at least in part by the conviction that understanding Bartók was both a condition and a sign of a higher level of cultural and *moral* development. Kovács had this to say about the concert of 12 February 1911, at which the Hungarian National Symphony Orchestra, under László Kún, performed Bartók's Romanian Dance for orchestra and the first of the Two Portraits, with Imre Waldbauer's violin solo:

> It was a red-letter day: they played Bartók. It was one of those great experiences that no one who had been gripped by them can ever forget. The Romanian Dance gleamed and glistened, crackled, sparkled, and tore along, inciting to wild exultation. The Portrait grew out of that single, skinny, naked voice, and the gigantic Joy grew, thickened, and swelled and swelled. It became clouded with clouds of clarity, it swirled, revolved; finally, it

flamed with pure flames, like a million lights. It tightened the
strings of attention, almost to the breaking point. We sat in a par-
oxysm of delight, our eyes wet from fever; we watched, out of
breath, with anguished hearts, frightened, as this titanic palace
of sound, these superhuman blocks of music, these heaven-
storming mountain peaks rose higher and higher and even
higher yet! All products of our day are dwarfed beyond words by
this sublime work, and if there is anyone in the past who can be
compared with it—in its proportions, in its virtues, in its directions [arányokra, erényekre, irányokra]—it cannot be anyone
else but John Sebastian Bach [Bach János Sebestyén]. . . .

In fact, words are awkward and useless if their subjects are ex-
cellences [jelességek] of such magnitude. If this art is after your
own heart, you will feel, as I do, how powerless words are if they
want to express either subjective impressions or evolutionary
values. And if the music does not speak to you, or does not speak
to you yet, you will not be converted by words, and it will take
more than words to convert you. We understand very well that
there are such people, even though we are not happy that this be
the case. Any empathy with Bartók's art presupposes a musical
culture that the audience and the majority of musicians don't
have, and a social and aesthetic culture that the musicians and the
majority of the audience don't have. And even of those who have
it, it demands [the experience of] having lived through Bartók's
development and witnessed the gradual emergence of the idiom
he speaks (an idiom we no longer understand). The uncomprehending I can understand. Critics who are dimly aware of
Bartók's significance but confess that he is alien to them evoke
our sympathy because at least they are sincere. But one cannot
have enough contempt for those who (with their thinly disguised
cloven hoofs) try to paint this uniquely great art in the pale colors
of mediocrity just because it cannot penetrate their obtuse
brains.[4]

Sándor Kovács (1886–1918) was one of the pioneers of Hungarian
musicology. Before his promising career was cut short by death at the
age of thirty-two Kovács had published a number of scholarly articles
in the field of music psychology, reporting on interesting experiments
in the field of melodic and rhythmic perception, among others. In his
review, however, he casts off scholarly objectivity to assume a highly
emotional and prophetic pose, in emulation of Endre Ady (1877–
1919), the greatest Hungarian poet of the time. The language of the

review, to which no translation could do full justice, teems with neologisms and nonstandard grammatical constructions that are reminiscent of Ady, whose art and personality left no literate Hungarian untouched.

Kovács saw in Bartók a cause that exemplified the struggle of old and new in general, and he participated in this struggle with an unusual vehemence and a zeal to "convert" (the repeated use of the word is revealing). He accused his opponents of not only intolerance and incompetence but also malicious intent, equating mediocrity with evil ("cloven hoofs"). It is interesting, however, that although Kovács was a passionate believer in the new, his rhetoric had a definite nineteenth-century flavor. He discussed Bartók in terms of a romantic paradigm inherited from the literature on Beethoven and Wagner, with the image of the composer as a heaven-storming genius as the focal point. No other metaphors could possibly do.

Kovács's ire was directed against such critics as Izor Béldi (1867–1926) of *Pesti Hírlap*, who played an infamous role in the press campaign against Bartók. The following sample, an account of a concert on 19 March 1910 devoted to Bartók's works, gives a good idea of the style and orientation of the opposing camp:

> After listening to Bartók's works presented at tonight's concert, we had only one wish, one irresistible desire: give us some aspirin! Because this music has the peculiarity of causing a monumental headache: it exhausts, torments, and unnerves the listener. (And the performer as well.) In Bartók's recent music, a logical train of thought is replaced by a wild chase of rhapsodic ideas, and form is supplanted by arbitrary juxtapositions. Tangled musical threads suddenly broken, interesting thoughts suppressed almost as soon as they are born and continually mixed up with other themes in different keys and opposite moods—thus might we characterize the latest works by Bartók, a genius gone awry. The description applies in particular to the ten bagatelles from Fourteen Piano Pieces, Op. 6, and the interesting but confused and rather empty Fantasy in C♯ minor and the Romanian Dance, which has an intriguing rhythm and starts skillfully but soon becomes incomprehensible. At the beginning, they played Bartók's new String Quartet Op. 7, in A♭ minor. This is a sort of *Elektra* in chamber music form, a veritable orgy of eccentric sound effects and a rhapsodic piling-up of a few incoherent musical thoughts. The first-movement Lento and the Allegretto following it sound at times as if all four players were simultaneously tuning their

instruments. The last movement is more sensible and more unified, but even there the composer seems to have worked in a de-
lirious state, with a few rare lucid moments.—Finally, they played
an earlier piano quintet by Bartók, which, after the quartet,
seemed like a work by Haydn or Mozart: so beautiful and melo-
dious, so pure and simple, so naive, natural, and immediate in its
effect. It is a pity Bartók abandoned the musical direction inau-
gurated at that time; it is a pity that he has turned to the worship
of false idols. Let us hope that he will return to artistic beauty, the
only redeeming religion. Any number of morphine, hashish, or
opium addicts have been cured of their disastrous ways; why
couldn't Bartók be cured of his worship of the ugly in music? For
if he were not cured, we should indeed mourn the great and irre-
trievable loss of an extraordinary talent. However, we would feel
equally sorry for our musical youth, whose training has been entrusted to this Bartók of today.

This review could have pride of place in the *Lexicon of Musical Invec-
tive,* yet it was not reproduced here as an addendum to Nicolas
Slonimsky's classic book. Rather, it is included to point out a startling
similarity between Kovács's and Béldi's reviews, namely the use of a
certain religious terminology: conversion and cloven hoofs on one side,
and the worship of false idols on the other. It seems that the contro-
versy surrounding Bartók amounted to an outright religious war between the disciples of a new "musical Messiah" and the "nonbelievers."
Even critics whose rhetoric was more sober viewed Bartók, right
from the beginning, in a larger context, as the composer who was
destined to write the next chapter of Hungarian music. One of the
most original critical voices of the early 1900s, Géza Csáth, passion-
ately espoused Bartók's cause as early as 1908. Csáth, a physician who
became known for his brilliant short stories, was also a trained musician. In contrast to the effusive and rhapsodic Kovács, Csáth was
somewhat more rational yet no less committed. The following excerpt
from his review of the Fourteen Bagatelles may serve as an example:

This music is entirely new in form, in its working-out, in its
sound, yet its roots and foundations may be found in every one
of us.
Every sensitive person has known these feelings! These halting
rhythms, these willful dissonant encounters between unrelated
tones! Even more: this abhorrence of the common, of dominant
and subdominant and cadences! These are subtle and far-out
states of mind, on the borderline of dreams and frenzy, which

have a right, and deserve, to be expressed, as only those can deny who fail to recognize that a person may and must express what he *can* express, and if this expression arouses interest, then art has its raison d'être.

Bartók set his peculiar moods for piano, and he notated all his intentions on the music paper. Dynamics has its own mysterious life here. The change of tempos reveals the secrets of an unusual nervous system. The strength of the melodies (without any las-civiousness and not "tuneful") bespeaks an ascetic depth. The harmonies represent the delights of a sophisticated, trans-formed, newfangled ear. These harmonies no longer move in the dimension of tonalities, as three-dimensional beings cannot live in two [dimensions]. . . . In all this there is rationality, musical substance, Hungarianness, and future. Yes, Hungarianness, though not the kind of Kálmán Simonffy and Béni Egressy,[5] who were excellent gentlemen and would certainly be saddened to learn that in Hungary, now as then, scold:ng and derision are the fate of those who continue the noble work of their ancestors rather than repeat it.[6]

Csáth was well ahead of his time in accepting Bartók's treatment of dissonance as an expression of artistic freedom, but even he, in the last sentence of his review, revealed his larger agenda and used Bar-tók as a stick with which to beat the conservatives.

The evolution of Bartók's musical style was paralleled by appropri-ate changes in the discourse about his music. From the late 1910s on, responses to Bartók's music became more scholarly as it began to be championed by some of Hungary's best musical minds. Antal Molnár, the original violist in the Waldbauer-Kerpely string quartet, who had played in the historic first performance of Bartók's First Quartet, pub-lished his earliest article on Bartók and Kodály in 1911.[7] Writing about *Bluebeard's Castle* in the year of its premiere (1918), Molnár sur-veyed the reviews of the first performance and summarized the con-servative positions with biting sarcasm: "Not all reviewers understand Bartók's epoch-making significance, but each one, without exception, recognizes his very great talent; many grant him, generously, the epithet 'genius.'"[8]

Molnár did not miss the ironic fact that many critics recognized Bartók's "genius" and yet rejected his opera. He pointed out that many conservative critics praised *Bluebeard* for what they perceived as its "strong Hungarian national character" but complained about the dissonant harmonic idiom and certain decadent, "morbid" tendencies. The critics hoped that once "reformed," Bartók would become Hungary's greatest composer. It is evident that Bartók was important to the conservative critics for ideological reasons: they saw him as a proponent of a Hungarian nationalism they espoused,[9] yet they were unable to accept the music.

In 1919 Molnár undertook a short but ambitious general essay on "Bartók's significance."[10] In this essay, he wrote:

> Bartók's significance lies in the fact that he has given voice to new material at the time of the mortal agony of the bourgeois establishment, namely the material of genuine folk music; in other words, he transferred the entire equipment of a compromised musical technique in the healthy direction of a new evolution, by combining it with the fresh utterances of a previously neglected social class. The technique was renewed in the process, and a new era began in the history of music. The folk material came into the foundry of form-giving as the healthy and fertile force that it is, raising art to a new, higher form of its evolution. . . . [Bartók] pointed his fist at the throat of a compromised, worn-out, thought-killing world. Morality instead of decay, simple strength, a life force leaving the stale air of a bourgeois room for the free outdoors, the pure confidence of a child whose new faith casts off the fatigue of old age: this is the significance of Bartók's direction.

The rhetoric of this paragraph dates it unmistakably: it must have been written during, or near, the short-lived communist regime of the spring of 1919; yet Molnár was certainly expressing his own feelings in his article. The references to social classes only couch in political language a basic thought that other writers formulated differently. The revolutionary rhetoric equates old with dying and new with young and healthy, providing a fresh set of metaphors for the same modern/conservative dichotomy we have seen in the reviews of Kovács and Csáth.

While the "religious war" was raging among critics, a new type of critical response began to emerge from an unexpected source: poetry. By the centenary of the composer's birth in 1981, more than a hundred Hungarian poems were inspired by Bartók and his music.[11] To the best of my knowledge, these poems have never been viewed in a musicological context before; yet they deserve a place in the composer's Hungarian reception history, as a complement to reviews, for at least two reasons. First, the very existence of so many poems is a rather unparalleled phenomenon. Second, the image of the composer that emerges from these poems is a fascinating complement to the reviews written by professional music critics. A complete study of this body of poetry would no doubt be an extremely valuable contribution to both the history of Bartók's reception and the cultural history of Hungary in general. Space, however, permits only a very selective sample here and now.

It is generally thought that the earliest Hungarian poem about Bartók was written in 1921 by Gyula Juhász (1883–1937).[12] An outstanding poet of his generation, Juhász lived in the city of Szeged, where Bartók had given a piano recital that year. Juhász's short, lyrical poem was soon followed by a more dramatic piece by Lajos Kassák (1887–1967), the poet and painter who was a key figure in the Hungarian avant-garde movement. Bartók had contributed musical scores to the periodical *Ma* (Today) edited by Kassák, and prior to his "Bartók" Kassák had published another poem dedicated to the composer.[13]

One of the most striking traits of Kassák's Bartók poem is how Kassák differed from many pro-Bartók critics who maintained that with repeated exposure and sufficient training Bartók could be fully appreciated, with the much-feared "dissonances" no longer in the way of understanding. Kassák did not try to neutralize the negative feelings associated with the music but rather made them the focus of the poem, somewhat like the unsympathetic critics had done. Yet Kassák was of course a fervent champion of the composer. His image of Bartók, however, was more diabolical than Messianic—in fact, he explicitly called Bartók "Satan" in the poem. (The roles have been reversed; it is Bartók who has cloven hoofs here.) The poem acknowledged a certain primal wildness in Bartók's music and associated it with destruction and catastrophe. Yet destruction was welcome, for it cleared the way for the emergence of something new.

Kassák's poem juxtaposes the fearful images of Bartók's music and the "diabolical" reputation of the composer with a rather unassuming and benign portrait of the man. The same juxtaposition occurs in a review published in the literary weekly *A Hét* (The week) a few years earlier. The reviewer, Gyula Fodor, a supporter of Bartók, had written in 1917, after the first performance of *The Wooden Prince*:

Eight years ago [pianist] Arnold Székely played the piano piece "Ma mie qui danse" in recital. It was a strange kind of waltz; people looked at one another in consternation, some hissed. A respectable German critic leapt up from his seat during the performance, slammed the door behind him, and said, "Scandal!" The piece was by Béla Bartók [his Fourteenth Bagatelle]. Bartók was instantly proclaimed a musical revolutionary, a Jacobin, a sansculotte, an anarchist, and a pathological case. Then the Philharmonic played his Second Hungarian Suite, making the witty critics moan about Texas, where there are signs in the concert halls asking [the audience] not to shoot at the musicians, but this request frequently goes unheeded. The careful spoke about a great talent regrettably gone astray. Those who were even more careful wrote, 'Bartók must have himself a good laugh when he says that some people actually applaud such horrors.' In the meantime, the situation became more complex. Some works by famous foreign composers were performed in Budapest. It had to be discovered—with a deeply saddened and broken heart— that there are composers abroad for whom tonality, the diatonic system, and its attendant harmonic theory are not the final point of evolution. Critics who thought they had done their duty by admitting the idiosyncrasies of Puccini among the things to be learned (alas!), had to pay homage to Strauss, Debussy, Reger, and Dukas, doing violence to their aversion to the new and to their love of comfort. Bartók, however, was still on the index. Musicians, if they played his scores at all, played him with revulsion and ill will. No Hungarian conductor would take up his cause. No wonder, if we remember that we are dealing with an individual gone astray, a perverted, pathological, disingenuous traitor to the fatherland, a decadent and a sansculotte. The species of pathological sansculottes, however, is unfortunately so rare in this country that we may devote a few words to its representative.

Who is this perverted composer? Who is this revolutionary gone astray? He is a short, slim, clean-shaven, gray-haired artist, wearing a pince-nez: the composer. He is a quiet, introverted, reserved, modest, delicate, kind, goodly man. His whole life is work. Only the nation's day workers have lived as does this prince of Hungarian music, born by the grace of God. He teaches piano at the Conservatory, and he trains not only the hands but the tastes, the minds, and the souls of his students. He is a flawless artist of his instrument, a perfect interpreter because he is an unselfish one. His musical knowledge has no limits. His knowledge is scholarship. In addition, this decadent traitor to the fatherland has spent many months in the countryside, traveling by carriage, eating nothing but bread and bacon. More than a thousand gramophone recordings, preserved at the folklore collection in the Városliget, document his collecting work, and his observations on the music of the Hungarians and the ethnic minorities of Hungary are more numerous and more valuable than anything done before in the field of folklore in Hungary.[14]

Fodor's article paints a somewhat idealized picture of the composer. Aside from its informative function, it also fulfills a poetic one as it appeals to the emotions as well as to the intellect.

As Bartók's international recognition grew in the 1920s and 1930s, there was a marked change in the composer's critical reception at home. Almost every professional critic now agreed on Bartók's greatness, yet this did little to alleviate Bartók's feelings of isolation in his own country. The critical legacy left by Kovács and Csáth, both now deceased, was taken up by younger men such as Aladár Tóth and Sándor Jemnitz, who combined passionate commitment with great erudition in their writings. At the same time, several important works, performed abroad, had to wait for years before they could be heard in Budapest. The performance of *The Miraculous Mandarin*, planned at the Budapest Opera for the composer's fiftieth birthday, was canceled; the work was never presented in Hungary during Bartók's lifetime. The *Cantata profana*, written in 1930, was not performed in Hungary until 1936 (the world premiere had taken place two years earlier, in London). It is typical of the atmosphere that Bartók, who had played the solo part in the world premiere of his Second Piano Concerto in Frankfurt in January 1933, declined to participate in the Budapest premiere later that year. He was replaced by Louis Kentner at the 2 June concert of the Budapest Philharmonic. And in 1936, the Kisfaludy Society, a conservative literary organization, awarded Bartók the Greguss Medal for his Suite for Orchestra No. 1, a youthful work written thirty-one years earlier. Again, it was clear that the Kisfaludy Society wanted to honor a man whose greatness they couldn't help but acknowledge, although they were unable to accept his mature music. Bartók's sarcastic response and his rejection of the medal are well known.[15]

In 1936, it was still possible for a critic, Fedor Dietl, to write from the position of the uncomprehending in public. His review of the Hungarian premiere of *Cantata profana* evokes the anti-Bartók diatribes of the 1910s:

> It wouldn't be fitting to report with patronizing superiority on the new work of a composer who has won fame and praise for Hungary abroad. We shall limit ourselves to pointing out that

even the title of the new "cantata" is a daring paradox—just as absurd as the piece itself, which goes exactly counter to everything classical tradition has made into law. Tradition, with which the definitive break occurs exactly in Bartók's music. This music, then, cannot be called music in the old sense, can it?

The story that inspired Bartók to write his cantata, first performed four years ago in London, is quite a meager affair. It is about the father, whose nine handsome sons come to a magical forest where they turn into stags. In vain does the father follow them to entice his enchanted sons back. The young stags coldly declare they have no intentions of returning to the home of their parents.

Who could say why Bartók chose this psychologically incomprehensible, confused story for his composition? After all, something similar is expressed much more simply and comprehensibly in the beautiful legend of Nimrod's sons and the giant stag.[16] At any rate, even the most attentive audience could not make out too many of the words. The utterly atonal voice leading of the double chorus precluded any emphasis on the vocal parts. But the chorus wasn't alone in being exposed to insurmountable difficulties. . . . The two soloists, Endre Rösler and Imre Palló, . . . had a heroic task, singing their parts, sometimes filled with wailing melismas without any orchestral support. The conductor, Ernő Dohnányi, did superhuman work! He outdid himself in watching every instrument and voice amid the maze of the chaotically cacophonous dissonances. But even his peerless musicianship could not prevent the chorus from losing pitch. One must admit, however, that almost no one in the audience noticed this tonal deviation. Just as no one would have noticed if the baritone solo had been switched with the tenor solo. . . .

The camp of Bartók's admirers, who always try to justify each new piece by the great composer, will certainly enthuse about the premiere of *Cantata profana*. For our part, not belonging to those who want innovation at any cost, we are ready to admit that the new work has one great and undeniable advantage. It is short! Finally, it will be interesting to mention that Bartók traveled to Turkey to escape the premiere.[17]

Dietl gave himself away when he said the *Cantata* was "about the father, whose nine handsome sons . . . " and so on. To almost all other reviewers, the piece was about the sons who had turned into stags. Just as the father represented the society that the sons rejected, Dietl evoked (not very intelligently, it has to be admitted) the authority of a "tradition" that Bartók had transcended. He couldn't understand new music any more than the father could understand his sons' decision to live in the forest. But in either case, there could be no amicable disagreement. The son threatens the father: "ízről porrá zúzódsz" ("you will be crushed to smithereens"); between the progressive and the conservative, the war was continuing.

The most eloquent and most influential critic to take up Bartók's cause between the two World Wars was without a doubt Aladár Tóth, who became the director of the Budapest Opera after World War II. Tóth wrote about Bartók and Kodály with the fervor of a zealot and with a sensitivity that can aptly be characterized, once again, as poetic.

This is not the place to discuss Tóth's music criticism in general.[18] One example, however, chosen from dozens, might exemplify his style and his approach. After the first Budapest performance of Bartók's Second Piano Concerto by Louis Kentner under Otto Klemperer, Tóth wrote:

Those who were present last night at the Hungarian premiere of Bartók's Second Piano Concerto, those who saw the extraordinary impact made by this grandiose masterwork on the Hungarian audience, could feel that the time is near when Hungarians will awaken to their highest calling in Bartók's art. Bartók may never before have spanned such enormous vistas in such a crystal-clear and concise form as he did in the four movements of this piano concerto.[19] One is amazed by the titanic form-giving force that was able to create a clearly outlined piano concerto style, one that might be considered a modern sibling of Bach's concertos, out of the most unbridled passions, the most pagan visions, the most unrestrained revolts of temperament and imagination. It is not easy to follow this music, where tremendous perspectives open up behind every note, where one may feel the awesome efforts of a genius's imagination that overcome the gigantic wilderness of the barbarous soul. But this exciting struggle gives rise to such enthralling poetic beauty that immediately captivates the listener at first hearing. We hope this composition will frequently figure on our concert programs, and then we will be able to write a more detailed appreciation. But we may as well make it clear now: Bartók's Second Piano Concerto is, next to his Fourth String Quartet, the greatest instrumental work of the twentieth century.[20]

The bold claim of the last sentence only summarizes the entire paragraph, bristling with superlatives. The comparison with Bach had been broached by Kovács twenty-five years earlier: the adjectives "titanic," "gigantic," "tremendous," "awesome," and so on also continue an earlier trend, though on a much higher level of intensity. Above all, Tóth reiterates perhaps more forcefully than ever a recurrent theme in Bartók's reception, namely the relationship between Bartók's music and what Tóth terms the "highest calling" of the Hungarian nation—in other words, the notion that Bartók's music, and the ability to appreciate it, are inseparable from a form of Hungarian cultural identity that is to be striven for; and although "it is not easy to *follow* this music" (my emphasis) it is a moral imperative to try to do so.

The discourse, placed on such a high cultural and moral plane, scarcely allowed for serious discussion in the field of musical criticism. The case of Fedor Dietl was an isolated one in the 1930s; even Emil Haraszti, another former opponent—one must say, much better trained and more articulate than Dietl—had become considerably more sympathetic by that time.

But Bartók's opponents did not give up the fight so easily. Fierce polemics involving him and Kodály were raging over issues other than his compositions. These polemics, which are well known, go back to at least 1919: that year, Bartók took Kodály's defense when the latter was under attack for his activities during the communist regime of 1919.[21] The all-inclusive nature of Bartók's ethnomusicological activities (the inclusion of Romanian and Slovak music in addition to Hungarian) repeatedly offended both Hungarian and Romanian nationalistic extremists.[22] And in 1937, the Catholic periodical *Magyar Kultúra* (Hungarian culture) attacked Bartók and Kodály for corrupting the schoolchildren by proposing to introduce folk song, and instructive works based on it, into the school curriculum.[23] As far as Bartók's compositions were concerned, however, the music critics, led by Aladár Tóth, were slowly making headway in their crusade.

While professional critics such as Tóth had recourse to elaborate poetic imagery to justify what was new in Bartók's music, one of Hungary's greatest poets, Attila József (1905–37), took a much more rationalistic approach in a projected but never completed study (1936), of which only thirteen brief theses survive.[24] On the question of dissonance, Attila József boldly proclaimed: "Creation is possible only through dissonance. Consonance is nothing but dissonance understood." He also asserted, in a statement that seems to respond directly to previous Bach-Bartók comparisons, that "some musicians try to explain Bartók by Bach. This is impossible. Bach is like custom. If one does something out of custom, one cannot understand the meaning of that custom unless one considers and solves an original situation (problem). Therefore, we may understand Bach from Bartók and not the other way around."

In rejecting an evolutionary approach in which Bartók's music was explained in terms of its historical antecedents, Attila József challenged "some musicians" and implied that the force of intuition could be greater than that of historical understanding. This is surely what he meant by "music understood from nonmusic," another of his cryptic theses. If Attila József had written and published his essay in 1936, it could have had a major impact on the discourse about the composer, since—as far as one can see from the thirteen brief theses—nationalistic considerations were completely foreign to his purview of the Bartók question.

As it was, Bartók continued to be discussed in terms of his moral message to the nation. A whole new generation of intellectuals had grown up feeling that they had to define their attitudes toward Bartók in order to understand themselves and their place in the world. The poet István Vas (1910–91), who in later years wrote several autobiographic volumes, described how he, as a young man in his twenties and a native of Budapest, had found a new sense of self-awareness by singing, at friendly gatherings, the peasant songs collected by Bartók and Kodály.[25] After the war, a younger poet, András Fodor (1929–), received a similarly formative influence from Bartók. In his case—Fodor was born in a small village in southwestern Hungary where he had evidently heard folk songs—the influence came from Bartók's compositions. In his book *Vallomások Bartókról* (Confessions about Bartók),[26] Fodor relates how he first came into contact with Bartók's music after his move to Budapest at age eighteen. Fodor describes the overwhelming impression Bartók's music made on him at the first encounter. His fascination was to result in many fine publications on Bartók's music and on twentieth-century music in general, including a monograph on Stravinsky. In 1948 (he was nineteen years old), Fodor published his poem "Bartók," a work frequently anthologized and that has come to be regarded as the document of an entire generation coming to grips with a composer with a difficult yet indispensable message.

> I do not remember when I uttered
> Your name for the first time, but
> Even then, there was a certain

Grave respect in it. We enthused
About the mere name, for it stood
For purity: professing faith, entirely
Akin, acting on our behalf;
We pointed him out proudly to
Mocking doubters: "He resembles us."[27]

It is clear from this opening paragraph that Fodor and his friends claimed Bartók as a spiritual guide even before they had found their way to the music. The rest of Fodor's poem describes initial responses to Bartók's works. Expressions like "fear," "horror" and "our hearts sank" crop up time and time again in the onomatopoeic evocation of several Bartók works (*The Miraculous Mandarin*, the Dance Suite, the [Second] Violin Concerto, *The Wooden Prince*, *Allegro barbaro*, *Cantata profana*, and *Divertimento* are mentioned by title). But Fodor also conveys his feeling of how the synthesis of various folk music traditions result in a "wider homeland": "Your music is an entire world, and I find my way home in it." The two strands—the recurrent references to fear on one hand and, on the other, images of home and kinship—are combined in the last sentence of the poem:

It made me understand that
Immortal is only he who fears,
And bequeaths his very fear
To us, his kin, as an encouragement.

Fodor wrote his poem three years after Bartók's death. Its success shows that the image of Bartók as a spiritual mentor who can be reached only after an arduous journey struck a deep chord in many of the composer's admirers. The last sentence contains an apparent paradox, suggesting that fear can serve as an encouragement. (In reality, it echoes the old wisdom that a hero is not one who knows no fear but one who overcomes it.) In this particular context, however, Fodor's closing sentence encapsulates the fundamental dichotomy between the fearsome aspects of Bartók's music and the encouragement inherent in his moral message.

Soon after Fodor's poem was published, the darkest chapter in the history of Bartók's posterity began. The fact that Bartók was not only one of the greatest composers of the time but also an ethnomusicologist who spent countless hours among villagers collecting folk music was not lost on the Communists. It could not be denied that Bartók had been strongly committed to the same "people" (*das Volk*) in whose name the Communists claimed to be ruling. And yet the old distaste for modernism could not be laid to rest so easily. It reappeared in an ideological guise as the Hungarian Stalinists, led by József Révai, the Hungarian Zhdanov, began to level charges against Bartók's music that were closely modeled on the "formalist" debates in the Soviet Union. (It is ironic but highly revealing that in 1919 revolutionary metaphors were used—in the previously quoted excerpt from Antal Molnár, for instance—to extol Bartók's music. After 1949, a similar revolutionary rhetoric was used to condemn him.)

In 1948, the year of the infamous Soviet Communist Party resolution against Shostakovich and Prokofiev, the Hungarian government awarded Bartók—posthumously—the Kossuth Prize, the highest distinction given by the state to an artist (Bartók was one of the first recipients of the prize). The same year, Budapest hosted an international Bartók festival and competition. But soon foreboding dark clouds started to gather on the horizon, and what has become known as the *Bartók-per* ("Bartók trial") got under way. As János Breuer explained in his 1978 essay,[28] Bartók's oeuvre was "torn in half." The works ostensibly based on folk music, those written with a pedagogical intent, and the more "classical" compositions of the last period were accepted as suitable for the "popular democracy," while works like the string quartets, the violin sonatas, and *The Miraculous Mandarin* were left unperformed for years. Their style was seen as decadent and an artistic dead end in Bartók's output. In the debates, culminating during the years 1950 and 1951 and finally subsiding by 1955, critics claimed that the "problematic" works were too complex and incomprehensible for the masses. Their "pessimism" and inherent conflicts also made them unsuited to the demands of a new society. The charges of complexity and pessimism were, of course, related, but they were also separated on occasion, as when Révai came around to accepting the first but not the second.[29] By the end of the debate, composer András Mihály—who had formerly advocated a selective approval of Bartók's music—realized that to criticize Bartók on the basis of "incomprehensibility" was merely to repeat what "bourgeois" critics had been saying all along.[30] The rhetoric had become shrewder and more subtle since Izor Béldi's desperate call for aspirin, and the motivation less personal and more political. It is evident that the writers were carrying out orders from the party. Nevertheless, the gallows and the altar were still exactly where they had always been.

In 1955, as the unfortunate "Bartók trial" was coming to an end, one of Hungary's greatest living poets, Gyula Illyés (1902–83) published his poem "Bartók," which has been frequently reprinted and recited by actors in public performances. The entire poem is based on the same duality we have encountered throughout this essay: the complexity and dissonance of the music versus its inherent moral message. Illyés's premise is that the music that "to them" is a "harsh discord" brings solace "to us." The entire poem is an elaboration upon this thesis: it is precisely through the apparent discords, so the argument goes, that the meaning of Bartók's music unfolds. Humankind has suffered deeply, and Bartók's music, by giving voice to that suffering, also shows the way to relief.

The poem has long been recognized as a landmark in postwar Hungarian poetry; yet its musical implications have, to the best of my knowledge, not been fully discussed. Illyés is a fervent champion of Bartók's music in this poem and engages in passionate polemics with the "unbelievers," who obstinately cling to their positions. At the same time, Illyés does not directly refute the charge that Bartók's music is characterized by harsh discords (the Hungarian term used, *hangzavar*, is even stronger, literally meaning "chaos of sounds" or "cacophony"). Rather, he accepts discord as a symbol of suffering and turns the charge into a praise for the composer who didn't hesitate to utter the horrible truth. But, compelling and sympathetic as it is, this argument still builds on the notion that Bartók's music is "discordant." In other words, Illyés provides a rationale for the *hangzavar* but does not deny its presence. To the contrary, he uses the concept in a series of startling oxymora near the end of the poem: "praying with blasphemy, sacrificing with sacrilege, wounding to cure."[31] The poetic images are extremely powerful, but one cannot help but wonder why *any* element in Bartók's music has to be perceived as blasphemy or sacrilege. The answer may be found in the circumstance that Illyés's poem was the poet's testimony in the "Bartók trial," and he built his defense of the composer incorporating (and turning around) elements borrowed from the prosecution.

The Illyés poem resembles the one by Kassák, written three decades earlier, in that both take up current perceptions of Bartók as cruel and cacophonous and turn them into praise for the composer. But there is a significant difference (aside from the styles of the two poems, which are light years apart): Illyés presents the "cacophony" as an ultimately beneficent force in the context of a fundamentally optimistic worldview, whereas Kassák, who did not offer any interpretation of the "cacophony," had positively reveled in the frightful imagery and, in the manner of an avant-garde enfant terrible, praised the composer for the very qualities the conservatives had rejected in him.

Kassák and Illyés were not the only poets in whom Bartók's music conjured up images of catastrophe. In the Second Piano Concerto, Gábor Devecseri heard Fate, approaching with big, thundering steps and treading humanity underfoot.[32] To Géza Képes, the four instruments in the Fifth String Quartet are four Greek Fates, spinning the thread of destiny. His poem is pervaded by images of death and the disintegration of human consciousness in a sea full of wild, colorful, animal life.[33] Sándor Csoóri expanded upon the generational conflict in the *Cantata profana* where the sons, transformed into stags, refuse to go home with their father. Whereas this refusal is ultimately presented in the *Cantata* as a victory of freedom in nature, Csoóri presents an extremely disquieting portrait of the abandoned father, sitting all shriveled up in his misery, and of the goose (the would-be supper) that bled to death in vain.[34] György Somlyó, for his part, took Bartók's farewell concert in Budapest before his emigration (8 October 1940) as his point of departure and reflected on the individual and collective responses to a tragic life situation elicited by that highly emotional evening.[35] In the sequel, "Bartók's Homecoming," Somlyó depicted a country that had risen to the challenge of Bartók's music. This poem, which is supposed to provide a positive counterpart to "Bartók's Farewell," still admits that the immediate effect of Bartók's music is somewhat painful: "Feszíts, az izmok bárhogy is sajognak" ("Stretch us, no matter how much the muscles may hurt").

It is remarkable that only a few poems express positive feelings inspired by Bartók. One of these, by Amy Károlyi, tells of the "geometrical pleasure" found in Bartók's music, but the poet also went out of her way to portray it as "abstract" music that does not express emotions of any kind. She seems to say that without such abstraction, a pleasurable reaction to Bartók's music would be impossible: the only possible pleasure to be derived from it is a "geometrical" one.[36]

How relevant are these poetic responses to Bartók's music? After all, many of these poets, as well as those not included here, bring their own personalities and concerns to the music. One might ask whether the poems do not actually say more about the authors than they do about Bartók. Granted, it is perhaps hard to share Devecseri's vision of a giant with thundering steps when listening to Bartók's Second Piano Concerto, or Képes's watery nightmare in connection with the Fifth String Quartet. Yet, as reactions of highly sensitive and articulate individuals who are not necessarily trained in music, the poems drive home the fact that certain phenomena in the music that presented no problems for the professional critics did cause concern in the nonmusician. They all had to find their own answer to a basic dilemma and reconcile their admiration for the man who preserved his moral integrity through difficult times with the overwhelmingly negative associations aroused by his music.

These associations were then, in turn, "legitimized" by the suggestion that the music is a valid and inevitable expression of very real tragedies that have happened in our time, but they are negative associations nevertheless. The uplifting, positive effect of the music on the listener is of course not denied, but its energy is often perceived as rough and wild rather than joyful and rambunctious. To some extent, Bartók is seen as a bitter medicine that the world sorely needs; and while it is conceded that his music is beautiful, it is only because of the aesthetic belief that *truth* is beautiful and not in terms of a direct, visceral response. The opera director Klára Huszár has written:

> If I need an example for the behavior to follow in difficult life situations, I think of Bartók. If I try to arm myself with music against wounds and humiliations that are inflicted too often and undeservedly, I can do so in three different ways. If I want to forget that humans can inflict wounds, not just receive them, I listen to Vivaldi and Purcell and feel light. If I want to accept that humans and the way of life they have created are what they are and are magnificent in their totality, I listen to Mozart. But if I revolt and want to change it, then I listen only to Bartók.[37]

To Hungarians Bartók's music has symbolized, and probably still does to some extent, a certain "hard beauty" that must be struggled through to be conquered, a challenge not only to the ear but to the mind and the soul in general, and therefore a phenomenon of surpassing importance in the spiritual life of the entire nation. This is no doubt part of the reason why Bartók's portrait is on the thousand-forint bill introduced in the 1980s and also why the reburial of Bartók's remains in Budapest in 1988 was publicized as a national event of the highest order.

In recent decades, as the documentation of Bartók's life and the historical and analytical understanding of his music have evolved by leaps and bounds, few have voiced any articulate dissent on the composer. Maybe the gallows has finally been removed from beside the altar. But because Bartók has always been much more in Hungary than just a composer, or even the country's greatest composer, it is very likely that this larger moral and spiritual context will always be an inalienable part of his public image in his native country.

NOTES

1. See Zsigmond Falk, "Uj magyar zenei géniusz" (New Hungarian musical genius), *Ország-Világ* 25, no. 3. Reprinted in *Bartók Béla tanulóévei és romantikus korszaka (1899–1905)* (Béla Bartók's student years and romantic period [1899–1905]), ed. János Demény, vol. 2 of *Zenetudományi tanulmányok* (Musicological studies), ed. Bence Szabolcsi and Dénes Bartha (Budapest, 1954), p. 416.

2. A nearly complete anthology of Hungarian Bartók reviews appears in vol. 2 (cited in n. 1), vol. 3 (*Bartók Béla művészi kibontakozásának évei I—Találkozás a népzenével [1906–1914]* [The years of Béla Bartók's artistic evolution, part 1–encounter with folk music (1906–1914)], ed. János Demény), vol. 7 (*Bartók Béla művészi kibontakozásának évei II—Bartók megjelenése az európai zeneéletben [1914–1926]* [The years of Bartók's artistic evolution, part 2—Bartók's appearance in European musical life (1914–1926)], ed. János Demény), and vol. 10 (*Bartók Béla pályája delelőjén—teremtő évek–Világhódító alkotások [1927–1940]* [Béla Bartók at the height of his career—creative years—world-conquering works (1927–1940)], ed. János Demény) of *Zenetudományi tanulmányok*, ed. Bence Szabolcsi and Dénes Bartha (Budapest, 1955, 1959, and 1962 respectively).

3. Bertalan Pethő, *Bartók rejtekútja* (Bartók's hidden path) (Budapest, 1984), p. 149.

4. *Zenetudományi tanulmányok*, vol. 3, pp. 388–89.

5. Kálmán Simonffy (1831–88), composer of popular songs; and Béni Egressy (1814–1851), composer and opera librettist.

6. Géza Csáth, "Bartók Béla új kottái," in *Ismeretlen házban: kritikák, tanulmányok, cikkek* (In a strange house: reviews, essays, articles) (Újvidék [Novi Sad], 1977), pp. 207–8.

7. "Neu-ungarische Musik," *Jung-Ungarn*, December 1911, pp. 1416–18.

8. "Bartók operája: A kékszakállú herceg vára" (Bartók's opera, *Duke Bluebeard's Castle*), *Zenei Szemle*, nos. 4–6 (1918). Reprinted in Antal Molnár, *Írások a zenéről* (Writings on music), ed. Ferenc Bónis (Budapest, 1961), pp. 27–35.

9. I am not concerned here with the extent to which this view was justified. On Bartók's nationalism, see Judit Frigyesi, "Béla Bartók and the Concept of Nation and *Volk* in Modern Hungary," *Musical Quarterly* 78, no. 2 (Summer 1994): 270.

10. "Bartók Béla jelentősége" (Béla Bartók's significance), *Thalia* (1919), pp. 108–10. Reprinted in Molnár, *Írások a zenéről*, pp. 36–38.

11. Two anthologies were compiled from these poems: *Csak tiszta forrásból: Antológia magyar írók és költők műveiből Bartók Béla emlékére* (Only from a pure source: anthology of works by Hungarian writers and poets in memory of Béla Bartók), ed. Ilona Fodor (Budapest, 1965); and *A szarvassá változott fiú* (The boy who turned into a stag), ed. Lajos Szakolczay (Budapest, 1981). It is noteworthy that both editors chose quotes from *Cantata profana* as titles;

this work of Bartók probably inspired more poems than any other. The poet András Fodor, whose own Bartók poem will be discussed later in this essay, published a brief survey article, "Bartók és a magyar költők" (Bartók and Hungarian poets), in 1986, reprinted in András Fodor, *Szülöttem föld* (My homeland) (Budapest, 1990), pp. 178–92.

My comments on a few Bartók poems here are not intended as a systematic survey of this large body of poetry; in fact, I am leaving out a few that by consensus are among the most important (those of Ferenc Juhász and László Nagy in particular).

12. Curiously, the first poem directly inspired by Bartók that I have come across was written in the United States by Amy Lowell (1874–1925), whose "After Hearing a Waltz by Bartók" was published in her volume of poetry entitled *Sword Blades and Poppy Seed* (Boston, 1914).

13. See p. 299 in this volume.

14. *Zenetudományi tanulmányok*, vol. 7, pp. 37–38.

15. See Béla Bartók, *Essays*, ed. Benjamin Suchoff (New York, 1976), p. 226. Bartók would have derived small comfort from the fact that his case was similar to that of Thomas Mann, who in 1929 had received the Nobel Prize for Literature for his first novel, *The Buddenbrooks*, even though by that time he had written much else, including *The Magic Mountain*.

16. The only element this story has in common with the *Cantata profana* is the presence of a stag. The story is the well-known myth about the origin of the Hungarians, whose ancestors followed a miraculous stag into the land where they eventually settled.

17. *Nemzeti Ujság*, 10 November 1936. Reprinted in *Zenetudományi tanulmányok*, vol. 10, pp. 568–69.

18. His reviews have been collected in the volume *Toth Aladár válogatott zenekritikái* (Selected music criticism by Aladár Tóth), ed. Ferenc Bónis (Budapest, 1968).

19. Tóth must have counted the Presto middle section of the second movement as a separate unit.

20. *Zenetudományi tanulmányok*, vol. 10, pp. 444–45.

21. See Bartók's letter to Baron Gyula Wlassics of 3 February 1920, in Béla Bartók, *Letters*, ed. János Demény (London, 1971), p. 151.

22. On the polemics surrounding Bartók's ethnomusicological work, see, in particular, nos. 26, 27, and 32 in Bartók, *Essays*.

23. See *Zenetudományi tanulmányok*, vol. 10, pp. 615ff.

24. They are given extensive, though not always successful, commentary in János Demény, "Medvetánc: 'A nem-zenéből értjük a zenét'" (Bear dance: "we understand music from nonmusic"), in Demény's collection of essays entitled *Rézkarcok hidegtűvel* (Engravings with a dry point) (Budapest, 1985), pp. 170–93.

25. István Vas, *A félbeszakadt nyomozás* (The interrupted investigation), quoted in Ferenc Csaplár, *Kassák Lajos Bartók-verse* (Lajos Kassák's Bartók poem) (Budapest, 1891), pp. 60–62.

26. Published in Budapest in 1978.

27. All translations are mine unless indicated otherwise.

28. János Breuer, "Bartók Béla pere" (Béla Bartók's trial), in *Bartók és Kodály: Tanulmányok századunk magyar zenetörténetéhez* (Bartók and Kodály: studies on Hungarian music history in the twentieth century) (Budapest, 1978), pp. 105–38, and notes on pp. 409–10.

29. Ibid., pp. 132–33.

30. Mihály, in ibid., p. 134.

31. Note the return of religious terminology.

32. "Döngő nagy léptekkel: Bartók Béla II. zongoraversenyének hall-gatásakor" (With thundering steps: listening to Bartók's Second Piano Concerto), in *Csak tiszta forrásból*, p. 40. For an English translation, see pp. 297–98 in this volume.

33. "Bartók: V. vonósnégyes" (Bartók's Fifth String Quartet), in ibid., pp. 41–42. For an English translation, see pp. 300–301 in this volume.

34. Sándor Csoóri, in *Várakozás a taraszban* (Expectancy in spring) (Budapest, 1983), pp. 189–91. For an English translation, see pp. 296–97 in this volume.

35. György Somlyó, in *Arión eneke: Összegyűjtött versek I (1953–1976)* (The song of Arion: collected poems, vol. 1 [1953–1976]). For an English translation, see pp. 301–2 in this volume.

36. Károlyi Amy, in *Csak tiszta forrásból*, p. 19.

37. Klára Huszár, in *Így láttuk Bartókot*, ed. Ferenc Bónis (Budapest, 1981), p. 210.

Bartók's Reception in America,

1940–1945

TIBOR TALLIÁN

TRANSLATED BY PETER LAKI

During my research trip in the United States in the first half of 1984, I was able to collect, almost in their entirety, all the concert, record, and score reviews as well as newspaper and magazine articles that document in print Béla Bartók's reception in America between 1940 and 1945. Based on these three hundred reviews and one hundred other articles, I shall try to contribute a few marginalia on the last five years of Bartók's life. I emphasize that they are no more than marginalia, lest I seem to rank the collection of raw material (for that is all this work is, and its result is not a finished product) higher on the scale of ideal musicological values than it deserves to be. This work is little more than an endurance test for the researcher, and I do not claim it as an indispensable norm in Bartók research, much less as a proclamation by a new musicological generation ready to trample on the cadavers of their predecessors. At the same time, my marginalia *are* relevant, for they contribute an ever so modest amount to what we were previously able to know about Bartók's later life and the way it gave rise to the last compositions. Not only has the collection of this data been the duty of Hungarian musicology; it has also been one of its outstanding debts. It has been decades since János Demény published the almost complete body of the Hungarian press material and a representative sample of foreign items in four large-scale studies,

This lecture, given at the Musicological Institute of the Hungarian Academy of Sciences on 11 April 1985, summarizes some of the main points in Professor Tallián's book *Bartók fogadtatása Amerikában* (Bartók's reception in America) (Budapest, 1988).

covering Bartók's career through 1939. His work needs to be completed by collecting the documents concerning the last five years of Bartók's life.

Bartók was traumatized by his new environment, so different from the one he had been accustomed to for sixty years. His position in relation to his environment was also different from what it had been, beyond comparison. Since 1920, Bartók had been able to ignore the Hungarian press. In a nondemocratic country like Hungary, the press did not count for much anyway. Nor was he dependent on market conditions. Things were different in America, where he had neither a job with retirement benefits nor a central place in cultural life as its greatest hero. As a result, he was forced literally to struggle for his existence. He found himself, at sixty, in a state of insecurity equal to or even greater than that during his greatest previous crisis, endured between 1904 and 1906, before his appointment to the Conservatory.

In this position of utter defenselessness, the press played, willy-nilly, a decisive role in the evolution of his career. The extent to which this was true may be seen from the reviews of the two-piano recital given in Chicago on 6 January 1942. The Bartóks must have played in a very ragged way that night, for the mildest expression in the reviews was "perplexingly informal recital"; and even Hans Rosenwald, the editor of *Music News*, who had a great respect for Bartók, suggested that "Bartók should not compete with two-piano teams but should limit his playing to renditions of his own compositions—that is enough for so versatile a man: player, writer, lecturer, composer, and research worker."[1]

Subsequently, the concert bureau of Boosey & Hawkes in effect quit acting as the Bartóks' agent, and when Bartók protested, they mercilessly reminded him of the Chicago reviews. There is no doubt in my mind that this humiliation and the cessation of concert possibilities were directly responsible for Bartók's first bout with illness, in the form of constant fevers, starting in the spring of 1942.

Since the days of "great remorse" following Bartók's death, we have generally considered his American years to be years of tribulations and a struggle with misery, disease, and indifference. This view did not originate in Hungary, despite attempts in this country to make cultural-political capital out of the master's American misfortunes. At the end of the 1940s Bartók's last years were seen in a bleak light in America as well, largely as a result of the contrast between Bartók's adverse circumstances during his last years and the posthumous triumph of his music. Only Benjamin Suchoff has tried to counter the general opinion.[2] According to Suchoff, what depressed Bartók the most during the tragic winter of 1942–43 was not his financial situation, or the nadir in the number of performances of his works, or even the end of his concert career. Rather, it was the hopelessness of his projects in ethnomusicology.

Be that as it may, it is indisputable that Bartók collapsed financially in early 1943. In the spring of that year, a small number of Bartók's friends turned to several arts patrons, including Elizabeth Sprague Coolidge, in a circular letter seeking support for the composer.[3] In a thoroughly unusual move, Irving Kolodin asked for the help of New York musicians in the *New York Sun* on 17 April 1943.[4] Columbia University undertook, contrary to its own rules, to disburse $1,500, raised by private individuals, to Bartók as an honorarium for university service.[5] In a desperate letter, Joseph Szigeti asked Serge Koussevitzky to program Bartók's Music for Strings, Percussion, and Celesta immediately, to help the composer cope with his crisis, which was as least as much emotional as physical.[6] Ernő Balogh rushed to ASCAP to raise money for Bartók's hospital treatment.[7] All these facts reveal that even if Bartók had not been literally in penury up to then, he lived from hand to mouth, and any accident, even if it were not a life-threatening illness, could invite a financial catastrophe and reduce him to utter destitution.

Occasionally, one can read opinions to the effect that the wartime difficulties of the United States were responsible for Bartók's fate. Distant wars, while they usually cause shortages in material goods, generally boost musical life, precisely because consumers compensate for the dearth of expensive material goods through the enjoyment of cheaper cultural goods. The music market in America, far from shrinking, had vastly expanded during this time. True, the supply had also grown. America was swarmed with immigrants. The League of Composers stated in its call for subscriptions at the beginning of the fall 1940 season: "In Europe, contemporary music, like modern painting and literature, is being rapidly outlawed. Can America, the last outpost of twentieth-century culture, stem this tide?"[8]

Native-born Americans voiced concern that competition from immigrants might nip American national music in the bud. But these fears proved unfounded. While the great American orchestras played the music of naturalized (immigrant) composers 114 times during the 1940–41 season (as opposed to 23 times in 1939–40), there was only a slight decrease in performances of works by native composers, from 107 to 93.[9]

Thus if Bartók was unable to break into either the concert scene or the university job market, it must have been for reasons other than adverse circumstances in general. We must look for a specific reason, or rather a set of reasons, to explain this phenomenon. I will not discuss the prospects of an academic career, or lack thereof, for I do not have any new data on that subject. The press sources, however, may help us understand the reasons for Bartók's failure as a concert pianist and composer and may clarify whether the indisputable tribulations really amounted to an outright fiasco.

First of all, any lack of success must be measured against Bartók's expectations upon arrival in America, and against the circumstances from which he was escaping. His first trip in the spring of 1940 was a short tour promising favorable results: he was invited to give a sonata recital with Joseph Szigeti at the Fifteenth Coolidge Festival, with a gross fee of $1,250.[10] His manager, Andrew Schulhof, who was subsequently to promise more than he could deliver, had arranged for other concerts. Bartók intended to promote *Mikrokosmos* in the American market, and some of his concerts were in part intended to serve that goal as well. He wanted to assess the possibilities for the dissemination of his works through the New York branch of Boosey & Hawkes. There were plans for recordings, including *Contrasts* with Benny Goodman and Joseph Szigeti. His most important objective, however, was to inquire about the likelihood of having his scholarly work published and, certainly, of a longer sojourn in the United States.

While planning his spring 1940 trip, Bartók had to weigh these chances against his fears that war in Europe would prevent him from returning to Hungary. In November 1939, Szigeti was able to allay those fears.[11]

The first tour—actually the second, since Bartók had previously visited the United States in 1928—was in fact successful, although a careful analysis might reveal the seeds from which later difficulties were to grow. Bartók gave ten concerts in two weeks:[12] a splendid average in comparison to the later sojourn, during which he would appear in public thirty-three times in two and a half years. But of these ten occasions three may be called "first and last"; it was to happen that neither the Coolidge Foundation, nor the League of Composers, nor the Chicago Arts Club would invite him back anytime soon after those ceremonial visits. University concerts and lectures constituted another category of appearances; these, too, could not be repeated at the same school, but at least they *could* take place on other campuses. Bartók's actual chances for succeeding in the college circuit were, however, questionable, because most of his university concerts in the spring of 1940 had been organized by personal acquaintances.[13] With the exception of the Washington recital, there was not a single major venue on Bartók's tour in the spring of 1940. It is difficult to comprehend, for instance, that no concert agent in New York should have been interested in having the three great stars Goodman, Szigeti, and Bartók perform a joint concert (the three were collaborating on the recording of *Contrasts* in the Columbia studios at the time); even later, this idea occurred to only one concert agent in Boston. Yet the recording enjoyed greater publicity than Bartók had ever seen— to be sure, because of Benny, the King of Swing, rather than Bartók. In his appeal for help, mentioned previously, Irving Kolodin reminded his readers of the ironic contrast between Bartók's dire situation in 1943 and the splendid press reception Columbia had organized to celebrate the release of the *Contrasts* recording in the spring of 1940.

The first visit also resulted in contacts with Columbia University, which offered him an honorary doctorate and promised him an appointment of some kind.[14]

Thus it was decided that Bartók and his wife would return to New York in the fall. Schulhof promised ample concert opportunities, and Columbia University held out the prospect of a job. Had these attractions not been enough, the premonition of war urging him to leave grew stronger and stronger.

As many of his letters reveal, Bartók had been struggling with the idea of emigration since the time of the Anschluss. After the outbreak of the war he felt like someone sitting on top of a dangerous fault line in the earth's crust, listening to the murmur of the imminent earthquake. As he put it in a letter sent to the United States in the autumn of 1939 (in the spirit of the "two-front" tradition in Hungarian liberal thinking),

> I wonder if you know our situation here? We see that small countries are invaded from one day to another quite unexpectedly by the most terrible armies and subjected to tortures of every kind. As for my own country, now, instead of one dangerous neighbor, we've got two of them; nobody knows what will happen the next day. It may happen, if I leave my country for America, that I cannot return, cannot even receive news from my family—I hope you will understand my state of spirit—[15]

Bartók left Hungary, then, because he could not stay. The personal tragedy of his final years derives from the fact that he went to the only place where he could go, and even there he felt: "I cannot live in this country. In this country—*lasciate ogni speranza.*"[16]

Bartók, who never saw the world through rose-colored glasses to begin with, gave up hope in America for good, at least so far as his practical life was concerned, after myriad insults, large and small. If we survey his various fields of activity, we must realize that he had in fact little reason to entertain high hopes from the start. Concertizing, as he did for a gross honorarium of about $200,[17] was an ordeal that carried little financial gain and no moral or spiritual benefits at all. He played for an audience of high-school students in the half-filled chapel of a small Mormon university town.[18] He was subjected to the "quiz kids" inquisition at Reed College on the western slopes of the Rocky Mountains,[19] or, at the other extreme, was at the mercy of the arrogance of *Time* and *Newsweek* (these magazines, competing with each other, reported on the premiere of the Two-Piano Sonata under the headlines "Kitchen Sonata" and "New Footwork by Bartók," respectively[20]).

Who could doubt, visualizing these depressing images, that only the instinct of self-preservation could carry Bartók along this thorny path, on the periphery of American concert life, for two concert seasons. He was able to play his Second Piano Concerto only three times. He had a single orchestral appearance in New York, and that was thanks to Fritz Reiner in January 1943, when everything was over anyway. Two concerts in the second-best concert hall in New York in the fall of 1940 and one better venue each for two-piano concerts in Boston, Chicago, and Baltimore could hardly compensate for dismal concerts mechanically rattled off at insignificant locales. The hopelessness of the situation even put a stamp on the production itself. The chamber music recital given in Boston by Goodman, Szigeti, and the Bartóks was described as "the driest program that had been presented in Jordan Hall this season—though it was not always easy to tell whether the miasma of the boredom which gradually enveloped the evening's proceeding was due more to the music itself or to the playing of it. Offhand, the honors might be divided about evenly."[21]

Such critical voices could be heard mainly after two-piano performances, which is regrettable since Bartók was less and less inclined to play alone. Great concert halls would in any event have been unavailable to a composer-pianist playing his own works. His solo recitals, frequently given on campuses, were often not even reviewed, unless there was a critic in town or nearby who, as an admirer of Bartók, was willing to make the pilgrimage and pay his homage after the concert. Such was the case of Alfred Frankenstein, the music critic for the *San Francisco Chronicle*, who took the trouble of going to Oakland, on the other side of the bay, to hear Bartók at Mills College. He wrote afterward: "Certainly few musical events in my experience could compare to this one for the intensity with which its central person impressed himself on his hearers, and at times the 'vibration' reached seismographic properties. It takes an earthquake only a few seconds to transact a most respectable lot of business, and so it was last night with many of Bartok's miniatures."[22]

To perceive art's minute earthquakes, however, one needs the right kind of seismograph, and those who did not have that tool could see nothing but miniatures in the twenty or thirty short movements making up Bartók's concerts, including sets from *Mikrokosmos*, Petite Suite, "Music of the Night," *Allegro barbaro*, Old Hungarian Dances, Rondo No. 1, and even the Suite Op. 14, with its sketch-sized movements. Admirers of the composer often said that these selections failed to reveal the true Bartók. Those with no special affinity to Bartók would not hesitate to judge him in a disgraceful way, as did an unknown concertgoer who wrote on a copy of a concert program, next to items from *Mikrokosmos*, "From my second childhood."[23]

The *Mikrokosmos* did not prove to be effective in winning over the audience. It was well known to be a pedagogical work; therefore the critics who had been justifying their antipathy to Bartók's music by calling it cerebral seized the opportunity to brand the pieces from *Mikrokosmos* as instructive studies lacking any musical merit. As Olin Downes wrote in the *New York Times* on 25 April 1940, "If these pieces are intended as technical studies they can be useful. If they are to stand as music it must be admitted that Mr. Bartok, on last night's evidence, has done better."

In the final analysis, Bartók's solo recitals and the two-piano performances given with his wife could hardly continue to propagate his oeuvre the way the earlier concert tours had been able to do. Following the first performance of the Two-Piano Sonata, the subsequent two-piano programs contained only four or five pieces from *Mikrokosmos*. The Bartóks introduced a new work, the arrangement of the Second Suite, on 6 January 1942, but this composition was played only three times, for the Bartóks were approaching the end of their concert career. It seems that no one was interested in the Two-Piano Sonata; granted, this was an impossible piece to take on tour, given its difficulties and the two percussionists required.

As for Bartók's solo piano music, it was no longer in need of advertisement. Yet—and this is peculiar—Bartók apparently never thought of appearing as a pianist except as a performer of his own works. Even if his repertoire could not compete with those of major concert pianists, he might have revived his virtuoso image by including some works by other composers in addition to his own. This, however, was one of the lines that the sexagenarian, whose personality was becoming increasingly rigid, was not prepared to cross. Aside from two works by Kodály, which he performed regularly, the only non-Bartók compositions on his last concert programs were blocks of transcriptions he had made of Italian baroque keyboard music.

The high points of Bartók's American concert career were his orchestral concerts. His appearances in Cleveland, Pittsburgh, and Chicago were at the center of the musical world's attention in all three cities, usually eliciting at least respectful reviews. The critics were visibly disturbed by the fact that Bartók played from the score, and sometimes drew the conclusion that he was a second-rate pianist (Bartók himself was dissatisfied with his performance in Chicago, incidentally). Yet the experience of the work and the personality reinforced what many professional listeners had heard only secondhand—that "a wispy, thin, gray-haired Hungarian pianist, Bela Bartok, is one of the great artists of the modern world."[24]

This statement would hardly have been a new discovery in the narrow circle that was aware of modern art and in the one, even narrower, that approved of it. The trinity Stravinsky-Schoenberg-Bartók had become something of a reflex with musical journalists wanting to name the greatest composers of the time. Minna Ledermann's journal *Modern Music*, the forum that discussed new music at the highest level, contains numerous hints showing that writers were keenly aware of at least some of the characteristic features of Bartók's style. Writing about neobaroque music, for instance, Manfred Bukofzer states that it had definitely helped Bartók to arrive at a high stylistic purity; in certain earlier works he had only groped in that direction, but he had finally achieved it in masterworks such as the Music for Strings or *Mikrokosmos*.[25] Another example: a reviewer, trying to define the character of a new American string quartet, calls it a work written in the Bartókian tradition, highly expressive but not neurotic, almost neoclassical in its structural purity and assurance.[26]

Yet the circle that appreciated Bartók in this way was exceedingly small. Mainstream musical thought was content with rather shopworn clichés: in most textbooks of new music, Bartók was placed in Stravinsky's shadow as one of the representatives of neobarbarism or one of the national-folkloristic composers. Bartók himself was in no small part responsible for the predominance of these clichés, since he never talked about his own music from any viewpoint other than that of its relationship to folk music. Even so, Bartók, the national composer, might have been expected to arouse more of a professional interest in the United States, where national music was very much on the agenda in the 1940s. Yet this possibility never materialized, for several reasons. First, Bartók's music and verbal statements lacked the national pathos, heroic and natural romanticism, and naïveté that informed American conceptions of nationalism. America during the war years needed romantic nationalism on a grandiose scale, whose models were Sibelius and Shostakovich rather than Bartók. No matter how much Bartók talked about folk music in his own oeuvre, he could fool no one—people could hear only avant-garde and modernism there, not folk music. Whereas this was considered a positive trait in avant-garde circles (in the eyes of Ernst Křenek, it even distinguished Bartók from other folklorists[27]), it did little to make Bartók's music either more suitable as a model to American composers or more attractive to large concert audiences.

There was another reason (a specifically political one) why Bartók's folklorism had little appeal in the United States. Although the less well versed writers on music always added the *epitheton ornans* "one of Hungary's leading composers" to his name (after the brief résumé distributed by the publisher), few people knew exactly where, or what, Hungary was. To make matters worse, the biography was peppered with names such as "Transylvania," "Yugoslavia," and "Bohemia" (meaning Slovakia)—places that were part Hungarian and part not. One music journal cut the Gordian knot of this geopolitical chaos by beginning Bartók's biography with the words "He was born in Hungary, which today is called Yugoslavia."[28] This nonexistent little Hungary could in no way serve as a model for the "great" music of America in search of its national identity. At most, it reminded the better-informed writers of gypsy music. Thus Bartók's *Mikrokosmos* recording was discussed in the *New York Times* in the company of Imre Magyari's *nóta* records under the heading "Gipsy Music," with Dinicu's "Nightingale" cited as the common denominator of the two.[29] Also, Hungary was an enemy country, even if no one in America took this very seriously. Yet even though Bartók's publisher emphasized the composer's antifascist stance whenever possible, this unclear political background contributed to his neglect—in contrast with the promotion of Martinů, for example—which was motivated in part by political factors.

Despite the respect he enjoyed in the circles of *Modern Music* and with certain critics, Bartók does not seem to have become a central issue to be resolved or analyzed by the public opinion of musicians. Although *Modern Music* reported on every Bartók premiere in a conscientious and unprejudiced way, and its reverence for Bartók's music is evident in every word, it published only one article devoted to Bartók between the autumn of 1940 and the time of the composer's death. (True, the spring 1940 issue had carried a theoretically oriented article by Tibor Serly and Henry Pleasants greeting Bartók on the occasion of his visit.[30]) The other professional journal, *Musical Quarterly*, published special articles on Shostakovich, Sibelius, Stravinsky, Revueltas, Milhaud, Gretchaninov, Martinů, Hindemith, and Schoenberg during these years but never on Bartók during the composer's lifetime. Other periodicals could not even be expected to publish in-depth articles. Although a few special articles did appear in other publications, they did not have much to say beyond rehashing data from the old biography. The only exception is the lengthy interview in the February 1941 issue of *Etude*.

The daily press ran feature stories before Bartók's performances in Boston, New York, Chicago, and Oakland. The composer received special attention at his first visit, which was, however, not always of the most fortunate kind. I would like to cite one of the most embarrassing incidents: Otto Gombosi tried to sum up Bartók's significance in the *New York Times*,[31] unfortunately slipping back into the messianic tone of Bartók worship characteristic of Hungary. Piling one mythological epithet upon another, he only inspired ironic commentaries on himself and his subject and could not convince his readers about Bartók's greatness. As the editor-in-chief of *Musical America* wrote after the publication of Gombosi's article,

"And what do you think of Bartok's music?" Over and over, for weeks and weeks, I have been asked that devastating question, and I have had to use all my ingenuity to turn the conversation on to Beethoven, Brahms, Victor Herbert or Alec Templeton. But now, the answer that I have been waiting for, has come to me, like a bolt from the blue. I thought of it while I was reading last Sunday's *New York Times*, and I can scarcely put it better than Otto Gombosi has put it in an article there. "Bartok's music is of an elemental strength: it is chthonic and orgiastic in its severity and its visionary poetry. Rhythm of extreme potency is one of its most characteristic features. This rhythm gives his music that Dionysian strain that produces its elemental effect, besides also giving it the strong backbone of the vision of sound. . . . It is difficult to foretell the way of human meteors. Bartok, who is now 59, will certainly write many surprising works. The surprise will certainly not consist of capricious breaks in the stylistic line, but of the still increasing expansion of his horizon and of his growing lapidarity of his means of expression." So this is what I will say the next time

I am seized by the lapel, and asked about Bartok. Well said! And believe me I shall make the most of "chthonic," "orgiastic," "Dionysian" and "lapidarity"—strange how the good Mr Gombosi should take those words right out of my mouth![32]

The fate of Bartók's works was hardly better in the concert hall than it was in the analytical literature. The assessment of a Chicago newspaper is valid for the entire country:

Although Mr Bartok has frequently been adjudged one of the most original and forceful composers of our day, he has received scant recognition in Chicago. Storm Bull, a pupil of the composer, played the Second Concerto with the Chicago Symphony Orchestra three seasons ago. The orchestra presented his "Dance Suite" 16 years ago and his First Suite for Orchestra 17 years ago, but beyond this slim representation his music has been ignored at Orchestra Hall. In five years only one Bartok work—the early Rhapsody for Piano and Orchestra—has found its way onto the usually adventuresome programs of the Illinois Symphony Orchestra. A few years ago the Kolisch String Quartet played all five Bartok string quartets in a cycle at the University of Chicago. Except for scattered and infrequent performances of small works, this is the complete Bartok record in Chicago.[33]

The 1940–41 season produced the greatest number of Bartók performances with leading American orchestras. He played his Second Piano Concerto in two cities. The St. Louis Symphony gave the American premiere of *Divertimento* on 8 November. The same work was programmed by the Philadelphia Orchestra, both at home and in New York, in January 1941. There was a total of five performances of Bartók works with major American orchestras during that season, as opposed to only two each in the 1941–42 and 1942–43 seasons. The latter season brought the premiere of the Two-Piano Concerto and the American premiere of the Violin Concerto in Cleveland. The 1943–44 season marked a return to the earlier level with six performances, all without Bartók's personal participation. The last season before Bartók's death, 1944–45, yielded the same figure.[34]

To appreciate these figures, we must compare them with the national statistics published annually in *Musical America*. In 1943–44, Shostakovich and Stravinsky had forty performances each, Sibelius thirty-four, Prokofiev thirty-one, and Hindemith and Milhaud sixteen each.[35] In the case of Soviet Russian composers, especially Shostakovich, one could feel an immediate political motivation, enthusiasm about the great ally. Commenting on its statistics for 1942–43, *Musical America* contained the following:

> The prominence of Shostakovitch in these findings undoubtedly should be taken with certain reservations. Through his politically inspired music, Shostakovitch has been a kind of diplomatic emissary, ex-officio, for the Soviet government since the beginning of the war. We have recognized him as such here in America, and we have given his compositions, especially his Seventh, or "Leningrad" Symphony, wide currency. This music might have been just as widely performed had there been no wartime diplomatic angle, but there is room for doubt.[36]

In view of the contrast between two performances for Bartók and twenty-eight for Shostakovich that year, the famous Shostakovich parody in the Concerto for Orchestra can hardly come as a surprise.

The scarcity of performances is striking, if one thinks of how dramatically Bartók's popularity was to grow after the war. We should not forget, however, that the later popularity was due mainly to the last two orchestral works, not yet written during the slowest years, and partly to the Violin Concerto. Bartók's oeuvre lacked *Firebirds* and *Petrouchkas*, early works for large orchestra that might have become hits with orchestras and audiences alike. We know about his fastidious reticence concerning the large orchestra, except in concertos. With Bartók, there could be no question of anything paralleling the various neo-romantic symphonic trends of the 1930s. The connoisseurs may have known, in the United States of the 1940s, that Music for Strings was the great classical symphony of the day.[37] But the large orchestras refused to accept this unusual work, both reduced and expanded in its scoring; it had only one performance during Bartók's entire American sojourn, and that was given by a semiprofessional ensemble directed by Rudolf Kolisch.

Divertimento did rate a few performances and garner enthusiastic reviews. At the 1942 International Society for Contemporary Music festival in Berkeley it enchanted listeners with its nobility, energy, conciseness, and lyrical momentum. The more sensitive ears perceived that in his late music Bartók was no longer as severe as he had been earlier but was growing more accessible: "Bartok's *Divertimento* might admirably serve as a commentary upon life in Europe in the last five years, but with a paean of faith in humanity as its coda."[38] Yet it seems that the general audience and average musician were not attracted to Bartók's aristocratic classicism from the end of the 1930s any more than they had been to the earlier "barbaric," expressionist Bartók.

The composer may have drawn a lesson from this when, given the opportunity, he wrote the Concerto for Orchestra the way he did: it was his largest multimovement orchestral work in forty years, a counterpart to his Suite No. 1 in form and sometimes even in content. He must have realized, at least, that a work for large orchestra was his only chance to break into the orchestra-oriented musical life of the United States.

After the world premiere and the first New York performance of the Concerto for Orchestra, all the critics observed the change in character from Bartók's earlier style. The *Globe* noted the "pleasant surprise to many of the Friday subscribers," who had previously considered Bartók an "awfully modern" composer, at this piece, which was easy to digest and easy to listen to: "The style is fairly light, the dissonance is expressive rather than idiomatic, and the five movements are, on the whole, engagingly emotional. And more than a few places seem to be in a joking mode." Comparing the work's nobility and purity to Bach, the *Herald* writer wrote: "His Orchestral Concerto . . . is a work which must rank as the composer's masterpiece, which is to say it must also rank among the musical masterpieces of recent years." According to the *Boston Post*, "The name of Bartók was once associated with all that was glum and gloomy, dour, dissonant and (to some) disagreeable. Of late years, however, his music has been much more likable and the new Concerto is a piece that should win many friends. . . . The second movement and the fourth, entitled 'Intermezzo interrotto' . . . are frankly light and might almost find their way into the Pops." And the *Christian Science Monitor* commented: "There can hardly arise complaint, though, that we have in the Concerto another one of those modern annoyances to the ear." *Modern Music*, for its part, pointed out—albeit with less enthusiasm—that the piece was written in the author's "least aggressive manner" and predicted that it would become a warhorse in Koussevitzky's repertoire and even in orchestral literature in general.

The piece was, of course, still too modern for the audience, and the reception, both in Boston and in New York, seemed polite rather than enthusiastic. Yet one newspaper said that if this piece was performed as often as "Shostakovich's antiquated sensations" it could become one of the audience's favorites.[39] As is well known, this soon came to pass. By 1948, the Concerto for Orchestra had had forty-nine performances worldwide, the Third Piano Concerto had been given thirty-nine times, and the Violin Concerto thirty-five times.[40]

Bartók's discovery by major orchestras and soloists had begun earlier, however, with performances of the Violin Concerto. After January

1943, when Tossy Spivakovsky gave the U.S. premiere in Cleveland, there were eight more performances before Bartók's death. Two of those were given by Spivakovsky, one by John Weicher, concertmaster of the Chicago Symphony, and five by Yehudi Menuhin, who even took Bartók and the Violin Concerto to the Hollywood Bowl. Critics of the Violin Concerto could find neither as great a simplicity in style nor such a predominance of emotional, popular expression as they could in the Concerto for Orchestra. Accordingly, there were more hostile voices, and more old charges were repeated. Nevertheless, the critical response was of a completely different order than those of earlier Bartók premieres. It was sensational for a new concerto to have had nine performances within two years and nine months. In addition, the New York premiere of the Violin Concerto gave rise to a beautiful and very sensitive essay by Jacques de Menasce in *Modern Music* about the technical and spiritual kinship between Bartók's and Berg's music.[41]

The Violin Concerto had made the rounds in the United States in such a spectacular way that it was no longer possible for any self-respecting writer on music to base his assessment of Bartók's music on a few works from the 1920s, or, rather, on discussions of them in old reviews and book excerpts. Bartók's complete oeuvre began to make its presence felt on the American horizon. Not only did people discover the new Bartók who had come closer to his audience; if reviews are any indication, audiences themselves came closer to the earlier "wild" Bartók.

To observe this phenomenon we must include performances other than orchestral ones in our investigation. The contemporaries already realized the central place of the string quartets in Bartók's oeuvre; thus any study of his reception would be incomplete if it did not include chamber music. This area is virtually impossible to survey in its entirety; nevertheless, the data available do yield a representative picture.

The Kolisch quartet led the way in the performance of Bartók's chamber music during this period as they had earlier. They gave the premiere of the Sixth Quartet in January 1941 and performed it several times along with the earlier ones. At the premiere, the reception of the Sixth Quartet was rather chilly; professional listeners grew more attuned to the work's emotional world by the second performance in New York in 1944. Marion Bauer's 1944 review echoes a motif already encountered in an earlier piece on *Divertimento*: "If one is looking for a contemporary expression of a mental state produced on a sensitive person by conditions of recent years, it is to be found in this poignant, profoundly sad work."[42]

"Conditions of recent years"—this phrase provides a focal point for our survey. Therein lies the main reason, a professional if not a personal one, behind Bartók's pre-1943 American ordeal. I would like to quote another variation on this theme, an anecdotal one reported by Virgil Thomson in an article written after Bartók's death. The title of the article is noteworthy in itself: "Bela Bartok's Music Beginning to Draw the Layman's Affection." Here is the story: "Visitors several years back to a Boston performance of some work of Bartok have recounted how at the end of the piece a neighbor turned to her husband and said: 'Conditions must be terrible in Europe.' She was right, of course. They were, especially in Central Europe, where Bartok lived. And she was right in sensing their relation to the expressive content of Bartok's music."[43] In her own way, the empathetic Boston lady was giving voice to the same thought that a critic in Chicago had expressed several years earlier upon hearing the First Sonata for Violin and Piano, with fierce hostility instead of empathy: "It is one of those fragmental, nihilistic, rhythmically reiterative pieces that really get on one's nerves. It was written shortly after the finish of the First World War, when most European composers were determined to be as disagreeable as possible. Few of them succeeded better than Bartok."[44]

Although John Cage, who was also present at that concert, had of course formed a completely different opinion,[45] the average musician surely agreed with the critic. Here was perhaps another reason why Bartók's path was particularly thorny, aside from the difficulties faced by all new music: Whereas progressive intellectuals in Europe and in Hungary in particular had shared Bartók's experiences and therefore considered his way of expression as having the force of law, in America these experiences were missing—a lack for which only a few were able to compensate by intuition and empathy with the force of the style. The average musician was averse to Bartók's music and, as we have seen, formulated the same charges against the composer and his modernism that Bartók had heard in Budapest around 1910: wanton dissonances, cacophony for cacophony's sake. But later, in an evolution possibly paralleling the deterioration of conditions in America, the understanding of Bartók, and of the wildest, most expressionist, most "unbearable" Bartók in particular, seemed to increase.

What makes this shift all the more interesting is that in musical circles works from the immediate past are always in a difficult position. The style of twenty-year-old pieces can seem as dated as twenty-year-old clothes, especially if the composer was as strongly influenced by his time as Bartók was. For instance, Andor Foldes was unable to help Bartók's Piano Sonata overcome the unfashionableness of the immediate past. Yet Yehudi Menuhin succeeded in doing the same to an astonishing degree, when he and Adolph Baller performed the First Sonata for Violin and Piano in New York on 28 November 1943 (a performance attended by Bartók) and subsequently in Chicago, San Francisco, and Los Angeles. There were critics even now (how could there not be?) who compared the last movement to the chatter of a magpie; in general, however, there is in the reviews a striking change in tone from two years earlier. Olin Downes, who was not exactly known for his admiration for Bartók (any more than for his admiration for Schoenberg; see Schoenberg's famous letter to him[46]), gave his review the subtitle "In Presence of a Master."[47] One San Francisco review bore the headline "Bartok's Great Sonata"; and in general, every honest reviewer in every city discussed the work and its performance as an event of the very first order. More and more came to perceive the dreams and visions that only two years earlier John Cage had been alone in perceiving. Certain critics were inspired by the sonata to write what were veritable psychoanalytic essays. Although the thirty-three hundred listeners at Carnegie Hall gave the composer only a polite applause, and the Chicago critic said, "Lay audience reaction to music of this kind is unquotable," the main point is that at least a few realized what this same critic put into words: "Only through artists and composers can our limits of present consciousness be expanded."[48]

Ultimately, then, the American ordeal was not a fiasco. For Bartók and his environment, it resulted in new works and new qualities in them; the music life in general received a chance to "expand the limits of awareness.' The gravely ill composer surely felt this himself, and perhaps the unusual serenity in his last works is partly attributable to this realization. As Olin Downes wrote after the performance of the Sonata for Unaccompanied Violin, "Bartók had the reason to feel courage." This courage is transmitted by the musical legacy of his final years.

NOTES

1. *Music News* 34, no. 2 (1942): 13.
2. Benjamin Suchoff, "Bartók utolsó évei Amerikában" (Bartók's last years in America), *Magyar Zene* 17 (1976): 190.
3. Undated typescript (copy) in the Library of Congress, Washington, D.C., Music Division, E. Sprague Coolidge Foundation ML 95 B 227.

4. "The Strange Case of Béla Bartók."

5. Columbia University, New York, Butler Library, Department of Rare Books, Bartók Collection, no. 11, 11 October 1943.

6. Joseph Szigeti's letter to Serge Koussevitzky, Library of Congress, Washington, D.C., Music Division, Koussevitzky Collection, box 188.

7. Ernő Balogh's letter to Ms. Rosenberg, 23 December 1945: "In view of the fact that I was the one who brought the Bartók case to ASCAP . . . " ASCAP archives, photocopy.

8. New York Public Library, Music Division, League of Composers Collection. Call for subscriptions to the 1940–41 season.

9. *Musician*, September 1941, p. 135.

10. See copy of telegram dated 6 March 1939, Library of Congress, Washington, D.C., Music Division, Coolidge Foundation.

11. Bartók's letter to Harold Spivacke, 3 December 1939.

12. The chronology of Bartók's American concerts between 1940 and 1943 may be found in Béla Bartók, Jr., *Apám életének krónikája* (The chronicle of my father's life) (Budapest, 1981). The following entries in that book stand in need of correction: on 17 November 1940 only Mrs. Bartók played (p. 428); and Bartók canceled his lecture of 17 April 1941 (p. 435). In addition, the chronicle has omitted the two-piano concert at Chicago's Orchestra Hall on 6 January 1942.

13. See Bartók's letter to Dorothy Parrish, 17 January 1940: "Now, I know that you secured a concert and a lecture for your College, it is—if I am right, the Juniata-College, *Huntingdon*, Pennsylvania . . . " Béla Bartók, *Letters*, ed. János Demény (London, 1971), p. 279.

14. Columbia University, New York, Butler Library, Rare Books, Bartók Collection. Copy of a telegram dated 1 April 1940: the university notifies Bartók of his nomination for an honorary doctorate. On 24 May 1940, the provost of the University, Frank D. Fackenthal, addressed an inquiry to the treasurer: "Is it likely that any of the recent Ditson bequest money will be available for 1940–41? There is an opportunity of doing a distinguished piece of work through Béla Bartók if we can provide a research associateship or some such position to him. It is assumed that if the appointment is made it should carry a stipend of about $4,000." The response was negative.

15. Bartók to H. Spivacke on 9 November 1939. Library of Congress, Washington, D.C., Music Division, Coolidge Foundation.

16. See Bartók, *Apám életének krónikája*, p. 455.

17. Todd Crow, "From Out of the Past, a Little Night Music," *Vassar Quarterly* 77, no. 2 (1981): 31. The figure is Hans Heinsheimer's estimate.

18. *Bartók Béla családi levelei* (Béla Bartók's family correspondence), ed. Béla Bartók, Jr. (Budapest, 1981), p. 613.

19. *Reed College Quest*, 5 December 1941.

20. Both on 11 November 1940.

21. *Boston Evening Transcript*, 5 February 1941.

22. *San Francisco Chronicle*, 7 February 1941.

23. New York Public Library, Music Division, League of Composers Collection. On a copy of the program from a concert on 24 April 1940, devoted to Bartók's works.

24. *Daily Northwestern*, 26 November 1941.

25. *Modern Music* 22 (1945): 152.

26. Ibid., vol. 21 (1944): 239.

27. Ernst Křenek, *Music Here and Now* (New York, 1940), p. 78.

28. Sydney Grew, "Some Notes on Belar [*sic*] Bartok," *American Music Lover*, April 1943, p. 161.

29. 13 July 1941.

30. Henry Pleasants and Tibor Serly, "Bartók's Harmonic Contribution," *Modern Music* 17 (1940): 131.

31. 5 May 1940.

32. *Musical America* 60, no. 9 (1940): 9.

33. *Chicago Daily Tribune*, 16 November 1941.

34. Kate Mueller, *Twenty-Seven Major American Symphony Orchestras* (Bloomington, 1973).

35. *Musical America* 64, no. 17 (1944): 12.

36. Ibid., vol. 63, no. 16 (1943): 8.

37. *Listen*, 3 July 1945.

38. Harry R. Burke in the *St. Louis Globe-Democrat*, 9 November 1940.

39. *San Francisco Chronicle*, 2 August 1942.

40. Statistics from Boosey & Hawkes catalog (London, 1948).

41. *Modern Music* 21 (1944): 76.

42. *Musical Leader* 76, no. 4 (1944): 9.

43. *New York Herald Tribune*, 20 March 1949.

44. *Chicago Daily Tribune*, 8 April 1942.

45. "The Sonata No. 1 for Violin and Piano by Bartok was good to hear. In this work ideas seem to be suggested but never grasped, every moment passes just as one begins to realize its presence. It makes for dreams and visions." *Modern Music* 19 (1942): 260.

46. Schoenberg to Downes. See Arnold Schoenberg, *Letters,* ed. Erwin Stein (New York, 1965), pp. 260–62.

47. *New York Times*, 29 November 1943.

48. *Musical Leader* 76, no. 3 (1944): 13.

Bluebeard as Theater:

The Influence of Maeterlinck

and Hebbel on Balázs's

Bluebeard Drama

CARL LEAFSTEDT

The works of a young creative artist often disclose marked affinities to those of selected predecessors or contemporaries. When they are young, their personal style springs naturally from the foundations of inherited tradition as they respond to the works of those forebears who, for them, provide the greatest inspiration. With time, influences that contribute to an artist's earlier style may recede in prominence, yielding either to new influences or to a more original voice that synthesizes those formerly external elements within the context of a new, individual style. This path toward artistic maturity may be found, with infinite variations, in the work of any young writer, composer, or artist.

Béla Bartók's first and only opera, the one-act *A kékszakállú herceg vára* (literally, *The Bluebearded Duke's Castle*) was composed in 1911, at a time when Bartók was beginning to crystallize his reputation as one of the leaders in a new generation of Hungarian composers. Bartók entered the opera in a national opera competition held in Budapest in early 1912. Had *Bluebeard* achieved the desired goal of winning this competition, Bartók's career over the following years would no doubt have turned out quite differently. Instead, the opera failed to win, and Bartók's public image as a composer, so tenuously established by that time, began to topple in the face of indifference and hostility. For the next four years he composed little. Its initial lack of success notwithstanding, *Bluebeard* represented a considerable musical accomplishment for the young composer. Since its premiere in May 1918, *Bluebeard's Castle* has come to be viewed as the crowning work of a certain period in Bartók's career, from 1908 to 1911, when Bartók first began to consolidate into a truly personal and original style the multitude of influences he had absorbed as a young man in the first decade of this century. Many compositions written before *Bluebeard* show ample evidence of the hurdles Bartók encountered as he attempted to reconcile the forms and language of Western musical tradition with those of Hungarian folk music. In *Bluebeard*, Bartók's style advances to a new level: influences of Strauss, Debussy, and Liszt, each in his turn a musical model for the younger Bartók, have begun to disappear from the surface of the music. In their place evolves an increasingly complex and original musical language that fuses a Western-derived vocabulary of early modernism with the rhythmic, harmonic, and melodic qualities of Hungarian folk music.

More than any other work written before it, *Bluebeard* seamlessly blends the divergent musical threads of Bartók's earlier years. It is at once a culmination and a point of departure for such later works as *The Wooden Prince* and the Second String Quartet. Ernő Lendvai has written that, in *Bluebeard*, Bartók's style sprang at once into existence. Such a claim, though grandiloquent and somewhat exaggerated, certainly contains a grain of truth. Befitting its special position in Bartók's musical output, *Bluebeard's Castle* has received considerable attention over the years from scholars and biographers. As a result, the development of Bartók's style in the years leading up to *Bluebeard* has been mapped out in detail. Bartók would later admit that the parlando rubato vocal style in *Bluebeard* owes a great deal to the example of Debussy's *Pelléas*. Following this lead, Elliott Antokoletz and others have looked to Debussy's music for further insights into the musical language of Bartók's opera, as well as of the piano works written from 1908 to 1911. Although *Bluebeard*'s stylistic connections with contemporary French music merit further examination, the basic elements of the opera's musical language are fairly well understood.[1]

But what of the libretto? Although we know a great deal about the types of music that interested Bartók in the years before *Bluebeard*, we know relatively little about the factors that contributed to the unusual dramatic style Béla Balázs adopted for his *Bluebeard* play. Balázs's dark, atmospheric play about the notorious folk character of Bluebeard shares with Bartók's music the fundamental attribute of looking both East and West at the same time. Certain of its textual features display a strongly national character that Hungarians have long recognized as deriving from the ancient folk heritage of the Transylvanian Magyars. Balázs openly modeled its recurrent eight-syllable lines and general dialogue style after the folk ballads of the Székely people in far eastern Transylvania. In other respects, though, *Bluebeard* remains a dramatic work whose essential spirit holds much in common with certain broad trends in early twentieth-century European theater, particularly with French and German drama. The *Bluebeard* drama's roots in the Western intellectual tradition are deep. Although often acknowledged, this aspect of the play's intellectual heritage is at once more complex and more revealing than has generally been recognized. Musicologists, drawn as they are to the opera by their predilection for musical or music-dramatic analysis, are often content to repeat unquestioned the accepted wisdom about the drama's aesthetic foundations: that it is the work of a young Hungarian writer who drank deeply from the fountain of French symbolism in his attempt to create a modern, authentically Hungarian dramatic style. This image of the play may be found throughout the Bartók literature. In its basic outlines, it is largely accurate. But if we look at *Bluebeard's Castle* as a work for theater in its own right, that is, as a self-sufficient play and not as a libretto wedded to musical expression, additional connections to the world of literature, some quite substantive, begin to appear.

When Balázs wrote *Bluebeard's Castle*, he was still a young man in his mid-twenties just beginning his literary career. He was extremely well versed in the work of other late nineteenth- and early twentieth-century European playwrights, such as Ibsen, Strindberg, d'Annunzio, Hofmannsthal, and Maeterlinck. It is quite natural that traces of the work of such prominent figures as these should filter into the expressive voice of the aspiring Hungarian writer. The symbolist technique of Maurice Maeterlinck's dramas forms the most recognizable influence on the style of Balázs's play, as many critics have noted. Additional literary and aesthetic connections may be detected, however. No turn-of-the-century dramatist could ignore the important new developments in theater represented by the work of August Strindberg, the Swedish playwright whose fantastic dream plays drew theater into the world of the subconscious; or Henrik Ibsen, the eminent Norwegian author whose *Ghosts* and *A Doll's House* gave the burgeoning nineteenth-century women's movement a strong theatrical voice. In subtle ways, each of these playwrights shaped Balázs's artistic conscience. Theories of tragedy propounded by the mid-nineteenth-century German playwright Friedrich Hebbel, though chronologically more distant, had a noticeable impact on the nature of tragedy in *Bluebeard's Castle*. On a purely theatrical level, the imaginative use of stage lighting in *Bluebeard* owes much to the revolution in lighting techniques that took place in the theater during the 1890s and early 1900s, as seen, for example, in the work of Adolf Appia and Max Reinhardt. And at the core of the drama's message lies something akin to the philosophy of Friedrich Nietzsche: Bluebeard, like Zarathustra, is ultimately resigned to the loneliness that is his fate.

All these influences, some more important than others, come together in the *Bluebeard* play. Two of the more powerful strands of influence are teased apart for discussion in this essay: the symbolist style of Maeterlinck's dramas, and Friedrich Hebbel's theories of tragedy. The Maeterlinck influence, often acknowledged as a significant factor in the creation of Balázs's own dramatic style, has never been examined in detail. The Hebbel influence is proposed here for the first time. Balázs's own published writings from the time of *Bluebeard*, still available only in the original Hungarian, reveal that the intellectual disposition of this young Hungarian dramatist was conditioned as much by a deep-seated attraction to German romantic drama as by the more immediate, and passing, influence of French symbolism. *Bluebeard*'s dramatic style flows from multiple sources in the dramatic world in which Balázs enveloped himself during his student years in Budapest. Awareness of the literary figures engaging Balázs's attention at the time he worked on the *Bluebeard* play enables us to understand better the sources of its symbolist language. Even more important, new reasons come to light that help explain one of the drama's lingering unanswered questions: why Judith submits so willingly to the fate of entombment in Bluebeard's gloomy castle.

·

In the pantheon of twentieth-century Hungarian literature, Béla Balázs (1884–1948) occupies a distinguished but sadly marginal position among the literary talents that blossomed in the decades before World War I, a golden age in the Hungarian arts. Born in Szeged to German immigrant parents, Balázs began writing poetry at an early age, even publishing some poems in a local newspaper under the *echt*-Hungarian pseudonym Béla Balázs, a name he adopted while still in his teens to conceal from the public his Germanic heritage, a potential liability in Hungary's chauvinistic sociopolitical climate at the time. His birth name was Herbert Bauer, and he encouraged his closer friends to call him by that name.[2] Balázs moved to Budapest in 1902 to begin studies at the University of Budapest and the Eötvös Kollégium, a prestigious teachers' training college. During his university years he combined studies in German and Hungarian literature, philology, and philosophy with a variety of his own literary projects. His roommate at the Kollégium, interestingly, was Zoltán Kodály, two years his senior. Kodály and Balázs became close friends. Out of this relationship Balázs was eventually introduced to Bartók, whom he met for the first time in 1906 when he accompanied Bartók on a folk song–collecting trip in rural Hungary. A common goal of creating new art forms based on authentic Hungarian folk idioms drew the two young men together. Bartók and Balázs were never truly close, however, despite their encouragement and support for each other's work. "Apart from his music," Balázs wrote of the composer in his diary, "I am able to enjoy little about him."[3]

Balázs's precipitous entry into Hungarian literary life took place in the years 1907 and 1908, while he was a doctoral student. He began to publish poems, drama reviews, and other short works in Budapest's literary journals, and in 1908 he contributed a number of essays to the inaugural issues of *Nyugat* (West), a literary journal that rapidly developed into Hungary's leading liberal cultural forum. That same year he received his doctorate in German philology from the University of Budapest for a dissertation entitled "Friedrich Hebbel's Pan-Tragicness, as a Result of the Romantic Worldview," a work that was soon published serially and in book form in Budapest from 1908 to 1909 under his real and presumably "official" student name, Herbert Bauer. Over the next four to five years, he wrote steadily for *Nyugat*. His first play, *Dr. Szélpál Margit* (1906), a three-act drama about a woman biologist who must choose between her career and her marriage, was performed in Budapest's National Theater on 30 April 1909. *Bluebeard's Castle*, his third completed play, was initially sketched out in late 1908, shortly after he completed his formal studies; the bulk of the writing was accomplished in 1909 and early 1910. The play was published for the first time in the theater journal *Szinjáték* (Stageplay) in two parts in April and June 1910, where it contained a dual dedication to Kodály and Bartók. Two years later Balázs republished *Bluebeard* and two other one-act plays from 1909 and 1910 in a collection of plays bearing the title *Mysteries: Three One-Acters*, which appeared around Easter 1912.[4] Throughout this time he continued to write poetry. An interest in dance led to *The Wooden Prince* in 1912, which Bartók began to set to music in 1914.

Though prolific, thoughtful, and blessed with an undeniable gift for writing, Balázs was never able to establish himself as a major writer in Hungary. Almost from the beginning he was viewed as something of an outsider to the main literary establishment in Hungary. His interest in German literature and culture was too pronounced for a nation then enduring an uncomfortable political relationship with Austria. The fact that he was Jewish may have had a negative effect on his acceptance by some contemporaries. His writing was perceived as too intellectual, or too unrelenting in its pursuit of deeper questions about life. Balázs, for his part, did little to dispel this perception. The volume with which he introduced himself to the Hungarian public in 1907, after all, had been graced with the singularly uninviting title *Death Aesthetics*. The *Bluebeard* play is itself a good example of his sober and intense writing style, which he would temper on occasion with a rather sardonic form of wit, as seen in the three-part essay *Dialogue about Dialogue* (1909–11). He enlisted in the Hungarian army in 1916 and afterward wrote a book about his experiences, *Soul in War: Diary of Béla Balázs, Army Corporal*. His alienation from the literary establishment intensified through the war years as his political leanings moved farther left. "The entire Hungarian literary world has become a unified, solidarized camp against me," he lamented in his diary in 1918.[5] Forced to leave Hungary in 1919 for his role in the short-lived communist takeover in March 1919, Balázs lived the life of an exile for the next twenty-five years, returning to Hungary only in 1945, where he died three years later. The remainder of his life was devoted to the genre of film. In Austria and then Germany he distinguished himself as a scriptwriter and as one of the first to make a serious study of film aesthetics.[6] His persona non grata status in Hungary throughout the 1920s and early 1930s caused him to lose contact with many former friends and colleagues, including Bartók and Kodály. Today he is remembered as much for his contributions to the history of film and film studies as for his authorship of the texts to Bartók's first two stage works.

·

In its dramatic style and means of expression, *Bluebeard's Castle* shows strong connections to the late nineteenth- and early twentieth-century symbolist movement in European literature, as critics have often remarked. Its reliance on atmosphere, portentous visual symbols, and lack of action is characteristic of the dramatic style pioneered by Maurice Maeterlinck in Paris in the 1890s and termed "symbolist" by later critics. Maeterlinck's dramas and their underlying philosophy had a profound impact on other dramatists of his day, many of whom, like Maeterlinck himself, sought meaningful expression of the perceived emptiness and tragedy of contemporary man's existence through the technique of allusion. Symbolist drama was an outgrowth of the nineteenth-century symbolist movement in French poetry. As a result, it is closely related to the techniques of expression found in poetry of writers as diverse as Baudelaire, Verlaine, and Mallarmé. Symbolist drama deemphasizes traditional dramatic essentials such as plot, characterization, and action. The suggestive use of words and language becomes an important factor in the overall effect, just as in symbolist poetry, where linear discourse is ruptured, dialogue is nuanced and nonexplicit, and expression is concentrated into small statements or mere words that may have multiple meanings.[7] What, specifically, makes *Bluebeard* a symbolist play? In what ways does it resemble Maeterlinck's dramatic style? Fortunately, Balázs left clear documentation of his symbolist leanings in the form of a remarkable essay published in 1908, entitled simply "Maeterlinck." This essay, which will be discussed presently, offers a revealing glimpse into the playwright's workshop as well as insight into the reasons behind Balázs's interest in symbolist drama.

It is immediately apparent to even the most casual observer that *Bluebeard's Castle* derives much of its effect from the use of visual symbols. Exactly what these symbols mean, however, or how we are to interpret them has been the subject of much unresolved discussion over the years. Suggestive but inconclusive links with biographical events in the lives of both Balázs and Bartók have been and will continue to be posed, but ultimately the play's message expands outward to address a more universal audience, aided in this purpose by the power and poignancy of Bartók's music. It is precisely because *Bluebeard* so readily evades straightforward analysis that it continues to fascinate. The language of symbols that it uses affects all aspects of the play. Perhaps the most striking symbol is the castle itself, with its seven large, forbidding doors, each of which opens to reveal another aspect of Bluebeard's life and identity. Colored light emanates from each of these doors. Red light pours forth from the torture chamber, golden light from the treasury, blue-green from the garden. As Judith advances deeper into Bluebeard's gloomy domicile, bringing light to its darkened hallways, it becomes increasingly evident that the castle doors and their contents have a symbolic significance far greater than outward appearances would suggest, and that the sequence of door openings has gradually assumed another level of meaning. Judith's entry into the castle, we realize, also represents the unfurling of Bluebeard's soul before the loving but firm advances of his new wife. The doors, therefore, represent windows into his soul; and the castle, man himself.

Dramatic symbolism like this becomes more inscrutable as Judith progresses deeper into the castle. The silent lake of tears that rises, gray and lifeless, behind the sixth door is interpreted by Judith as the tears of Bluebeard's former wives; but it seems just as likely that these tears are Bluebeard's own, wept in anguish over his lost loves. From behind the seventh and last door step the three former wives, splendidly adorned with jewels and rich fabrics. A kneeling Bluebeard symbolically designates them Morning, Noon, and Evening. Judith, by opening the seventh door, has passed beyond the same mysterious, unspoken threshold that also claimed each of these women before her. To know that the former wives exist is to become one—to move, in effect, from present into past, receding into the dreamscape of Bluebeard's memory. Bluebeard symbolically anoints Judith "Night," thereby bringing about a completion of the twenty-four-hour cycle and, presumably, closure to his fruitless attempts to find love. The darkness that had been slowly creeping back into Bluebeard's castle after the sixth door was opened now becomes complete as Judith takes her place next to the former wives, and the stage lights ebb to blackness.

In a never-used introduction to the *Bluebeard* play dating from around 1915, Balázs partially explained the meaning behind his symbols: "Bluebeard's castle is not a realistic stone castle. The castle is his soul. It is lonely, dark, and secretive: the castle of locked doors. . . . Into this castle, into his own soul, Bluebeard admits his beloved. And the castle (the stage) shudders, sighs, and bleeds. When the woman walks into it, she walks into a living being."[8] Befitting its central role in Balázs's conception, the castle was included on the list of dramatis personae in the first published version of the play, just after the names Judith and Bluebeard, as if it, too, were a participant in the drama. (Bartók removed the castle from this list.) Dialogue between Judith and Bluebeard frequently alludes to the castle's human qualities. When Judith's hand strays against the castle's wet walls at the beginning, she remarks that "the castle is weeping." And following Judith's declaration of love in the second door scene, Bluebeard speaks as if the castle itself were alive and responding to her: "My castle's dark foundations tremble / From within its gloomy rocks, pleasure shivers. / Judith, Judith.—Cool and sweet / Blood flows from open wounds." The castle sighs when Judith turns the key in the first and sixth doors. Repeated references to the castle's "coldness" and "darkness" emphasize the icy loneliness of Bluebeard's solitude. Bluebeard's human attributes are thereby transferred to the castle, which becomes implicitly identified with its owner.

Withdrawal from the world of dramatic realism, as seen in *Bluebeard's Castle*, necessarily elevates the element of stage lighting to new importance as dramatic moments are now created and defined not by language but by atmosphere. Lighting effects themselves become significant symbols in *Bluebeard*, bearers of meaning that help shape the progression of events on stage. The play begins and ends in total darkness. In between, the stage slowly lightens with the opening of each successive door up to the fifth, after which the castle's gloom gradually returns. This arc from darkness through light and back to darkness mirrors the progression of Bluebeard's and Judith's hope for love. The glimmer of brightness occasioned by Judith's entry into the castle slowly increases in magnitude through the first five doors. The blinding white light streaming forth from the fifth door represents the conquering of darkness in Bluebeard's soul and the triumph of hope; it is Judith's compulsion to open the remaining two doors, and Bluebeard's acquiescence to her wishes, that causes darkness to return. As Judith steps toward the sixth door, the hall darkens slightly—"as if a shadow were cast over it," the text reads. Deepening shadows from here to the end parallel the extinction of hope in Bluebeard's soul. Bartók's musical setting reinforces the symbolic opposition of light and dark in Balázs's play with its overall F♯–C–F♯ tonal plan, where the beginning and end of the opera are cast around the tonal center F♯, and the brilliant dramatic moment when Judith opens the fifth door is presented in the contrasting tonal center of C.

A specific color of light is associated with each door. When Judith opens a door, the audience sees only a sudden shaft of colored light emanating from the opening in the wall. The actual contents themselves are not visible, apart from an occasional small, suggestive stage prop. Judith describes the door's contents aloud, her words confirming the symbolic impression of the light's color. By replacing scenes of splendor and horror with appropriately colored shafts of light, Balázs reduces the stage to utmost simplicity. This helps focus the audience's attention on the two characters before them. The contents of the doors are not themselves important, Balázs seems to say; it is what each door represents to Bluebeard and Judith that determines its dramatic significance. His use of colored light to represent symbolically the doors' contents also neatly sidesteps what could have become a real impediment for stage producers. The multitude of vivid scenes would crowd the drama psychologically; but, perhaps more important, it would also require a large stage with impressive resources to portray all these scenes both simultaneously and convincingly. Balázs's decision to represent the contents of the doors with colored beams of light reveals an awareness of practical matters of stage production.

The Nature of Balázs's Interest in Maeterlinck

Balázs's interest in the expressive possibilities of Maeterlinck's dramas has long been recognized as an important factor in the shaping of his own style. Most discussions of *Bluebeard* in the secondary literature at least mention Maeterlinck as an influence on the young Hungarian playwright. Unfortunately, many of these discussions point to Maeterlinck's *Ariane et Barbe-bleue* (1899) as the primary source of inspiration for *Bluebeard*, either implying or stating outright that this drama also provided the inspiration for the symbolism in Balázs's work. *Ariane* was first performed, in an operatic setting by Paul Dukas, in Paris in 1907. "Béla Balázs was primarily influenced by Maeterlinck's *Ariane et Barbe-Bleue*," writes Simon Broughton.[9] An unsympathetic Emil Haraszti asserts, "Béla Balázs attempted to compress Maeterlinck's three-act tragedy into a one-act drama."[10] In fact, very little in *Bluebeard* can be traced to this play, as I shall argue here. Far more important in their influence on Balázs's drama are Maeterlinck's symbolist plays from the early 1890s, works such as *L'Intruse* (The intruder, 1890), *Les Aveugles* (The blind, 1890), and *Intérieur* (Interior, 1894). The one-act format of these plays, combined with their dreamlike atmosphere and virtual lack of action, shows them to be the true stylistic predecessors of *Bluebeard's Castle*, even though they claim no connection with the Bluebeard story.

Maurice Maeterlinck is far from a household name in the later twentieth century. His dozens of plays and volumes of thought-provoking essays, extremely popular and influential at the turn of the century, have fallen into a state of near-oblivion from which it does not appear they will be rescued anytime soon. Only *Pelléas et Mélisande* (1892) still keeps his name before the public, and that is due primarily to Debussy's opera. In the 1890s, however, few dramatists generated more excitement in European literary circles or inspired as many followers as did this Belgian playwright. Maeterlinck's career traced a meteoric path from the moment his first play, *La Princesse Maleine*, was published in Paris in 1889. Heralded exuberantly by Octave Mirbeau, a leading Parisian author and critic, as one of the most notable playwrights since Shakespeare, Maeterlinck rapidly emerged as a leading figure in late nineteenth-century French drama. His plays addressed the mystic aspects of humans powerless to control their fate, of souls battling with universal forces they could neither understand nor alter. Pessimism and darkness pervade the works that established his reputation: *L'Intruse, Les Aveugles, Intérieur,* and *Pelléas et Mélisande*. Maeterlinck's was an exciting new style of theater in fin-de-siècle Europe.

In contrast to the naturalist style of theater championed in France by Emile Zola and his followers, where the emphasis was on the accurate, realistic portrayal of dramatic situations as they occurred in daily life, Maeterlinck moved the drama inward to portray the psychological states of people captured in tragic situations not of their own making. Little action occurs in Maeterlinck's plays, and pregnant pauses expand into silence as the characters haltingly address one another. In a book of essays published in 1896, Maeterlinck expressed an admiration for "tragedies without movement" in which "events are lacking," a quality he discerned in Greek drama and likened to his own theatrical style.[11] In his view, words function as language-transcending, external symbols of an inner dialogue between souls. "It is idle to think that, by means of words, any real communication can ever pass from one man to another," he once expressed in an essay entitled "Silence."[12] Maeterlinck's personal philosophy brightened through the 1890s and 1900s as his dramatic output became more optimistic in tone and less overtly symbolic, a shift that directly affected *Ariane et Barbe-bleue*. He won the Nobel Prize in Literature in 1911 for his play *The Blue Bird* (1909) and toured the United States at that time in the wake of his now-worldwide celebrity.

Béla Balázs was an early apostle of Maurice Maeterlinck in Hungary. In 1908, at the time he was beginning to contemplate the play that eventually became *Bluebeard's Castle*, Balázs contributed a substantial essay on Maeterlinck to the inaugural issue of *Nyugat*.[13] In this well-crafted essay, Balázs reviews Maeterlinck's dramatic and literary output in light of its ability to express the mysteries of human existence. All Maeterlinck's work, in Balázs's opinion, is unified by its attempt to express life's profound, unknowable depths. Different dramas and essays are merely alternative ways of projecting the mystic forces that govern our actions. Thus plays like *Aladine et Palomides*, *Pelléas et Mélisande*, *Les Aveugles*, and *L'Intruse*—which Balázs describes as "fable names and fable scenarios"—all exhibit a fundamental spiritual similarity to one another:

Somewhere nonexistent so that they may exist anywhere. For who knows? That silence, that motionlessness locked up in those sullen castles, does it not undulate around me here as well? That invisible, all-ruling great mystery. For *that* is the hero of Maeterlinck's plays. Within that protracted silence where nothing happens, the invisible force is active which holds back this life, the silence which depicts its movements. And as for the vast Unknowable, within whose breast we live as if in a dark forest: its most visible, most dramatic manifestation is death. Death is the hero of these dramas. But death here is not the terrible sad end, not burial pit and skeleton, but the dark secret, the lurker. *It is only a symbol of the great mystery.* It is the invisible, *living* figure which walks among us, caresses us and sits down at the table as an "uninvited guest." Nothing happens in these plays. Life happens.[14] (Emphasis in the original)

The last two sentences in this quotation sum up Balázs's attraction to Maeterlinck's dramatic style. Balázs pursues this observation to the logical conclusion that, as Maeterlinck has written, action is but a surrogate. "Depiction of eventless motionlessness is the ideal," he asserts.[15]

Balázs was fascinated with the possibilities for dramatic expression that Maeterlinck's plays offered. His article's liberal peppering with phrases like "the Great Secret," "the Vast Unknowable," and "the Great Mystery" shows him to be primarily interested in the mystical side of Maeterlinck's philosophy, which manifests itself in Maeterlinck's choice of stories and settings for his dramas, the sketchily drawn nature of his characters, and his attempt to express, through silence and a minimum of stage action, what cannot be seen or described. But as a dramatist himself, Balázs was also interested in how Maeterlinck successfully transferred this mystic philosophy to the stage. Literary historian Ivan Sanders, examining this same essay, concludes that it is "clear that its author has become an advocate of this new, plotless, often voiceless theatre of mood, nuance and effect."[16]

Balázs's published observations about Maeterlinck resonate deeply with the dramatic style of *Bluebeard's Castle*. The heavy, mysterious atmosphere of Balázs's play, in which characters barely move in response to the portentous dramatic events enacted on stage, is clearly inspired by Maeterlinck's example. The figures of Bluebeard and Judith themselves seem modeled after Maeterlinck's dramatic characters. Maeterlinck had conferred the title "marionettes" on the characters in his early plays, referring to the manner in which their actions were controlled by an external fate instead of their own internal thoughts or motivations. Balázs elaborates on this designation: "For indeed they are marionettes. Because the true, principal, and only character is that force within each of them which pushes and pulls them, the 'force we do not see.'"[17] Bluebeard and Judith appear to exhibit somewhat greater internal complexity than Maeterlinck's marionettes. Their thoughts evolve as they weigh the import of Judith's discoveries. Taints of blood behind each door force an increased awareness of her situation upon Judith, and her thoughts develop accordingly. She is not a "single immobile mood from beginning to end," as Balázs describes Maeterlinck's characters.[18] But at first glance, Judith and Bluebeard could be called marionettes, too, in the sense that "forces we do not see" push and pull them, conditioning their actions and responses to each other. They often fail to signal in words the reasons for their actions. They exhibit the same lack of personality and individualization that Balázs perceives and admires in Maeterlinck's characters.

Balázs's pronouncements about drama in his Maeterlinck essay radiate a passionate interest in inexpressible, mystic profundities of the human soul. Balázs is always interested in the dramatization of internal thoughts and emotional states. In another essay from 1908, this time discussing the plays of Strindberg, Balázs waxes enthusiastic about "visible thought, visible feeling, atmosphere. Surely this is the dramatic ideal."[19] In true symbolist fashion, Balázs yearns for the expressive capabilities of music in his Maeterlinck and Strindberg essays:

> Yet why is the mystical music that is breathed toward us from Maeterlinck's dramas . . . so inconceivable? Perhaps because it's music? Perhaps because it's mystical? It is my eternal envy that musicians need not speak and my eternal love that in drama it is likewise possible not to. (Balázs, "Maeterlinck," p. 450)

> Music and drama are the agents of expression of the undefinable areas of life. (Balázs, "Strindberg Paradoxonok," p. 518)

Music, drama, and the mystic expression of human longings would later intersect in Bartók's opera based on the Bluebeard play. Balázs's choice of the title "Mysteries" for his collection of three one-act plays written from 1909 to 1911 becomes more understandable in light of his clearly expressed admiration for the mystical aspect of Maeterlinck's dramas. That he chose such a title is a clear indication that *Bluebeard's Castle* and its two companion plays were written under the influence of this dramatic aesthetic. Interest in mysticism was widespread in Europe at the turn of the century. Balázs was not the only dramatist exploring this vein around 1910. Gabriele d'Annunzio labeled his *Le Martyre de Saint Sébastien* (1911) a "mystère," and Frank Wedekind subtitled his *Franziska* (1912) a "modern mystery." Russian composer Alexander Scriabin, a man thoroughly steeped in the spirit of mysticism, worked for years, until his death in 1915, on a grandiose composition entitled *Mysterium* that would engage all the arts and human senses in a profound synesthetic experience.

Bluebeard Compared with Maeterlinck's *Ariane*

In exploring the literary background of the Bluebeard drama, music historians and other writers trace two distinct lines of influence to their source in Maeterlinck's writing: the libretto's style and its subject matter. The stylistic influence is general in nature, based on similarities between language, atmosphere, and aesthetic, as discussed earlier. The subject matter, it is often suggested, derives more specifically from a single antecedent: Maeterlinck's own version of the Bluebeard story, *Ariane et Barbe-bleue*. The accrual of critical attention on *Ariane*, as opposed to any other of Maeterlinck's dramas or his style in general, has created a somewhat lopsided situation in the historiography of *Bluebeard*. *Ariane*'s obvious connection with the Bluebeard legend obscures the fact that stylistically it bears little resemblance to *Bluebeard's Castle*. Literary historians have long recognized *Ariane* as a fundamentally different type of play from the early plays of Maeterlinck's symbolist period. To seek stylistic connections between *Bluebeard* and the three-act rescue drama *Ariane et Barbe-bleue*, then, is to seek connections that are, at best, barely present. The "mystery" in Balázs's mystery play could not have come from *Ariane*.

Maeterlinck wrote *Ariane et Barbe-bleue*—a work he described as a "simple libretto, a canvas for the musician"—during the spring of 1899.[20] Along with *Soeur Béatrice*, completed later in 1899, *Ariane* represented a new direction for the Belgian playwright: it was specifically created as an opera libretto, for an as-yet-unnamed composer. (*Pelléas* had not been intended as a vehicle for music; Debussy adapted the existing play.) Unlike the plays that brought Maeterlinck acclaim earlier in the 1890s, *Ariane* features considerable dramatic interaction between the characters. It is also less overtly symbolic than previous plays, less mysterious, and less gloomy. Oblique allusions to life's eternal mysteries are correspondingly few.

Maeterlinck gave a subtitle to this work that captures the essence of his treatment of the Bluebeard story. Its full title is *Ariane et Barbe-bleue, ou la délivrance inutile* (Ariadne and Bluebeard; or, the useless rescue). *Ariane* is a rescue drama in which Ariane, Bluebeard's assertive, heroic new wife, liberates her predecessors from their entombment behind the seventh door and offers them the choice: to follow her and leave the castle, or to remain. The five imprisoned wives choose to stay. Ariane then boldly leaves, simply walking away from Bluebeard and his castle at the end. The plot unfolds through three acts, engaging a full cast of peasants, the two principal roles, Ariane and Bluebeard, Ariane's nurse, and the five former wives. Though ostensibly a retelling of the Bluebeard story, the drama actually centers on the strong leading figure of Ariane, whom one writer has described as "the prototype of the liberated woman."[21] Ariane's determination to rescue Bluebeard's five former wives meets little effective resistance from Bluebeard, who seldom appears on stage. The figure of Ariane dominates the drama. She is a woman of heroic will and clear conscience whose decisions never cloud with uncertainty, and whose actions alone impel the drama to its surprising conclusion. Bluebeard, in contrast, does little except glower helplessly when thwarted by Ariane or the peasants. He is an almost pathetic individual. Ariane's gesture of imperial indifference at the end, when she signals that Bluebeard should be liberated from the ropes that bind him, emphasizes that the noble traits of heroism and honor belong not to Bluebeard in this drama but to her.

Maeterlinck's approach to drama varied as the 1890s wore on. The life and destiny of the human soul, always the center of Maeterlinck's philosophy, retained its deep mystery for the playwright, but around 1895 the tone of his dramas began to change from the pessimism of his symbolist plays, where characters are mere marionettes controlled by a destiny they cannot understand, to a more affirmative life view in which humans can find happiness in pursuit of their unknown destiny.[22] In an 1894 essay, "The Modern Drama," Maeterlinck explicitly redefined his artistic credo: "To penetrate deeply into human consciousness is the privilege, even the duty, of the thinker, the moralist, the historian, novelist, and to a degree, of the lyrical poet; but not of the dramatist. . . . Do what one will, discover what marvels one may, the sovereign law of the stage, its essential demand, will always be *action*" (Maeterlinck's emphasis).[23] Maeterlinck's aesthetic redirection stresses the fundamental importance of action in drama. "With the rise of the curtain," he continues, "the high intellectual desire within us undergoes transformation; and in place of the thinker . . . there stands the mere instinctive spectator . . . the man whose one desire it is to see something happen."[24] When the human rabble rushes in to save Ariane, or when Ariane shatters the darkened window of the wives' underground tomb to show them the way to freedom, *Ariane et Barbe-bleue* gives evidence of how far Maeterlinck's conception of drama had evolved away from that of his earlier, more overtly symbolist plays.

Connections between Balázs's version of the Bluebeard tale and Maeterlinck's *Ariane* seem increasingly distant the more closely these two plays are examined. Superficial similarities do exist. Balázs may have borrowed certain ideas from Maeterlinck's play—for example, the seven doors and the symbolic contrast between lightness and darkness. As in *Ariane*, behind the seventh door the former wives are not dead but living, a situation that allows each playwright to contrast Bluebeard's newest wife with earlier wives. Also, Judith, like Ariane, brings light to Bluebeard's dark castle, so there may be a parallel between the two female protagonists. Ivan Sanders feels that a similarity also exists between the animism of the two castles.[25] These resemblances can all be viewed as part of a shared symbolist vocabulary, or, alternatively, as the result of something as innocent as both plays being based on the same folk tale. Many writers who drew upon mysticism in their literary work used symbols similar to those found in Maeterlinck's and Balázs's plays. When one reads in Flaubert's novel *Salammbô* (1862) of a "long vaulted hall" in which "seven doors" were displaying against the wall "seven squares of different colors," one realizes how much the nineteenth- and early twentieth-century devotees of mysticism imbibed a common language of symbols and numerology, and how difficult it is, therefore, to posit specific precedents for any aspect of a given work.[26] Once one starts looking, similarities can be found almost anywhere. The castle in *Bluebeard* could just as easily have been modeled after Klingsor's magic castle in *Parsifal*.

The differences between *Ariane* and *Bluebeard's Castle*, on the other hand, are profound. Balázs changed nearly every aspect of plot and characterization. The opening of the seven doors, to pick only one example, becomes the central focus of *Bluebeard's Castle*, whereas in *Ariane* this action occupies only the first act and is of secondary importance to the main plot. The quality of the differences between the two plays has caused one writer to question whether Balázs even used *Ariane* as a source: Miklós Szabolcsi feels Balázs wove his version of the Bluebeard story directly from Charles Perrault's original fairy tale.[27] This view is too extreme. It is far more likely that Balázs drew upon his knowledge of both the original Bluebeard story and Maeterlinck's play to fashion the outlines of his own version. Some elements of Balázs's play, too, could not have come from Maeterlinck. The recurrent blood motif, for example, clearly originates in Perrault's folk tale, where Bluebeard's newest wife cannot remove the blood stains from the magic key she accidentally drops upon viewing the horrors of the seventh door.[28] Halsey Stevens aptly characterizes the distant relationship between *Ariane* and *Bluebeard*: "Although Maeterlinck's play furnished the initial inspiration for Balázs's libretto, there are fundamental differences in both treatment and point of view."[29] Balázs himself held *Ariane* in high regard. He referred to it in his 1908 essay as Maeterlinck's "most profound play" ("Maeterlinck legmélyebb darabja"), but such open admiration did not necessarily translate into close connections between the two plays.[30] Balázs transformed the Bluebeard story into a pessimistic drama of human irreconcilability. Aspects of Maeterlinck's drama filter into his conception, but they are radically altered in meaning. Perhaps the most basic connection between *Bluebeard* and *Ariane et Barbe-bleue* is that both were conceived with the idea that they would eventually be set to music.

For the true stylistic precedent to the *Bluebeard's Castle* drama, we must turn our attention instead to the example of Maeterlinck's early one-act symbolist plays. In *L'Intruse*, one of the more well-known of these plays, the invisible figure of Death is introduced early on. Characters gathered around a table in a small, quiet room hear the sound of a scythe being sharpened outside in the garden but fail to recognize the source of that noise. For the remainder of the play, the audience is aware of the presence of Death. The family on stage appears oblivious, however; they think the noises they hear are those of a relative coming over to visit. Only at the play's end does Death enter the house, still unseen, to claim its victim, the sick mother in the adjacent room. Death surrounds the family, but they do not perceive it for what it is. The halting, disjunct dialogue in *L'Intruse* is laden with frequent heavy pauses. An anxious atmosphere suffuses the theater. The sharpening scythe heard at Death's first appearance early in the play shapes the expectation that some character will die—the only question is who.

Bluebeard's Castle achieves a dramatic result similar to this through its symbols of blood and instruments of torture. Symbols of Death in both plays (blood, torture, the scythe) are first found near the beginning and resurface from time to time to remind the audience, if not the characters, that Death lurks behind all the actions taking place on stage. Balázs's blood symbol is considerably more overt than Maeterlinck's allusive, offstage hints of Death. Nonetheless, the technique by which he injects an element of tension into the drama is similar. Future criticism of Balázs's drama must be deflected away from the supposed model of *Ariane*, which has received the lion's share of attention to date, and onto the more elusive but real connections with these early symbolist plays.

PART I: ESSAYS

Balázs's Personal Interest in Hebbel and German Romantic Drama

When Judith steps forward to assume her place next to Bluebeard's former wives at the end of *Bluebeard's Castle*, the tragedy of her failure to bring love to Bluebeard is brought home to the audience with great power. Why must she be entombed? She has done nothing morally wrong in opening the doors. And why does she succumb so willingly, with such resignation? Shouldn't she struggle more against Bluebeard? She has done nothing to warrant such punishment other than press Bluebeard into making concessions he does not want to make. Answers to these questions expose the presence of an entirely different sense of tragedy in Balázs's drama. It is in his drama's tragic conclusion that Balázs transcends the symbolist style of Maeterlinck. There is an attempt to express something more profound and meaningful. Where does this come from?

Balázs, it has been remarked, was a student of German culture.[31] He grew up in a German-Hungarian household, and throughout his life he moved easily in the world of German arts and letters, albeit from a geographically distant vantage point. His proclivity for things German would manifest itself repeatedly in his literary career. Perhaps the most outward example of this personal inclination may be found in his 1914 *Nyugat* essay "Paris or Weimar?" where he contemplates the relative merits of French and German culture and comes down firmly on the side of German culture, feeling that Hungary could benefit from its influence; he hopes for its eventual victory in the newly begun World War.[32] From 1906 to 1908, his doctoral studies focused on the dramas and dramatic theories of Friedrich Hebbel, the mid-nineteenth-century German dramatist whose ideas were drawing renewed attention across Europe, predominantly in German-speaking lands. The mere fact that Balázs chose to study Hebbel for his doctoral program is indicative of his German-oriented intellectual alignment at this time. At the same time that he was writing articles revealing his fascination with the symbolism of Maeterlinck, Balázs was personally absorbed in a major study of one of Germany's great romantic dramatists. The different quality of his symbolism results from his attempt to impart greater metaphysical depth to the symbolist aesthetic.

Evidence that Balázs viewed German literature and philosophy as more profound and worthy of emulation surfaces repeatedly in his writings from around 1910. This attitude is present even in the otherwise Francophilic essay on Maeterlinck. There, attempting to put into words the mystic philosophy that emanates from Maeterlinck's plays, Balázs notes that these plays lack the spiritual depth that results from rational thought. Instead, he explains, their depth results from the playwright's ability to suggest or allude to the inexpressible forces of fate that guide humans in their lives. Balázs expresses this qualitative difference as the difference between French and German thinking: "This German woman [Anselma Heine, author of a Maeterlinck biography] wants at all costs to extract the German from within Maeterlinck. Frightening! . . . What Germanicism is there in this *thoughtless* depth? Maeterlinck's diving bell is not thought; his depth is not related to the depth of Goethe's, of Hebbel's. He wishes to grasp those thoughts that 'we think without thinking'—this is not a German craft"[33] (original emphasis and punctuation). Here Balázs specifically contrasts Maeterlinck with Goethe and Hebbel, finding "thoughtless depth" in the former and thought*ful*, rational depth in the latter two. The flavor of his comments demonstrates how Hungarian writers at this time viewed French and German literature as separate channels of influence possessing their own distinguishable national identities. In finding a lack of "Germanicism" (*germánság*) in Maeterlinck's dramas, Balázs wishes to make it clear that just because Maeterlinck's aesthetic appears to be deep and profound it is not the result of keen insight into the human condition. Maeterlinck's delicately nuanced style is akin to those of "Verlaine and Debussy, Monet and Carrière," Balázs exclaims, "not the Germans!"[34]

For the same issue of *Nyugat* in which the Maeterlinck essay appeared, Balázs also wrote a short essay assessing Friedrich Hebbel's impact on modern drama.[35] This was in truth his first contribution to the journal, and an offshoot of his dissertation work. In this essay, Balázs eloquently stresses that the dramatic theories of Friedrich Hebbel form a worthy point of departure for modern dramatists seeking to impart deeper metaphysical significance to their dramas. He places himself directly in the tradition of dramatists who found inspiration in Hebbel's writings: "The last great theoretician of drama was Hebbel. That which he dreamt and thought of, the great drama of the future, he himself could not realize. . . . Yet to this day we have not reached the goals that Hebbel the theoretician had set, which live on as unsolved problems, disquieting secret thoughts in the souls of those contemplating the fate of drama. . . . *He initiated things which have not yet been finished*"[36] (my emphasis). Balázs shares the excitement of these unnamed Germans who sensed the considerable potential of applying Hebbel's ideas of tragedy to their own work. Later, his concluding statements reveal that his own dramatic outlook is conditioned by Hebbel and German romanticism: "Our long-starved metaphysical instincts are beginning to torture us and the problem of drama disquiets us, for its pangs of birth and groping for direction have never been so obvious as in our own time. *And we return to the [German] romantics, to begin where they left off so as to find a modern form of expression for our modern feeling of transcendence*"[37] (my emphasis). Such demonstrable enthusiasm for Hebbel confounds our neat picture of Balázs as a symbolist dramatist. His interests were clearly capable of pulling him in several directions at once.

In his attraction to both German romanticism and French symbolism, Balázs was not alone among Hungarian intellectuals and writers working around 1910. György Lukács also felt a spiritual kinship with German romantics like Schlegel, Tieck, and Novalis, a feeling brought about by his realization that symbolism, at its core, remained incapable of communicating the reality underlying human existence. Lukács and Balázs were close friends at this time. The ultimate failure of the symbolist aesthetic in the eyes of Lukács drove him backward to nineteenth-century writers, in whose writing he sought inspiration for a more affirmative cultural and spiritual outlook.[38] According to Mary Gluck, by 1910 Lukács and other young Hungarians "confessed themselves to be paradoxically related to the romanticists, whose failed task they felt they would finally bring to fruition."[39] Balázs's Hebbel article from 1908 seems to epitomize this relationship with German romanticism. As a dramatist, Balázs's attention naturally came to bear on the great German romantic tragedician who, as he wrote, "initiated things which have not yet been finished." Balázs emphasizes repeatedly how Hebbel's ideas looked ahead to the future of drama. The "metaphysical instinct" is being "reborn" among contemporary German writers, he proclaims, and "romanticism is experiencing a renaissance."[40]

Balázs harbored a lingering attraction to the symbolist aesthetic long past the time when Lukács had rejected it on philosophical grounds, probably because he was at heart a creative artist, not a philosopher like Lukács. In Hungary, symbolism was only beginning to emerge as a new artistic trend in the first decade of the twentieth century.[41] The application of French symbolist techniques in the poetry of Endre Ady starting in 1906 powerfully demonstrated symbolism's viability and relevance for Hungarian writers. Nonetheless, Balázs—perhaps influenced by Lukács—was sensitive to the empty spiritual core at the heart of Maeterlinck's symbolist dramas, as his comments in the 1908 Maeterlinck essay demonstrate.

Because of their German cultural orientation, Balázs and Lukács approached symbolism not through French poetry and drama but instead through the German literature of Goethe, Novalis, Wagner, and the German romantics.[42] This approach brought about an entirely different focus. Unlike most of their contemporaries in Hungary, who were attracted to symbolism for its novel use of language, Balázs and Lukács were interested in the philosophical and metaphysical aspects of symbolism as well.[43] The eventual realization that symbolism rested on little more than a vague mystical philosophy led both men, in their individual ways, to search for firmer metaphysical foundations in the work of German romantic writers. As a result, both became increasingly alienated from the mainstream of Hungarian literature, which was strongly Francophilic at the turn of the century. Balázs's plays and poetry were "too speculative, too abstract, too 'German' for Hungarian tastes," suggests Ivan Sanders.[44]

The perception that his works were shrouded in a fog of German-inspired metaphysics dogged Balázs from the beginning of his career. Mihály Babits, one of Hungary's most prominent men of letters, reviewed *Bluebeard's Castle* and the other *Mystery Plays* in 1913. He admits that the title of the collection worried him; he expected to read "works of a vague, German type . . . like Hofmannsthal's creations."[45] He goes on to express qualified approval of these new dramas because of their Hungarian spirit. "My fears should have been unfounded," he writes: "Balázs . . . took care to seek his homeland tradition, and, with truly splendid poetic taste, it wasn't in drama that he sought true dramatic form, but, as he once expressed to me, 'he tried to enlarge the fluidity of Székely folk ballads for drama.' "[46] Babits is relieved to see this new aesthetic direction in Balázs's writing. He contrasts these "Maeterlinckian symbolical dramas," as he calls the *Mystery Plays*, with some of Balázs's earlier works, "which under a strong German influence wanted to express metaphysical abstractions, the mystical breaths of life."[47]

Predictably, György Lukács took exception to Babits's negative view of the German influence on Balázs. He rallied to Balázs's defense in a series of essays gathered together in 1918 under the remarkable title *Béla Balázs and Those Who Do Not Want Him.* This volume, in a striking coincidence, appeared around the same time *Bluebeard's Castle* was achieving its first operatic performances in Budapest. The contrast between Bartók's ascendant career and Balázs's own descent from public favor could not have appeared sharper. "I have esteem for this outstanding wordsmith and philologist [Babits]," Lukács wrote in the preface to this volume, "but in his attitude toward Béla Balázs I see a deep prejudice . . . against Germanicism."[48] Lukács questions whether Babits actually knows what Germanicism is. He suggests that Babits has unjustly equated George, Rilke, Dehmel, and Werfel, as if they may all be lumped into one generalized category of German literature. Significantly, Lukács takes for granted the fact that Balázs's dramatic style was strongly influenced by Hebbel. But "the connection between the tragedician Hebbel and the tragedician Balázs, which, it must be added, is never simple or straightforward, does not apply here."[49]

Balázs's interest in nineteenth-century German drama may be one reason why so many Wagnerian dramatic themes can be seen in *Bluebeard's Castle*. Judith's curiosity about what lies behind the last two doors, and her persistent questioning of Bluebeard, who begs her to stop, recalls Elsa's curiosity about Lohengrin's name in *Lohengrin*. Judith, like Elsa, is motivated to action by love. And as in *Lohengrin*, the strength of her feeling for Bluebeard and the certainty that she must press ahead regardless of the consequences drive the drama toward its tragic conclusion. As dramatic characters, Bluebeard and Lohengrin are similar, too, in that they both place extreme demands on their new wives; secrets exist, Judith and Elsa are informed, that should not be asked about. Another Wagnerian notion in *Bluebeard's Castle* is that of human redemption, specifically the redemption of man's love through the agency of a woman. Bluebeard is clearly a stricken soul. Like the Dutchman in *Der fliegende Holländer*, he repeatedly seeks the one woman whose faith and grace will redeem him from his misery. Dark, brooding, mysterious, lonely, and passionate, Bluebeard is in many ways modeled on the Dutchman type. He represents the archetypal masculine man. Judith, a modern-day Senta, in turn represents an idealized feminine type: the "Ewig-Weibliche" for whom Bluebeard unrealistically yearns. Wagnerian connections like these merit further study. Although Bartók's opera is usually described as anti-Wagnerian in conception, the text itself draws noticeably from the world of German romanticism.

Hebbel's Dramatic Theories and Their Effect on the Bluebeard Drama

Balázs's strong interest in the works of Friedrich Hebbel had a perceptible effect on the nature of tragedy in his Bluebeard drama. This is an influence on *Bluebeard* that has not yet been recognized. Friedrich Hebbel (1813–63) was well known as a poet and dramatist in mid-nineteenth-century Germany. In addition to his biblical tragedies

Mary Magdalene and *Judith,* which he retold with an added psychological dimension, his play *Genoveva* was later adapted and set to music by Robert Schumann. His essays about drama, notably the 1843 "My Word Concerning Drama," set forth the view, manifested repeatedly in his own dramatic work, that human life was fundamentally tragic. Hebbel expressed the nature of human tragedy as the conflict between individual and universal wills. The opposition of individual and universe invariably seeks an equilibrium within which the individual is subsumed. The tragedy of existence lies in the fact that strong individuals are incompatible with the sense of general world balance, and that the more they assert their individuality, the more force the universe applies to restore the balance. From this basic conflict arises Hebbel's concept of "tragic guilt," which occurs when an individual has unknowingly upset the balance and must pay the price for his or her action; the "guilt" stems not from having sinned or from having made a moral transgression but from having endangered the universal whole. Hebbel expresses this tragic guilt as "Nothwendigkeit," or necessity.[50]

One of the more puzzling aspects of *Bluebeard's Castle* is found in the concluding actions of Bluebeard and Judith in the seventh door scene. When Judith sees that her fate, too, is to be entombed within Bluebeard's castle, she does not struggle violently against this unjust sentence, as any normal person might do. Instead, she submits with little struggle as Bluebeard bedecks her with crown, mantle, and jewels. Judith seems to recognize that such an end is inevitable, rendering further contest useless. A Hebbelian interpretation throws considerable light on her actions. Judith is an individual who asserts herself increasingly throughout the drama. After the crucial fifth door scene, her continued desire to open more doors (to get closer to Bluebeard's soul) passes the point that the universe broadly recognizes as the limit of harmonious love between man and woman. Had she stopped at this point, some sort of compromise would still have been possible. But because Judith is driven to tragic self-assertion and demands the keys to the last two doors, the universe sets in motion a counterbalancing force that ultimately destroys the individual. Bluebeard and Judith are both caught in the larger web of human experience, participants in a drama that has been acted out countless times by other lovers. In this case it is the woman who attempts to penetrate man's soul, but it could easily take place the other way around. The stage gets darker immediately upon the opening of the sixth door. The poignancy of Judith's tragic decision to continue lies in her simultaneous awareness of and disregard for the dangers that lurk ahead:

"Be it my life or my death, Bluebeard / Open the last two doors," she states before the end of the fifth door scene, her words evoking the familiar hero's words ("Életemet, halálomat . . . ") of Hungarian folk tale.[51] Once the universe has set in motion the corrective counterbalancing force, the process grinds forward until the individual is extinguished. The universe's counterbalance here takes the shape of entombment behind the seventh door. What is Hebbelian about the conclusion of *Bluebeard's Castle* is the way in which Judith, after the fifth door scene, drives the drama forward to its tragic conclusion and ruins herself in the process.

Judith embodies the idea, it might be said, of Hebbelian tragic guilt. She has not sinned morally in pressing to open the last two doors, for moral or ethical issues do not come into play in this drama. Nor can she be faulted for her desire to open the last two doors, though several critics have demonstrated their readiness to do so.[52] There is no doubt that Judith is the actual agent that brings about the collapse of hope after the fifth door scene. In the face of her determination, Bluebeard responds with passive, weary resistance. Judith may be guilty of forcing the drama to its tragic conclusion, but does this mean she is morally guilty, too? No. In attempting to gain greater knowledge of Bluebeard's soul, she has stumbled onto the realization—a universal truth to Balázs, Bartók, and their circle?—that full and total knowledge of man's soul by a woman is possible but only at the terrible cost of their mutual love (and the woman's life or freedom). The wives before Judith had also made this discovery but, like her, made it too late. Judith stands caught between the honesty of her intentions and their tragic results. Her actions, oddly, conflict with the normal "curiosity" motive of the Bluebeard story. Only before the last door does Judith seem to show a fearful curiosity; the act of opening the previous six doors is motivated less by curiosity than by her urgent and clear-sighted desire to let no impediments stand in the way of their love.

The conclusion of *Bluebeard's Castle* thus seems to have a perceptible Hebbelian cast to it. Balázs extracted the essence of Hebbel's ideas, as presented in his dramatic theories, and subtly transferred it to the modern stage. He was influenced by the philosophical ideas behind Hebbel's plays, not the plays themselves. Hebbel's concept of tragedy is present in *Bluebeard* in abstract form. The Hebbel influence may exist on several levels, however. Additional specific parallels can be seen between Balázs's Judith and the biblical figure of Judith found in Hebbel's own 1840 drama *Judith*. Although the topic is too large to

investigate here, this raises the very real possibility that Balázs modeled his female character in some way after Hebbel's well-known
tragic heroine.

.

The text to *Bluebeard's Castle* reflects Balázs's multiple interests in the
years around 1910. Two of the stronger influences on his operatic text
are Maeterlinck and Hebbel. In deriving his dramatic aesthetic from
these two sources, Balázs demonstrates strong connections to broader
trends in European drama at the turn of the century—one essentially
French in origin, the other essentially German. This bivalent influence may explain why we can see connections with both French symbolist drama and German expressionist drama in *Bluebeard*. In one
sense, then, *Bluebeard* is international in outlook, part of a general
trend toward internalization of the drama in the decades before
World War I. *Bluebeard*'s mixture of a modern symbolist style with a
nineteenth-century conception of tragedy is not as unusual as it might
first appear. Miklós Szabolcsi notes that as the symbolist movement
spread outside of France, it often coexisted with "certain neo-
romantic, even neoclassicist trends."[53] As a dramatist interested in
creating a new, identifiably Hungarian dramatic style, Balázs drew
upon what he found most interesting in Western European dramatic
trends and synthesized these disparate elements into a modern drama
of considerable theatrical power. The fact that Bartók changed so
little of Balázs's drama is a testament to the drama's intrinsic merits,
and proof that Balázs created a work that spoke deeply to Bartók's
own conscience.

NOTES

1. *Bluebeard's Castle* has been the subject of surprisingly few full-length
studies. Many insightful comments are sprinkled throughout the Bartók literature, however, often in general studies of his music or in biographies. Of the
principal studies devoted specifically to *Bluebeard*, György Kroó's seminal article on the opera ("Duke Bluebeard's Castle," *Studia Musicologica* 1 [1961]:
251–340) remains by far the most thorough appraisal of the opera and its
dramatic text. Elliott Antokoletz's valuable study of Bartók's music, *The Music
of Béla Bartók* (Berkeley and Los Angeles, 1984), discusses the general compositional links between Bartók and Debussy. He turns more specifically to Debussy's influence on *Bluebeard* in his later article, "Bartók's *Bluebeard*: The

Sources of Its 'Modernism,' " *College Music Symposium* 30, no. 1 (Spring 1990): 75–95. Ernő Lendvai includes a major chapter on the opera in his appraisal of the theoretical foundations underlying Bartók's music, *The Workshop of Bartók and Kodály* (Budapest, 1983).

2. All the Balázs books in Bartók's personal library, for example, are inscribed to Bartók by "Herbert." Anti-German sentiment began to crest at the turn of the century when ethnically pure Hungarians developed a sharper intolerance for Hungary's recent immigrants, often German in origin. (Witness Bartók's chiding letters to his family in 1903, in which he urged them never to speak in German to one another.) In 1913 Balázs formally changed his name from Herbert Bauer to Béla Balázs. The primary source for biographical information about Balázs is Joseph Zsuffa's monumental study *Béla Balázs: The Man and the Artist* (Berkeley and Los Angeles, 1987). Greater detail about the biographical events sketched here may be found by consulting Zsuffa's book, primarily chapters 1–3. In my recent Ph.D. dissertation ("Music and Drama in Béla Bartók's Opera *Duke Bluebeard's Castle*" [Harvard University, 1994]) I examine the nature and extent of Bartók's and Balázs's working relationship.

3. Béla Balázs, diary entry from 5 September 1906. Balázs kept a detailed personal diary for most of his adult life. This diary represents a valuable chronicle of the concerns of his generation and is preserved, along with Balázs's other papers, at the Library of the Hungarian Academy of Sciences. Many entries deal extensively with Bartók and the first two stage works. Excerpts from Balázs's diaries have been published in English in István Gál, "Béla Balázs, Bartók's First Librettist," *New Hungarian Quarterly* 55 (Autumn 1974): 204–8. The original diaries themselves are published in abbreviated form as a two-volume set, *Béla Balázs: Napló* (Diary), ed. Anna Fábri (Budapest, 1982).

4. A more detailed account of the publishing history of the *Bluebeard* play may be found in Kroó, "Duke Bluebeard's Castle," pp. 274–80. The "Prologue of the Bard" led a somewhat separate existence for two years until it was united with the body of the play in the 1912 edition. In April 1913, after Bartók had temporarily shelved the operatic score following its poor showing in two opera competitions, Balázs staged a theatrical performance of *Bluebeard's Castle* in Budapest under the sponsorship of *Nyugat*. Bartók helped with the performance by playing some of his piano music at the intermission between *Bluebeard* and the other drama presented that evening, *The Blood of the Virgin Mary*. Balázs recorded the details of this production several months later in his diary (*Napló*, vol. 1, p. 604).

5. Quoted in Zsuffa, *Béla Balázs*, p. 66.

6. It is a singular feature of Bartók's biography that both men who wrote texts for his stage works, Balázs and Melchior Lengyel, would later go on to greater successes in the film industry. Lengyel turned his back on the lurid world of the mandarin to pen the delicately humorous *Ninotchka*, one of Greta Garbo's signature roles in the late 1930s. Balázs received acclaim first as a film

critic in Vienna, then as one of the founders of modern film theory following the 1924 publication of his influential study of film aesthetics, *The Visible Man; or, the Culture of Film*. He participated in the production and writing of dozens of films, including *Die Abenteuer eines Zehnmarkscheines* (1926), *Das blaue Licht* (1930), starring the famous and soon-to-be-infamous Leni Riefenstahl, and the film version of Kurt Weill's *Die Dreigroschenoper* (1930). Balázs's film years are extensively documented in Zsuffa's biography.

7. André Karátson, "A Translation and Refraction of Symbolism: A Survey of the Hungarian Example," in *The Symbolist Movement in the Literature of European Languages*, ed. Anna Balakian (Budapest, 1984), p. 165.

8. Béla Balázs, "A Kékszakállú Herceg Vára: Megjegyzések a szöveghez" (Duke Bluebeard's Castle: notes on the text), in *Balázs Béla: Válogatott cikkek és tanulmányok*, ed. Magda Nagy (Budapest, 1968), p. 35. Balázs's original unpublished text is in German and was intended as an introduction to a German production of the play that never materialized. It is preserved in the Béla Balázs Collection of the Hungarian Academy of Sciences. The only published version of this text is in Hungarian translation, from which the translation given here in the text has been made.

9. Simon Broughton, "Bartók and World Music," in *The Stage Works of Béla Bartók* (English National Opera Guide no. 44), ed. Nicholas John (New York, 1991), p. 19.

10. Emil Haraszti, *Béla Bartók: His Life and Works* (Paris, 1938), p. 72.

11. Maurice Maeterlinck, *Le Trésor des Humbles* (1896), published in English as *The Treasure of the Humble*, trans. Alfred Sutro (New York, 1916), pp. 106–7. One essay from this volume, "The Tragical in Daily Life," is particularly relevant to the study of Maeterlinck's philosophy.

12. Maurice Maeterlinck, "Silence," in *The Treasure of the Humble*, p. 4.

13. Béla Balázs, "Maeterlinck," *Nyugat* 1, no. 1 (1908): 446–54. This essay is a major document of Balázs's intellectual affinities in the years before he wrote *Bluebeard's Castle*.

14. Ibid., p. 448. This English translation was prepared by Adam Tolnay. All further citations from Balázs's Maeterlinck essay are taken from this translation, which appears in its entirely at the end of my "Music and Drama in Béla Bartók's Opera *Duke Bluebeard's Castle*."

15. Ibid., p. 449.

16. Ivan Sanders, "Symbolist and Decadent Elements in Early Twentieth-Century Hungarian Drama," *Canadian-American Review of Hungarian Studies* 4, no. 1 (Spring 1977): 27.

17. Balázs, "Maeterlinck," p. 450..

18. Balázs further states that Maeterlinck's characters "do not develop and do not move. . . . They are like children within the giant stillness which surrounds them." Ibid., p. 449.

19. "Strindberg Paradoxonok" (Strindberg paradoxes), *Nyugat* 1, no. 1 (1908): 517–19. Here Balázs reviews three one-act plays by Strindberg (1849–1912): *Creditors* (1888), *The Stranger* (1888–89), and *Playing with Fire*

(1892), all of which were performed in Budapest by the Berlin Hebbeltheater. Two years earlier, in 1906, Balázs had mused in his diary about the possibilities of "a new dramatic form: showing internal pictures, too. The struggles which lie within dialogue" (*Napló*, vol. 1, p. 357). Had Balázs known any of Strindberg's later plays, such as the *Road to Damascus* trilogy, *A Dream Play*, or any of the late chamber plays like *The Pelican* and *The Ghost Sonata*, he might have found the mysticism and symbolism in those plays more akin to his own outlook.

20. A good general discussion of the history of *Ariane et Barbe-bleue* and its place in Maeterlinck's dramatic output may be found in W. D. Halls, "Les débuts du théâtre nouveau chez Maeterlinck," *Annales du Fondation Maurice Maeterlinck* 3 (1957): 45–58. It was first published in German translation in 1900; its English translation appeared in 1902, the same year as the first French edition. These dates are often misrepresented in literature about *Bluebeard's Castle*. Because the music rights to the drama had already been assigned to Paul Dukas in 1901, its first performance had to wait until 1907. Balázs probably first knew of the play in its German translation. It is extremely likely, though unprovable, that he witnessed one of the premiere performances of Dukas's opera in Paris in 1907.

21. Sanders, "Symbolist and Decadent Elements in Early Twentieth-Century Hungarian Drama," p. 30.

22. According to W. D. Halls, Maeterlinck's personal philosophy had already begun to change to a more positive outlook after 1895; the years from 1890–95 represented Maeterlinck's "symbolist period" (W. D. Halls, *Maurice Maeterlinck: A Study of His Life and Thought* [Oxford, 1960], pp. 43 and 167ff.). Elsewhere, Halls describes *Ariane* as an "intermediary between the symbolist theater and the works of 'the second style' (Halls, "Les débuts du théâtre nouveau chez Maeterlinck," p. 53). Some of Maeterlinck's earliest biographers also recognize the plays from this era (roughly 1890–95) as distinct from his later plays, though the term "symbolist" is not used. See Edward Thomas, *Maurice Maeterlinck* (New York, 1911), p. 95.

23. Maurice Maeterlinck, "The Modern Drama," in *The Double Garden*, trans. Alexander Teixeira De Mattos (New York, 1911), p. 126.

24. Ibid., pp. 126–27.

25. Sanders, "Symbolist and Decadent Elements in Early Twentieth-Century Hungarian Drama," p. 30.

26. Gustave Flaubert, *Salammbô* (New York, 1929), p. 127. Flaubert's epic novel about the Carthaginian princess was written in 1862.

27. Miklós Szabolcsi, "On the Spread of Symbolism," in *The Symbolist Movement in the Literature of European Languages*, ed. Anna Balakian (Budapest, 1984), p. 188.

28. Reportedly, Balázs had studied the original Perrault folk tale of Bluebeard while still a student at the Eötvös Kollégium in Budapest (i.e., before 1906). See Kroó, "Duke Bluebeard's Castle," p. 273.

29. Halsey Stevens, *The Life and Music of Béla Bartók*, rev. ed. (New York, 1964), p. 287.

30. Béla Balázs, "Maeterlinck," p. 449. Balázs prefers to overlook the stylistic differences between *Ariane* and the earlier plays. He sees them as all part of a unified dramatic aesthetic.

31. Sanders, "Symbolist and Decadent Elements in Early Twentieth-Century Hungarian Drama," p. 26.

32. Béla Balázs, "Párizs-e vagy Weimar?" *Nyugat* 7, no. 2 (1914): 200. Zsuffa briefly summarizes this article in his biography (Zsuffa, *Béla Balázs*, p. 53). This is the source of my description.

33. Balázs, "Maeterlinck," p. 452. Balázs takes Anselma Heine's recent German-language biography of Maeterlinck as a point of departure for his own essay.

34. Ibid.

35. Béla Balázs, "A tragédiának metafizikus teóriája a német romantikában és Hebbel Frigyes" (Friedrich Hebbel and the metaphysical theory of tragedy in German romanticism), *Nyugat* 1, no. 1 (1908): 87–90.

36. Ibid., p. 88. This translation was prepared by Adam Tolnay.

37. Ibid., p. 90.

38. Mary Gluck, *Georg Lukács and His Generation, 1900–1918* (Cambridge, Mass., 1985), p. 138. Gluck describes the reactions of Lukács, Balázs, and others to what she labels "the Crisis of Aestheticism" that gripped many young Hungarians in the decade 1900–10. She provides penetrating insight into a topic that is far too complex to cover here. Lukács's rejection of symbolism based on its lack of spiritual content resembles the position taken by some German intellectuals around 1910, who rejected impressionist art and literature because its beautiful external surface was not matched by inner substance. (Richard Sheppard, "German Expressionism," in M. Bradbury and J. McFarlane, eds., *Modernism: A Guide to European Literature, 1890–1930* [London, 1991], p. 277).

39. Mary Gluck, *Georg Lukács and His Generation*, p. 131.

40. Balázs, "A tragédiának metafizikus teoriája," p. 80.

41. André Karátson identifies the period of symbolist poetry in Hungary as the years from 1906 to 1914. The buds of symbolism bloomed relatively late, he writes, "but the flowering was spectacular and beautiful thanks to a generation that was gifted to the point of genius" ("A Translation and Refraction of Symbolism," p. 166).

42. Sanders, "Symbolist and Decadent Elements in Early Twentieth-Century Hungarian Drama," p. 26. Balázs and Lukács both came from German Jewish families who had settled in Hungary during the great influx of German settlers in the nineteenth century. Historically, many Jewish families retained their German cultural affinity despite their voluntary acculturation within Magyar Hungary. Balázs and Lukács's taste for German literature and philosophy thus developed out of a number of overlapping personal and cul-

tural factors. The social history of Jews and Germans within Hungary is presented in greater detail in John Lukács, *Budapest 1900: A Historical Portrait of a City and Its Culture* (New York, 1988), pp. 84–107.

43. Sanders, "Symbolist and Decadent Elements in Early Twentieth-Century Hungarian Drama," p. 26.

44. Ibid.

45. Mihály Babits, "Dráma," *Nyugat* 6, no. 1 (1913): 166. It has been suggested to me that Babits's choice of the word "German" here was probably intended as a euphemism for "Jewish." Undercurrents of anti-Semitism may therefore be present in Babits's review.

46. Ibid., pp. 166–67.

47. Ibid., p. 166.

48. György Lukács, preface to *Balázs Béla és Akiknek Nem Kell* (Gyoma, 1918), p. 11.

49. Ibid. Lukács reviews Balázs's *Mysteries* in a separate essay reprinted in the 1918 book on Balázs. His comments are of a general nature, intended to bolster Balázs's position as a leading Hungarian dramatist. He does not describe *Bluebeard's Castle* specifically, nor does he examine Balázs's connections with Hebbel other than grandiosely to compare Balázs's dramatic "aphorisms" with those in Sophocles, Shakespeare, Corneille, and Hebbel ("Misztériumok," in *Balázs Béla és Akiknek Nem Kell*, p. 58). Lukács's staunch support of Balázs's poetry and dramas caused many to question his judgment on literary matters. Arpad Kadarkay, author of a superb recent biography of Lukács, explains that Lukács's "untiring efforts to promote the fame of Balázs . . . amounted to a headlong rush into critical martyrdom" (*Georg Lukács: Life, Thought, and Politics* [London, 1991], p. 124). Two chapters in Kadarkay's biography (chapter 6, "Don Juan in Budapest," and chapter 7, "In Bluebeard's Castle") document and analyze the friendship between Balázs and Lukács.

50. The ideas summarized here are taken freely from two sources: Hebbel's own 1843 essay, "My Word Concerning Drama," translated and reprinted in *Three Plays by Hebbel*, ed. Marion Sonnenfeld (Lewisburg, Pa., 1974); and the chapter "Conception of Tragedy" in Edna Purdie's *Friedrich Hebbel: A Study of His Life and Work*, 2d ed. (Oxford, 1969), pp. 255–69.

51. This passage is often mistranslated because of the difficulty of rendering Balázs's truncated Hungarian phrase "Életemet, halálomat, Kékszakállú" into English. John Lloyd Davies's translation of this line, "I will fear no danger from you, beloved," is typical in its complete alteration of the meaning of Judith's words (*The Stage Works of Béla Bartók* [English National Opera Guide no. 44], p. 56).

52. György Kroó is especially forceful in his negative comments about the character of Judith. He sees her as a blindly passionate, instinctive woman who brings about her own ruin (Kroó, "Duke Bluebeard's Castle," pp. 302–3 and 307).

53. Szabolcsi, "On the Spread of Symbolism," p. 184.

The Miraculous Mandarin:

Melchior Lengyel, His Pantomime,

and His Connections to Béla Bartók

VERA LAMPERT

The name of Menyhért Lengyel, or Melchior Lengyel, as he preferred to be called outside of his native Hungary, sounds familiar to those who know Béla Bartók's stage work *The Miraculous Mandarin*. Very few, however, know that Lengyel wrote more than forty plays and was a popular film scriptwriter in England and North America during the first half of the century.

Born in 1880, the second of six children in a Jewish family, Lengyel spent his childhood in rural Hungary, in Sajóhídvég, where his father supported the family as a farming supervisor.[1] After finishing his secondary schooling, he found employment as a clerk at the First Hungarian General Insurance Company in Kassa (now Košice, Slovakia), a small town in the northeastern part of pre–World War I Hungary. Later he served at the company's headquarters in Budapest.

Attracted to literature from his early childhood, Lengyel experimented with poetry from the age of fifteen, and he avidly frequented the permanent theater in Kassa after it had opened its doors in 1900. As the reviewer for one of the local papers, he spent all his free time in the theater and was fascinated by all its aspects. In 1905 he traveled to Budapest to see one of the Sunday matinee performances of the short-lived avant-garde theater Thalia, opened in the previous year. This theater was organized by three progressive young intellectuals, one of them the nineteen-year-old György Lukács, to perpetuate the works of the founders of modern drama—Hebbel, Ibsen, Strindberg, Hofmannsthal—in defiance of the traditional programs of Budapest's establishment theaters. Lengyel's visit led to a decisive turning point in his life. "I saw Ibsen's *Wild Duck* there first. Both the play and the performance made a tremendous impression on me. A new world opened before me. I felt that the drama was the medium where I could really express myself. I took the train back to Kassa in a daze, and I hardly spoke to anyone for days. After that, I stayed home most of the time at nights, sitting at my desk until sunrise. I wrote my first play."[2]

It took Lengyel two years to summon enough courage to approach Thalia's stage director, Sándor Hevesy, with the manuscript. But much to his astonishment, the play, A nagy fejedelem (The great prince), was accepted at once and performed by Thalia in 1907. This event earned Lengyel six months' paid absence from the insurance company. He used part of this time to go to Berlin to study the work of Max Reinhardt, whose productions he knew from the regular guest performances of Reinhardt's company in Budapest.

> A born stage director, he stood at the beginning of his rising ca-
> reer. Everything he touched, whether it was a modern comedy or
> a classical drama, was illuminated by his brilliant talent. . . . As
> stage director, he revitalized the theater. He was the inspired
> master of stage action. Gradually every theater professional and
> Western stage director went to study with him. . . . He concen-
> trated not only on the great roles and scenes but on every detail
> neglected before, through which he gave new light and meaning
> to the performance. I was watching this closely because he invited
> me to his rehearsals; and there, in the darkness of the audi-
> torium, was born the true interpretation of the work, right before
> my eyes.[3]

The observation of the director's work—attendance at drama performances—was the most valuable training a novice playwright could hope for, Lengyel stressed later: "The only way to really learn the profession of drama writing is to sit in the theater and watch plays until the dynamics of the drama become a habit. I went to this high academy of the dramatist."[4]

Upon his return from Berlin, Lengyel finished his second play, A hálás utókor (Grateful posterity), which, in spite of its criticism of the backward conditions of Hungarian society, was performed in 1907 not in Thalia but in the National Theater, the foremost theater in the country. The premiere was well received and won Lengyel great acclaim. His employer, impressed by his success, freed him once and for all of his clerical duties while providing his salary and, after ten years of employment, a pension so that he could devote himself entirely to writing. In 1909 three new Lengyel plays were premiered in Budapest. The third of them, *Taifun* (Typhoon), was an enormous hit, and after its Budapest premiere it was translated into several languages and performed in Berlin (1911), Paris (1911), Turin (1911), and London (1913), and later also in Japan, bringing the author worldwide recognition.

After the success of *Taifun*, hardly a year went by without a Lengyel premiere in Budapest during the second decade of the century. His plays, however, were not received with unanimous recognition. The stage directors, aiming for sure success, urged him to make concessions to the tastes of the audience; his critics, on the other hand, looked with suspicion at everything that pleased the public. Lengyel, always distrusting his own capabilities, suffered greatly from the insecurity and the unpredictable reception of his work throughout his life. At the beginning of his career his fears became pathological and forced him to seek medical help. He was the first patient of Sigmund Freud's Hungarian pupil Sándor Ferenczi. Then he turned to Freud himself. He wrote to a close friend in 1908: "Since my condition sometimes was downright unbearable and I was afraid of a catastrophe happening at any moment, I went to Vienna to see Professor Freud. He diagnosed the symptoms of hysteria and psychoneurosis, which require lengthy treatment with his psychoanalytical methods."[5]

Whether Lengyel underwent the lengthy treatment is not known. But in spite of his recurrent depression and despair, he continued writing. Besides writing his plays, which appeared regularly on the stages of Budapest and other European cities, he became one of the most prolific contributors to the radical literary review *Nyugat* (West). *Nyugat* was started in 1908 and became the most respected and significant forum on the Hungarian literary scene until it ceased publication in 1941. Lengyel was present in *Nyugat*'s columns from the beginning, and even became its secretary for a while. His contributions, over a hundred in number, include literary criticism, theater reviews, essays, sketches, plays, and excerpts from his diary.[6] Especially noteworthy are a series of short articles, under the title *Egyszerű gondolatok* (Simple thoughts), published during the period of World War I, between 1914 and 1916. For Lengyel, war was an incomprehensible, incredible absurdity. Written in a colorful, easy-flowing, passionate, and witty style and showing Lengyel's prose at its best, these articles are his protest against the war and the expression of his deep concern for humanity. Much later, preparing to republish these articles in his memoirs, he recalled the state of mind that had compelled him to write his *Egyszerű gondolatok*:

An enormous responsibility weighed upon me and has never left me for a minute, because we have to do something, we have to warn people, yelling and crying, not to let themselves be carried away into that monstrosity that may bring the killing of innocent people, the collapse of the whole world, which is bestial horror and contrary to all humanity. Behind the frantic excitement I felt the smell of death, I saw vast burial grounds, the swelling of a sea of blood, and the roaring of world-shattering storms fueled by the moans of suffering. One cannot keep calm. Something has to be done. . . .

I took up the fight with my only weapon, my pen, from the first day of the war. I started to publish my pacifist articles in *Nyugat*. People, even some of my friends, did not quite understand my great agitation. On the streets there were mass demonstrations, started by paid demonstrators, but soon almost everybody was hoaxed into the "patriotic" adventure, banners fluttered, young people sang, drafted soldiers joining the army were surrounded by enthusiastic people—because basically everyone was convinced that the whole thing would be finished in six weeks. . . .

But I sensed immediately that as soon as the demons, dormant in the depths of human instincts, are awakened—and the power slips totally into the hands of those whose vocation, glory, and profession is war—a terrible tragedy will afflict the world. And I started to write.[7]

During the war Lengyel left Hungary for Switzerland, working as the correspondent of the Budapest daily *Az Est* (The evening). Switzerland was the refuge of the European pacifist literary movement during that time,[8] providing a nurturing environment for Lengyel's antiwar writing. He became one of the most respected Hungarian representatives of this literary movement. In 1918, he was asked to be the editor of the pacifist Hungarian journal *Europa*. Among his plays, *A hős* (The hero), written in 1917, is the first to give voice to his pacific conviction. Although it was never performed, Lengyel always considered this play to be his best literary effort.[9] His two plays from 1918, *Charlotte kisasszony* (Miss Charlotte) and *Sancho Panza királysága* (The kingdom of Sancho Panza), also express his ideas about the futility of war. Both works were performed in Budapest with great acclaim shortly after their completion.

Lengyel followed the events of the socialist revolution of 1918 and the communist regime of 1919 with sympathy but reserve and doubts. In Lengyel's plebeian play *Sancho Panza királysága*, Don Quixote's servant is given a governorship for the amusement of the prince. Sancho proves to be a wise governor and wins the support of the people. Wanting to help the poor, he plans to distribute the prince's hunting fields among his subjects when he discovers the hoax. At the people's request the prince offers him the governorship for real, but he refuses and returns to his village. In the one-act play *Névaparti estély* (On the Neva), written in 1919, Lengyel makes his audience laugh at the changed situation of the Russian aristocracy caused by the Bolshevik Revolution, but he also shows compassion for them. Both plays, along with *A hálás utókor*, belonged to the most frequently played stage works in Budapest during the communist regime. Fearing retribution, Lengyel emigrated to Germany right after the fall of the regime, in August 1919, and visited America in 1920. Although he returned to his home country periodically during the next twenty years (he even became a theater director in Budapest for a short time in 1929), he lived mostly in Germany during the 1920s, then moved to London in 1931 and finally settled in the United States in 1937, where he eventually became an American citizen.

Although he never abandoned the stage—the catalog of his works compiled by József Vinkó lists twenty-four plays written between 1922 and 1963—from the 1920s Lengyel turned his attention toward the movie industry and soon became a well-known and frequently employed screenplay writer. He wrote about sixty movie scripts.[10] Though some of these have never been realized, several were produced by the most celebrated film personalities of the era—Ernst Lubitsch, Paul Czinner, Thomas H. Ince, Alexander Korda, Georg Cukor, Otto Preminger and others—with such stars as Greta Garbo, Marlene Dietrich, Gregory Peck, Fred Astaire, and Cyd Charisse. Besides his original screenplays, many of his works written or intended for the stage eventually became film scripts, some of them repeatedly.[11] In many cases, however—as in the famous and still-appreciated *Ninotchka*, produced and directed by Lubitsch in 1939—Lengyel supplied the original story, whereas the screenplay itself was written by others.[12] The significance of Lengyel's contributions to the history of the film has not been assessed so far.

From 1960, Lengyel resided in Italy near his daughter, who had lived there since her marriage. About this time, at the age of eighty, he decided to publish his memoirs, based on the diaries he had kept from the early 1910s, but was able to complete only the first part (until 1913) of the ambitious project before his death. He returned to his homeland in 1974, shortly before he died at the age of ninety-four.

After World War II Lengyel was almost entirely forgotten in Hungary. Between 1937 and 1963, there were no productions of Lengyel's plays in Budapest. Only *The Miraculous Mandarin*, with Bartók's music, kept his name alive. In the 1960s, however, the slow rediscovery of his accomplishments began. Since 1963, several of his plays have been performed, either in their original form or in adaptations both on stage and on television.[13] In 1978, a comprehensive evaluation of the first part of his career appeared in a series of essays on Hungarian playwrights of the twentieth century. And in 1984, a collection of his works, containing seven dramas, was published in Budapest; and in 1987, his recollections appeared, along with a selection from his diaries.[14] In spite of the problems inherent in the nature of these works, they are an indispensable source for the research of Lengyel's life and career.[15] It is, at the same time, a touching document of the struggles of creative work, and it offers insight into the thoughts of a warm and interesting personality who witnessed almost an entire century.

The Miraculous Mandarin

The Miraculous Mandarin was written in 1916 and appeared in 1917, in the 1 January issue of *Nyugat*.[16] The story takes place in a big city where three thugs force Mimi, their companion, to lure visitors into their attic room so that they can rob them. After they throw out two penniless visitors, a rich Chinese mandarin enters the room. He makes a stunning impression with his strange calmness and indifference. But the girl's dance awakens a tremendous passion in him. As he chases the fleeing girl with an ever wilder force, the thugs try four times to kill him; he will not die, however, until he can fulfill his desire.

Although Bartók later called the story marvelously beautiful,[17] its shocking subject of crime and prostitution is often singled out in the Bartók literature as the main obstacle to the work's success. The 1926 Cologne premiere of Bartók's composition resulted in such a scandal that it was banned after the first performance, as were several later projected performances. With one exception, the original text is examined only in terms of its divergences from Bartók's version, and not in its own right. That exception is Annette von Wangenheim's study, in which the libretto is explained in the context of the German expressionist one-act drama that flourished during the first two decades of the century.[18]

One of the main characteristics of the expressionist drama is abstraction: the characters are not realistic imitations of particular individuals but embody principles that the author considers to be important.[19] This principle in *The Miraculous Mandarin* is the importance of the sexual instinct, and its indestructible strength in its clash with society. With this sensitive subject, Lengyel followed the mainstream of expressionist drama, which, influenced by the emergence of psychoanalysis, often dealt with the previously avoided subject of sex and had a predilection for the prostitute as heroine.[20] The conflict of nature and society was one of the main concerns of the expressionist artists as well. The symbol of modern society, the great city, was seen as the focus "of all imaginable types of decadence," "the 'doom and death' of the Volk and of culture, the epitome of the disintegrated 'society' in which each person lives alienated and dissociated."[21] Bartók the ethnomusicologist, in particular, must have found the representation of the city as the enemy of humanity irresistible as a vehicle for venting his frustration about civilization's destructive tendencies, including the war, which had been raging for years when the piece was written.

If the characters of the expressionist drama merely symbolize ideas, the action is extremely compressed and restricted to only crucial situations. In many plays, fatal decisions are made, changing the life of the protagonist; or an event or illumination is experienced that alters the course of the hero's life forever.[22] Both protagonists of *The Miraculous Mandarin* experience this sudden and fundamental change: the mandarin, when his passion is born by the touch of the girl; and the girl, when she decides to yield to the mandarin's desire.

Other elements of the expressionist drama are also present in Lengyel's pantomime. One is the opposition of extremes, static and dynamic, cold and hot, like the mandarin's initial calmness set in sharp contrast to his frighteningly intensive passion. Another frequently used expressionistic device employed in *The Miraculous Mandarin* is the grotesque—using distortions and exaggerations not to induce laughter but to frighten and shock. Lengyel's mandarin is frightfully grotesque, both in his fishlike coldness and in his frantic pursuit of the girl, as "he moves provocatively, starting to dance with fantastic movements. A strange, grating noise rises from his throat. . . . He is crying—tears streaming down his cheeks. . . . He is completely beside himself—spinning, whirling, with increasingly alarming speed. . . . He is now like a huge spinning top, fanning a whirlwind around him."[23]

Shock is also induced by violence, mentioned disparagingly more often than not in the Bartók literature in connection with *The Miraculous Mandarin*. In fact, since Bence Szabolcsi's pioneering essay,[24] most analyses point out a connection between Lengyel's text and the style of Grand Guignol, a popular theater active in Paris from the late 1890s well into the 1960s. Although some naturalistic moments—such as the bulging eyes of the suffocated mandarin, or the vivid description of the knife passing through his body—undeniably occur, these are a far cry from the indulgence in naturalistic displays of horror on which the plays of the Grand Guignol were almost exclusively built.[25] Violence is an integral part of Lengyel's drama: the extraordinary strength of the mandarin's desire proves itself through his immunity to murder.

Bartók found the story beautiful but was aware of the shock it would cause to the public, when he made a sarcastic remark about the honorable audience in connection with the hellish introductory music of the composition.[26] It seems that Lengyel, attacked and condemned so many times for the sentimentality of his successful stage works, consciously wanted to achieve the opposite impact in the tale of *The Miraculous Mandarin*. Something he once wrote in one of his undated letters to his friend, the writer and literary scholar Lajos Hatvany, might be seen as a reference to *The Miraculous Mandarin*: "If I can ever afford the luxury, I will write such an impossible and odd thing, expressly for their vexation, that their jaws will drop."[27] In retrospect, in his late memoirs he saw *The Miraculous Mandarin* in a more subdued light: "The true message of *The Miraculous Mandarin*, of course, is not the excessive eroticism but the apotheosis of pure, almost unearthly desire and love."[28]

Although none of Lengyel's works was fashioned after the expressionist drama as closely as *The Miraculous Mandarin* was, the latter nevertheless reveals similarities to his other plays in several ways and fits well into the series of the works he created during the first decade and a half of his career. One of the main peculiarities of Lengyel's plays in this period is the recurrence of a certain protagonist, already identified by Lajos Hatvany in a 1916 essay, the first evaluation fully devoted to Lengyel's dramatic output. This typical Lengyel hero is described through the Japanese characters, and Dr. Tokeramo, the main character of *Taifun*:

> Lengyel's main interest is not in the Japanese people or in the Yellow Peril but in these seemingly weak but obstinately strong, introverted, distrustful, lonesome, talented, strong-willed people with a hidden passion, who may bear some similarities in their appearance to the Japanese; still, in the bottom of their soul, they are certainly more closely related to that timidly brave, humble

revolutionary, to that stubbornly determined county archivist even in his great oppression, in whom Lengyel gave his own likeness already at the time of *The Great Prince*.[29]

Among Lengyel's other works, the main characters of *A hálás utókor*, *A hős*, and *Charlotte kisasszony* are, in one way or another, incarnations of the same figure. The strongest and most extreme of them all is *The Miraculous Mandarin*. He is an alien: as Tokeramo, he also comes from another part of the world. His initial indifference and coldness puzzles the girl and the thugs. His suddenly erupting emotions are also strange and frighteningly powerful. In his fight to reach his goal, the mandarin shows a superhuman determination that cannot be defeated.

Another chief concern in Lengyel's dramas is the fate of women in modern society: how they fight their battle against the roles into which circumstances force them, how emancipation changes their life, creating various conflicts that either are overcome with triumph or destroy them. The heroine of the 1908 play *Idyll at the Countryside*, the educated German bride of a Hungarian constable—called anti-Nora by one of Lengyel's commentators in reference to Ibsen's *A Doll's House*[30]—becomes a victim of the backwardness of Hungarian society whose lethargy finally swallows her up. In *A szűz* (The virgin, 1909), the conflict is caused by chastity. Guarded as a treasure before marriage in bourgeois society, it proves to be a burden for the young bride in the play. Three further plays, *A cárnő* (The tsarina, 1912), *A táncosnő* (The ballerina, 1915), and *Charlotte kisasszony* (1918) throw light on women who gain independence through professional work. This empowers them to act with liberty, formerly a privilege reserved exclusively for men (*A cárnő*, *Charlotte kisasszony*), but also gives rise to tragic conflicts between their calling and their personal life (*A táncosnő*).[31] The female protagonist of *The Miraculous Mandarin*, Mimi, belongs to the periphery of society. Far from being independent, she is at the mercy of the thugs, who force her to become a party to their crime: her body is used as a decoy to entice the future victims of their robbery. At the climax of the work, the girl is the one who recognizes that the mandarin is indestructible because of his great passion, and she acts on her own to quench his desire. Her victorious smile after the mandarin's death can be interpreted as the triumph of the feminine but also as the sign of her transformation from a defenseless creature into the mandarin's equal and her awakening to a new life.[32]

What sets *The Miraculous Mandarin* apart from the rest of Lengyel's stage works is that it is a dumb show: a drama without words. Lengyel called it a *pantomime grotesque*, an increasingly popular artistic genre during the first two decades of this century. Several channels fueled the predilection toward this peculiar dramatic form, which did away with words and relied exclusively on the expressive movement of the human body. During the first decade, Michel Fokine and the Ballets Russes revolutionized classical ballet, replacing its stereotypes with a more naturalistic approach to movement. The founder of modern dance theory, Rudolf von Laban, opened his school of dance in Munich in 1910, and the Dalcroze Institute was founded the next year in Hellerau to propagate a new method of music education emphasizing the awareness of the rhythmic element of music through the accompaniment of body movements. This was also the time when the silent movie, another art form relying on mime and gesture, began to flourish. Pantomimes were not only staged in musical theaters as alternatives to traditional ballet productions, employing dramatic actors rather than dancers;[33] they were also included in the regular programs of prose theaters. Two of Reinhardt's most acclaimed productions, which conquered most of Europe and America in a short period of time, included Friedrich Freksa's *Sumurûn* (1910) and Karl Vollmoeller's mysterium play, *The Miracle* (1911),[34] both without words. Writing about Bartók's *Miraculous Mandarin*, the British music critic Philip Heseltine spoke of a craze for modern ballet to which Bartók had also yielded.[35] The power of the expressive gestures of the human body clearly exerted an irresistible attraction for creative artists in all genres.

For Lengyel, the medium of pantomime could have been the ideal form of expression. From very early on, he recognized that he did not belong to those dramatists who handle words with virtuosity. He was a simple storyteller, an inventor of tales. His *Miraculous Mandarin* is one of his most memorable tales—Lengyel himself called it a "pantomime tale" in his memoirs—which, typically for the dramatist Lengyel, takes the form of a play, although the characters don't have words and the story unfolds only through forceful dramatic action.[36] Nevertheless, *The Miraculous Mandarin* remained Lengyel's only pantomime, in retrospect a bridge between his first dramas and the film scripts he would produce in the subsequent decades of his career.

The Lengyel-Bartók Connection

Were it not for Bartók's music, *The Miraculous Mandarin* would have shared the fate of Lengyel's other works, especially that of his prose writings: no one would know about it; no one would read it. In the concluding part of this essay I shall try to reconstruct the path that took Lengyel's tale from the pages of *Nyugat* to Bartók's compositional workshop and to document the relationship of the two authors of *The Miraculous Mandarin*.

As Lengyel recalled, *The Miraculous Mandarin* was written in the heat of an inspiration, and—as he noted not once but twice—he wrote the story without any specific plan.[37] By "without any specific plan" Lengyel probably meant that he did not submit it to any theater for performance, but the statement also implies that it was written neither on commission nor with the intention of having it set to music. This, however, contradicts two different documents pertaining to the history of the work. Three weeks after *The Miraculous Mandarin* appeared in the 1 January issue of *Nyugat*, the Budapest daily *Esti Újság* (Evening newspaper) claimed that it had been commissioned by Diaghilev, director of the Ballets Russes.[38] The company gave performances in Budapest back in 1912, and thus Lengyel could have seen them there, or in Paris during his many visits to that city. He was most likely aware of their significance and might have been influenced by their performances as he wrote *The Miraculous Mandarin*, but there is no documentary evidence for his direct contact with the company at that time, and it is very unlikely that he wrote the pantomime for them.[39] The other contradictory statement comes from Elza Galafrés, a Viennese actress living in Budapest from 1915, who was Ernő Dohnányi's mistress and became his second wife in 1919. According to her memoirs, "Lengyel . . . had sent a libretto to Dohnányi, but the latter was unable to undertake it, first because his two operas were still unfinished, and second, but more important, he thought the theme, on a grand Guignol subject, was more suitable to Bartók's style. Bartók accepted the assignment."[40]

Because, however, there are inaccuracies in the rest of these late recollections,[41] in addition to inconsistencies with Lengyel's diary statements, it is most likely that Lengyel did not offer the text to Dohnányi or anyone else. Nevertheless, Galafrés's memoirs may contain a grain of truth after all. She was a dramatic actress of great acclaim before she settled in Budapest. Because she did not speak Hungarian but wanted to continue her acting career, she had to turn her attention to pantomime. In 1916 she and Dohnányi performed André Wormser's pantomime *The Prodigal Son*. She was also interested in taking a role in Bartók's ballet *The Wooden Prince*, which was staged at the Budapest Opera in 1917, and she became the pantomime artist of the Budapest Opera a little later.[42] It is conceivable that Lengyel's libretto in *Nyugat* caught Dohnányi's attention, since he was looking for suitable texts for Galafrés. He may even have briefly considered composing it but dropped the plan because of the subject or lack of time.[43] If this is true, then it was probably he who later called Bartók's attention to *The Miraculous Mandarin*.

Bartók was also a member of *Nyugat*'s readership: his library contains complete runs of the journal for several years. The copy in which *The Miraculous Mandarin* appeared has also survived, although it does not contain any of Bartók's annotations or markings.[44] If he noticed it at all when it appeared, there are no indications that he was struck by it at first sight. At that time Bartók was working intently on the orchestration of *The Wooden Prince*, which was scheduled to have its first performance at the Budapest Opera during the coming spring season. The unexpected success of the 12 May premiere resulted in plans for a stage production of his long-neglected opera, *Bluebeard's Castle*, written in 1911.[45] Moreover, yet another stage work was commissioned by the Budapest Opera for a text of Sándor Bródy, the most successful Hungarian playwright of the time.[46] Bartók eagerly accepted the commission, in order to create a Bartók triple bill. Bródy, however, proved to be far from an ideal cooperator. In a letter addressed to his wife on 21 July 1917, Bartók noted sarcastically: "*Az Est* has already blazed out that Bródy is writing for me a Hungarian puppet play called *László Vitéz*, commissioned by Bánffy. Now at least I know the title of my future opus! The dailies serve their purpose after all!"[47]

The project did not show much progress during the following year. In spite of another press release on 16 January 1918 and Bródy's enthusiastic interview after the premiere of *Bluebeard's Castle*, in which he mentioned his collaboration with Bartók on a new work, the original topic was dropped and replaced with another.[48] Although Bródy's deadline for supplying the text had expired in the middle of June 1918, in his only extant letter to the composer, written on 27 June 1918, he apologized for not working on the libretto as promised and indicated that he was sending the sketch of only the second scene.[49]

It is not surprising that in these circumstances Bartók remained open to other ideas. If he read Lengyel's story when it was published, he might have remembered it when he started losing his patience with Bródy. It is also possible, and a little more probable, that someone reminded him or recommended Lengyel's libretto to him later, once Bródy's collaboration proved to be a fiasco. If so, then Dohnányi, perhaps more than anyone else, may have been that person. During the fall of 1917 Dohnányi for the first time included some of Bartók's piano pieces in one of his Budapest recitals. Bartók was present and was delighted with the performance. Not long after the recital, at the end of November, the Dohnányis invited Bartók and his wife for a visit.[50] The topics of conversation that evening certainly included Bartók's future compositional projects, and he cannot possibly have avoided mentioning his frustration with Bródy's delay in providing the text for his new stage work. If they were in fact the ones who called Bartók's attention to Lengyel's work, the Dohnányis were not completely disinterested. As is known from later correspondence, Elza Galafrés hoped to play the role of the Girl in the future production of the Budapest Opera.[51]

Whether or not it was on Dohnányi's recommendation, Bartók did start to think about *The Miraculous Mandarin* around this time. By the end of March 1918 he decided to pursue the matter, and he asked his friend and former piano teacher at the Academy, István Thomán, to intercede with Lengyel for him. Thomán's postcard of 28 March 1918 came with the following message: "Menyhért Lengyel would be delighted if you set the *Mandarin* to music. Please let me know when you are coming to dinner—I'd like to invite him also to meet you."[52]

Bartók, however, did not take the opportunity immediately but instead postponed their meeting until after the premiere of the opera. Lengyel was present at the premiere. The entry in his diary, jotted down the following day, on 25 May, testifies to his enthusiastic impressions and his genuine recognition of the importance of the event:

A first night. An evening in the Opera. Bartók's *Bluebeard's Castle*. I am as knowledgeable about music as anything else; for example, I admired Van Gogh and Cézanne at an age when I hardly had a notion about painting. I instinctively felt what real values were. Music can excite me so much that it exhausts me. I felt this last night too. I looked around in the theater. Did they know that genius was present? Absolute genius, which dissolves the message that we, ordinary people, have to express in words. How shall I convey that the sun is shining outside? If I use too many words, it will be forced. I am lucky if I find a new epithet, because words go the way of all words and get worn out with overuse, and you don't have to be a poet to replace hackneyed words by fresh ones; it's only a question of a little ingenuity and resourcefulness, and you will be regarded as a good writer. But all this is utterly incapable of conveying the thrill of life, the tingle that is impossible to name, for that can only be done by the man of music! Perhaps no one can do it like Bartók. And what a sad fate this work has had!

It was shelved for six years. How did they dare not to perform it? By force of what law?

Let's be careful, and let's be tolerant. Let's take a good look at anything new. And if we are not receptive enough, let's trust finer ears.

There was hardly any applause. The theater was not full, in this year when people rushed to every false sensation. When *The Woman and the Goose* was a hit. Remarkable!

(After *Bluebeard's Castle* they sang *I Pagliacci*. It seemed as simple as the paintings of Viktor Madarász.)[53]

Barely a month later, on 21 June 1918, about a week after Bródy's deadline for providing the libretto for the work commissioned by the Budapest Opera expired, Bartók met with Lengyel and signed an agreement with him about setting *The Miraculous Mandarin* to music. The event is recalled in the writer's later memoirs:

Not long after the first night of *Bluebeard's Castle* I met with Bartók. It was he who wanted this meeting, which was mediated by Béla Reinitz, composer of Ady's poems.[54] Bartók read my *pantomime grotesque*, *The Miraculous Mandarin*, published in *Nyugat*, which I wrote without any specific plans in mind, in the heat of an inspiration, and he asked me whether I would let him set it to music. "With pleasure," I said. "Then let us take care of it," he said. We wrote and signed a short letter in which I gave Bartók permission to set the piece to music. That was all. "I will let you know if I have made some progress," he said. We thought, of course, both he and I, that the play would be staged in the Budapest Opera during the next season at the latest."[55]

The letter, written by Lengyel, contains the following conditions:

Agreement.

1. Mr. Menyhért Lengyel gives the exclusive right of setting to music *The Miraculous Mandarin* to Mr. Béla Bartók.
2. Mr. Menyhért Lengyel agrees to acknowledge the relevant sections of the contract between Mr. Béla Bartók and the Viennese publisher Universal Edition to be binding for him in connection with the work's publication and staging.[56]
3. From the royalties of *The Miraculous Mandarin* due to the authors after stage performances, publications of the score, and the piano reduction (except of those scores that present

sections of the work without text) two-thirds is owed to Mr. Béla Bartók and one-third to Mr. Menyhért Lengyel.

4. This agreement is also extended to the authors' heirs.

Budapest, 21 June 1918   Béla Bartók
                                     Menyhért Lengyel[57]

Neither Lengyel's recollections nor the agreement mentions the later alterations of the text, but this was probably the occasion when Bartók got permission to change whatever he needed to change in the story for his composition. Although he still expected to hear from Bródy during the summer,[58] he began to work on *The Miraculous Mandarin* at the beginning of September 1918: "I am now thinking about the *Mandarin*, too. It will be hellish music if I succeed. The prelude before the curtain goes up is going to be very short and will sound like horrible pandemonium, din, racket, and hooting: I lead the honorable audience from the crowded streets of a metropolis into the Apaches' den. Bródy, thank God, is mute as a fish. Much good may it do him as well as me."[59]

By June 1919 the composition was finished, and Bartók, keeping his promise to Lengyel, presented the music to the writer.[60] There is a short entry about this occasion, dated 5 July 1919, in Lengyel's diary: "The other day Béla Bartók played for us on the piano the music of *The Miraculous Mandarin* . . . in the apartment of our mutual friend Professor Thomán. Only Thomán, with his closest family members, and the two of us were present. Wonderful music! Incomparable talent!"[61]

Soon after, in August 1919, Lengyel left for Germany, where, after a short stay in Munich, he settled in Berlin. Bartók himself considered emigration at this time. He made inquiries about the possibilities in three countries: Romania (Transylvania), Austria (Vienna), and Germany. As he wrote to his mother on 23 October 1919, Géza Révész, a music psychologist who also emigrated to Germany around that time, took with him the German translations of all Bartók's ethnomusicological writings (on Hungarian, Romanian and Arabic folk music) to establish contacts for him there.[62] Lengyel tried to arrange a performance of *The Miraculous Mandarin* in Berlin: he certainly recommended it to Max Reinhardt, because in his memoirs he recalled that Reinhardt often inquired about the pantomime and asked him to convince Bartók to go to Berlin.[63] The following exchange of letters between Lengyel and Bartók, their only correspondence known to date, is from these difficult times. *Seherezáde*, mentioned in both letters, is the opera libretto that Lengyel wrote in the spring of 1919, expressly for Bartók.

> Berlin W. Meineke str. 10 I.
> 20 November 1919

My dear Sir,

I am very happy to be able to write to you through our mutual friend, who is going home. What are you doing? Aren't you thinking of coming here? Life is favorable here, one can work, and, most important, work brings results. Now that Tango has left Pest, I think the prospects of the mandarin are not favorable; here, on the other hand, there is a good chance of a performance. Of course, you should be here for this to happen—would that be possible? Are you dealing with the *Seherezáde*—can you work at all? I would be thankful if you could write me shortly; and if I can do anything for you, I would do it with great pleasure.

> Yours truly,
> Menyhért Lengyel[64]

> Rákoskeresztúr, 10 January 1920

Dear Sir,

I received your letter safely, in fact already in the middle of Dec.; the reason I didn't answer it earlier is that it was hard to bring myself to—complain.

But I cannot avoid complaining if it is a question of trying to explain why I have not worked and will not be able to work for who knows how long. We live in great misery; true, there are no material shortages now, but whatever is available is unaffordable for poor people like us. As a result, I spend the whole winter with my family in one room, in our smallest, where I cannot even work on orchestration.

Not only am I unable to think of the *Seherezáde* but there is not a single sheet of the score of the *Mandarin* finished yet. The transportation situation is such that we can get into Pest only by foot. I am on leave until April. How it will be after that, I cannot even fathom; renting an apartment in Pest is out of the question; on the other hand, I cannot stay here if I want to keep my job.

Of course, I would go to Germany gladly, if I only had the courage! But I do not dare set out into the uncertainty—all the less since I believe the living conditions are not the best there either. And I cannot even imagine what kind of a job I could have there. Miserable private lessons? I would not help myself much with those. Révész wrote to me that he met you; he probably informed you about the nature of my plans for emigration. I gather from Révész's letter that unfortunately there is little prospect in Germany of realizing my plans. He might have also told you about my plans oriented toward the East (with which he does not agree at all). But it is impossible to get information from that direction; maybe after the signing of the peace agreement.

I don't have the money to go to Germany for only a short time, just "to look around a little"; my income is hardly enough to meet the only luxury we have, not going hungry. Unfortunately I think I cannot expect any help from the West; my only hope is the East.

I would be glad to get news from you once in a while; the normal mail traffic has resumed in Rákoskeresztúr, so you can safely address your letters here (28 Teréz St.).

With many regards,
Béla Bartók[65]

Bartók did visit Berlin between February and 1 April 1920, and it is possible that Lengyel's letter helped sway him in favor of making the trip. In Berlin he established many connections, played *The Miraculous Mandarin* at least twice,[66] and met Reinhardt; and although Reinhardt did not undertake to stage the work in his theater, he wanted to commission Bartók to write the incidental music to his staging of Aristophanes' *Lysistrata*.[67]

Bartók and Lengyel, however, probably did not meet in Berlin, as the following letter indicates.

Munich, 28 February 1920
Ludwigstraße 22

My dear good sir,

I was waiting for you impatiently for weeks; I did not answer your letter because I thought you would be arriving before you could receive my letter, and now fate's inscrutable, evil turn made me leave Berlin right when you arrived there. Death took my dearest brother, at a hopelessly remote place from me, and in my deep sorrow I can find or hope to find some consolation with my family here.

But I hope I will find you in Berlin when I return. I write to you now to testify, in case you might not notice it, how much you are appreciated and esteemed in Berlin, and I firmly believe that Berlin will be the best soil for your magnificent art! I beg you not to be discour-

PART I: ESSAYS

aged, even if at the beginning you encounter some difficulties—your complete recognition, especially in such a musical center as Berlin, is only a matter of time, a short time at that, I am convinced.

I am sure that your concert today was a great success. In this hope and in the expectation of seeing you again soon in Berlin,

I am faithfully and sincerely yours,

Menyhért Lengyel[68]

Bartók's and Lengyel's paths crossed again in 1931, when the Budapest Opera reconsidered the performance of *The Miraculous Mandarin*. Lengyel recalls:

Both Bartók and I were in Budapest, and we participated in the rehearsals. There was a hostile atmosphere in the Opera, however, and the staging did not represent the true spirit of the work. Bartók, who strove for perfection in everything, especially in music, in his growing dissatisfaction finally banned the performance, which was full of mistakes—with my consent. The Opera, instead of correcting the mistakes, took us at our word right away and removed *Mandarin* from the program once and for all.[69]

By the time the Budapest Opera made another failed attempt in 1941 to stage the work, both Bartók and Lengyel were in the United States. When in 1946 the first Hungarian production finally materialized—after Aurel Miloss's choreography had been successfully performed in Italy—Bartók was no longer alive. This entry in the playwright's diary marks the composer's death:

Béla Bartók died. He was the second genius I met. (The first was Ady.)[70] . . . What a talent, and in what heartbreaking circumstances he had to live—with worries of everyday life, in poverty! What kind of a society is it that cannot or doesn't want to give the same living conditions to a recognized genius that every skillful grocer easily obtains for himself and considers essential? In every discipline of art (literature, painting, music, science) there are no more than five geniuses in the whole world. Bartók, the musician, *was one of the five.* . . .

He was not kind—he was rather professorlike—but one had to like him because he was such a pure spirit and an artist of the highest order. What a shame that the toady director of the Hungarian Royal Opera—I don't even remember his name—did not perform his works. They ought to have encouraged him to write a new opera or ballet every year—he should have been commissioned; then today the world's music would be richer by five or six great musical stage works![71]

NOTES

1. The following summary of the events of Lengyel's life and career is based on his *Életem könyve* (The book of my life), ed. József Vinkó (Budapest, 1987).

2. Ibid., p. 51. Unless stated otherwise, all translations from the Hungarian are mine.

3. Ibid., p. 59.

4. Ibid., p. 48.

5. *Levelek Hatvany Lajoshoz* (Letters to Lajos Hatvany), ed. Mrs. Lajos Hatvany (Budapest, 1967), no. 13.

6. See *Nyugat repertórium* (Repertory of Nyugat), ed. Ferenc Galambos (Budapest, 1959).

7. Lengyel, *Életem könyve*, p. 86.

8. J. M. Ritchie, *German Expressionist Drama* (Boston, 1976), p. 85.

9. The second act was published in *Nyugat* 2 (1918): 806–22.

10. Lengyel, *Életem könyve*, pp. 495–500 and 11. József Vinkó's list of Lengyel's screenplays lists only works mentioned in the text of *Életem könyve*. This catalog can be regarded as tentative at best and is clearly in want of further investigation.

11. *A cárnő* (The tsarina), written in 1912 with Lajos Bíró, was adapted in three movies: *Forbidden Paradise* (Ernst Lubitsch, 1924), *Catherine the Great* (Paul Czinner, 1934), and *A Royal Scandal* (Otto Preminger, 1945); *Ninocska* (Ninotchka), written in 1937, was adapted in Ernst Lubitsch's *Ninotchka*, released in 1939, and in Cole Porter's Broadway musical *The Silk Stockings* (1954), filmed in 1957. See Lengyel, *Életem könyve*, pp. 496 and 500.

12. Charles Brackett, Billy Wilder, and Walters Reisch, *Ninotchka* (New York, 1972).

13. Lengyel, *Életem könyve*, pp. 11 and 495–500.

14. Péter Nagy, *Drámai arcélek: tanulmányok a huszadik századi magyar drámairodalom köréből* (Dramatic profiles: studies from the literature of twentieth-century Hungarian drama) (Budapest, 1978); and Menyhért Lengyel, *Taifun* (Budapest, 1984), and *Életem könyve*.

15. Although Lengyel kept his diaries until the very end of his life, several important facts and events are not recorded in it. Another problem is that in the published version original entries are not distinguished from later corrections, additions, and amendments, which impairs its authenticity, especially in the case of the account of earlier events. Some of his letters were also published (see *Levelek Hatvany Lajoshoz*).

16. Lengyel, *Életem könyve*, p. 156, and *Taifun*, p. 523.

17. In an interview in 1919. Reprinted in *Bartók Béla válogatott írásai* (Béla Bartók's selected writings), ed. András Szőllősy (Budapest, 1956), pp. 338–39.

18. Annette von Wangenheim, *Béla Bartók. Der wunderbare Mandarin* (Overath bei Köln, 1985), pp. 64–78.

19. Ritchie, *German Expressionist Drama*, p. 15.

20. Roy Pascal, *From Naturalism to Expressionism* (New York, 1973), pp. 235–36.

21. Ibid., p. 152.

22. Ritchie, *German Expressionist Drama*, p. 21.

23. Menyhért Lengyel, "The Miraculous Mandarin," trans. István Farkas, in *The Stage Works of Béla Bartók* (London, 1991), p. 99.

24. Bence Szabolcsi, "Bartók's Miraculous Mandarin," in *Bartók Studies*, ed. Todd Crow (Detroit, 1976), pp. 22–38. The original Hungarian essay, "A csodálatos mandarin," appeared in *Zenetudományi tanulmányok* 3 (1955): 519–35.

25. John M. Callahan, "The Ultimate in Theatre Violence," in *Violence in Drama* (Cambridge, 1991), pp. 165–75.

26. Letter to Márta Ziegler of 5 September 1918, in *Bartók Béla családi levelei* (Béla Bartók's family correspondence), ed. Béla Bartók, Jr. (Budapest, 1981), p. 282.

27. In the Manuscript Collection of the Hungarian Academy of Sciences, MTA MS 385/F/95–188. The original is in Hungarian.

28. Lengyel, *Taifun*, p. 524.

29. Cited in ibid., p. 23.

30. Nagy, *Drámai arcélek*, p. 130.

31. Ibid., p. 137.

32. See Jürg Stenzl, " 'Wer sich der Einsamkeit ergibt . . . ': zu Béla Bartóks Bühnenwerken," *Archiv für Musikwissenschaft* 39 (1982): 110; and Everett Helm, "Bartók on Stage: Fresh Light on a Long Undervalued Dramatic Trilogy, *High Fidelity* 14, no. 11 (1964): 86.

33. The Budapest Opera, for example, staged several pantomime productions with the dramatic actress Elza Galafrés. See Bálint Vázsonyi, *Dohnányi Ernő* (Budapest, 1971), pp. 81, 86, 112, 134, 142.

34. J. L. Styan, *Max Reinhardt* (Cambridge, 1982), pp. 26 and 93.

35. Cited in Malcolm Gillies, *Bartók in Britain* (Oxford, 1989), p. 123. Note that Heseltine refers to the *The Miraculous Mandarin* as a ballet. Sometimes there was no clear distinction in the terminology between pantomime and modern ballet. Bartók himself called his ballet *The Wooden Prince* a pantomime occasionally, as did its librettist, Béla Balázs. (See Bartók's letter to Philip Heseltine of 24 November 1920, published in "Vier Briefe Bartóks an Philip Heseltine," *Documenta Bartókiana* 5 (1977): 139; and Béla Balázs, *Napló, 1903–1914* [Budapest, 1982], p. 583.) In the case of *The Miraculous Mandarin*, however, Bartók used the pantomime designation more consistently. When Universal Edition advertised it as a ballet, he observed that "this work is less a

ballet than a pantomime, since only two dances actually occur in it"; then, a few months later, "The piece must not be turned into a ballet show; it is intended as a pantomime, after all" (unpublished letters to Universal Edition, 3 March and 22 June 1925, both in Peter Bartók's estate, cited in György Kroó, "Pantomime: The Miraculous Mandarin," in *The Bartók Companion*, ed. Malcolm Gillies [London, 1993], p. 373).

36. *Levelek Hatvany Lajoshoz*, no. 47 and p. 156.

37. Lengyel, *Taifun*, p. 523, and *Életem könyve*, p. 156.

38. Cited in Ferenc Bónis, " 'The Miraculous Mandarin': The Birth and Vicissitudes of a Masterpiece," in *The Stage Works of Béla Bartók*, ed. Nicholas John (London, 1991), p. 81.

39. A few years later he came to know Nijinsky through the dancer's Hungarian wife, Romola Pulszky, and wrote a film script about their story at their request. See Lengyel, *Életem könyve*, p. 254.

40. Elza Galafrés, *Lives, Loves, Losses* (Vancouver, 1973), pp. 236–37. The two operas are *Vajda tornya* (The tower of the Voivod) and *A tenor* (The tenor).

41. "Later [he] showed the score to Dohnányi, who tried to draw his attention to what he thought must be a mistake in the introduction. Lengyel had set the first scene against the background of Paris. Bartók began immediately with exotic music, thus precipitating the atmosphere which should begin to make itself manifest only with the appearance of the Mandarin, and should depict his strange character and strange world." See Galafrés, *Lives, Loves, Losses*, p. 237. As Bónis pointed out, this part of the recollections is incorrect, for Dohnányi could not have commented on the lack of city atmosphere in the introductory music to the piece that was exactly Bartók's idea when he started composing. See Bónis, "The Miraculous Mandarin," p. 81. See also Bartók's letter to Márta Ziegler of 5 September 1918, in *Bartók Béla családi levelei*, p. 282.

42. See Bartók's letter to Márta Ziegler of 2 March 1917 and Márta Ziegler's letter to her mother-in-law of 14 May 1919, in *Bartók Béla családi levelei*, pp. 258 and 295 respectively. According to the first letter, Bartók wanted to postpone the premiere of his ballet until after January 1917 "because of the Galafrés combination." Because Galafrés gave birth to her son in January 1917, this could only mean that he wanted her to be part of the performance. See also Balázs, *Napló, 1914–1922*, p. 203.

43. The daily *Esti Újság* also claimed to recognize that a composer of European fame, who was reluctant to shed his incognito, was setting *The Miraculous Mandarin* to music. This clearly refers to Dohnányi, who was the most famous Hungarian musician at that time. Bartók had withdrawn from public appearances around 1912, after his opera failed to win the competition for which it was submitted. His fame was established only after the premiere of his ballet in 1917. See Bónis, "The Miraculous Mandarin," p. 81.

44. Budapest Bartók Archives, BH VII/131.

45. Bartók wrote a letter on 17 June to the director of the Budapest Opera about his submitting the score of the opera the following month. See Béla

Bartók, Jr., *Apám életének krónikája* (The chronicle of my father's life) (Budapest, 1981), p. 157.

46. The contract was signed on 27 May 1918, three days after the premiere of *Bluebeard's Castle*. Bródy agreed to supply the text of the three-act ballet *Anna Molnár* by 15 June 1918. Bartók's deadline for submitting the score was 30 June 1919. See Arisztid Valkó, "Adatok Bartók színpadi műveihez" (Documents relating to Bartók's stage works), *Magyar Zene* 18 (1977): 433–39.

47. Letter to Márta Ziegler of 21 July 1917, in *Bartók Béla családi levelei*, p. 272.

48. János Breuer, "Bródy Sándor nyilatkozata Bartókról és operájáról" (Sándor Bródy's statement about Bartók and his opera), in his *Bartók és Kodály* (Bartók and Kodály) (Budapest, 1978), p. 45 and 46–50.

49. *Documenta Bartókiana* 3 (1968): 103.

50. Bartók, *Apám életének krónikája*, p. 160.

51. See Bartók's letter to his mother of 9 June 1919, in *Bartók Béla családi levelei*, p. 299.

52. Quoted in Bónis, "The Miraculous Mandarin," p. 82.

53. Lengyel, *Életem könyve*, pp. 126–27. In the first three paragraphs the translations are taken from Bónis, "The Miraculous Mandarin," p. 82. The same entry also appears in *Taifun*, p. 523, with slightly different wording and in a shortened version. Viktor Madarász (1830–1917) was a renowned painter of Hungarian historical subjects.

54. Reinitz was another mutual friend. His connections to Bartók were very strong at that time. He became minister of cultural affairs during the communist regime of 1919 and planned to name Bartók as head of the folk music department of the National Museum, a department to be newly created.

55. Lengyel, *Taifun*, p. 523.

56. Bartók had held negotiations with Universal Edition since April 1918. Their agreement about stage works was formulated on 4 June, and the contract was signed in September. See Bartók, *Apám életének krónikája*, pp. 162–63 and 165.

57. Manuscript in the Budapest Bartók Archives, BBA 4610. The original is in Hungarian. I am grateful to László Somfai, director of the Budapest Bartók Archives, for providing me with material housed in that institution.

58. "Bródy did not show up with the text." See Bartók's letter to Márta Ziegler of 20 August 1918, in *Bartók Béla családi levelei*, p. 279.

59. Letter to Márta Ziegler of 5 September 1918, in ibid., p. 282. This translation partially follows Bónis, "The Miraculous Mandarin," p. 83; and Kroó, "Pantomime," p. 373.

60. Márta Ziegler's letter to her mother-in-law of 9 June 1919, in *Bartók Béla családi levelei*, p. 298.

61. Lengyel, *Életem könyve*, p. 156. By "the two of us" Lengyel was probably referring to his wife, Lidia Gerő, a former Sorbonne student, daughter of Károly Gerő, playwright and secretary of the National Theater in Budapest. They were married in 1917.

62. *Bartók Béla családi levelei*, pp. 299–300.

63. Lengyel, *Taifun*, p. 523.

64. Manuscript letter in the Budapest Bartók Archives, BBA 1039. The original is in Hungarian. Egisto Tango, conductor of the premieres of *Bluebeard's Castle* and *The Wooden Prince*.

65. The original Hungarian is published in *Bartók Béla levelei* (Béla Bartók's letters), ed. János Demény (Budapest, 1976), pp. 256–57. This translation partially follows the excerpt published in Bónis, "The Miraculous Mandarin," p. 85. Bartók lived in Rákoskeresztúr, a village near Budapest, from 1911 until May 1920.

66. Letter to Márta Ziegler of 6 April 1920, in *Bartók Béla családi levelei*, p. 306.

67. Letter to Márta Ziegler of 4 March 1920, in ibid., p. 303.

68. Manuscript letter in the Budapest Bartók Archives, BBA 1038.

69. Lengyel, *Taifun*, p. 526. The passage contradicts Gusztáv Oláh's recollections ("Bartók and the Theatre," in *Tempo* [London] 13–14 (1945–50): 4–8), in which he clearly states that the performance was banned by the censors.

70. Endre Ady (1877–1919), Hungarian avant-garde poet and leading personality of the progressive Hungarian intelligentsia during the first two decades of the century.

71. Lengyel, *Életem könyve*, p. 371.

Bartók and Stravinsky:

Respect, Competition, Influence,

and the Hungarian Reaction to

Modernism in the 1920s

DAVID E. SCHNEIDER

The relationship between Bartók and Stravinsky was one-sided. For Bartók, Stravinsky represented variously a putative ally, a competitor, a threat, an inspiration, a musical resource, and an emblem of modernity and sophistication. Stravinsky's importance for Bartók waxed and waned, but the number of scores of Stravinsky's music in Bartók's possession[1] and references to him in Bartók's writings, correspondence, interviews, and music indicate that Stravinsky was more important to Bartók than any of his other contemporaries, with the possible exception of Kodály. On the other hand, whatever regard Stravinsky might have had for Bartók as a musician and pianist, as a composer he regarded him as a nonentity, a poor "country cousin." Though Stravinsky's crude reaction to the news of Bartók's death, "I never liked his music anyway,"[2] should almost certainly be considered an unfortunate, private slip of the tongue, another statement, intended for publication, demonstrates a similarly dismissive attitude:

I met [Bartók] at least twice in my life, once in London in the nineteen-twenties and later in New York in the early forties, but I had no opportunity to approach him closer either time. I knew the most important musician he was, I had heard wonders about the sensitivity of his ear, and I bowed deeply to his religiosity. However, I never could share his lifelong gusto for his native folklore. This devotion was certainly real and touching, but I couldn't help regretting it in the great musician.[3]

In fact, the meeting "in London in the nineteen-twenties" was two Parisian encounters in April 1922, one at the home of Henry Prunières, the other at the Pleyel company. Despite these factual details and Richard Taruskin's argument that Stravinsky denigrated Bartók's attachment to folk music to deflect attention from his own,[4] one sentiment expressed here rings true—Stravinsky does not seem to have been significantly affected by Bartók. Even a cursory comparison of the two composers' work lists suggests, however, that Bartók may have been less immune to Stravinsky's influence. The list here includes a few examples of a curiously consistent trend: Bartók's compositions often appear several years later than Stravinsky's essays in the same genres.

Stravinsky: Comparable work of Bartók:

The Firebird (1909) .... *The Wooden Prince* (1914–17)

Petrouchka (1911) ....

The Rite of Spring (1913) .... *The Miraculous Mandarin* (1918–19) (riots

Le Rossignol (1914) ....   greeted both premieres)

Les Noces (1922) .... Village Scenes (1924; orchestrated in 1926)

Sonata for Piano (1924) .... Sonata for Piano (1926)

                                            .... First Piano Concerto (1926)
Concerto for Piano and Winds (1924) ....
                                            .... Second Piano Concerto (1931)

Perhaps as striking as the potential correspondence between any two works is that Bartók's tendency to follow in Stravinsky's footsteps does not end with Stravinsky's "Russian period," in which folk (or folklike) music played a significant role. The trend extends at least to 1926, when, in a seeming response to Stravinsky's "neoclassical" works, Bartók's music also gravitated in a similar direction. The intersection of their oeuvres makes Stravinsky's work especially useful for understanding Bartók's, for by viewing his compositions from a perspective informed by Stravinsky, their Hungarian-hued individuality comes into sharper relief.

After a brief consideration of Bartók's relationship to Stravinsky before 1926, I will consider Bartók's First and Second Piano Concertos in light of Stravinsky's Concerto for Piano and Winds. Stravinsky's concerto and its reception in Hungary provide a context that

enables us to understand Bartók's two concertos as mediations between traditional Hungarian attitudes toward "serious" music and the
notions of the "objective" and "neoclassical," so important to modern
music in the 1920s.

.

Through nearly the end of the First World War, Bartók was frequently preoccupied with folk music research and often isolated from
developments in Western Europe. Though he was familiar with a few
of Stravinsky's compositions they do not appear to have had an important influence on his music, nor was Stravinsky's music or reputation a
significant force in Hungarian musical life until the latter part of the
1910s. Stravinsky's first important works for the Ballets Russes do,
however, bear enough superficial similarities to Bartók's own first ballet to warrant a brief consideration of the evidence for a relationship
between them.

The precise origin of Bartók's acquaintance with Stravinsky's music
is unclear. The Ballets Russes performed *The Firebird* at its first appearances in Budapest on 30 December 1912 and 4 January 1913.[5]
Bartók, however, was in the countryside collecting folk music until 31
December, and we have no record of his having attended the January
performance. At this time Bartók was living in "self-exile" in Rákoskeresztúr, a distant suburb, and almost never went to Budapest for concerts. Furthermore, a Hungarian reaction to Stravinsky at this time is
virtually impossible to come by, because the local reviewers covered
only the dance, to the exclusion of the music.[6] Stravinsky's star had
not risen in Budapest by the winter of 1912–13, so we have no reason
to doubt Bartók's testimony from 1920, which omits *The Firebird* from
the few works of Stravinsky that he knew from before the war.[7] Nevertheless, it is fortuitous that Béla Balázs's scenario for *The Wooden
Prince*, written at Bartók's request, was published just in advance of
the Ballets Russes' first Hungarian engagement.

That the scenario of *The Wooden Prince* shares several surface connections with *The Firebird* as well as with *Petrouchka* and *Le Rossignol* is
probably a result of their common folk or quasi-folk inspiration: as
the magical King Kashchei of *The Firebird* initially blocks the union of
the Princess and the Tsarevitch, the magical fairy of *The Wooden Prince*
foils the union of the Prince and Princess; like Petrouchka, the
wooden prince is an animated puppet; and in *The Wooden Prince* and
Le Rossignol, mechanical doubles—the imitation prince and the toy
nightingale—are, for a time, unjustly favored over the living originals. These correspondences must be considered coincidental without

strong evidence of a specific musical connection. Still, in conjunction with the folk quality of these scenarios Bartók and Stravinsky both turned to folk music for inspiration. A comparison of roughly analogous sections of *The Wooden Prince* and *The Firebird* highlights significant differences between Bartók's and Stravinsky's treatment of folk song, differences that are rooted in Russia's and Hungary's divergent nineteenth-century musical legacies.

As is well known, nineteenth-century Russian opera had a long tradition of representing supernatural figures with chromatic music, which differentiated them from human characters associated with simpler folk or folklike diatonic themes.[8] Stravinsky adopts this technique directly in *The Firebird* with diatonic music for the Tsarevitch and the Princess and chromatic music for the magical Firebird and evil King Kashchei.

In contrast, Hungarian opera in the nineteenth century had a tradition of juxtaposing two other sets of characters: pure Hungarians and immoral foreigners. The former displayed their noble patriotism with music in the style of the heroic Hungarian dance known as the *verbunkos*; the latter voiced their impure desire in an Italianate, international operatic idiom. The locus classicus for this practice is *Bánk Bán* by Ferenc Erkel (1810–93), which was well established as the Hungarian national opera by the time Bartók entered the Academy of Music in 1899.

As Stravinsky had appropriated musical topoi from Rimsky-Korsakov's operatic tradition in *The Firebird*, Bartók had also drawn directly on the *verbunkos* tradition as practiced by Erkel to lend a heroic Magyar character to several of his early instrumental works.[9] But after Bartók discovered a group of pentatonically based Hungarian peasant songs in 1906, the nineteenth-century distinction between Hungarian versus foreign musical styles changed in his work. The important distinction for Bartók became the contrast between "authentic" Hungarian peasant music, strong enough to maintain its pentatonic backbone even in the face of Western influence, and what Bartók regarded as the ersatz, foreign-influenced folk music of the gypsy-gentry *verbunkos*, which according to his analysis maintained no uniquely Hungarian underlying structure. What had been considered positive in the nineteenth century became negative in the mature works of Bartók, but the underlying opposition between native and foreign musical styles remained.

Bartók, like Stravinsky, uses chromatic music to depict the supernatural in his ballet; but the primary musical dramaturgy of *The Wooden Prince* relies on the distinction between "pure" and "impure" folk song.

Example 1a. The melody that accompanies the Princess's entrance. Note the sixteenth-note triplet turns, a characteristic *verbunkos* gesture.

The Princess's "fake" folk music, infected with sixteenth-note triplets, telltale symbols of the *verbunkos*, illustrates her vapid pretensions (example 1a). In contrast, the robust, monophonic, modal music introducing the Prince is clearly indebted to "real" Hungarian folk song. It immediately defines him as a strong, virtuous hero (example 1b).

Both Bartók and Stravinsky accompany the resolution of the dramatic conflict in their ballets with a climax clearly indebted to folk song. Taking his melody whole from a collection of folk songs published by Rimsky-Korsakov,[10] Stravinsky builds an entire tableau of rejoicing out of repetitions of the tune (example 2a). In contrast, Bartók uses not folk song proper but a five-note pentatonic motive distilled from the most characteristic feature of the oldest type of Hungarian melodies. Sequences of the pentatonic motive initiate the music accompanying the climactic embrace of the Prince and the Princess (example 2b). In both ballets the apotheosis of folk song represents something positive and human. But whereas Stravinsky revels in this human display, repeating the tune over and over in a gradual crescendo until the final curtain, Bartók's music gradually pulls back from the climax of emotional intensity. The human, emotional aspect of the music—embodied in motives derived from folk song—gradually dissolves into a texture made up of a simple C-major chord.

By analogy to the opening of the ballet, the "white-note" purity of the closing C major represents nature and provides another clue

Example 1b. The D-mixolydian melody that accompanies the Prince's entrance. The tune is doubled at the octave but otherwise monophonic.

David E. Schneider

Example 2a. The tune Stravinsky uses to build to a climax in the final scene of *The Firebird*, notated as it appears in Rimsky-Korsakov's 1877 collection *100 Folk Songs*.

Example 2b. The climactic embrace of the Prince and Princess in *The Wooden Prince*.

to the difference between Bartók's and Stravinsky's use of folk song in these two early ballets. In *The Firebird*, folk song articulates the diatonic extreme in the dichotomy between chromatic supernaturalism and diatonic naturalism. In *The Wooden Prince*, folk song represents an expressive, human middle ground between a different set of opposites: nineteenth-century Hungarian sentimental expression (gypsy-style *verbunkos*) and the static, unemotional purity of nature (C major).

.

After the premiere of *The Wooden Prince* (12 May 1917), and especially in his years of extensive touring after the war, Bartók became more keenly aware of musical developments in Western Europe than he had been previously. During this time Stravinsky also became more important to Bartók in a complex variety of ways: from the late teens through 1920 Stravinsky seems to have acted as an inspiration and vindication for Bartók's own work; from 1921 through early 1926 Bartók appears to have been troubled by the mood of Stravinsky's latest compositions and his shift away from folk-inspired music; and from the middle of March 1926 through the completion of Bartók's

Second Piano Concerto (1931) Stravinsky elicited competition, homage, and criticism in Bartók's music and writing.

Studying the reception of the premiere of *The Wooden Prince*, we learn that by 1917 Stravinsky had already achieved a secure reputation in Hungary. Stravinsky appears to have been well enough known that at least one Hungarian critic evoked Stravinsky in order to help explain Bartók's music to his own countrymen. The association of Bartók with Stravinsky in the press seems designed to lend Bartók the prestige tacitly granted Stravinsky. János Hammerschlag, the critic for the German-language *Pester Lloyd*, writes: "[Bartók's] music, which is understandable even to the layman, best displays a relationship with the music of Igor Stravinsky, whose works have been played here several times."[11] On the other hand, Stravinsky (presumably because of his use of folk music) could also be seen as a threat to Bartók's reputation as an innovator. Antal Molnár, reviewing the premiere of *The Wooden Prince* for the Hungarian music review *Zenei Szemle*, defended Bartók against the potential charge of lack of originality: "Bartók entirely unconsciously discovered numerous methods that similarly occurred to other outstanding composers without knowing about one another. This is the point where the original creator differs from the epigone. This said, the mutual effect can only be healthy; it is very natural that Bartók gladly studied Stravinsky."[12]

Bartók's own actions were not in the least defensive. Basking in the warmth of the tremendous success of *The Wooden Prince* and his resulting short-lived position of favor at the Hungarian Opera, Bartók seems to have felt particularly generous toward Stravinsky. Bartók's first wife, Márta Ziegler, recounts that during the rehearsals for the premiere of *Bluebeard's Castle* in 1918, Bartók "carried the four-hand piano score of Stravinsky's *Le Sacre du printemps* around with him constantly, waiting for an opportunity to play it for the intendant and so to persuade him to stage the ballet."[13] These efforts at the Opera on behalf of Stravinsky were unsuccessful, but Bartók continued to express his admiration for Stravinsky in writing. Responding to a letter in which English critic Philip Heseltine had encouraged him to concur with a disparaging article about Stravinsky in the *Sackbut*, Bartók preferred to defend him:

> Concerning Stravinsky, I only know his arrangement for piano of the "Rite of Spring," of the "Rossignol" and the score of his "3 Chants japonaises" [*sic*]. But these three works have made a great impression on me. It is true, I see in him also the traces of such manners which are too often repeated and the lack of a big con-

ception; but these faults are not so important with him until now. I would like very much to know how he has developed since 1914, but—alas—in our situation we can afford neither a book nor a score that comes from abroad.[14]

Bartók's enthusiasm for Stravinsky's work did not, however, necessarily extend to more recent and less clearly folk-inspired compositions. As Bartók wrote in his next letter to Heseltine,

Lately I had opportunity to see several new publications of Stravinsky, and I must tell you: I am quite disappointed. The only works I like of all these are the "4 Chants russes" and the "Pribaoutky"; But other works: his Rag Time for 11 instruments, his pieces for piano "à 4 mains" etc. are not even curious. I had expected something of real grandness, of real development; and I am really very sad for not finding at all what I imagined.[15]

Despite this disappointment, Bartók did help keep Stravinsky's name in front of the Hungarian public by performing the Piano-Rag-Music, Four Russian Songs, and Three Tales for Children at the Academy of Music on 23 April 1921. In addition to the lack of "grandness" mentioned to Heseltine, it seems that Bartók was uncomfortable with the joking tone of some of Stravinsky's work. Couched in praise, Bartók's own report of the concert hints at this dissatisfaction:

Stravinsky's songs had, for all their originality and modernity, a decided success with the audience—so much so that one of them, the *Chanson pour compter*, was encored. In this, however, the public was mistaken: in my opinion the last of the *4 Chants russes*, the *Chant dissident*, is full of moving intimacy, and it lacks all those jokes and extravagances that we meet so often in Stravinsky's works.[16]

Surely Bartók's interest in Stravinsky had been initiated by Stravinsky's incorporation of folk music into a modern musical idiom. The clearest testimony to this is Bartók's analysis of the last song from Stravinsky's *Pribaoutky* in his 16 October 1920 article for *Melos*, "The Influence of Folk Music on the Art Music of Today."[17] Here Bartók describes the way Stravinsky's folklike melody determines the tonality of the piece despite a disorienting accompaniment. The same analytic observation could have been made about many of Bartók's own compositions. By using Stravinsky as his example, Bartók follows the rhetorical ploy already used in the Hungarian press—implicitly justifying and elevating his own music by analogy to Stravinsky's. The traces of folk music in Stravinsky's work had encouraged Bartók to think of him as an ally; Stravinsky's move to a new style after the war meant the loss of Bartók's most prestigious, if unwitting, support.

If in 1921 Bartók had suspected that Stravinsky was turning away from folk music, Stravinsky confirmed this when the two composers met in Paris a year later. Upon his return to Budapest Bartók spent a large portion of an interview given to Aladár Tóth discussing this encounter with Stravinsky. Tóth reports:

> Stravinsky naturally expounded to Bartók that [Stravinsky's] music is the most objective absolute music; it does not depict, does not symbolize, it does not express anything, it has nothing to do with emotional life, it is just line, harmony, and rhythm. This "objective" theory of music is spreading dangerously. . . . [Bartók], by the way, by no means identifies himself with Stravinsky's theories. . . . In the midst of their conversation in Paris, when Bartók [complimented *Le Sacre*], Stravinsky did not renounce his earlier work, but he assured Bartók that the *Rossignol* was the last in this style; after that he already turned to the road of "completely objective" music.[18]

Bartók, unlike Stravinsky, wanted to distance himself and his music from the rhetoric of "objectivity." He shows this desire as well as a frustration with the narrowing definition of modernism in a letter regarding a lecture associated with performances of *The Wooden Prince* and *Bluebeard* in Weimar. Bartók requests that the lecturer emphasize that his music "is absolutely tonal" and that "it has nothing to do with the 'objective' and 'impersonal' tendencies (so, in fact, it is not at all 'modern!')."[19]

Bartók shared Stravinsky's professed rebellion against the hyperexpression of Wagner and Strauss but regarded the radical concept of a music entirely devoid of human expression to be a logical contradiction. In May 1925 in response to Dezső Kosztolányi's statement that "every art is human by necessity," Bartók replied, "This is natural. Otherwise music would turn into machine music. Bach also expresses something, a few moments of life. . . . If I write a deep note and then a higher, that is already rising; if I strike a high note, and after that a lower one, that is already sinking: the one undoubtedly merriment, the other despair."[20] Concomitant with the "objective theory of music," one of Stravinsky's postwar ideas most foreign to Bartók was the denigration of Beethoven as a "romanticist." Asked about the direction of new music in 1925, Bartók again makes it clear that he does not want to be associated with the latest trend as represented by

Stravinsky: "One of the slogans is: away from romanticism! The other: neoclassicism! They even consider Beethoven a romanticist. The tendency began already with Debussy and is reaching its peak with Stravinsky, who proclaims that Beethoven might have been a great person, an outstanding personality, on the other hand was absolutely not—a musician."[21]

Bartók's surprise that Beethoven (a "classicist" in the Hungarian canon) should be denigrated as a "romanticist" and his expectation that the best music should be "grand," "emotional," or "free of jests" are commensurate with his Hungarian training. If Bartók's incorporation of peasant music into a modern musical idiom had been a radical rebellion against his conservative, Brahms-oriented education at the Academy of Music, in a more general sense he had never abandoned a deeper Hungarian tradition, one that at once burdened and privileged art music with a weighty *ethical* obligation.

.

Bartók's ambivalent reaction to Stravinsky's latest compositions and to the rhetoric that accompanied them was shared even by the Hungarian critics most sympathetic to Stravinsky. These critics responded to the threatening, alien, and for them oxymoronic idea of "musical objectivity" by making their basic assumptions about the expressive and serious nature of art music explicit. This process comes to light in Hungarian reviews of Stravinsky's performance in Budapest in 1926 and in Antal Molnár's philosophy of modern music, *Az új zene* (The new music), published in Budapest in 1925.[22]

Molnár, a follower of Bartók in collecting folk songs and a performer of Bartók's music as the former violist of the Waldbauer Quartet, would be entrusted by the composer to provide an analysis of his First Piano Concerto for the Universal Edition pocket score (1927). This trust surely owes something to Molnár's vigorous defense of Bartók in *Az új zene*.

In this work Molnár's principal criterion for judging composers is the extent to which their work displays "ethical" responsibility. This, according to Molnár, should be demonstrated by fulfilling two abstract obligations: music should have "social content" and should "express the personal feelings of the composer."[23] Molnár capitalizes on the amorphousness of these obligations, for it allows him to justify a specific hierarchy among modern composers through the musical elements he claims satisfy these requirements. The first obligation provides a rationalization for the use of folk music in modern composition. Folk music is, in Molnár's formulation, a "human universal," and therefore he considers it axiomatic that music incorporating folk music has "social content." This reasoning serves to privilege the music of Kodály and Bartók as well as Stravinsky's Russian works over those of Schoenberg. The second obligation, that music "express the personal feelings of the composer," is specifically directed against "objectivity" and the music of Stravinsky. With this formulation he sidesteps having to make his own interpretation of Stravinsky's music and judges instead the rhetoric associated with it. Molnár's argument results in a victory for Bartók (Kodály having been shuffled out of consideration), who emerges as the true representative of "new classicism," Molnár's highest category for new art (note how Molnár's formulation resonates with Bartók's belief in the expressivity of Bach's music):

> New classicism cannot be "objective," properly formulated: to compose with an indifferent spirit; indeed we find objectivity in Bach's music, but this is objectivity of belief in God, which is beyond every individual subjectivity, not the objectivity of neutrality. For just this reason Bach's music—in spite of all its objectivity—pours the heat of the waves of emotion. Eternal music is not "inhuman"; . . . [Stravinsky] is the battering ram of new classicism, the blind strength, but not the spirit of new classicism.[24]

By the time of Molnár's study, "new classicism" was a badge of prestige intimately associated with Stravinsky; Molnár attempts to co-opt Stravinsky's prestige for Bartók by creating a specifically Hungarian definition of "new classicism."

This Hungarian appropriation of "new or (neo)classicism" may also be seen through Molnár's language. From the description of Stravinsky as the "battering ram of new classicism" it is clear that Molnár's phrase "új klasszicizmus" (new classicism) is intended to evoke the French "néoclassicisme." There is, however, a nationalistic component to his translation of "néo" as "új" (new) instead of simply using the Latin "*neo*klasszicizmus" more common in Hungary. Molnár's insistence on "*new* classicism" is a symbol of his polemical attempt to adjust the term and its implications to a Hungarian model.

For Molnár and Bartók, "classicism" meant primarily Viennese classicism: Haydn, Mozart, and especially Beethoven, who best represented the profound, ethical side of music so important to Molnár. Implicit in Molnár's discussion of Hungarian "new classicism" is a strong link between Beethoven and Bartók, a link that was not part of the concept of neoclassicism associated with Stravinsky. Bartók takes

Molnár's distinction between himself and Stravinsky one step further. In his formulation, which wisely avoids any reference to the confusions of "new classicism/neoclassicism," the difference between Kodály's (read: Bartók's) and Stravinsky's relationship to the past constitutes an antithetical position in the present:

> In general two opposite [approaches to new music] crystallize in practice: one (for example, Stravinsky) is revolutionary; that is, on the one hand, it shows a sudden break with the music of yesterday, and on the other, it throws the whole range of dazzling novelties and new departures into the music of today. The other type seems rather to be comprehensive: a summation of all the elements available up to now. It is thus not a revolutionary break with yesterday, for it even rescues everything it can use from romanticism . . . that is, whatever has vitality. The most characteristic representative of this is the Hungarian Kodály. Which of the two will better withstand the test of time, the innovators or the summarizers, remains to be decided by the future. If, however, we think of parallels in music history, we would be inclined to rule in favor of the great comprehensive art.[25]

This passage, part of a draft Bartók probably intended for use in a preconcert lecture in 1928 or 1929, is a rare competitive jibe at his more successful contemporary.

If Stravinsky's renown in Hungary by 1925 had challenged Bartók's position of dominance enough to warrant Molnár's reformulation of neoclassicism in Bartók's defense, then Stravinsky's personal appearance in Budapest on 15 March 1926 turned abstract threat into palpable reality. With this concert the Budapest Philharmonic honored Stravinsky with an entire evening devoted to his work (*Rossignol*, the Concerto for Piano and Winds, and *Petrouchka*), something they had never done for Bartók. Furthermore, in his role as piano soloist, Stravinsky encroached on a domain that previously had been exclusively Bartók's. Bartók the composer/pianist was now both literally and figuratively confronted on his own turf.

Aladár Tóth, who in his September previews of the opera season had for many years been demanding productions of Stravinsky's ballets,[26] was perhaps the person most responsible for keeping Stravinsky's name alive in Hungary after the war. Despite Tóth's general support for Stravinsky, a patriotic loyalty to Bartók demanded that he use the Stravinsky concert as an opportunity to educate the public about Hungary's own composer-pianist: "We know well the power of barbaric, wild rhythms, for here among us lives well the greatest master of them: Béla Bartók. But Stravinsky's rhythm is something entirely different: it resembles Bartók's only in its demonic verve. Bartók's rhythm is always deeply poetic. . . . Bartók soars when he plays the piano, Stravinsky remains earthbound." Later in the same review Tóth resorts to damning Stravinsky with faint praise—again we are given evidence of the importance of Beethoven to the Hungarian canon: "[Stravinsky] really wrote this music for ballet. Ballet music, easy, characteristically pantomime dance music—not in the sense that Beethoven's *Prometheus* or Bartók's *Wooden Prince* want to reform the art form into a poetic manifestation equal to opera and symphony, but in the sense that Lully or Delibes writes ballet music."[27] As a Stravinsky supporter, Tóth could afford to defend Bartók at Stravinsky's expense on this occasion because the audience had received the performance so enthusiastically. As Bartók reported, "The biggest event [of this year's musical season] was, without question, Stravinsky's evening concert, which the audience in Pest received with great understanding. . . . Stravinsky's latest works, which he calls neoclassical . . . seemed dry to me after their first reading, but they were enriched for me after his concert."[28] But even Bartók's words of praise appear to belie the profound effect of the concert when read in the context provided by an account of the event by his second wife, Ditta Pásztory:

> Monday was the Stravinsky concert. Now I know quite exactly what the new direction is. Imagine, Mama, for yourself such a music, in which there is absolutely no room for feelings, in which you can find no part that causes tears to come to your eyes. You know bare rhythm, bare hammering, bare some-kind-of-timbre. I can say that the whole thing, as it is, really carries one away. Stravinsky is a magnificent genius, and we very, very much enjoyed the evening; truly one gets caught up in his miraculously beautiful-timbred machine music, music of pulsating rhythm—but if Béla would make such music, then for Béla I would not be able to be the artist that I am and always will be. Because this music is not my homeland. Mine is Béla's music, where there is also the profound pulsating rhythm, the timbre, but where the feelings live and are, and which has soul.[29]

Ditta's account is a bundle of contradictions. She and Bartók were clearly moved, "carried away," "caught up" by Stravinsky's music and performance. Yet, with expressions such as "bare hammering," "no room for feelings," and the sentiment that Stravinsky's music lacks "soul," Ditta parrots epithets that were already in general circulation.

That her brand of negative criticism of Stravinsky's music was in fact a commonplace in the Hungarian reception of Stravinsky is demonstrated by comparing her description with the following passage:

> [Stravinsky's] playing was bare rhythm, without color, spirit, and soul. It is possible that by the time our earth cools and there is ice on the equator, at that time this will be considered music too. But as long as feeling and spirit live in man, as long as feelings and passions find a home in our hearts, this mechanical clattering, this rhythmical but colorless ticking, this mixing of tones without melody or harmony cannot be considered music.[30]

This excerpt is from the only consistently negative review of Stravinsky's concert known to me—that of the widely read *Pesti Hírlap* (Pest news). The review appeared two days before Ditta penned her letter.

Ditta Pásztory, Antal Molnár, and Aladár Tóth all implied that Bartók's music combined the profundity of Beethoven ("soul") with the modernity of Stravinsky. Although they wrote about this as a past achievement, it was, in the context of Stravinsky's latest style, only a future possibility.

Bartók's First and Second Piano Concertos represent two different stages in Bartók's reaction to Stravinsky. The First Concerto I read as a still-raw struggle to balance Beethovenian symphonic weight with elements of Stravinsky's "neoclassical" concerto style. The Second Concerto emerges as a less fraught, more direct response to Stravinsky. It seems to embrace a more mature mediation between Bartók's dedication to folk music and his desire to participate in the latest Western European musical trends. A device Bartók uses for the first time in the Second Piano Concerto, the embedding of themes in formal structures derived from folk song, appears concomitantly with a more flexible interpretation of Stravinsky's work. The Second Piano Concerto signals a new stage in Bartók's development, one in which he has been freed from the need to address Stravinsky directly in composition.

In the three years preceding the fateful Stravinsky concert, Bartók had virtually retired from composing. During this time he had written only one work, a folk song arrangement called Village Scenes (1924), and had never written anything comparable to Stravinsky's Piano Concerto in mood and scope—for over twenty years he had been relying on his early Rhapsody, Op. 1, for engagements with orchestra. Bartók badly needed a piano concerto of his own, and Stravinsky's concert in Budapest must have made this need even more urgent. When he began work on his First Piano Concerto a few months after hearing Stravinsky, his long absence from composition had left Bartók unusually unsure of his own direction:

> To be frank, recently I have felt so stupid, so dazed, so empty-headed that I have truly doubted whether I am able to write anything new at all anymore. All the tangled chaos that the musical periodicals vomit thick and fast about the music of today has come to weigh heavily on me: the watchwords, linear, horizontal, vertical, objective, impersonal, polyphonic, homophonic, tonal, polytonal, atonal, and the rest; even if one does not concern oneself with all of it, one still becomes quite dazed when they shout it in our ears so much.[31]

Despite his professed resistance to new trends, the compositions of 1926 mark a change in style that does seem to have been affected by the barrage of rhetoric surrounding musical modernism. Bartók refers to this aesthetic shift when he looked back on his compositions of 1926 several years later: "In my youth my ideal for what was beautiful was not so much Bach's or Mozart's creations as those of Beethoven. Recently this has changed to a certain extent; in the past few years I have been very occupied with music preceding Bach, and I believe that traces of this are revealed in the Piano Concerto and the Nine Little Piano Pieces."[32]

The circumstances of its genesis suggest that Bartók's First Piano Concerto may be read as a musical analogy to Ditta's impassioned, if ambivalent, reaction to Stravinsky's concert. Although this concerto reveals Stravinsky's influence at times in both detail and mood, the influence is rarely straightforward. In the First Piano Concerto Hungarian attitudes about serious music, and with them Beethoven's legacy, are mixed with Stravinskian echoes. The result is a work beautifully layered with meanings culled from evocations of folk music, nineteenth- and twentieth-century topoi—a work difficult to classify, and simply too *difficult* to be very warmly received in the European concert halls of the late 1920s and early 1930s. An examination of points of intersection in three sections from the first movement of Bartók's and Stravinsky's concertos (introductions, primary themes, and culminating climaxes) highlights some telling similarities, which in turn bring their differences into more meaningful relief.

Both Stravinsky and Bartók begin their concertos with a borrowing from another musical genre. Stravinsky's Largo introduction to the main Allegro of the movement recalls the tradition of the French baroque overture; the implications of the dotted rhythms of the Largo march were not lost on Aladár Tóth, who wrote that Stravinsky "cut a noble, festive robe for himself from Handel's punctuated rhythms."[33] In A, the introduction establishes the key of the Allegro. For orchestra alone, this music metaphorically paves the way for the entrance of the king, the soloist—in this case Stravinsky himself.

Especially given the rarity of slow introductions in concertos, it hardly seems coincidental that Bartók too chooses to begin his concerto with an introduction set off from the main Allegro by its slower tempo. In fact, Bartók's introduction may be seen to challenge its predecessor by taking Stravinsky's idea of "objective" orchestration one step further: strings are entirely absent from this introduction. Here the prominent role for the percussion, including the percussive use of the piano, would seem to outdo Stravinsky at his own brittle game. Comparison of the opening bars of the Allegros of each concerto makes Bartók's inspiration more apparent: Both passages begin with a long series of repeated A's that require an outstretched hand position clearly intended to generate a percussive attack. The rhythms of the accompaniments to these passages are identical; Bartók is quoting or at least alluding here (example 3).

But if Bartók seems to have been inspired by Stravinsky's instrumentation, use of rhythm, choice of pitch, and the opening gambit of an introduction, his introduction has roots in a very different tradition from Stravinsky's. Bartók's introduction symbolically reenacts the process of creation by gradually building a distinct shape from amorphous musical material. This gesture belongs to a topos commonly associated with large-scale works of the nineteenth century. Bartók had already drawn on this tradition in the opening of *The Wooden Prince*, which, like the famous E♭ chord that opens Wagner's *Das Rheingold*, begins with a long C pedal to accompany an image of nature's awakening. Although it is not the first such example, the most influential model for this kind of "creation" image is surely the beginning of Beethoven's Ninth Symphony, whose legacy includes Mahler's First Symphony among others.

The "creation" openings of Beethoven's Ninth, *Das Rheingold*, Mahler's First, and *The Wooden Prince* all begin with long pedal points that provide a backdrop for metaphorical birth, the crystallization of the musical material. Bartók's First Piano Concerto continues this tradition, but with a twist that identifies the gesture as a product of the 1920s. Instead of one continuous pedal, Bartók employs two (B and

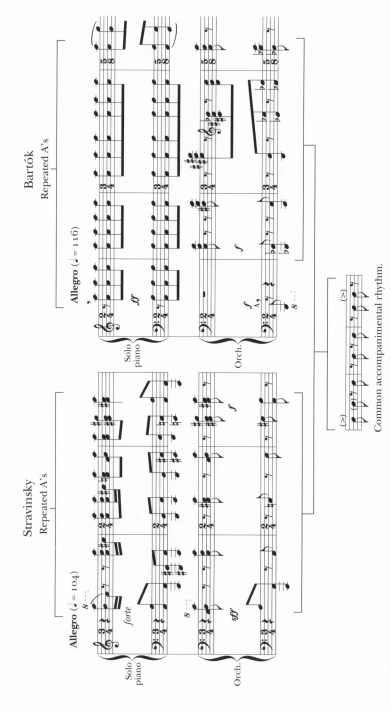

Example 3. The opening bars of the first movements of Stravinsky's Concerto for Piano and Winds (left) and Bartók's First Piano Concerto (right). Note the similar repeated A's in the piano and the identical accompaniment rhythms.

A), set to sharply contrasting rhythms. The two pitches dissonantly beat against each other as they are drummed out by the timpani and solo piano. In alternation with this increasingly energetic rhythmic exchange, Bartók presents the elements of music one by one—after drumming, a lone, stark chord in the brass, then a primitive melody in several orchestrations, before the percussive energy of the dual pedals bursts into full bloom, the vital first theme of the Allegro.

Both Stravinsky and Bartók return to ideas presented in their intro-ductions to effect a climactic point of return just before the end of the movements. Stravinsky's climactic *Largo del principio* recapitulates the introductory march, now intensified by the inclusion of added layers of rhythmic activity in the piano (example 4a). The resulting rigid metrical matrix emphasizes the mechanical, or more exactly, the pro-portional aspect of the music: the bars of 2/4 are at once divided into quarter notes in the orchestra and quarter-note triplets in the piano's left hand while each large division of the bar is respectively supported by its own subdivision, sixteenth notes in the dotted melody in the orchestra and sextuplets in the piano right hand.[34]

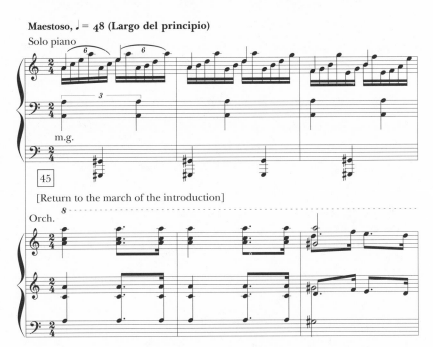

Example 4a. The climax of the first movement of Stravinsky's Concerto for Piano and Winds.

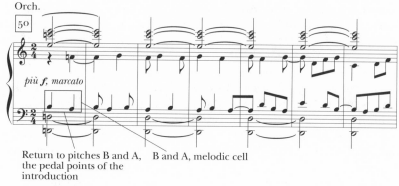

Return to pitches B and A,   B and A, melodic cell
the pedal points of the
introduction

$\hat{5}$–$\hat{4}$–$\hat{1}$ melodic folk cadence

Example 4b. The climax of the first movement of Bartók's First Piano Concerto.

For the climax of the first movement of his concerto (example 4b), Bartók does not literally repeat the music of the introduction but instead returns to a metaphor for the image of creation. The pitches B and A, which had been so productive as the dual pedals of the introduction, return to bear musical fruit—this time with a melodic function in a higher octave. Beginning with a simple alternation of B and A Bartók expands this embryonic whole-tone cell to a pentatonic protomelody, which in turn erupts into a full-throated tenor-range tune whose modality (E dorian), Hungarian rhythms (♩♩♪; ♫.), descending melodic profile, and $\hat{5}$–$\hat{4}$–$\hat{1}$ melodic cadence betray its debt to Hungarian folk song. Accompanied by block chords, Bartók's climactic phrase revels in melody as Stravinsky's had in counterpoint—in human song, Bartók (or Tóth) might have said, as opposed to musical clockwork.

But this clear distinction between Bartók's and Stravinsky's style evaporates if we choose to compare the conclusions of the first movements rather than their climaxes. Just as Bartók had quickly retreated from the expressive, folk-inspired music representing the embrace of the Prince and Princess in *The Wooden Prince*, the climax of the first movement of the concerto quickly retreats to an alienating coda. At the $\hat{5}-\hat{4}-\hat{1}$ melodic folk cadence Bartók closes the door on the high-tenor, human quality of the orchestra's "song" and shifts to a ticking eighth-note accompaniment that paves the way for the piano's marcato entrance in a "music box" register. Bartók follows with a contrapuntal treatment of the piano's tune that closes the movement with a neatly interlocking stretto.

Despite the antithetical orientation of their climaxes, the first movements of Stravinsky's and Bartók's concertos end, so to speak, on the same "objective" note. But, as was the case in the final scene of *The Firebird*, Stravinsky's climactic and closing gestures in the first movement of his piano concerto are one and the same, whereas Bartók separates these two events in his concerto, as he does in *The Wooden Prince*.

That the first movement of Bartók's First Piano Concerto requires, in effect, *two* endings (one emotional, one mechanical) should perhaps come as no surprise. Not only did the introduction introduce two pedal points, but it was a combination of two topoi: a traditional nineteenth-century metaphor for "creation," oddly coupled with dissonant and percussive gestures identified with the "objective" music of the 1920s. This peculiar combination seems to have been born of the double weight of Bartók's ideals of "grandness," "emotional expression," and profundity coupled with his obligation to meet the challenge of Stravinsky.

Predictably, both Molnár and Tóth claimed that Bartók's concerto represented a great melding of styles, a new "classicism." For them Bartók had succeeded in challenging the neoclassical Stravinsky while staying true to the Central European belief in music's "soul," its moral obligation, its debt to Beethoven. Molnár could take the folk elements in Bartók's concerto as its human element—fulfilling the requirements for musical "classicism": "This general human characteristic [folk music] raises Bartók's concerto above the phenomenon of fashionable 'neoclassicism' and confers on it the status of an independent *classical* work, in which the artist succeeds in drawing out something of absolute value from the 'indifferent' mood of the time."[35] Tóth's review of the Budapest premiere of the concerto again defends Bartók as if Stravinsky's concert in Budapest had preceded Bartók's by two days or weeks rather than by two years: "What remained in the 'neoclassical' Stravinsky of the *Sacre du printemps* from barbaric Asia?

Virtually nothing: Stravinsky's barbarism was nothing more than a movable set, which he left out of his music the closer he came to French neoclassicism. The more 'classical' Bartók is, however, the more . . . complicated, the more 'barbaric,' all the more 'Asia.' "[36]

Tóth and Molnár represented, however, a minority opinion. Despite Bartók's twenty-odd performances of it over five years, this concerto seems never to have achieved more than a succès d'estime. What Bartók's Hungarian apologists considered great depth was frequently regarded as simple confusion; the Hungarian public was not sympathetic to Bartók's concerto. Rather than the genuine enthusiasm that had greeted Stravinsky's concerto two years earlier, the Budapest audience received Bartók's with polite, perfunctory applause. According to Emil Haraszti of the *Budapesti Hírlap* (Budapest news), "The public of tonight's Bartók premiere was perplexed. They did not understand the piece; they scolded, belittled, mocked. . . . The believers also, with few exceptions, voiced only banal commonplaces. . . . Béla Bartók's piano concerto is one of the composer's less successful works."[37] The reaction of the Hungarian audience was typical; and as a Dutch critic suggests, the work's lukewarm reception throughout Europe may have been partially attributable to its odd mix of nineteenth- and twentieth-century topoi:

> We cannot condemn the audience in its judgment. Béla Bartók is a serious thinker and exceptional composer, but his desire is different . . . from his knowledge. In his piano concerto he made use of lessons from Stravinsky . . . but his mentality is different; his tools are not in agreement with his temperament, which is still romantic. So there is a gulf between the mode of expression and the content; for this reason the piece is not convincing.[38]

Bartók's First Piano Concerto was not the composition to meet successfully the challenge posed by Stravinsky, and Bartók implicitly admitted its failure with the public by dropping the work from his repertoire as soon as his Second Piano Concerto was ready for performance in 1933. In 1939 Bartók publicly proclaimed that the First Concerto was "a bit difficult—one might even say very difficult!—as much for the orchestra as for the audience. That is why some years later (1930–31), while writing my Second Concerto, I wanted to produce a piece which would contrast with the first: a work which would be less bristling with difficulties for the orchestra and whose thematic material would be more pleasing."[39] But, as is often the case with composers' pronouncements about their own works, what Bartók left unsaid about the relationship between the two concertos appears to be more significant than what he did say. For, in the Second Piano Concerto, Bartók again confronts Stravinsky—this time more explicitly and with greater control than he could while navigating in Stravinsky's turbulent wake in 1926.

.

The evocations of Stravinsky in Bartók's Second Piano Concerto represent a new stage in Bartók's relationship to Stravinsky. These allusions are so direct that they must be regarded as intentional, and with this intentionality comes a sense of measured purpose vis-à-vis Stravinsky that is absent from the First Concerto. Here Bartók shows off his virtuoso technique by incorporating material inspired by actual Russian folk tunes from Stravinsky's works into music that seamlessly fuses the structures of Hungarian folk music with the percussive linearity of Stravinsky's own "neoclassical" style.

Bartók evokes Stravinsky in the first movement of his Second Piano Concerto by omitting the strings, a reference so obvious it would be apparent to any listener who knew only the title of Stravinsky's Concerto for Piano and Winds. Two other evocations, of *The Firebird* and *Petrouchka*, become apparent when viewed or heard next to their models (examples 5a, 5b, 6a, and 6b). Less immediately apparent are the possible meanings of these evocations suggested by Bartók's integration of them into structures indebted to Hungarian folk song.

In spite of its Dorian modality and range of a minor seventh—two characteristics of Hungarian folk song—the motto associated with *The Firebird* does not particularly recall Hungarian folk song, because its rhythms and melodic profile have no precedent in that tradition. Bartók, however, finds a way to unleash the motto's latent Hungarian characteristics at the point of climactic arrival just before the cadenza.

Example 5a. The opening seven pitches of "By the Gate," the folk song Stravinsky uses in the final scene of *The Firebird* (transposed to G; cf. example 2a).

Example 5b. The opening motto of Bartók's Second Piano Concerto, and its retrograde inversion. The box designates the Hungarian *short*-long rhythm.

Example 6a. The opening of Stravinsky's "Danse russe" from *Petrouchka*.

Example 6b. The opening of the piano's theme in the first movement of Bartók's Second Piano Concerto.

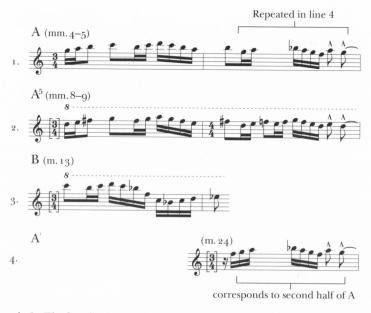

Example 6c. The four-line Hungarian folk song structure of the piano's opening theme in the first movement of Bartók's Second Piano Concerto.

Here the motto becomes a clearly Hungarian gesture by the addition of a pointedly Hungarian *short*-long rhythm and the transformation of its melodic shape through the use of the retrograde inversion of the motto (examples 5b and c). Bartók also brings the reference to *Petrouchka* into the sphere of Hungarian music by embedding it within an AA⁵BA (A⁵ = A a fifth higher), four-line structure codified by Bartók in his study of Hungarian folk songs (example 6c). Typically for Bartók, who had an aversion to exact repetition, he abbreviates the return to A analogous to the fourth line of the song.[40]

The first movement of Bartók's Second Piano Concerto may be read as a homage to Stravinsky's Russian period and a corrective criticism of his neoclassical style. For in the process of evoking two of Stravinsky's best-known Russian-period works Bartók shows how folk song can even form the background to a lean, contrapuntal style, dominated by winds and percussion. This time Bartók judged his potential audience correctly—the Second Concerto received a relatively consistent stream of kudos, starting with its premiere in January of 1933.

But the Second Piano Concerto does not only represent homage to and criticism of Stravinsky. For Bartók, completion of this work seems to have coincided with a less rigid understanding of Stravinsky's rhetoric. At approximately the same time as the completion of the Second Piano Concerto, Bartók finds a way to justify his relationship to "objectivity"—a term that earlier had seemed so antithetical to his concept of music. In a lecture on 10 March 1931 Bartók declared that "peasant music contains everything that more recently they like to call 'objectivity' and what I would call the absence of sentimentality."[41] As the style of his Second Piano Concerto suggests, Bartók seems to have found common ground between his reliance on folk music and the leading credo of modern music in the years between the two World Wars. Bartók's ability to see this intersection coincides with an important advancement of his technique: the adoption of the formal features of folk music (such as AA⁵BA) into his own compositions. This level of abstraction allows Bartók the freedom to incorporate a wide range of musical styles while maintaining the connection to folk music so important to him in the justification of his work.

·

Except in connection with Béla and Ditta Bartók's performances of Stravinsky's Concerto for Two Solo Pianos at the end of the decade, Stravinsky's name almost disappears from Bartók's interviews and correspondence of the 1930s. In February 1943 Bartók followed in

Stravinsky's footsteps for the last time when he held a series of lectures at Harvard University, as Stravinsky had some three and a half years before. In these lectures Bartók confirms his retreat from the position of the late 1920s. By 1943 he no longer saw Stravinsky as a revolutionary, his own antithesis, but considered both himself and Stravinsky representatives of a similar artistic "evolution."

In his Harvard lectures, Bartók's references to Stravinsky return to their rhetorical function of the early 1920s—to justify Bartók's own use of folk music in his original compositions. In 1943, however, Bartók primarily refers not to Stravinsky's Russian period but to his "neoclassic" style. Bartók justifies Stravinsky's abstractions from the music of the seventeenth and eighteenth centuries in just the same way that he often explained his own abstractions from folk music:

> The opinion of some people that Stravinsky's neoclassical style is based on Bach, Handel, and other composers of their time is a rather superficial one. As a matter of fact, he turns only to the material of that period, to the patterns used by Bach, Handel, and others. Stravinsky uses this material in his own way, arranging and transforming it according to his own individual spirit, thus creating works of a new, individual style.[42]

By this time Bartók was far from relying on press reports of Stravinsky's music. In addition to the earlier-mentioned works that he knew and others that he must have heard, Bartók owned an album of Stravinsky's selected compositions for piano solo (Marks Music, 1941); the *Concerto en Ré* for violin and orchestra; the *Concerto per due pianoforti soli* (which he played in 1939 and 1940); Etude for piano; *Histoire du soldat* (both the full score and the arrangement for clarinet, violin, and piano);[43] *Les Noces*; *Petrouchka* (both the full score and the arrangement for piano); *Renard* (both the score and the arrangement for voice and piano); and the *Suite de Pulcinella* and *Symphonies d'instruments à vent* (arranged for piano).[44]

In his Harvard Lectures Bartók recalls an exchange that had not appeared in his descriptions of his meetings with Stravinsky in 1922: "When I once met Stravinsky in Paris, he told me that he thinks he has the right to incorporate into his music any music he believes to be fit or appropriate for his purposes."[45] At first glance, the recollection seems to be yet another example of Bartók's old rhetorical ploy to invoke Stravinsky's practice as a justification for his own reliance on folk music. Given the intimate connection between Stravinsky's work and Bartók's first two piano concertos, however, this passage might also be read as the Hungarian composer's justification for his own debt to a most inspirational model, Igor Stravinsky.

NOTES

1. See Vera Lampert, "Zeitgenössische Musik in Bartóks Notensammlung," *Documenta Bartókiana* 5 (1977): 142–68.

2. Statement of 27 September 1945, as reported in Vera Stravinsky and Robert Craft, *Stravinsky in Pictures and Documents* (New York, 1978), p. 648.

3. Igor Stravinsky and Robert Craft, *Conversations with Igor Stravinsky* (London, 1958), p. 74.

4. See especially Richard Taruskin, "Russian Folk Melodies in *The Rite of Spring*," *Journal of the American Musicological Society* 33, no. 3 (1980): 501–43, and "Stravinsky and the Traditions: Why the Memory Hole?" *Opus*, no. 3 (1983): 10–17.

5. János Breuer, "A magyarországi Stravinsky-kultusz nyomában" (In search of the Stravinsky cult in Hungary), *Bartók és Kodály* (Budapest, 1978), p. 315.

6. Ibid.

7. See his letter to Philip Heseltine of 24 November 1920 (*Documenta Bartókiana* 5 [1977]: 140).

8. See Eric Walter White, *Stravinsky: The Composer and His Works* (Berkeley and Los Angeles, 1979), pp. 182–89.

9. Bartók's works employing the *verbunkos* style are his *Kossuth Symphony*, the Rhapsody for Piano, Op. 1, and the Suites for Orchestra Nos. 1 and 2.

10. "By the Gate," no. 21 of *100 Folk Songs* (St. Petersburg, 1877).

11. *Pester Lloyd*, 13 May 1917. In *Bartók Béla művészi kibontakozásának évei II—Bartók megjelenése az európai zeneéletben (1914–1926)* (The years of Bartók's artistic evolution, part 2—Bartók's appearance in European musical life [1914–1926]), ed. János Demény, vol. 7 of *Zenetudományi tanulmányok* (Musicological studies), ed. Bence Szabolcsi and Dénes Bartha (Budapest, 1959), p. 46. (All translations are my own unless otherwise noted.)

12. *Zenei Szemle* (Music review) 1, no. 4 (Temesvár, 1917): 128–29. In *Zenetudományi tanulmányok*, vol. 7, p. 34.

13. Márta Ziegler, "Über Béla Bartók," *Documenta Bartókiana* 4, (1970): 175.

14. Letter to Philip Heseltine of 24 November 1920 (*Documenta Bartókiana* 5 [1977]: 140). Original in French.

15. Letter to Philip Heseltine of 7 February 1921 (ibid., p. 141). Original in English.

16. "Budapesti levél" (Letter from Budapest), a Hungarian translation of the Italian "Lettera da Budapest," published originally in *Il Pianoforte* 2, no. 9 (September 1921): 277–78. My English translation here is based on András Szőllősy's Hungarian version in *Bartók Béla összegyűjtött írásai* (Béla Bartók's

collected writings) (Budapest, 1966), p. 744. A different translation appears in Béla Bartók, *Essays*, ed. Benjamin Suchoff (New York, 1976), p. 480.

17. Bartók, *Essays*, pp. 316–19.

18. "Bartók külföldi útja" (Bartók's foreign tour), *Nyugat* 15, no. 12 (1922): 830–33. Reprinted in *Zenetudományi tanulmányok*, vol. 7, pp. 219–22. See pp. 282–89 of this volume.

19. From Bartók to Ernst Latzko, 16 December 1924. In *Bartók Béla levelei* (The letters of Béla Bartók), ed. János Demény (Budapest, 1976), pp. 311–12.

20. Dezső Kosztolányi, "Bartók Béla megjelenése az európai zeneéletben" (Béla Bartók's appearance in the musical life of Europe), *Pesti Hírlap* (Pest news), 31 May 1925; reprinted in *Zenetudományi tanulmányok*, vol. 7, p. 349. See also pp. 228–34 of this volume, esp. p. 232.

21. Ibid.

22. Antal Molnár, *Az új zene: A zeneművészet legújabb irányának ismertetése kultúretikai megvilágításban* (The new music: the review of music's newest directions in the light of the ethics of culture) (Budapest, 1925), p. 359.

23. My summary of Molnár's position is taken primarily from "Újabb zenemozgalmak" (Newer movements in music), chapter 4 of *Az új zene*, pp. 96–110.

24. Ibid, p. 204.

25. "Béla Bartók's Proclamation about Progressive Musical Creation," ed. László Somfai, *Magyar zene* 16, no. 2 (1975): 115.

26. Breuer, "A magyarországi Stravinsky-kultusz nyomában," p. 319.

27. *Pesti Napló* (Pest journal), 16 March 1926, pp. 14–15.

28. "Conversation with Béla Bartók," interview in *Kassai Napló*, 23 April 1926. *Zenetudományi tanulmányok*, vol. 7, pp. 395–96. See pp. 235–39 in this volume.

29. Letter to Mrs. Paula Voit Bartók of 18 March 1926, in *Béla Bartók családi levelei* (Béla Bartók's family correspondence), ed. Béla Bartók, Jr. (Budapest, 1981), p. 375.

30. Izor Béldi, "Casals és Stravinsky" (Casals and Stravinsky), *Pesti Hírlap*, 16 March 1926.

31. Bartók to his wife, Ditta Pásztory, on 21 June 1926, in *Bartók Béla családi levelei*, p. 381. My translation follows that in Tibor Tallián, *Béla Bartók: The Man and His Work*, trans. Gyula Gulyás (Budapest, 1988), p. 140.

32. Bartók to Edwin von der Null, in von der Null, *Béla Bartók, Ein Beitrag zur Morphologie der neuen Musik* (Halle, 1930), p. 108.

33. Aladár Tóth, "Béla Bartók's Piano Concerto on Monday's Philharmonic Concert," *Pesti Napló*, 20 March 1928. In *Bartók Béla pályája delelőjén—teremtő évek–Világhódító alkotások (1927–1940)* (Béla Bartók at the height of his career—creative years—world-conquering works [1927–1940]), ed. János Demény, vol. 10 of *Zenetudományi tanulmányok*, ed. Bence Szabolcsi and Dénes Bartha (Budapest, 1962), pp. 269–71.

34. My interpretation of this passage of Stravinsky's concerto is indebted to Richard Taruskin's "The Pastness of the Present and the Presentness of the

Past," *Authenticity and Early Music*, ed. Nicholas Kenyon (Oxford, 1988), p. 176.

35. "Béla Bartók: Piano Concerto—On the Occasion of Its Premiere, 1 July 1927," *Melos* 6, no. 6 (June 1927): 256–57. Reprinted in *Zenetudományi tanulmányok*, vol. 10, p. 218.

36. Tóth, "Béla Bartók's Piano Concerto on Monday's Philharmonic Concert," *Zenetudományi tanulmányok*, vol. 10, pp. 269–71.

37. 20 March 1928. Ibid., p. 272.

38. *Nieuwe Rotterdamische Courant*, 9 November 1928. In ibid., p. 291.

39. "Analysis of the Second Concerto for Piano and Orchestra," in Bartók, *Essays*, p. 419.

40. The relationship between the opening of the Second Piano Concerto and the four-line structure of Hungarian folk song was first described by László Somfai in "Statikai tervezés és formai dramaturgia a 2. zongoraversenyben" (Static planning and formal dramaturgy in the Second Piano Concerto). In Somfai, *Tizennyolc Bartók-tanyulmány* (Eighteen Bartók studies) (Budapest, 1981), pp. 194–217.

41. "A parasztzene hatása az újabb műzenére" (The influence of peasant music on the art music of today), in Szőllősy, *Bartók összegyűjtött írásai*, p. 674. The text quoted was part of the version of this essay given as a lecture in Budapest on 10 March 1931 and published originally on 10 May 1931 in *Új Idők* (New times).

42. Bartók, *Essays*, p. 360.

43. The trio arrangement of *L'histoire du soldat* was originally scheduled for Bartók's concert on 27 February 1923, but he never performed it. See Breuer, "A magyarországi Stravinsky-kultusz nyomában," p. 312.

44. See Lampert, "Zeitgenössische Musik in Bartóks Notensammlung," pp. 142–68.

45. Bartók, *Essays*, p. 360.

PART II
WRITINGS
BY
BARTÓK

.

Travel Reports from Three Continents:

A Selection of Letters from

Béla Bartók

TRANSLATED BY PETER LAKI

Béla Bartók, Jr. (1911–94), the composer's older son, published *Bartók Béla családi levelei* (Béla Bartók's family correspondence) in 1981 (Editio Musica, Budapest). The volume contains no fewer than 918 letters by Bartók. The first letter, a birthday poem for his mother, dates from 1889, when the composer was not quite eight years old; the last one was written in the United States in 1941. A final supplementary letter, written by Bartók's younger son, Peter, informs Béla, Jr., of the circumstances of their father's death.

A new English-language edition of Bartók's letters, edited by Malcolm Gillies and Adrienne Gombocz, is forthcoming. This volume will provide the English-speaking reader with unprecedented insights into the composer's everyday life and his personality. The present selection of letters, not included in the Gillies-Gombocz edition, can offer only a modest sampling of this veritable treasure trove and is a small addendum to the more comprehensive collection that will soon become available. In the five letters relating to Bartók's travels in Europe and his emigration to the United States, Bartók describes his current environment to close family members who are far away. The letters from Remete and from the estate of Baron Kohner are to his first wife, Márta Ziegler; those from the Swiss Alps and Cairo are to his second wife, Ditta Pásztory. The Christmas letter from New York was addressed to his two sons. The letters to Fritz Reiner are taken from *Bartók Béla levelei* (Béla Bartók's letters), ed. János Demény (Budapest, 1976).

Bartók's letters cover a wide array of topics, from ethnomusicology to nature to his American diet. The composer, so reticent about discussing his music, discloses a great deal about himself and his reactions to people and situations. The playful, punning tone of the letters is also revealing. These letters add an important dimension to our understanding of a man whose personality has, in spite of an extensive biographical literature, in many ways continued to elude researchers. [Ed.]

A Letter from Remete

Köszvényes Remete, 12 April 1914

Yes, this is what a Székely village is like. I am out and about all day, and now since eleven o'clock I have run out of being out and about—it's High Mass—and until it's over, even those who have stayed home would not sing half a tune, lest the Virgin Mary take offense. I say, the Romanian clergy is much better than these hypocrites, who have fed the people such nonsense. But let's begin the story at the beginning.

Upon arrival at Marosvecse, the carriage that had been ordered—wasn't there. I had to pass the time in the waiting room from six to eight, then go to the notary's office, where the carriage was inquired after by telephone. Word came from Felső-Répa that "it had just left." So by ten o'clock it was there—until then, I watched the Maros (which doesn't flow there calmly at all[1]), vowing that if they weren't outstandingly polite and amiable to me in Felső-Répa, then I'd be rude and threatening. I arrived by noon. They said they had ordered a carriage at the proper time but the driver hadn't kept his word (I don't believe it). The notary is a sickly, angry man, but at least his family did everything to make up for this unpleasant reception.

There was slight trouble with the first singers: there were about six women; one started a song, and the others accompanied her with confused mumbling. It took some time before I realized that the other five, even though they had come to *sing*, had no ear at all and were incapable of any musical performance. I eliminated them and amused myself with the remaining woman for about two hours. She is illiterate, and yet she sang a few composed songs;[2] she even knows this one:

! I obtained no colindas, in part because I didn't

want to bother the notary, sickly as he is. (That night I shared a room with an asthmatic old man.)

Next came Idecspataka, where twenty colindas turned up, mostly very different from the ones I'd known. There were songs, too, but the gypsies played miserably. It turned out that the second violin was

tuned 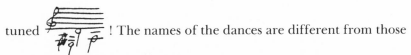 ! The names of the dances are different from those

in Répa. (That night I shared a room with mice.) Collecting was very pleasant, because I was able to do it by myself all day in a peasant house, with women, without any disturbing circumstances.

From here, I traveled twenty-six kilometers by carriage (partly in the rain) to Libánfalva. Oh, Libánfalva and Hodák! What beautiful memories! The notary having been fired, a Hungarian "gentleman" notarizes on a temporary basis (Madaras); he received me with the greatest affability (as had the one in Répa; one can see the influence of deputy sheriffdom[3]). But he had imagined the collecting Hungarian-style; they order the people to come up and then order them to sing, sparing no attendants,[4] and other coercive means! Aside from that, he knows only Hungarian and kept nudging the good Romanians in Hungarian, in true Magyar fashion—with the most serious face. They, of course, didn't understand a single word of his talk. (A notary such as he thinks that he alone will turn six thousand souls into Hungarians if he keeps speaking Hungarian to them.) When it turned out that I was not getting anywhere at the notary's office because the people who had been called in (and clumsily chosen) knew nothing, I declared that we'd have to go to the peasant house. So we took off— me, the notary, the deputy notary, the public tutor, three scribes, the notary's younger brother, and two teachers—and we all went to a peasant house, to a woman who was apparently completely "peasant" and who could sing well (on the way, we stopped at a gypsy's; we thronged in his little hut for about half an hour, about thirty of us, including the poor notary with his elegant smile and aristocratic profile). So the woman opened her mouth, and her voice boomed over us like the howlation[5] of a prima donna. I declared that it was utterly impossible to record anything from her. Before we left, the woman suddenly wanted to boast of a few broken fragments of German. We asked, where did she learn German? "I was in Vienna," she said! That's the kind of singer they got for me in Libánfalva (it is true, she couldn't read or write). I had to go to Görgényhodák, where I did have some success after all. A few girls came together; before *each* song, they had to be egged on for about half an hour. The next day, I had a rendezvous with one of the teachers at half past ten. I go; the house is locked. I go to the inn to have dinner: well, who is there, merrily playing cards with the two priests and the innkeeper, but the teacher? The Orthodox priest helped me very much in everything.

From here on, the period of omelettes and milk began. That's all I had at the teachers' houses in the next three villages! But at least they helped me, with great zeal. A few even remembered a notice about my lecture,[6] which contained, so they said, an invitation for the esteemed Romanian public to support me in my work. I read an article in a weekly paper myself: it was written by an eye- and earwitness who had even talked to the five people from Hunyad. The communication is so thorough, he even says how much the society paid each singer; the only small lapse that crept in was that the lecture had been given by "Professor Konti." "Professor Konti," the earwitness further says, "has visited most of the Romanian countryside," etc., etc.

At any rate, it's a good thing that the Romanian teacherdom begins to be aware, here and there, of who I am and what I want.

I have traveled on awful roads, in terrible carriages. It is true that the earth here is like a sponge soaked with water. We walked from Orsova to Kincses right during the great rain on Thursday. From there, also on foot, we went to Felső-Oroszi, where they know, make, and use the Alphorn, but—they make it out of the bark of a tree, freshly scaled off or pulled off, and this tree is ready to be scaled in only two weeks! I curse the Academy of Music! In a few more villages, the same pleasantness was repeated: the women hardly wanted to begin singing, and not just before the first song but before each one. I don't know what kind of savage people they are! In the last village, they have dances such as: I. a) "de-a-lungu" (first boys only, girls later; a round dance, but without holding, in which the dancers face the direction of the motion; when the girls join, they form a second, outer circle) and b) "împcelecata" (= halting), similar to the de-a-lungu, an irregular couple dance that has steps, a stop, and slow turns in it; and II. a) "bătută" (= "învârtiţă"), an irregular turn in couples that goes over into b) "tiganeasca," which is a slower, irregular turn in couples (of Hungarian origin, it seems), and then they return to the faster-turning batuta. This is a dance cycle.

In addition, there is "brâu," danced by women only, at weddings, in closed circles and holding tightly together. (In Libánfalva, Kincses, and Orsova they have a dance called "marioară" instead, which may be identical to brâu.

Plus, they know the Hungarian "bărbunc."[7]

There are many melodies for *Turka*[8] dances, belonging to two groups: "de-a-lungu Turcii" and "bătută Turcii."

The dirges can be divided into two categories: "la prevedj," lamenting at the house—several melodies, sung in the evening—and "de glǎsit," one melody sung at burials. As I approached Székely country, Székely elements began to turn up one after another: first the bodice, then Székely jugs, Székely tiles with Hungarian *fecit* ["made by"], and finally bǎrbunc, and the strangest thing—that bridal laments are called "siratau"[9] in Oroszi.

So one arrives in Székely country with the greatest expectations, and there one sees neither bodice, nor jugs, nor "şiratǎu."

To make things promising right at the start, the gypsy was reluctant to play: he could not, he this, he that. Then he played—all kinds of abominations: horrors like "sima sebes" or "forgató." In my misery, I recorded it. Fortunately, we found a pipe player who was the first to produce "cum se cade"[10] Hungarian dance music. I learned that the Székely pipe players here call *that* hole on the pipe "zegna." (What kind of word could that be?) Unfortunately, that is the only result so far in Remete. The "good old singing women," those wenches dressed in servants' garb, sing in such a shaky voice, are so insecure, and giggle so much that they forget notated tunes from one day to the next (I whistle it to them in vain; they are unable to sing them after me)—in a word, they are hideous. On top of it all, they talk about forints. At first I thought that in this *big city*, where I have to pay for my room and board, at least the singers won't demand money. But if they do, and then for the most part sing melodies that I've already transcribed a hundred times already—then goodbye Székely collection. The certitude that I won't find anything entirely new is depressing anyway; after all this begging, all I'll get are mostly variants suffering from old-age deformity.

Tomorrow, *Tuesday*, I'll try my luck in Köszvényes, then on Wednesday in Jobbágytelke, not so much for the sake of the songs as for that of the dance music with pipes. Afterward, maybe I'll visit a few Romanian villages. And if I can't collect there because of their Holy Week, then I'll show up in Vásárhely[11] one fine day.

At any rate, I will be home Tuesday morning at a quarter to seven, when *the concierge should be at the summer station*. If one can't collect in Remete, at least one can eat, although I'd prefer it the other way around. It is true, things could be even worse, if one could neither collect nor eat.

So this is the end of the Hungarian collection for me. I have no desire to go fishing in hogwash and pick misshapen bones. At most, I will collect Hungarian in mixed-language villages from now on, if I can find any, and there I can recoup with Romanian, and I won't be forced to spend days in a single place completely in vain.

These two strange flowers[12] grew on the Kincses meadow. One resembles a cyclamen, but is larger. It turns out that in Gyergyóalfalu [a pure Hungarian village] they still use Alphorns. God forbid I should go there: the horn players would surely be ashamed to blow the horn, and if they did, after a long entreaty, taps would come out.

Remete, April 13

Wouldn't it be possible to hire a domestic in Vásárhely? Maybe a Romanian one? Many go, for instance, from Felső-Oroszi to Pest, to be servants.

A Letter from the Estate of Baron Kohner

[24] August 1918

I have gotten quite used to having a butler push the chair under me when I sit down to dinner; I am becoming quite good at dishing out the food onto my tray and not beside it; nor do I feel too much *gène* in the big leather chair after dinner. Even so, it gets stranger by the day what big apparatus is used for everything: what a to-do for every single meal! When they set the table and put out all those innumerable plates, when the butlers get dressed in their gala outfits! When everything is ready they don their impeccably white gloves, open the doors wide, and then *feierlicher Einzug der Gäste zu Tisch*.[13] So much ado, so much work, so much ceremony before each stuffing! What an artificial lifestyle! What highfalutin manners!

3 butlers + a few maids + who knows how many kitchen workers; 4–5 people work in the laundry room at all times: they wash on Monday and Tuesday, they fold on Wednesday, they iron on the other days. I know this exactly, because I've camped there a lot, having found a good source in one of the ironing women, who gave me some "fine" songs. Another time we visited the tomato-cooking girls, where I kept on transcribing until 11 at night; a "Mr. Manager," with a characteristically black beard, was hobnobbing with the girls and ensuring order in a somewhat brusque voice. They sang various seasonal workers' songs about a bailiff, Mr. József Májer, and "Adolf Kohner's carriage" (*sic!*); occasionally the baron himself showed up with his family, or Lolla on horseback with her entourage.

It was with the Slovaks, though, that we came off the most oddly.

We went into their shed: the floor is sticky mud from the plains. There is no table, the seats are muddy. We nonetheless managed to obtain a clean bench, and collected a few songs with great difficulty, as well as—something else, with no difficulty at all. Even while we were there, people kept touching their legs and their waists. But by the time we got back to the castle!— Two of Lolla's nephews competed in removing the fleas from her white dress, or making them jump off, so she ran in horror to change her clothes. Since then, we have been catching fleas all the time; I, for one, had a booty of 20 a day for three days, and they are still not completely gone.

We had a pleasant surprise tonight. We were sitting in front of the castle at 9 in the evening. Suddenly the seasonal worker girls showed up to say goodbye in song. An accordion (!) started to play, and the girls began to dance. Then one girl left the ranks and—with the words "honorable baron"—asked Kohner for a dance. The little Kósa[14] was the briskest dancer of all, shaking a leg now with Lolla, now with Wanda,[15] now with both at the same time. All of a sudden they started a strange hand-waving and clapping dance to some Czech melody: "I don't speak, you don't speak, it doesn't become you to speak."

Wanda arrived here on the 20th. They are giving her a hard time because of the loss of some document or other. Did you know about this? I didn't. Ani did a fine number, too: she lost her purse, with 100 crowns and Wanda's silver cigarette holder!

Kató[16] is wherever there is a chance for a prank: she irons in the laundry room, crawls under the table and scares the girls, and crawls into the cauldrons when they cook tomatoes; she "helps" and drives everyone to despair.

There are as many guests here as in a grand hotel. Hardly a day goes by without someone arriving or leaving. Adolf Fényes came today, and Kornstein is coming tomorrow.[17] I am leaving the day after tomorrow (the 26th). I've gathered everything collectible, I've been all over, I've read a Maupassant novel—*der Mohr hat seine Pflicht getan, der Mohr kann gehen.*[18] I give *you* "time off," though, as long as Elza[19] needs you.

So I've given you a brief sketch of my life here. Let's leave the rest, the detailed report, until September, so something is left over for then.

By the way, I've been weighed. I weigh 52 kilograms gross. That's enough!

B.

A Letter from the Swiss Alps

Arolla, 11 July 1930

My sweet little one!

In my postcard written three days ago I forgot to tell you that the previous day I had received your 2 July letter—the one in which you got up early, at 4:45. Your next letter, in which you wrote about Weisshaus,[20] came yesterday. I was amused to read your first letter, because 2 July was the worst day so far. I got up early—not at 4:45, though (I would never do *that*). By the way, the position of the sun here at 4:45 corresponds to about 3:45 in Budapest. Anyway, I got up at about 6:30 and left at 8; you know the rest. You behave very well, as far as letter writing is concerned; you apply yourself, which is very good. Now, of course, when I go to Pontresina, there will be a slight irregularity with my mail, so there will be a longer pause before I get your news. Especially if the weather should be bad on the 14th, in which case I would have to postpone my departure by a day. Or shall I take my *umbrella* to Haudères? I'll think this over. For no matter how beautiful it is here, I would like to see other landscapes too, as soon as possible. For I've already gone or climbed to all the places that are accessible to me, some of them even twice. So now I can only have repeats. One may say, I can go myself as high as 3,000 meters; whatever is higher is so wild and steep, or else so icy, that it can be tackled only with a guide. And I balk at that. Since I last got soaked on (I think) 4 July, I was able to stay dry on every excursion. In the last four days it hasn't rained at all; one could say the weather was *too* good, because I was out all day four days in a row! I couldn't just watch the beautiful blue sky from home. Don't worry, though. These excursions are not as big as those in Davos or Montana. There I had to climb at least 1,000 meters each time before I reached the right altitude. Here, 600 will do it, because my starting point is higher. Thus I am much less tired after my excursions—in fact, I am not tired at all. That's how it was possible to have excursions four days in a row. Here are the results of my sojourn:

First day, 29 June. Ascent of Mont Dolin, 2,960 meters. With less than complete success.

30 June. The same, with more success (edelweiss plucking).

1 July. Rest.

2 July. Rain.

3 July. Excursion to Plan Bertol (2,700 meters) There I picked out a

peak that I thought I could climb. There wasn't enough time to do so, though; therefore on

4 July I returned there and almost made it to the top of the chosen mountain (maybe 2,900 meters).

5 and 6 July. Rest or rain?

7 July. Ascent to the bottom of the Glacier de Torgnon (2,500 meters at most) along a glacial drift. A glacial drift is the broken stone that the glacier has been carrying along and accumulating since ancient times, often in the form of a very long mountain ridge. N.B.: There is a noticeable little path along that debris of stone. A great fog, clouds, hardly any sun. Dissatisfaction. No view. For this reason, on

8 July I repeated the same trip, with better weather. I saw another alpine hen, even two together; one was certainly a rooster. This time, one of them said *krrrr, krrrr* and waddled along those bloody large masses of stone with magical skill.

9 July. I went around Mont Dolin and returned passing through the mountain pass between Mont Dolin and La Roussette, amid fantastic masses of stone and rock (2,600 or 2,700 meters?). Although I had previously inquired whether this pass could be passed, I still looked from the pass toward Arolla with some trepidation: didn't there lurk some unconquerable obstacle on the way back? Because if there had been, I'd have had to turn around, which would have been a lot more tiring. But fortunately there wasn't, and so the round trip was successful.

10 July. I passed by the pass called "Goat's Track" (2,850 meters) and looked down from there on the neighboring valley where a gigantic glacier sprawls sluggishly. One moment it cleared up, and the next it got cloudy again; occasionally the weather seemed quite critical, and there was even a slight drizzle on my way back, but it didn't begin to rain until 7:30, with thunder and lightning—and this morning, the familiar picture: fresh snow on the mountains as far down as 3,000 meters. Tell Peter that it has snowed on the mountaintops, but down in the valley it has only rained. It's accordingly cold. But for today I had planned a rest anyway. What's more, I won't go very far in the next two days, either.

Well, thus it has been so far. On 7 July a large and noisy family arrived: father, mother, and *five* children, the youngest could be 7–8 years old. All wearing "mountain climbing" shoes. Happy about their arrival, they made so much noise until late at night that I got angry and wanted to leave the next morning. But it turned out that they are very respectful. In the morning they only whisper and have calmed down at night, too, so my anger evaporated. Yesterday, two Snow Whites came. Well, their skins are in for a rough time, unless they are going to wear gloves and veils. The Frenchman (a bank employee) and the two German dames are still here; they will leave about the same time I will. The flower identifications continue, with the help of a book. I will send the remainder of my collection next time, before I leave.

I found out that the main profession of the lady of the house is—midwife! Namely, in Evolena. She is asking the good Lord and the women of Evolena to plan the childbirths for the winter, when she lives in Evolena, not during the summer season. If her clients should give birth now, they call her on the telephone (there is a telephone at the hotel!), and she can mule her way[21] down to Evolena, leaving guests and everybody else in the lurch. But we also have a cook and a waitress now. I think I could have called you on the telephone from here, I really felt very much like it, but it is so uncertain when you are home! (Out of the bathtub.) Yesterday I discovered with some consternation that some of my handkerchiefs modestly lack a mark. Modesty is nice, but in this case I would prefer to be a little ostentatious.

I wanted to start some very onerous work yesterday: darning! Well, my goodness! What teeny-tiny needles these are, with openings that even a microbe would find it hard to creep through. How on earth is one supposed to thread that thick brown yarn through that opening; is there a living creature able to do that? No, there isn't! I acquired, in the store, a needle as big as a smaller larding needle; I will be able to work with that one. The only result of my exertions last night: I pricked my finger!

Of course, I have midafternoon snacks. I have them every day, only I eat differently from usual. The butter has been so abominable so far that I could only get it down at breakfast. I had crackers with tea for my afternoon snack (during excursions, too). Since yesterday, the butter has been better. A few times I had milk and crackers for my snack. Besides, I drink milk before going to bed and before getting up. The food is pretty good—I eat enough, as you can see: I am sufficiently well nourished.

Of course, this is the cheapest of the five hotels; that is why I chose it. But it is really good. They are working on the bathroom (only the tub is still missing), and there will be electric lighting (but only after I'm gone). Now I received a kerosene lamp. I use it for work. So far I finished nine pages of score. Not a lot. But the weather has been too nice! I, too, am very glad of Abbazia. I have already written that your departure should be on *28 July*, haven't I?

Well, now, I've written a lot too, haven't I? How is swimming?!
I hug and kiss you many times, very many times indeed.

Daddybéla

I received the cigarette papers.

A Letter from Cairo

Cairo, 19 March 1932

My sweet Ditta!

My head has become quite large, larger than a barrel, what with all that has gone into it these past four days. I'll begin with the landing—which wasn't as easy as in England, for example. This is a different continent, after all, and it is harder to disembark here, harder even than in America. The ship stopped outside the port to take a European-looking gentleman brought on board in a motorboat by several soldierlike types wearing fezzes, with nice clean uniforms but barefoot. He sat down in the lounge, and we dutifully sat around him. He was the district physician. They brought him coffee (maybe even liquor?); he drank it, then inquired about the number and state of the passengers, the ship's capacity, itinerary, and schedule, and then the passengers were counted in his presence. His duty was thereby done, and he left. It all took half an hour; I thought this was fairly simple. But in the meantime the passport committee came. They even asked questions of the passengers and behaved in a very authoritative manner. They stamped the passports and said, "All right." I thought it was all right, but it wasn't. In the meantime the ship had come to anchor, but no one moved; we were just waiting. We were waiting for the city doctor, who was late, despite the demented hollering of the porters and hotel employees standing on the shore. At length he came and sat down, and we thronged around him. All of a sudden I heard a voice behind my back: "Monsieur Béla" and "Congress." It turned out that a committee from Alexandria had come to fetch me and liberated me from the ship in a second. They took my picture upon landing (I'll bring it home). Well, I thought to myself, we're off to a funny start; what else is yet to come? We quickly got into a cab and took off. All of a sudden it was stop again! Get off, get the luggage out, it's the customs house. I was freed again soon, thanks to my protectors; the only question I was asked was whether I had any instruments with me. I said no, I forgot to bring my piano. We arrived at the train station, and I boarded the train with my entourage, who were teacherlike Arab gentlemen and stayed faithfully at my side until departure.

· 213 ·

They strongly discouraged me from using the train restaurant and made me buy bread and eggs instead (I still don't know why). Finally I started out toward the delta of the Nile. No sooner had we begun to move than a mass of rags came rolling toward the door of the compartment: it was a beggar, crawling on his hands and bottom, holding out the mere stump of his leg into the compartment. (This is just what you would have needed!!)

Before long, we saw villages with mud walls, camels, bisons, donkeys, all kinds of strange things. Palm trees. And Arabic inscriptions everywhere, in Arabic first. This is really Arab country, not just fake Arab like Algeria. We arrived at the first station. Great noise, lots of vendors—you could barely look out the window, so emphatically were they offering their merchandise. A lot of strange, big, eagle-like birds circle above the cities. I learned that these fulfill a sanitary mission: they do away with meat scraps, carcasses, and whatnot. Cairo is full of them; you are awakened by their screeching in the morning. I arrived in Cairo at 4 o'clock.

I was greeted at the Cairo train station by the obligatory din and Takács.[22] There was no official Arab reception. We took a cab. Two Arabs climbed on board without being asked (they were hoping to help carry the luggage upon arrival at the house). Takács had a hard time prodding them off the coach with my umbrella!!

Shortly after my arrival at the inn, Hefni, the secretary of the congress came; apparently he hadn't found me at the station (no wonder, in that chaos). He immediately invited me to a session, but I didn't go until about 6 o'clock, after being given directions by Takács. Just then, Iraqi musicians were blowing, fiddling, plucking, and striking away in my subcommittee. (There are about seven subcommittees; everyone chooses one for himself.) Hindemith and the quarter-tone Hába are also here. The schedule is like this: sessions from 9 to 11 and from 4 to 7 in the afternoon, concerts at 9:30 (with in- and out-digenous Arabs playing).

I'll tell you in person about how the work was going. In our group there are a lot of debates, but in some of the other subcommittees they've nearly come to blows. The Arabs want to modernize everything, and the Europeans (with a few exceptions) want to preserve the old. The discussions are led in a rather confused way; all this chaos is enough to give you a headache. We haven't seen any prominent personalities, and it seems that there will be no official receptions, parties, and similar things.

I have seen little so far—it is true, time has been short as we are only free from 1:30 to 4. One day Takács and I strolled around in the bazaar area, and another day someone took me to the closest pyramids (the ones with the sphinx) by car. Yesterday we saw the dance of the whirling dervishes, as an official program, from 3 to 5; afterward we visited a mosque and an uninhabited private dwelling (in the old city). In the evening, supper with the Takácses, and then, at 11, a car ride by moonlight to—the Dead City. This is a cemetery, but—*what* a cemetery! Streets winding among small houses (one story, two at the most); the walls have doors and windows on them. The graves are behind them. This is a whole separate large part of the city; silent, empty streets all entangled in one another. Here and there, a large, domed edifice: the grave of a caliph. Or else: a crumbling old mosque. And great silence. Yet smack in the middle of this big, big Dead City there are a few streets alive, like a small island. The island of the living in the Dead City, with cafés, shops, everything that the living need. This was something entirely strange, especially at midnight! Then we left and returned to the city, through the desert. All of a sudden we entered an area of ever-stronger odors and smoke. What's that? It was the trash of Cairo being burned! What on earth could it be, the smoke of which we inhaled?! This afternoon I was supposed to go to see a Byzantine (Greek Orth.) church service, but this was too much of a good thing. I stayed home and am writing a letter!

What is this Cairo like? In the "European" section, there are large houses (as many as 6 or 7 stories), with European shops, streetcars, buses, policemen (traffic and otherwise). But in the street you see mainly Arabs. Every shade of color from black to light brown. The lower classes wear big, white shirtlike whatevers and turbans; the "intelligentsia" wears European clothes with fezzes. The women are half-veiled. You can't go 10 steps without being pestered by street vendors. But there are hardly any beggars! The shops in the smallest streets are pretty Arabic-looking, with an odd clientele. The better cafés are also full of Arabs wearing fezzes and smoking the *nargileh*. The old city is, in some places, pure Orient: garbage, excrement, other rubbish in the narrow streets (covered in the bazaar area), swarming with people. Odd, protruding wooden cages with bars on the second and third floors of the houses (harem windows), and lots and lots of mosques. They don't pester you here, though; at most they give you a good look. Some stores have Armenian inscriptions in addition to the Arabic ones. The day before yesterday I almost stepped on a dead cat (there are no dogs!); today I saw a blanket on the sidewalk somewhere. It was teeming with flies. What could it be? I went closer; well, it seemed that a sick person was lying there, out in the street, and a woman was cowering at his side, taking care of him (for continuation, see above). Such are some of the things one sees here! It's a completely different world after all. Hornbostel, whom I have known for a long time, has never been in "the Orient" before. He is happy as a child. The poor man suffers from the heart; he came here with his doctor's permission and is so glad of everything, the sunshine, the warm weather, the music, the bazaars, the narrow streets. I am glad, too, but would very much like to hear some news from home. Today is Saturday; maybe I'll get something on Monday. This letter will be taken by Monday's ship; you may get it next Saturday. Send it on to Mama and Aunt Irma (to whom, by the way, I shall write a postcard today).

Many kisses
Béla

Today was the first *nice* and warm day. Tomorrow morning I will be taken by car to see some pyramids lying farther south.

So far, I have written you postcards from Saloniki and Athens, a letter from Alexandria, and a postcard from Cairo. This is my fifth mailing.

These are the Arabic numerals! They are on the telephone dials, too!

A Letter from New York

The address: 110–31, 73 Road,
    Forest Hills,
    Long Island,
    N.Y.
    U.S.A.

The address should be like this, in 5 lines; we will stay in this apartment through May 7.

24 December 1940

Dear Béla and Péter!

I write to both of you, in two copies; I will mail one copy to you, Béla, today, and the other one to you, Péter, in a week. If you, Béla, receive it, show it to Aunt Irma and then send it on to Péter, if you haven't yet received his copy in the meantime. And you, Péter, send yours on to Béla, if you haven't yet received his copy.

It is 1 P.M. here, and Christmas night where you are. Of course, we think of you a lot, wondering who is spending Christmas where. We also think of past Christmases and—are lonely. The postal service is totally unreliable, which is very bad. We have received a single letter from you, Péter (written at the end of October, arrived by clipper about four weeks ago); from you, Béla, we have a postcard sent from Kolozsvár on 1 Nov., received four days ago. At the same time came Elza's postcard written in Pest at the end of Oct. (as well as a letter from Julis written at the same time).

So far we have written you, Péter, about three letters from here, and about as many to you, Béla. In addition, I sent $250 by cable on 27 Nov.—this is the dollar sum received from the [Hungarian] National Bank. In two of my letters I wrote about the issue of my passport, telling you to go to [the Ministry of] Internal Affairs and press for the extension of my passport; this was sent over by the Hungarian main consulate here under file number 5823. If they have processed it, then pay Internal Affairs for the cable expenses, so they cable the main consulate here to that effect. And write us only by air mail (as long as it's possible to do so), the letter takes 2 months by boat!—

On 7 December we took a furnished apartment at the above address. This is about 16 kilometers from the center of New York, but the subway stop (express) is right in front of our door, so for 5 cents we can be downtown in 20 minutes anytime. The trains run frequently, day and night, without interruption. It is much more pleasant to live here than downtown: the streets are broad; you can see fields, woods, and ponds; the car traffic is great but not noisy. Only the subway rumbles every minute. We have stores and every comfort. The heating system is so strong that we have to turn off three-quarters of the radiators. One of the windows in our bedroom can be left wide open (if there's no wind). We have started to become Americanized, for instance, in our meals. In the morning, we have grapefruit, cereals[23] with cream, dark bread with butter, egg or bacon or fish. At some point between 2 and 4 in the afternoon we have coffee with bread and butter or something else (this is not American style, though, for the Americans eat something light at 1). Our main meal is between 8 and 10 at night: raw carrots, lettuce, radish, olives, and whatnot with bread and butter, maybe soup; meat; maybe some pastries. Cooking takes up a bit too much time; but there are all kinds of restaurants here (we haven't tried them yet). We have been having some linguistic difficulties with words such as "yeast" or "caraway seed"; but we're getting over them. My head is full with a lot of new words, with the names of streets and subway stations, with maps of train networks and the multiple possibilities of changing trains—all things necessary for life here, but otherwise fruitless. We live on the sixth floor;[24] there are no more floors above us. The lobby[25] of the house has a low ceiling but is long and wide, heated, and furnished with couches, small tables, and lights that are perpetually burning. Here are the residents' mailboxes; everyone goes to get his mail himself. The concierge is Mr. Janoško, that is, pán Janoško, a Slovak from near Kosice, he still speaks Hungarian pretty well (and, of course, Slovak), although he has been here for 30 years. He has been a widower for 12 years and has 11 living children, who all speak only English. One of his sons-in-law—a minor office employee with an electrical company—took us on an outing to the seashore in his comfortable 4-seat car. We stopped at their 4-room[26] apartment, provided with every comfort; they treated us to cold pork in aspic, prepared by Janoško (it was lunchtime). This is what the offspring of concierges are like here. We have had a lot to learn in order to handle the various electric and gas appliances, corkscrews, can openers, etc., as well as means of transportation, but we are beginning to cope. Only occasionally do mishaps occur—like, for instance, the other day, when we wanted to take the subway to New York's southernmost point; I wasn't sure where to change to what (the signs aren't exactly conspicuous; they are rather incomplete and confusing), so that we traveled back and forth underground for 3 hours, until our time ran out and we returned home without accomplishing anything, with our tails between our legs, and of course always underground.

I became doctorized[27] on 25 Nov. What a ceremony it was! To begin with, I had to have my measurements taken, in yards, feet, and fathoms; I had to have my head size and my shoulder width measured and to send in the figures. At the university, we were all dressed up in gowns and cloaks, and then proceeded to march in ceremoniously, to the peal of discreet organ music. I had strict orders to rise when I heard my name, to take off my gown when addressed by the president, and to start walking in his direction to accept my diploma when he was finished with his speech. In the meantime they would hang the pink velvet ribbon of the order of music on my back; afterward I could go back to my seat. And that's how it all happened.

Fortunately we, the recipients, didn't have to give speeches.

A deanlike person pointed out, in his preliminary speech, how beautiful it was that Columbia University was able, in these troubled times, to bestow this title on a native of the Hungarian *puszta*, a son of France, a scientist from England, plus a professor from the United States.

We have played a few times in New York; on 1 Dec. I went to Cleveland and thereabouts for 8 days. There somehow I met Oszkár Jászi.[28] The Cleveland Hungarians threw a big party: with gypsy music and *palotás* (!!).[29] Hungarians here, Hungarians there, Hungarians everywhere; but we can't be too happy about this, because the second generation barely speaks the language any more.

We think of you both a lot and can hardly wait for news from you, Aunt Irma, and Elza. Who knows how much longer we'll have mail service, if something isn't going to happen next spring to end even this imperfect way of communication!

To satisfy the law, we appeared at—the post office in Jamaica, which was the closest to us (4–5 subway stations, but farther out). They duly took our fingerprints (we had to wash in benzine afterward) and put us on oath. It took us 3–4 hours, what with the crowd that was there. They expected 3 million foreigners, but they've had 4 million so far; it is possible that the final figure will be close to 5 million.

On 9 Dec. we received a cable from Lisbon on 9 Dec. [*sic*], to the effect that our luggage will be sent on its way from there on the 13th, aboard the Excambión. This ship came in yesterday, but we still don't know whether our luggage has arrived; there were shipments for 3,000 people, and as of noon today nothing could be found out. Tomorrow is a holiday, so we won't know anything until the day after. Isn't this annoying? And we thought we'd have everything by Christmas!

Of course, one can't write about what's most important; but maybe that's not a bad thing after all. No one knows anything for sure anyway, people just talk without any rhyme or reason. Only the tone is completely different, across the board.[30]

We kiss all of you many times,

Dad

It's 6 P.M. now; X-mas night is over where you are. How was everything—for everyone?! Since yesterday, we have been thinking about home all the time, almost every minute.

Hugs to all of you,

Ditta

I just wanted to add that on the day of our arrival, 30 Oct., we sent the following cable to you, Béla:

"Safely arrived notify everyone."

It seems you never got this cable!

We don't have a Christmas tree; the building has one, downstairs in the lobby, lit by lightbulbs according to the local custom; pán Janoško set it up and ornamented it.

There are Christmas trees in the streets, on the squares, in department stores, even at train stations.

Bartók's Letters to Fritz Reiner

Budapest, 29 October 1928

Dear friend,

Thank you very much for the greeting telegram you and Murray sent me. But don't think you were the first to break the news: the news agency *Est* beat you to it, announcing on 2 Oct. that I had won $6,000![31] This looked suspect to me, and it wasn't until I had received your telegram the same night that I was reassured of having really won something after all. A few days later I learned from foreign newspapers that at least four of us had won something; from the many contradictory reports it was impossible to figure out who had won how much. So I waited patiently until a few days ago, when the letter from Philadelphia came, with an exact description of the matter (plus a check). I don't have to tell you how much this money came in handy. We may breathe a little easier now—not to mention the publicity. One can barely imagine the sensation created in Budapest. Six thousand dollars! I kept telling everyone from the beginning that it couldn't be such a large sum, but no matter, public opinion has it that I won $6,000. I had no longer even expected to win, since things had been dragging for so long. The very day before the arrival of the news I had sent the *Druckvorlage* to Universal Edition for printing. The surprise was all the greater and more pleasant. After the official-looking commentaries, like those I had read about the four works in the *Musical Courier* a few days ago, I begin to marvel that in fact I won at all.

I had been meaning to write to you anyway, but I didn't know where you were. Finally I heard from someone in the fall that you were conducting in Cincinnati for another season. I am very sorry that the Budapest business came to nothing, although who knows whether you would have been able to stand it here. As for membership in the Upper House, that's the only thing that—in my opinion—should not have been asked for. This wasn't discussed when we spoke about the matter last winter, so I'm not even sure it was really part of your conditions.

I have played my Piano Concerto several times since my return. It was given the most divergent performances and the most divergent receptions!

The Budapest performance was rather thorough for Budapest (though the brass could never muster enough power). The one in Berlin—under Kleiber—had great *Schwung*, but there *were* quite a few accidents in the orchestra. Of course, none of the European performances were so precise or had as much assurance as the one in Cincinnati. Next week it will be performed in Amsterdam (with Monteux! Mengelberg apparently doesn't feel like it!). I wonder how it will be.

Many greetings to both of you, in true friendship—

Bartók

P.S. In the meantime I have composed another string quartet, a much lengthier one in five movements (isn't there another competition somewhere, by any chance?!!).

.

The Buckingham
101 West 57th Street
New York
17 May 1940

Dear friend,

I send you my warm greetings once again before my departure and thank you very much for the nice pictures.

I hope to be able to return to the "free" country by October at the latest.

Until I see you again, yours truly,

Béla Bartók

Schulhof[32] would like to have the Pittsburgh dates as soon as possible!

.

110–31, 73 Road, Forest Hills
Long Island, N.Y.
18 January 1941

Dear friend,

After many misadventures—all our luggage is still stuck in Lisbon—we made it here at the end of October. I am very glad that we can see each other next week and make music together.

I will arrive in Pittsburgh at 9:20 P.M. on 22 Jan. and will stay at the Schenley Hotel. Should you wish for a so-called "piano rehearsal," I will be happy to be at your disposal. Please send word to the Schenley if that be the case. I would also like to know if I should come to rehearsal at 10 A.M. or later the next day, on the 23d.

Until then, many greetings,

Béla

Denver, 16 February 1941

Dear friend,

I want to let you know, in accordance with our agreement, about my relationship with Columbia University: "Visiting Associate in Music." The appointment is for this semester (and, as the official letter states, will expire unless it is extended). I shall get $1,500 for this period and shall do scholarly work (its nature depends on me, or rather on a mutual agreement). I am to give no regular lectures, only one or two at most, if I am asked to.

Of course, I want to earn my salary: I will work about three times, five hours a week, but will be happy to do so, because this is my favorite type of work.

It is all but certain that my appointment will be extended to the next academic year. Still, as long as one doesn't have it in writing, one cannot count on it with unconditional certainty.

For this reason, and also because my relationship with my manager is deteriorating more and more, I would be very happy and grateful if you tried to do what you once mentioned concerning the Curtiss [sic] Institute. I think four or five hours of teaching per week would be enough, so I could go to Philadelphia once a week.

Of course, this does not fall under my manager's jurisdiction, so any information regarding this matter should go to my address.

My permanent address is 110–31, 73 Road, Forest Hills, Long Island, N.Y. (We shall return there from our tour on March 12.)

My warmest thanks again for all the good things you showered upon me in Pittsburgh, especially for the excellent performance, and I send many greetings to you and your wife.

Yours truly,
Béla

Permanent address: 3242, Cambridge Avenue, Bronx, N.Y. Summer address until 31 Aug.: Riverton, Vermont

28 July 1941

Dear friend,

Excuse me for disturbing you during your summer vacation. It is for the following reason.

Several months ago, I applied for a *preexamination*, i.e., for a *nonquota immigrant*[33] visa. The Washington lawyer who was retained managed skillfully (perhaps intentionally) to procrastinate with the arrangement of this matter until early July. Then I received acceptance of my request for preexamination; but in the meantime, as of 1 July, a new regulation was enacted. This requires two sponsors of American nationality to issue a moral and financial affidavit. The "moral" part is not a serious problem, but the financial sponsorship is formulated as follows: *that I personally promise and agree that I will save the U.S., counties, towns (etc.) thereof harmless against any losses and damages which may be suffered by reason of the fact that the person above mentioned will become a public charge*, etc. . . . *I shall assume responsibility for their support,*[34] etc.

Of course, the sponsors must authentically prove their financial standing.

I would like to ask you, then, if you could find two people who would agree to this.

To us this is an extremely unpleasant matter, and if it were only for my sake I would drop it all like a hot potato.

Let me just be a *visitor* until they chase me out (where they chase me should be the problem of the chasers). But bringing our minor (seventeen-year-old) son here is at stake, and apparently that is possible only on the basis of my nonquota immigration.

Columbia University has extended my employment through next year (I do some extremely interesting work there), so this would be all right, but this contract is no longer enough for the immigration authorities.

We send our warmest greetings to you and your wife.

Béla

·

Riverton, Vermont, 8 Aug. 1941

Dear friend,

Thank you very much for the kind help you offered. I am enclosing the forms. My only fear is that this whole matter is much more complicated than you believed! Read it, and you'll see what you can do. Of course, I could fill in only the data concerning myself.

They make these things exceedingly difficult and (unnecessarily) complicated now. I've enclosed a Form B and a Form C for you, and another Form B and Form C for Wallerstein, and a letter to him. I would like to ask you to very kindly forward these to him, with a short letter, maybe, since I don't think I know him personally.

N.B.: I don't have an attorney; that is, I used to have one, who, after mismanaging everything, basely deserted me. Therefore I'm asking you to please return these documents directly to me.

Don't forget that the forms may be filled out *by typewriter only*; the instructions say so in the most explicit terms.

We thank you for your kind invitation, but I think it would be simpler to travel there from New York.[35] From here, on our way back, there are only two, not very convenient, trains per day.

Fondly,
Béla

3242, Cambridge Avenue
Bronx, N.Y.
8 October 1941

Dear friend,

The papers have arrived; we've sent them to Washington, where they have been duly taken care of. Now everything depends on the good graces of the consul in Montreal.

Thank you once more for your help!

With my best wishes for the new season, I send both of you my warmest greetings.

Béla

3242, Cambridge Avenue
Bronx, N.Y.
27 October 1941

Dear friend,

Excuse me for disturbing you again, but the following complication has arisen.

My wife's immigration papers have somehow found their way to Washington separately from mine. They now demand sponsors for her too. I would like to ask you to tell me quite frankly if it would be very unpleasant for you and the other gentleman (I can't think of his name right now) to take on this sponsorship too. If the same people were the sponsors, then their financial and moral trustworthiness wouldn't have to be proved again. We could simply say that this has already taken place in regards to my application, and the relevant documents are already at the Washington office. I have a lawyer friend (in Budapest) who would do all the paperwork. All you two would have to do is sign it.

Many greetings
Béla

.

3242, Cambridge Avenue
Bronx, N.Y.
2 August 1942

Dear friend,

We thank you very much for your kind letter and invitation. However, we will be able to accept the latter, with great pleasure, only in Sept., if you are still in Westport at that time as we hope. As a matter of fact, I have not been very well since April. I run a fever up to 38 (in English, 100) degrees every blessed night. The most meticulous examinations, in the hospital and otherwise, have been in vain. The sages of medical science are unable to determine the cause. Of course, this necessitates a certain special care. I will try some change of air and environment: an acquaintance invited me to the Massachusetts coast for a few weeks. Maybe this will help, and bring me greater strength and increased mobility by September. Maybe you'll be also interested in knowing that the resolution of my immigration proceedings still remains shrouded in remote obscurity! But more of this, and many other things, in person in September.

I have written to Heinsheimer;[36] I told him to notify you when he can send you the score.

Many greetings to both of you,

Béla

NOTES

1. Allusion to the well-known *magyar nóta*, or pseudopopular song, "Maros vize folyik csendesen" (The Maros flows calmly). [Ed.]

2. The term *műdal* (art song) is used as the opposite of *népdal* (folk song) and refers here to the genre *magyar nóta*. [Ed.]

3. The local administrative office of *alispán* was often held by members of the (lower) nobility. [Ed.]

4. *Hajdú*, a liveried attendant to a local dignitary. [Ed.]

5. *Üvöltmény*, a word of Bartók's coinage. [Ed.]

6. On 18 March Bartók had given a lecture in Budapest entitled "The Musical Dialect of the Romanians of Hunedoara." [Béla Bartók, Jr.]

7. This word is the Romanian version of the Hungarian *verbunkos*. [Ed.]

8. I.e., Turkish. [Ed.]

9. The Romanian version of the Hungarian word *sirató* (dirge). [Ed.]

10. The Romanian equivalent of the French expression "comme il faut." [Ed.]

11. Bartók's wife was staying in that town (Marosvásárhely, or Tîrgu-Mureş, in Romanian). [Ed.]

12. The flowers, wrapped in paper, were included in the letter. [Béla Bartók, Jr.]

13. Festive entrance of the guests to table [Béla Bartók, Jr.]. This is an allusion to Wagner's *Tannhäuser*. [Ed.]

14. György Kósa (1897–1984), a pianist and composer who studied piano privately with Bartók and Dohnányi and composition with Kodály. [Ed.]

15. Wanda Gleiman, a friend of Bartók's. She wrote the text to one of the songs in Bartók's Op. 15. [Ed.]

16. Kató Kohner (1906–64), one of the baron's daughters. Bartók made an arrangement of the folk song "I don't speak, you don't speak" and dedicated it to the twelve-year-old Kató. See Béla Bartók, *Letters*, ed. János Demény (London: Faber and Faber, 1971), p. 141. [Ed.]

17. Adolf Fényes (1867–1940), an important Hungarian painter; and Egon Kornstein (1891–1983), violist of the Waldbauer-Kerpely quartet, who later changed his name to Egon Kenton and became a noted musicologist in the United States. [Ed.]

18. "The Moor has done his duty, the Moor may go." [Béla Bartók, Jr.]

19. Elza Oláh-Tóth, *née* Bartók, the composer's sister (1886–1955). [Ed.]

20. Imre Weisshaus (1905–), composer and pianist who studied with Bartók. He later moved to France and changed his name to Paul Arma. [Ed.]

21. Another of Bartók's whimsical coinages: *öszvéregelhet*, or "she may ride a mule." [Ed.]

22. Jenő Takács (b. 1902), Hungarian composer from the Austrian province of Burgenland, who at this time was living in Cairo. [Ed.]

23. Because cereals are not a staple of the Hungarian diet, Bartók uses a rather convoluted locution to describe them: "pattogatott *buza*" (or "pop-*wheat*"), with the second word in italics to stress that it is not "pattogatott kukorica," or popcorn, with which Béla and Péter would be familiar. [Ed.]

24. Bartók notes the difference between American method of counting floors and that in Europe, where the first floor is not counted: the sixth floor would have been the fifth in Hungary. [Ed.]

25. Bartók gives the English word "lobby" in parentheses after the Hungarian equivalent (which, incidentally, happens to be another word of English origin: "hall"). [Ed.]

26. After the European fashion, Bartók did not count the kitchen and bath with the rooms. [Ed.]

27. Bartók facetiously uses the newly coined *doktorosítottak meg*. He is referring to the honorary doctorate he received from Columbia University. [Ed.]

28. Oszkár Jászi (1875–1957), leading progressive politician. He left Hungary in 1919 and emigrated to the United States in 1925. [Ed.]

29. Old Hungarian dance, related in style to the *verbunkos*. A famous example occurs in Erkel's opera *Hunyadi László* (1844). [Ed.]

30. This oblique paragraph refers to the political situation, which was not safe to discuss in a letter. [Ed.]

31. Bartók's String Quartet No. 3 won the $3,000 prize of the Musical Fund Society in Philadelphia. [Ed.]

32. Andrew Schulhof was Bartók's American agent. [Ed.]

33. The italicized words are in English in the original. [Ed.]

34. The italicized material is in English in the original. [Ed.]

35. The Bartóks had to travel to Montreal to have their nonquota immigration applications processed by the American consulate there. [Ed.]

36. Hans Walter Heinsheimer, musicologist representing Boosey & Hawkes. [Ed.]

37. Hans Walter Heinsheimer, musicologist representing Boosey & Hawkes. [Ed.]

Béla Bartók: An Interview

by Dezső Kosztolányi

TRANSLATED BY DAVID E. SCHNEIDER

One of the most important Hungarian poets of Bartók's generation, Dezső Kosztolányi (1885–1936) made his reputation with his first collection of poems, *Négy fal között* (Between four walls) in 1907. His five novels—including *Édes Anna* (Sweet Anna), recently translated into English (New York, 1991)—appeared between 1921 and 1926. Kosztolányi also worked as a journalist and, together with his circle of university friends in Budapest, founded *Nyugat* (West), Hungary's foremost literary journal (1908–41).

The present interview for the *Pesti Hírlap* (Pest news) was conducted in Bartók's apartment in Buda (Szilágyi Dezső tér), shortly after Bartók had returned from a meeting of the International Society for Contemporary Music in Prague (15–19 May 1925). It is notable not only for Bartók's recollections of his earliest musical experiences and his views on the musical trends of the early 1920s but also for Kosztolányi's vivid description of the composer. [Trans.]

·

Silver head. The fine head of a silver statue which the smith has worked to perfection with a tiny hammer over the course of many years. The body, which lifts the forty-four-year-old head, fragile, small, nearly disappears in the room where a lamp burns even during the day. He barely moves. What would movements even be for? Every strength, impetus, is needed for his art, for his music, where it is possible to gesticulate freely, with arms extended to the heavens, to move in ecstatic dream. Only his eyes live on the calm surface of his face underneath a forehead white as virgin snow—sparkling, attentive, dark eyes, the seeing brain, which leaps out from the farthest summit of our skull, and, in the desperation of the thirst for knowledge, breaks two holes for itself to peek through, to look into the world, to see what is around it. I hate the approach that seeks the artist in everyday life. I know there were great composers who better resembled pot-bellied sacristans or cow herders or prize wrestlers than the fanciful picture the amateur paints for himself. But this man who sits in front of me is harmoniously proportioned, taut and sonorous in body; he reminds me of his compositions. His surroundings: a Bösendorfer grand, which was put at his disposal by the Bösendorfer company; a table from Kalotaszeg, on which a Transylvanian peasant carefully carved "Bartók Béla"; and, up on the wall on a sky-blue stand, three sky-blue Hungarian peasant plates. Out of place with this are several foreign music journals on the piano (League of Composers Review, Der Auftakt, *etc.*).

—What instrument did you play first?

He. The drum.

—The drum?

He. Yes. I got a drum when I was two. Mother says I drummed all the time. I tried out rhythms on it.

—Later?

He. The piano. I must have been four years old—Mother tells this also—I plunked out Hungarian popular songs with one finger.

—And after that?

He. My first printed music. I got it for my fifth birthday. I remember this. My father—a member of the gentry[1] of Gömör county and the director of an agricultural school in Nagyszentmiklós, Torontál county[2]—loved music and composed. My mother liked to play the piano. Both of them encouraged me. But practicing scales bored me. Like every child, I was bored to death. Mother said, "Learn to play the piano, my son. If company comes over and they ask you to play the piano for a dance, what a shame it would be to say you don't know how. And how nice if somebody plays the piano." *(A pause.)*

—When did you start to compose?

He. When I was nine. These were sort of dance pieces, Viennese waltzes, csárdáses, sonatinas, imitations of Mozart. Mother keeps them in Pozsony.

—Today *(I glance at the Bösendorfer, which, full of past melodies and dormant storms, is meaningfully silent in the room)*, do you play the piano frequently?

He. If I must. Sometimes days go by—no—also weeks, weeks, and I don't sit down. *(He, too, looks at the piano.)* Only before my concerts. I am forced to give concerts. *(His voice is soft, colorless.)* I've just come from Prague *(where he concertized and represented Hungary triumphantly in the international music competition).*[3]

—Which is the first composition you truly consider your own?

He. The Fourteen Pieces for Piano.[4] The First Quartet.

—The *Kossuth Symphony*?

He (making a gesture). Not that. Its form is not yet mature. *The Wooden Prince* I like least from this point of view.

—How do you work? Systematically?

He. I can say this: I don't like to mix work. If I begin something, then I live only for it until it is finished.

—At the desk? At the piano?

He. Between the desk and the piano.

—Is the collection of Hungarian folk songs still continuing?

He. I have not been on a collecting expedition since 1918. The work is difficult in the occupied territories.[5]

—Before your appearance, Hungarian music had a kind of Kazinczy era—an international, European epoch—which was elevated into a Petőfi-Arany era by your activities.[6] It is interesting that this movement occurred only a half-century later in music than it did in literature.

He. However—I think—knowledge of folk songs is even more important in music [than in literature], because folk songs can be better integrated with music. I mean that peasant music continually inspires the composer. Do not imagine that we are thinking of the transplantation, the assimilation, the annexation of peasant music into the classical musical inheritance. No, no. We think that peasant music gives our music its character. Furthermore, if one hears songs from peasants in their original environment, one understands them much better; they inspire him much more than if he were familiar with them only from written collections or recordings. The atmosphere also affects us. Foreigners have also written a lot about the role of folk music in our music. But more recently—especially in America—they are spreading the (in my opinion incorrect) idea that reliance on folk music is harmful.

—How did the peasants react to the collectors?

He. Distrustfully. The nature of collecting meant that I could turn only to older people, mainly to older peasant women, because only they knew the old songs. They had to sing into the phonograph, and I made notations. The Hungarians and the Székelys quickly understood what it was all about.[7] They smelled money, but they didn't ask. Out of modesty, out of pride. But how difficult it is to persuade an old woman to sing. Why should she sing, just to be mocked by men from the city [i.e., the collectors]? Every one of

them suspected something, a trap, which they didn't want to fall
into. We had to resort to cunning, to talk and talk. Finally the old
peasant woman would give in. She would begin to sing, but in the
middle she would suddenly give up. She changed her mind. She
wouldn't sing after all. What for? Then we had to begin a new line
of attack, another tack with other pretexts, until the recording succeeded. Everywhere the peasants are reserved before the upper
classes. Collecting goes somewhat more easily among the Slovaks,
but with the Romanians even the young people could hardly be
persuaded to sing. With these two peoples, however, the song had a
"fixed price." As soon as I arrived, news got out that a "traveling
agent for songs" was among them, and they made sure they were
paid properly. It went most smoothly with the Arabs—in 1913 I
collected in Biskra—I had a letter of introduction to the sheik, who
ordered his subjects to sing. They belted out the songs like opera
singers.

—What kind of journal is this? *(I take the* League of Composers *from
the piano, in which I happen to find a long and enthusiastic article entitled
"Magyar Explorers," about Béla Bartók's and Zoltán Kodály's pioneering
work. He calls my attention to one passage. Together we read it.)* "Because
it is well known that there are no people so unmusical as the Hungarians . . . "

He (quite angrily). What thick-headed ignorance. This, even in America. All peasants sing; it is part of human nature to love songs. That
our peasants don't know polyphonic songs? The Arabs, Romanians,
Slovaks, and a bunch of peoples don't know them, either. Anyway,
what is this, that a people is musical? That its peasant music is valuable, or that it gives the world great composers? If I look at it the
first way, then the English are musical; if the second, then they are
not. Our roots are indeed in peasant music; this preserves the Asian
five-note scale, the pentatonic.

—I wish we also had such an ancient memory in literature. Are such
ancient musical roots also found with our related people, the Finns?

He (making a gesture of resignation). Finnish folk music doesn't offer
anything interesting. It simply echoes Swedish-European music.
Here among the neighboring peoples we stand alone with our music, like an island. In Europe there is pentatonicism only in the music of the peoples who are originally Asian, like the Cheremisses.[8]
Here is an example, in this Cheremiss song. *(Months ago his pioneering work on the Hungarian song was published, the result of many years of
artistic-academic research, with musical notations, columns of figures, re-*

ports. We had not yet heard about it, but the proofs of the German edition were already lying on the table; it will be publicized in extensive studies abroad, which will perhaps be translated for our benefit.)

—In what direction is new music proceeding?

He. One of the slogans is: away from romanticism! The other: neo-classicism! They even consider Beethoven romantic. The trend already began with Debussy and is reaching its peak with Stravinsky, who states that Beethoven might have been a great man, an excellent character, but on the other hand was absolutely not—a musician. Naturally I don't agree. Maybe it's possible to assert that he doesn't orchestrate like Mozart, but I enjoy the *Eroica* as much today as I ever did. Undeniably, there is a big reaction against the romantics. The whole world cries out, "Stop!"—it turns back to Bach and to even earlier composers; it desires objective, un-programmatic music, which doesn't represent definite feelings but is absolute music. Before the war the Germans were on the fore-front of the movement with Schoenberg, the expressionist. But after the war it was as if German music had stagnated. Now new talents crop up—the twenty-eight-year-old Hindemith, the twenty-four-year-old Křenek, one of whose compositions I just heard in Prague. Concerto Grosso. (The Handelian title also emphasizes neoclassicism.) With regard to Stravinsky, I was enthusiastic about his previous works. His latest works, however, I feel are dry; they don't warm me up.

—In painting this revolution already ran its course decades ago, when with the expression "abstract painting" geometric forms started to appear on canvas. But here it also turned out that every art is human by necessity. It is not possible to make art completely independent of the human being, of the feeling, of the source of that feeling.

He. This is natural. Otherwise music would turn into machine music. Bach also expresses something, a few moments of life. We can see that in his compositions with text he tries to express this. If I write a low note and then a higher one, that is rising; if I strike a high note and then a lower one, that is sinking: the one undoubtedly merriment, the other despair. I must admit, however, that there are certain advantages to this turnaround, because the outgrowth of musical romanticism with Wagner and Strauss became unbearable. That's why people are searching and experimenting. This journal from Prague gives news of an invention, the *Farbenlicht-Musik*, which performs music and color. In addition—taking into consideration the slower rate of perception of the eyes—it emits just one color for several pitches and makes the spatial art of painting temporal. So the light instrument works simultaneously with the musical instrument. *(He reflects.)* Light instrument. Strange word. It engages the eyes, as music does the ears. Anyhow, its inventor is Hungarian, László Sándor.

—Don't you think this blending of styles, this test tube work, this great self-consciousness—in music and in other arts as well—demonstrates the sterility of the age?

He. No. I'm inclined to think self-consciousness isn't bad. Why, there are many examples of ages of great artistry that were also self-conscious: they escaped to preexisting forms and styles; they poured their content into these molds. I'll mention just one: the Renaissance.

Béla Bartók stands in the doorway of the foyer without moving, like in his portraits in the Manchester Guardian *or* El Sol. *I open the door; the latch squeaks. From another floor emanates a nauseating music hall song, mercilessly beaten out on a bourgeois piano. Amid these rattlings, these unmusical scrapings, lives the composer, who carries music in his head. The noise of the world surrounds him, which he in turn, paying attention to his inner order, pushes away, forgets. Just like the writer, who, while walking down the street thinking about a poem, reads on the wall the text of an official muzzling order formulated with a strict compactness.*

[This interview appeared in the 31 May 1925 issue of *Pesti Hírlap* (Pest news) and has been reprinted in Hungarian in *Bartók Béla művészi kibontakozásának évei II—Bartók megjelenése az európai zeneéletben (1914–1926)* (The years of Bartók's artistic evolution, part 2—Bartók's appearance in European musical life [1914–1926]), ed. János Demény, vol. 7 of *Zenetudományi tanulmányok* (Musicological studies), ed. Bence Szabolcsi and Dénes Bartha (Budapest, 1959), pp. 347–49; in Dezső Kosztolányi, *Írók, festők, tudósok* (Writers, painters, scholars) (Budapest, 1958), vol. 2, pp. 244–50; and in *Új Hang* (New voice) in May 1956. A loose and extensively abridged English translation appeared in *Living Age* 340 (March–August 1931): 565–68.]

NOTES

1. Bartók's father was not born into the gentry class but created a gentry title for himself—Szuhafői. Szuhafő, in Gömör county, northern Hungary, is the home of a Bartók family of noble extraction. The composer's family was, however, from Borsodszirák in Borsod county. (See Tibor Tallián, *Béla Bartók: The Man and His Work*, trans. Gyula Gulyás [Budapest, 1981], pp. 8–9.) [Trans.]

2. Present-day Sînnicolau Mare, Romania. [Trans.]

3. Bartók went to Prague not to perform but to attend a meeting of the International Society for Contemporary Music, at which his Dance Suite was enthusiastically received. [Trans.]

4. I.e., the Fourteen Bagatelles, Op. 6. [Trans.]

5. Bartók refers here to territories that had been taken away from Hungary by the Treaty of Trianon (1920). [Trans.]

6. Ferenc Kazinczy (1759–1831), a poet and writer, was the leader of the movement to rejuvenate the Hungarian language to make it suitable for literature. Poets Sándor Petőfi (1823–49) and János Arany (1817–82) brought Hungarian literature to a new level of excellence. [Trans.]

7. Székelys, a Hungarian-speaking people of southeast Transylvania. [Trans.]

8. Cheremisses, a Finno-Ugric people of the central Volga region. [Trans.]

A Conversation with Béla Bartók

TRANSLATED BY DAVID E. SCHNEIDER

AND KLÁRA MÓRICZ

Extreme inflation in Hungary following World War I, and the added financial responsibility of a second child (Peter, the composer's son by his second wife, Ditta Pásztory, was born in 1924), may have provided some of the impetus for Bartók's extensive concertizing in the 1920s. The following interview was given on 20 April 1926 to a writer for the Hungarian-language *Kassai Napló* (Kassa journal) following a concert in Košice, Slovakia (formerly Kassa, Hungary). Only the interviewer's initials, M.Ö., have been identified. The interview is especially noteworthy for the documentation it provides of the audience's sensitivity to the provenance of Bartók's folk sources, and Bartók's admission that Stravinsky's concert in Budapest just over a month earlier (15 March 1926) caused Bartók to reevaluate Stravinsky's "neoclassical" compositions. Bartók's program in Kassa consisted of Beethoven's Sonata in E♭, Op. 31, No. 3; three Scarlatti sonatas; Chopin's Nocturne in C♯ minor; Debussy's *Pour le piano*; and several works by Bartók: Variations on a Hungarian Peasant Song (no. 6 of Fifteen Hungarian Peasant Songs), Old Dance Tunes (nos. 7–15 of Fifteen Hungarian Peasant Songs), Four Dirges, the *Allegro barbaro*, the Sonatina, "Evening in Transylvania," "Bear Dance," the Second Burlesque ("A Bit Drunk"), and a Romanian Dance (which the program erroneously listed as a Slovak dance).

.

After the concert I had the opportunity to speak with this truly great master, who not only is the greatest phenomenon of Hungarian music but is considered to be one of the most significant composers of modern European music even outside of Hungary.

Everyone who heard the concert left the hall with memories of a great experience, but I was also given the pleasure of getting to know a great individual through our conversation after the musical event. Bartók received me during his dinner in the *Schalkház*. His voice is soft, his words simple, and his eyes also explain; he must be a great teacher. Clearly he enjoys having the opportunity to talk about his favorite subjects.

A good part of his concert on Tuesday consisted of folk songs or pieces based on folk song motives.

I mention that the Slovak members of the audience claimed to have detected Slovak motives even in the Hungarian pieces.

He smiles.

You see, in Pest, I have to cope with precisely the opposite belief; there they sense Hungarian motives in my songs of Slovak origin. Of course, both opinions are superficial, based on surface features. Undeniably, there are influences. But it so happens that the Hungarian pieces I played today are purely Hungarian in origin. I divide these folk songs into three groups. The pieces belonging to the first group are purely Hungarian, and their influence can be detected only in Romanian folk songs. These songs are generally of ancient origin; they go back centuries. In the second group the origins are already so mixed that it is difficult to classify them (these demonstrate borrowings from Slovak folk music). This group includes songs that are found in both Slovak and Hungarian folk music, yet they are Western European in origin. Examples of these are "Debrecenben kidobolták" (They announced it in Debrecen) and "Szeretnék szántani" (I would like to plow). There are purely Slovak songs—for example, "Azt mondják nem adnak" (They say they won't send me). But mutual influences are so widespread that my acquaintances who were prisoners of war in Russia heard what they suspected were typically Hungarian songs even there. It is impossible to determine how far back the origins of these songs reach. The third group consists of folk songs of newer origin. It can be shown that those that came into being before 1850 are of purely Hungarian origin, and their influence on Slovak and Romanian folk songs is easily demonstrable. Perhaps this influence is the result of common military service, or of the migration of Slovak harvesters who went down to the great Hungarian plain for work and returned to their villages with Hungarian songs.

Unlike Zoltán Kodály, however, I am interested not only in Hungarian folk songs but in the peasant music of all nationalities. Before the war I was in Biskra, among the Arabs, for a long time.[1] You might say that I have been occupied with the folk music of almost every people. Of course, it is difficult to separate the music of the semieducated gypsy from peasant song, just as it is difficult abroad to distinguish music of the village from that of the city. As everyone knows, peasant music of various peoples has been a great influence on me. I am interested not simply in their musical motives but also in their formal structures, which particularly fascinate me. Had I obtained them only secondhand, these songs' influence would not have been so immediate and strong. But because in the course of my collecting I simultaneously received impressions of both the songs and their environment—the atmosphere of the village—the experience had a full impact.

I cannot say exactly the same thing about the black music that is so fashionable nowadays. Jazz is very interesting music: its rhythm and composition, like that of all folk music, is fascinating. I am, however, bothered by its banal harmonization and the strangeness of its instruments.[2] But, more important, its motives and melodies are frequently banal to the point of boredom. I don't believe it will have a greater influence on modern music than gypsy music had on the works of Brahms or Liszt in the last century.

Let me repeat: all peasant music deeply interests me, and my goal is to extract the essence from it.

Modern music is not following the road of folk music. Two of its outstanding figures, Stravinsky and Schoenberg, are taking divergent paths. Of the two, Stravinsky stands closer to me. I barely know the younger generation, Antheil[3] and his contemporaries. Stravinsky's recent works, which he calls neoclassical and which indeed resemble the music of Bach's time, seemed dry to me at first reading, though after his concert in Budapest I found a lot more in them.[4] Stravinsky's switch to neoclassicism is intimately bound to current developments in other arts. Although Stravinsky stands under the influence of Picasso, I do not believe things can be explained so simply; the arts have been developing concurrently ever since romanticism. I believe that I belong to the generation of Ady. Kassák and his circle,[5] however, are mistaken when they consider my music to be in the spirit of their journal, since the driving force behind my work is a Rembrandtesque conception.

I have not yet formulated for myself a unified picture of my concert tours or my achievements as a composer. In England, where I arrived through the connections of my musical friends, I had a decisive moral success. My compositions were played several times by the Waldbauer Quartet and by English musicians. But the Dance Suite was my only real public success. My concerts in Germany have been more significant. My folk song transcriptions, however, were not really understood anywhere abroad. They barely sense their significance. Although

I have had only a few opportunities to play my Sonatas for Violin and Piano, their success has been more important because of where I played them.[6] Three years ago at my first concert in Kassa it was a mistake to play my Sonata with Waldbauer. Today the audience here in Kassa understood my program much better.

Among the young Hungarian composers only the talented György Kósa and Zoltán Székely are significant.[7] Kodály naturally has many students because he teaches composition at the Academy.

This year the musical season in Pest has been quite lively. Without a doubt the biggest event was Stravinsky's concert, which the audience received with great understanding. The greatest Hungarian musical work of the last years is Kodály's *Psalmus hungaricus*. Its performance also took place this year.

It was late by the time Bartók finished this informative conversation, which I believe will provide a fitting interpretation of Tuesday's concert.

[Source: M.Ö. (identity unknown), "A Conversation with Béla Bartók" (Beszélgetés Bartók Bélával), *Kassai Napló*, 23 April 1926; reprinted in vol. 7 (*Bartók Béla művészi kibontakozásának évei II—Bartók megjelenése az európai zeneéletben [1914–1926]* [The years of Bartók's artistic evolution, part 2—Bartók's appearance in European musical life (1914–1926)], ed. János Demény), vol. 7 of *Zenetudományi tanulmányok*, ed. Bence Szabolcsi and Dénes Bartha (Budapest, 1959), pp. 395–96.]

NOTES

1. The time he spent collecting in Biskra was in fact two weeks, from 11–24 June 1913. Bartók had to cut the collecting expedition short because of illness. [Trans.]

2. It is doubtful that Bartók had more than a very superficial acquaintance with jazz by this time. Although the interviewer's recording of Bartók's objection to banal harmonization rings true, Bartók's supposed objection to the strangeness of the instruments seems to be a misunderstanding. Bartók generally enjoyed discovering unusual instruments. [Trans.]

3. George Antheil (1900–1959), American composer best known for incorporating jazz elements into his music. [Trans.]

4. The translation of this paragraph up to this point mainly follows that in Tibor Tallián, *Béla Bartók: The Man and His Work*, trans. Gyula Gulyás, (Budapest, 1988), p. 138. [Trans.]

5. Lajos Kassák (1887–1967), a poet, writer, and painter who was an important representative of the avant-garde in Hungary and the founder of the radical periodical *Ma* (Today) (1916–25). [Trans.]

6. Bartók gave a number of performances of his First and Second Sonatas

for Violin and Piano in prestigious venues prior to 1926. Performances of the First Sonata include those with Jelly Arányi in London's Aeolian Hall (24 March 1922) and at a London International Society for Contemporary Music concert (7 May 1923), and with Zoltán Székely in Budapest's Vigadó (24 November 1925). Significant performances of the Second Sonata include those with Imre Waldbauer (7 February 1923, for subscribers to *Melos* in Berlin), with Székely in Amsterdam's Concertgebouw (28 April 1923), and with Arányi in Aeolian Hall (7 May 1923). Perhaps most significant for Bartók was the performance of the First Sonata with Arányi in Paris at the home of Henry Prunières for a group that included Stravinsky, Ravel, Szymanowski, Honegger, Milhaud, Poulenc, and Roussel (8 April 1922). [Trans.]

7. Zoltán Székely (1903–), violinist to whom Bartók dedicated his Second Rhapsody for Violin (1928) and Violin Concerto (1938). [Trans.]

PART III
WRITINGS ABOUT BARTÓK

.

Recollections of Béla Bartók

MRS. PÁL VOIT, *NÉE* ÉVA OLÁH TÓTH

TRANSLATED BY PETER LAKI

I was born at Sziladpuszta, in Békés county, where my father, Emil Oláh Tóth, managed the estates of the Wenckheim family. My mother, Erzsébet Bartók, was Béla Bartók's only sibling. As a child I spent much time with Bartók.

Uncle Béla often visited with us. My nannies were among those whose folk songs he recorded. Their names—Róza Kocsis, for instance—may be found in the files of the Bartók folk song collection. Péter Garzó's name also occurs in many songs—he was the coachman.

When I was very young, I often saw Uncle Béla sitting in front of a huge pile of music paper and writing. I wasn't allowed to walk or run around except in the greatest silence—something a child obviously didn't like very much. Because we lived in the country, however, there was plenty of room.

In 1921 we moved to Szőllőspuszta, to another Wenckheim estate. My father had to look after some farms that had been badly neglected. I spent a great deal of time with him, because I loved nature and animals. When Uncle Béla saw that I was studying the life of small insects, he explained a lot to me but also listened to what I had to say. He was spending the summer in the country with his wife, Ditta, and their son, Péter. We used to take a chair and a stool to the orchard, and I saw him write music there. What he wrote, I don't know. He put a wet handkerchief on his head, tying it into knots on the four corners—this makeshift hat was his protection against the sun.

There were some young girls from the village of Endrőd who had been hired to work on the farm for the summer. Two of the girls stayed with us all year round; both had fine voices and liked to sing. I remember that sometimes they sang songs for Uncle Béla that I knew myself. I wanted to sing, too, but Uncle Béla motioned for me to keep quiet and let Maca and Hermina sing. I didn't understand why my singing wasn't good enough. After all, I had learned those songs from these two girls! Today I understand, of course. Later, cataloging the sheets of the Bartók folk song collection at the Bartók Archives, I discovered with great pleasure the names Maca Farkasinszky and Hermina Haluska on some of the pages.

At night, when everything was quiet, we would sit in the garden. Uncle Béla told my mother the names of the stars. On the great Hungarian plain you get a wonderful view of the Milky Way; the bright stripe, made up of so many stars, seems to cut the sky in half. On these starry nights, Uncle Béla taught me to identify the Big and the Little Dipper and the Pleiades.

In 1926 I went to Budapest to continue my studies. I spent a lot of my free time with Uncle Béla and Ditta. During the November holidays, Uncle Béla made arrangements so that I could go home to Szőllőspuszta, accompanied by his older son, Béla, Jr.

In September 1929 I switched schools and enrolled in the Teacher's Training College in Cinkota, near Budapest, an institution that had relocated from Pozsony (Bratislava). My grandmother had taught in the same school—in Pozsony—until 1906. My mother graduated from there in 1904, so it was logical that I should attend the same school. Both my grandmother and my mother insisted that I should have a profession; we were inspired by the example of my grandmother, who, widowed at an early age, would not have been able to raise and educate her children had she not had a teacher's diploma.

In September, when the school year started, Uncle Béla came with me to Cinkota (my mother was ill and couldn't be there). He was the one who talked to the director of the school, Ida Tabódy. We took the suburban train. Béla, Jr., was also with us. The trip took one hour, and from the station we had to walk to the institute. I wasn't in the mood for talking very much. They were trying to reassure me: I would be able to leave this institute more often than the previous one, and they would take me to concerts. I tried to hold back my tears when we said goodbye. Uncle Béla stroked my face but said nothing. What he said to the director, I don't know.

The same year, my grandmother and her sister, Irma, who lived with her, moved from Pozsony to Budapest. I was very happy to visit them in their apartment on Krisztina Boulevard. I would tell them about my life at the institute and write letters to my mother. My grandmother showed me the postcards that Uncle Béla sent from his concert tours abroad.

My last year at the institute arrived. On 18 May 1934, Uncle Béla came to Cinkota with his mother, Ditta, Péter, and Béla, Jr., and played for the students in the music room of the institute. Afterward, Uncle Béla and his family had dinner with the members of the faculty, and I was allowed to attend as well—I considered this a great honor indeed.

After I had finished my studies, I often came to Budapest to visit my grandmother. I was a frequent guest at the elaborate dinners Aunt Irma prepared for Uncle Béla twice a week. After dinner, Uncle Béla and his mother would go to one of the rooms to talk. They read his reviews together. My grandmother had a book in which she wrote down the dates and places of Uncle Béla's concerts, and what he had played. Later, when my grandmother found writing too difficult, he dictated his programs to me.

My fiancé, Pál Voit, and I were frequent dinner guests at the Bartóks' on Csalán Street. I remember one occasion when we listened to some unusual recordings. My grandmother was also there. They were Negro recordings, perhaps. My poor grandmother listened to the record with great consternation and made a miserable face. Uncle Béla got a big kick out of this. This music seemed very strange to us then.

Péter and I would often walk behind Uncle Béla, watching his steps very carefully in order not to tread on an insect, when he went hiking on Gugger Hill. When he saw an unusual plant, he indefatigably explained it to us over and over again.

We went to hear his concerts, but in those days I did not have a real feeling about his greatness yet. It was natural for us to be there and hear him.

IVAN ENGEL

TRANSLATED BY PETER LAKI

I first became acquainted with Bartók's works during the 1920s. The memorable concert at which Bartók's Dance Suite and Kodály's *Psalmus hungaricus* were premiered took place in November 1923. This historic concert had a strong impact on me.

It was in the same year that I first heard Bartók play the piano. He played his own Sonata No. 1 for Violin and Piano, with Imre Wald-

bauer. That evening, something happened that was strangely characteristic of Hungarian musical life in those days. It revealed the total
incomprehension of new Hungarian music in a most unusual way. At
the beginning of the second movement, the policeman who was there
on duty got up and left the Great Hall of the Academy of Music with
heavy, resounding steps. Apparently, he had been barely able to put
up with the first movement. Many people in the audience turned
around when they heard the strange noise, and a few jumped to their
feet. A veritable panic broke out. In those days, the atmosphere was
always tense and explosive whenever one of Bartók's works was performed. Someone shouted, "It's nothing; only the policeman left—
please sit down!" Order was gradually restored, and the two musicians calmly started the movement over and finished it without any
further interruptions.

After the concert I was invited to the house of my teacher, István
Thomán. Bartók was there, too. I asked him how it felt to see such a
scandalous scene from the podium. Bartók replied, "I'm not surprised; there is always something happening."

Between 1932 and 1940 I was privileged to visit Bartók at his house
often. When I entered, he always offered me cigarettes that he himself had filled. The conversation invariably began with difficulty. His
personality exuded calmness and tension in equal measure. But
whenever he looked at me with his wonderful eyes, the tension decreased. His voice had a warmth and a flavor that can scarcely be
described.

Once I played his Four Dirges for him, before a performance in
London. After he had approved the tempos, I drew his attention to
an erroneous metronome marking. To prove my point, I took out my
Swiss metronome watch. I immediately saw the great interest with
which he watched it work. It was a new device to him. I happily offered him the little gadget as a gift, because I knew his interest in
everything that had to do with rhythm. He was visibly pleased. He
corrected the erroneous marking and wrote the correct one into my
copy himself.

Once I mentioned to him that I couldn't get the piano score of *Duke
Bluebeard's Castle* in Budapest. So he presented me with his own copy. I
still have this copy in my possession; in it, one accidental has been
corrected [by Bartók]. This is how he reciprocated for the little
metronome.

On another occasion, he notated the exact rhythm of one of the
Romanian Folk Dances on an empty page in one of his printed scores.
I cherish this valuable manuscript as well:

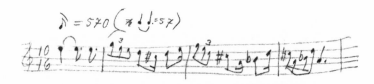

Once he took me to his room, where we listened to complicated Bulgarian rhythms from a recording. "What is the exact rhythm?" he asked me. I was unable to tell. He observed, laughing, "Simple Bulgarian peasant women dance to it."

We were together in Basle in January 1938, where he and his wife were preparing the premiere of his Sonata for Two Pianos and Percussion. We attended all the rehearsals, admiring the patience of Bartók, who was working hard with the two percussionists to make them understand and precisely execute the rhythms, which they were not used to.

The premiere was an extraordinary success. Rarely had I seen such a rage in the city of Basle! We met afterward, and I asked Bartók where his works had been performed the best. He said, "At the BBC and in Basle." "Why?" I asked. "Because they have enough rehearsals."

A year later, we met the Bartóks in London at the great International Society for Contemporary Music concert. We visited the National Gallery together. In one of the rooms he greeted a man in his middle years and introduced us to him. He was the Czech composer Alois Hába, who became famous with his quarter tone theory and compositions. After the visit to the museum, we went to a typical London tearoom with the Bartóks. Bartók was in high spirits. He watched the patrons with great interest and jokingly said about the waitress, "How good her English is."

It is the great fortune of my life that I was able to see Bartók so often both at home and abroad. His every word, his every gesture, remains unforgettable to me.

GÉZA FRID

TRANSLATED BY PETER LAKI

I had the privilege of being a close witness of Bartók's life for two decades, from 1920 to 1940. I saw him in many different situations, but I couldn't call myself his friend—because of the age difference, if for no other reason.

After my graduation from the Liszt Conservatory as a pianist and composer, I continued to take piano lessons from him for another year. After the completion of his First Piano Concerto, he asked me for assistance in preparing the work for performance. For several months, I played the orchestral parts on a second piano as he was practicing the solo part. I am still proud that Bartók entrusted me with the proofs of some of his greatest works: I read the galleys for *The Miraculous Mandarin*, the Dance Suite, the First Piano Concerto, the two Rhapsodies for Violin and Piano, and *Cantata profana*. I was thus the first to see these scores before publication.

In 1937, when Bartók and his wife, Ditta, were preparing the Sonata for Two Pianos and Percussion, he invited us to his house—my wife and I were spending our honeymoon in Budapest—to hear a preview of the work.

A year and a half later, he wrote his great Violin Concerto for Zoltán Székely. In January 1939, Bartók sent the score and the piano reduction to Holland, to Székely and me, so we could prepare the work for the March premiere. By the way, the last measures of the Violin Concerto were completed at my house in Amsterdam, on my Bechstein piano. The ending had caused the composer some difficulty, as endings often do. Finally he chose, among several possibilities, the version known today. I made bold to suggest that he add a two-note pickup before the theme of the first movement. Bartók just smiled at my suggestion; yet years later, when the score was published, I saw that he had taken my advice.

The most striking feature of Bartók's personality was his unimpeachable integrity. He was obsessed with truth and justice, regardless of how he himself or others were affected by the outcome. No matter whether the issue was friends or relatives, piano playing or teaching, folk music or composition, theory or practice, finances or politics, he accepted no compromises. If he found someone guilty of the slightest lie, he—normally a gentle and genial man—suddenly turned ice-cold and withdrew into himself, even if this was detrimental to his career.

This meticulousness to a fault characterized him as a teacher and as a pianist as well. There are fewer and fewer of us alive who have heard him play the piano. This is why I want to talk more about Bartók the pianist. First, a word of warning: there exist some recordings of Bartók as soloist, chamber musician, and accompanist. Without debating the documentary value of these recordings, I must stress that they do not come even close to re-creating the fantastic effects Bartók's live playing produced. Therefore Bartók the pianist must not be judged on the basis of his recordings. This is true not only because recording technology was rather primitive in those days; even the best mechanical reproduction could never recapture Bartók's playing. His highly convincing and suggestive style, the irresistible and incredibly rich nuances, are impossible to reproduce. This is true of Bartók's performances of his own works as well as his renderings of works by other composers.

What was the secret of Bartók's piano playing? First of all, his powerful personality, his human greatness, and the purity of his character. Those who knew him well can never forget the profound fire in his eyes. When Bartók sat at the piano, you could feel, right from the very first note, that you were listening not to an instrumentalist but to a prophet who uses his instrument as a means to a revelation.

He was a revolutionary in composition. Likewise, his piano playing was under the sign of innovation. Routine was completely foreign to him. His two piano cycles, *For Children* and *Mikrokosmos*, bear witness to this searching spirit as well as to his pedagogical bent. He was a pioneer in introducing numerous piano works by foreign composers—Debussy, Ravel, Stravinsky, Schoenberg—to Hungary. The performance of Kodály's works was also a pioneering act.

At the same time, he had a high respect for tradition. He carefully studied every style, every composer. As a pianist, he entered their world with natural ease. His editions of Bach and his arrangements of other baroque masters are among the best. . . . The harpsichord, an instrument out of the museum, was not favored by Bartók in the concert hall.

One could speak at length about his Mozart playing, which was incredibly light and supple but, especially in the later works of the Salzburg master, also full of dramatic accents. One could speak at length, too, about his interpretation of the romantic masters, virtuosic and always constructively musical. No one played Liszt better than Bartók, but he was also one of the fieriest interpreters of Schumann and Brahms. I never heard him play Schubert or Mendelssohn, and Chopin only once: it was a miraculously powerful interpretation, significantly different from those of known Chopin players, and perhaps at variance with the ideas of that poet of the piano. He never played the piano music of composers leaning toward salon music (Tchaikovsky, Rachmaninoff, Grieg, even César Franck).

Bartók's most outstanding achievements as a pianist were certainly his interpretations of Beethoven. I don't think there could ever be a better Beethoven interpreter than Bartók, save Beethoven himself. If you closed your eyes, you could believe that Beethoven himself was sitting at the piano; we heard incredibly strong accents alternating with moments of utmost tenderness. Much has been written about the kinship of Beethoven and Bartók as composers; it is true that, besides Bach, Beethoven was the composer who had given the most to Bartók's unspeakably rich musical palette. No wonder Bartók the pianist could express himself in the works of Beethoven with the greatest perfection!

Whoever has heard Bartók perform the piano part of the "Kreutzer" Sonata (I turned pages for him on three occasions, with different violinists each time: in Budapest with Henri Marteau, in London with Zoltán Székely, and in Rome with Joseph Szigeti) will never forget the way he interpreted the first movement. There were primal forces at work here. . . . Space and time became irrelevant; one felt as if one were in heaven and hell in turn, until one came back to earth at the end. The thirty-second note variation in the Andante was conjured out of the piano with a magical attack, in a performance that can only be called transcendent. But the most unforgettable of all moments was the A-major chord that opens the last movement. No one could ever have imagined the sonority that was born here under Bartók's hands: this finale was mighty, victorious, and optimistic, a celebration of joy.

With my mind's eye, I can still see the delicate, gray-haired master at the piano, a visionary glance in his eyes. He plays his *Allegro barbaro*, this key work among his piano compositions. Or else I hear him as the soloist in Liszt's *Totentanz*—this was one of his favorite pieces. This was more than piano playing, this was MUSIC itself in its primeval form, the most mysterious manifestation of human spirit.

I would like to end with a letter I received from Bartók in April 1938. After the German occupation of Austria, Bartók wanted to quit his publisher, appropriated by the Nazis, and the Composers' Association, which had met with the same fate. Here is the letter:

Dear Mr. Frid,

I am writing to you with a request: could you discreetly inquire at the Netherlandish Composers' Association whether they would accept me as a member? I assume you belong and could inform me as to whether this association functions normally and whether it is completely independent. You will probably guess easily why I am asking all this.

Last February, I wrote to the "old" U.E. [Universal Edition] in Vienna that I would agree to have you orchestrate the cello version of my Rhapsody No. 1. Unfortunately, I have to rescind this now, since I will never authorize the "new" U.E. to publish any transcriptions whatsoever. I hope you haven't started work yet!

I look forward to hearing from you and send my best wishes to you both,

Béla Bartók

SÁNDOR VERESS

TRANSLATED BY PETER LAKI

I was nine years old when I first met Bartók, not personally but through his music. "Evening in the Country" was the first piano piece of his I started to play, entirely on my own.

My mother was a very gifted singer; she also played the piano well. There was a very musical atmosphere in our home. But when I started playing "Evening in the Country," it had an effect on my mother as though she had just lost her son. My mother had grown up in the spirit of old music, and this music was terribly new and upsetting for her. It wasn't long, however, before she discovered the flavor and beauty in "Evening in the Country" and gradually became used to her son's new avant-garde tastes. Later, few were more enthusiastic about Bartók and his music than she was.

I did not meet Bartók personally until much later, when I was a student at the Conservatory. Around 1927, when I was still a composition student of Kodály, I began an internship under László Lajtha at the Museum of Ethnography. I finished my studies with Kodály in 1929. I had also studied piano at the Conservatory. My piano teacher for the first three years had been Emánuel Hegyi. Of dead people, one should speak well or not at all. Still, I cannot help pointing out that this student-teacher relationship was evolving in a direction antithetical to my musical development. The tension between us grew to the point that I dropped out of my third year of study, and prepared my examination for the fourth year by myself, without any help. I passed the exam. By then, I had long wished to become Bartók's piano student. I called on him, requesting admission to the teachers' program.

Bartók may have already heard of me as a composer: with Pál Kadosa and Ferenc Farkas we had formed the Association of Modern Hungarian Musicians. Ferenc Szabó was also a member of our group. It was at that time that he wrote two of his fine works: a piano sonatina and a sonata for unaccompanied violin. István Szelényi also belonged to this group, as did poor Laci Kaufmann—the young generation of those days, which started on its path being rather abandoned. We had no support at all; we had to create everything ourselves. It cost immense sacrifices to organize a concert in the small hall of the Conservatory; and as for the reception, we could count on very little understanding.

It is possible that Bartók knew my name from these sporadic concerts. Be that as it may, he received me very kindly when I approached him with my request to be his student in the teachers' program. He accepted me, so I spent two years studying with him, which was a great experience for me in many respects. But I could not really get close to him.

Bartók was extremely withdrawn and did not easily let people near him. He had a hard time warming up. He was always fair and polite, but there was always a wall between him and his students. The atmosphere around him was very different from that surrounding Kodály. Kodály didn't hobnob with his students either, yet there was a very warm human relationship between him and his students, even though Kodály sometimes raked us over the coals. He was right; he did a good deed. Bartók never did anything like that; he was separated from his students by a higher and thicker wall than Kodály was. I was no exception during my two years in the teachers' program.

He started to warm up when I returned from my Csángó[1] folk song–collecting expedition. This created some surprise and even a small sensation, because no one had known about my plans in advance. I wasn't sure myself if I could realize them, so I didn't mention them to anyone. I left for Bucharest on 1 June 1930 and continued from there to the Csángó region. It wasn't until my return in the first weeks of August that people found out where I had been and what I had been doing. Of course, Kodály and Bartók were both eager to see my results. I remember that when I went to see Bartók to tell him about my experiences I found a completely different person: someone very kind, friendly, and open. This made my activities as his piano student very pleasant. It gave our relationship a more humane character and helped me considerably with my development as a pianist.

My piano playing had gotten quite out of control when I first went to Bartók. As I have said, I had prepared my fourth-year exam entirely on my own—this was not an ideal situation. Moreover, I had a technical problem that greatly hindered my pianistic activities.

Let me say a few words about Bartók as a pedagogue here. He really was no piano teacher. His activities in this field served mainly to provide him with a secure financial base. Bartók was not the kind of pedagogue, not the kind of passionate educator, that Kodály was. He gave his lessons very conscientiously, and he cared about his students very conscientiously, but his heart was not really in his teaching. In those days, around 1930, one could feel that he considered piano teaching a burden. He had a hundred more important things to do: organization of the folk song collection, his own concerts, his tremendous development as a composer. It is understandable that he was not overjoyed to listen to the good, not so good, or downright poor playing of his students.

As a matter of fact, Bartók should have been the director of an artists' program, teaching interpretation to students who were already accomplished technically. In that, he was splendid.

What were his piano lessons like? He assigned his students the entire year's program. This was an old custom at the Conservatory. Thomán[2] had done it; so did Bartók. It was up to the student to decide what to bring to each lesson.

When we brought something in for the first time, Bartók said nothing. He listened, then he sat down at the piano and gave a concert-level performance of the piece, whatever it might have been. Whether it was a Chopin etude, a difficult piece by Liszt, an etude by Kramer, or a sonata by Mozart, he played it with the same concentration as at his concerts. It was invariably a great experience. He said, "Play it like this!" Then we went home and tried to "play it like that."

I brought in the piece for a second time, two or three weeks or even a month later. Then Bartók thoroughly worked it through, with regard to form, dynamics, articulation, everything. Then I went home again, trying to shape the piece according to the directions received.

The third playing-through came whenever we were ready for it. If at that point the piece did not sound approximately the way Bartók had wished and demonstrated, then he didn't like to continue working on that particular piece. He probably thought that if after three such "treatments" students still could not play the piece as Bartók thought it should be played, then it was no use; they'd better bring in something else.

Bartók was not a born piano teacher—this was evident from the fact that he never addressed technical problems such as bad hand position or bad tensions in the mechanism. Such issues are integral parts of the teaching of great piano pedagogues. Bartók was not interested in this aspect of piano teaching. If someone was struggling with a technical problem, he tried to correct it by sitting down, playing the section in question, and then saying, "Now play after me!" That's easy to say, but if a student has a technical problem, he or she is hardly able to play after him. Bartók evidently did not get to the bottom of the technical problem; this shows that, despite his extreme conscientiousness, he wasn't a born piano teacher.

It wasn't until later that I understood why this was so. Bartók was probably such an instinctive pianist that he had never had a technical problem in his life, either as a child or later. He must have solved all technical problems in an instinctive way, without any difficulty. Therefore, not knowing the problems, he wasn't able to correct them in others.

It was an important moment in my career as a pianist when I brought in my own First Piano Sonata, which I was preparing for an Association of Modern Hungarian Musicians concert. Bartók was immediately interested. I played without music; he took the score and followed my performance. He especially liked the first movement of the Sonata, which contained numerous new technical devices, including ones that I could play well. Bartók gave me a few hints concerning interpretation and even attended the concert in the small hall of the Conservatory. This was a turning point in my life. As a pianist, I had risen by one notch in Bartók's esteem.

A little later I passed my final exam, which went reasonably well. This marked the end of my pianistic contacts with Bartók. We continued to have contact, however, in the field of folk music.

It goes without saying that my friends and I still attended every recital and premiere by Bartók. Afterward, we would discuss these momentous events at the Edison Café, at "Saturday night gatherings" that lasted until two or three in the morning. This café, on Teréz Boulevard, was our favorite hangout. Who was there? Pál Kadosa; Gyuri Hannover, the magnificent violinist who could play anything at sight; Vili Palotai, the outstanding cellist, later a member of the first Végh Quartet, who had just returned from Prague. Ödön Pártos, the excellent violinist, was there, too. I dedicated my Solo Violin Sonata to him; he learned it in a very short time and played it wonderfully at the premiere. Sándor, the waiter, knew us all well. We didn't even have to order; he knew what to bring to everyone. He always brought two eggs in a cup to me, and egg noodles to Vili Palotai—after his wooden-platter steak. In one word, there was good company. We discussed all the events of the week. If someone had written something that week he brought it in if he felt like it—we criticized it together. These gatherings went on for years; we would take the first tram in the morning to go home.

In those days, my meetings with Bartók always revolved around folk music. When he retired from the Conservatory in 1934 and went to work at the Academy of Sciences to prepare the folk music collection for publication, he invited me to be his assistant. We spent three afternoons a week in his office at the Academy of Sciences. He would sit at one end of the large, horseshoe-shaped table wearing headphones, revising earlier transcriptions, while I organized the material according to various criteria. He always had me work on material never before processed, like Polish songs or Ruthenian ones (but not from his collection).

Bartók spent exactly the same amount of time at the Academy of Sciences as he had previously spent teaching at the Conservatory: fifteen hours a week, divided among three afternoons. Three times a week he showed up at the Academy of Sciences at exactly three o'clock, and worked there until eight. Then he put on his pince-nez, lit a cigarette, said goodnight, and went home. Thus it went for a couple of years.

The first recordings of Hungarian folk music were made in the 1930s, on the Pátria label. At the recording sessions, which took place at the radio station, I spent a great deal of time with Bartók. One of the most interesting recordings was made in 1938, when we succeeded in bringing some Csángó singers out of Moldova. On their passport application, they had stated that they were coming to the Eucharist Conference. So we were able to bring a few families whom I had visited. Three families came to Budapest, from grandparents to grandchildren. Many of the women had never seen a train before, much less traveled in one. They had never dreamed of a city the size of Budapest. Bartók played a very active part in these recordings. This is the origin of the Pátria recordings, preserving original Csángó singing, including the beautiful laments.

I remember that Mrs. János Péntek sang the most wonderful laments. It was very hard to persuade her. We were three in the studio: László Lajtha, Bartók, and myself. Bartók had agreed with Mrs. Péntek that everyone would leave the studio, because she would not sing a lament otherwise. We all left; of course, she didn't know that we were listening from the control room. Mrs. János Péntek remained alone in the studio and visualized the day she had mourned for her mother. And she improvised such an authentic lament that all three of us were deeply moved.

I then had the opportunity to admire Bartók's ability to deal with these people, his understanding of their souls, and the kindness he showed toward them. He, who was so reserved with everyone—except with Kodály and a few close friends—was completely at ease with the peasants. I saw how well he knew their language and how he moved about in their midst. He had a kind word for everyone. This was a great experience for me, as well as an unforgettable lesson in ethnography: how to make authentic folk music recordings. For these people had to be treated this way to achieve that natural, relaxed state of mind without which authentic recordings would have been impossible.

On one of the recording sessions I was accompanied by my wife, who in those days spoke very little Hungarian.[3] Bartók began to speak to her in English. He was very kind to her but, already at their first meeting, asked her many questions about the English names of different things. Did she know what various parts of a particular type of sea vessel were called in English? He asked a lot of peculiar things of this sort, words you wouldn't know even in Hungarian.

This little story goes to prove Bartók's incredible knowledge of languages and his intensive study, whenever possible, of the most diverse languages. He had studied Arabic, knew Romanian well, and also knew Slovak fairly well. When he was preparing for his field trip to Turkey, he was learning Turkish. For months, wherever you saw him—on the bus, for instance—he had a Turkish dictionary in hand. Whenever he wasn't transcribing folk songs or practicing for a concert, he was reading his Turkish dictionary. This was part of the incredible meticulousness of his mind: he tried to become as familiar as possible with the languages of the people whose folk music he collected and studied.

His meticulousness and conscientiousness were unequaled. When he started working on Bulgarian folk music, he completely immersed himself in Bulgarian folk music collections. He had received some very nice collections from Sofia. The Bulgarians were then ahead of us in their publications. It was as a result of these studies that various Bulgarian rhythms were later incorporated into Bartók's music. Once I asked him at the Academy of Sciences, "What is Bulgarian folk music really like?" He replied: "I can't answer that question yet, for I have seen only five thousand Bulgarian folk songs so far."

Late in 1938, I went to London. We wanted to settle there. By the summer of 1939, the premonitory signs of the war's approaching catastrophe could be strongly felt in London. I wrote to Bartók, asking for his advice and his perspective on the situation. Should I go home, or stay in London? That's when he wrote me the letter, now published several times,[4] in which he reflects on the torment we were all experiencing at the time. I felt the same struggle after the outbreak of the war. After England declared war on 3 September 1939, we stayed in London until mid-November, when we returned to Budapest. I rejoined Bartók at the Academy of Sciences.

The Bartóks left Budapest on 12 October 1940. I was with him at the Academy of Sciences through late evening on the 11th. Then Kodály came, who had taken over Bartók's collection of Hungarian folk music, arranged and classified according to rhythmic criteria. As far as Bartók was concerned, this collection was ready for publication.[5] That was the last time I ever saw Bartók.

ERNŐ BALOGH

TRANSLATED BY PETER LAKI

I can discuss Bartók's American years not only because I was a close eyewitness but also because I was responsible for the preparation of his first American tour.

Bartók crossed the Atlantic three times—each time by boat—to visit the United States. The first time was in December 1927, next in April 1940, and finally in October 1940, never to return [to Europe]. He died in New York on 26 September 1945 and was buried there.[6]

Neither of his trips took place at the invitation of an American musical organization. Although Bartók had a great reputation in American musical circles by the end of the 1920s, his audience was not large enough to cover the expenses of a great trip, much less make it financially profitable.

The story of his first American trip begins with my visit to Frankfurt in the summer of 1927 to attend the festival of the International Society for Contemporary Music. Bartók was playing the premiere of his First Piano Concerto there under Furtwängler's direction. When I inquired after his health and his financial situation after one of the rehearsals, Bartók told me that he had been repeatedly ill in past years but had fortunately recovered each time. He would need money, however, to have his piano, which he had been using for more than twenty years, rebuilt.

The representative of one of the American piano manufacturers, Mr. William Murray, also happened to be in Frankfurt. At my suggestion, he showed willingness to invite Bartók to America, pay all his travel expenses, and guarantee the $3,000 honorarium for which Bartók was asking. Bartók's American tour in 1927–28 was far from bringing in that sum—nor did the piano manufacturer expect that it would.

It is a tribute to Bartók's reputation, that when he gave his American debut (he was playing his Rhapsody for Piano and Orchestra [Op. 1] with the New York Philharmonic) the audience at Carnegie Hall rose to its feet to greet the forty-six-year-old master. Few artists had been so honored by this crowd of three thousand: Paderewski, perhaps, at one of his rare appearances, or Toscanini at his New York farewell concert.

The Rhapsody had been programmed in lieu of the First Piano Concerto, which had been scheduled originally. The latter work had to be canceled because of insufficient rehearsal time. The Concerto was later performed by Bartók's loyal friend Fritz Reiner, who was then the director of the Cincinnati Symphony. This was early in 1928.

I think Bartók's personality is best revealed in his own words. Here is one of his letters, written to me after his first American tour:

Budapest, Szilágyi tér 4, 20 March 1928

Dear Ernő

It's not fair that I haven't written to you until now, to you who have done so much for me in New York and looked after me so well. But it has been entirely impossible for the following reasons: I got home on the 10th without any major problems but completely exhausted, having caught a cold on the boat on the last day of the trip and traveled from Cherbourg to Budapest in a feverish state (both literally and figuratively) with a flu, in constant fear of getting stuck and being unable to continue my journey. As soon I arrived in Budapest, I got better, but I was of course in poor shape. I rested as well as I could but not as much as I should have, since the rehearsals with the Philharmonic were about to start and I had a recital on the 16th, so I was up to my neck in work. Now my Budapest concerts are finally over!

The sea voyage was otherwise very pleasant; the weather was exceptionally calm. I diligently practiced my French with the Schmitzes, Casals, and Corti to bone up for my Paris performance, which should have taken place on 23 March but was canceled for most unusual reasons. So I am going only to Cologne the day after tomorrow, and on 20 April I am playing in Berlin under Kleiber (concerto). The Budapest orchestra and Dohnányi applied themselves and did their very best: the performance was quite good, excellent even by European standards, surpassing my expectations. My mother and sister came to

Budapest for these performances: there was great happiness. We couldn't find enough words for your praise—it *is* true, what you did for me was really too much! But you know this; I told you a number of times in New York—my mother thanks you for thinking of her, as do my wife and my son, Béla.

Now that I have the financial records of my American trip in front of me, I must confess that I cannot be satisfied with this. On the boat I received some valid data on what other people have made in America. Even someone like Tansman made more money than I did. There is something wrong here: either I didn't command the respect in America that I deserved, or the financial aspect of the matter had been poorly handled. Of course, it is vain to speculate after the fact, but one thing is certain: were I ever to undertake a similar trip again, I would do so only under much more favorable financial conditions.

In spite of all this, now that the American trip is over, I am glad to have gone; I don't even mind the trouble, which incidentally doesn't even seem so terribly great, in hindsight and viewed from so far away. One is inclined to forget all the inconvenience and remember only the good things.

Once more, thank you very, very much for all your help, and many greetings,

Béla

Bartók came to America for the second time during the spring of 1940. He was motivated not by money but by the desire to serve the cause of folk music. He wanted to publish one of his great folk song collections and studies. Since such things interest only a handful of specialized scholars, he could not find a publisher. So he decided to print the work at his own expense, for which he needed $1,500. He could raise this sum only through an American concert tour. Andor Schulhof, an impresario who had visited Budapest in 1940, offered him just such an opportunity. I later met with Schulhof in New York and did everything I could to realize this project. At my New York apartment I dictated a letter to Schulhof that he sent out to fourteen of my friends and acquaintances whom we deemed capable of helping us organize Bartók's concert tour. As is well known, this tour came to pass in the spring of 1940.

All of us who were concerned about Bartók's fate were trying to persuade him to move to the United States during the time of the war, which was already raging in Europe. We knew that he could neither live nor work in the Hungary of those days, an ally of Hitler's. We were trying to persuade him not even to return after his spring tour, the ocean being threatened by German submarines. Of course, Bartók went home to fetch his wife and the manuscripts of his works.

In the autumn of 1940, then, he undertook the great journey for the third time, to spend the war years in America. Although the United States itself entered the war soon afterward, Bartók at least was able to live out his last years far from the turmoil and the fascist regimes.

When Bartók and his wife, Ditta Pásztory, first visited us after their arrival, I took Mrs. Bartók aside and asked her to let me know if they had any problems, financial or otherwise; I thought I would be able to find a way to help Bartók in New York. I had to take Mrs. Bartók aside, for I knew that it was virtually impossible to "help" Bartók, who was too proud to accept any kind of financial assistance, even in the form of an advance.

The five years Bartók spent in America can be divided into two periods: pre-ASCAP and post-ASCAP years. The intervention of ASCAP, a turning point in Bartók's American life, occurred approximately halfway through this five-year period.

Bartók was not a member of ASCAP—nor could he be, for he was not an American composer. I, on the other hand, knew—having been a member for decades—that ASCAP was the largest and strongest composers' association in the United States and that it had a financial aid department that helped members in need in the strictest confidence. I was hoping that this organization would stand behind Bartók if necessary.

The first half of Bartók's American life—about two and a half years—were not spent in the best circumstances. In the beginning he had some concerts, which accounted for the greater part of his income. Later, the number of concerts decreased. He received invitations to serve as a professor of composition, famous composer that he was, but he turned these invitations down, because he had never taught composition in his life. In those days one couldn't make a living with ethnomusicology in America. Yet Bartók not only was an ethnomusicologist of the very first rank but considered this the most important aspect of his activities.

Two of America's most famous universities expressed an interest in Bartók. Harvard invited him to give a series of lectures. The only musicians other than Bartók to receive this honor in Harvard's three-hundred-year history were Stravinsky, Hindemith, and Aaron Copland.[7] The other famous school, Columbia University in New York,

entrusted Bartók with the transcription of the Serb folk song recordings in their collection. Bartók embarked on this project with great
gusto. They gave him an office at the university where he could work
as much as he wanted, whenever he pleased. Columbia was the only
university in the world to award him an honorary doctorate, an honor
that he accepted with ostensible pleasure. I will never forget how, during one of our visits, he brought in the cap and gown he had worn at
the ceremony.

Bartók later contracted a serious illness. He did not write a single
note during the first half of his American sojourn. He was treated
in New York by the same Hungarian physician—free of charge, of
course—who had been his doctor in Budapest. Yet he kept losing
weight and running a fever, at first in the evening only, but later during the day as well.

That was when Mrs. Bartók gave me a phone call. She told me how
serious Béla's illness had become. His weight had dwindled to forty
kilograms; the doctor had given him six weeks to live, at most, if his
condition kept deteriorating. Their financial situation was so bad that
they had money for only two weeks.

I was glad that Mrs. Bartók had caught me at home. As a concert
pianist I was on tour most of the time during the concert season.

I don't want to bore my readers with the details of how the urgent
assistance of ASCAP was obtained. Everything was urgent—not only
money but also someone to take the entire Bartók case in hand and
secure doctors, sanatorium, medication, nurses, and later a new and
better apartment, vacations, transfers, everything. Mrs. Bartók spoke
little English at that time, and moreover she was completely exhausted
from attending to her sick husband day and night.

The financial aid committee of ASCAP sent Bartók to the best and
most expensive rehabilitation center. They made sure that he was
seen by the best doctors. They put Bartók back on his feet so that he
could write, in the last two years of his life, his Sonata for Unaccompanied Violin, his Concerto for Orchestra, and his Third Piano Concerto, and could sketch the Viola Concerto.

Bartók's entire life situation changed from this moment. The greatest artists commissioned works from him, so at last he was able to hear
his works in ideal performances. He received more commissions than
he could honor. To the best of my knowledge, the Bartlett-Robinson
piano duo commissioned a concerto for two pianos—he couldn't even
begin to write this work. The great violist William Primrose commissioned the Viola Concerto, which remained unfinished because Bar-

tók had put it aside to finish the Third Piano Concerto first—for his wife.

In 1945 his condition became critical again. He was brought back to New York City from Saranac Lake and taken to the hospital. It was too late. His white blood cells had proliferated beyond control, and his strength declined quickly. He literally wasted away within a single week. In his last days he barely spoke; no visitors were allowed in his room. He was unconscious most of the time; death finally came around 11:45 A.M. on 26 September 1945.

The funeral was organized in accordance with Bartók's wishes. There were so many journalists present that ASCAP had to set up a separate room for them, with typewriters, telephone, and telegraph.

In keeping with its rules, ASCAP never revealed the amount spent on Bartók's medical bills. His doctors told me, however, that ASCAP must have spent at least $16,000 on physicians, medication, and hospitals and at least $30,000 on his sustenance. It never committed that much money to one of its members, either before or since. And Bartók was not even a member.

I would like, finally, to quote Bartók's final letter to me. During the last years we did not write to each other, since we lived in the same city and saw each other frequently. He wrote to me when he was out of town—as in this case, when he was in Saranac Lake.

4 October 1944

Dear Ernő,

Thank you for your letter of 20 Sept. I am going to New York tomorrow; I will call you sometime after Friday. The newest problem—for there always has to be a problem—is that we can't find an apartment in New York, not even a place to stay. Ditta keeps checking the Woodrow, but all rooms are occupied for now. Ditta lost the studio apartment she had last year, but fortunately she found another apartment, a larger one, in the same building (309 West 57th, apartment 503). The temporary solution is that I move there. Of course, even so we will be cramped in those two rooms, me with my many belongings and Ditta with her piano. But at least the piano is there in case I need to practice.

I am awaiting the negotiations with Elkan with keen interest. I will settle the date with you in N.Y.; as a matter of fact, I am free anytime.

I've been trying to practice here; it seems that I can still play the piano. I say this with reference to the planned gram[ophone] recordings. Suite Op. 14 (9½ minutes), Sonatina (4 minutes), perhaps two or three burlesques (2 minutes apiece), First Romanian Dance (4½ minutes), some of the fifteen peasant songs—these can be considered, for I have not recorded them with either Continental or Columbia. Maybe other things as well. I don't know if they've got *Allegro barbaro* or the "Bear Dance."

As far as my health is concerned, you can call it health from certain points of view. At least, the local doctor says that my lung problem from last year, several times misdiagnosed as [tuberculosis], has completely vanished. From another point of view, however, it is more "halfth" [fél-ség] than health [egészség]. My spleen, my blood, and I don't know what else, require periodic checkups. But this supposedly has to do with age (senescence? I don't care, whatever it is). I *have* been working, though not what was expected of me.

But I can't work on two things at a time, any more than a person with healthy eyes can squint simultaneously in two directions.

To make a long story short, I have been working only on those Romanian texts, and I have written an essay on them. I hope it will be "epoch-making," or at least "seminal"; too bad it interests no one in a position to appreciate it. But I don't care about that either. As I told you in N.Y., this is the working-off of my last (six-month) Columb. University appointment. So the effort wasn't entirely wasted.

Summer is good here; sometimes the heat is 96 degrees, not as chilling as last year. In addition, we got to enjoy the earthquake; Ditta, in particular, got her share of the tornado, too. So we've had enough entertainment.

Until we see each other (*so long! see you later!*[8]),

Many greetings,
Béla

The words "I *have* been working, though not what was expected of me" means that he knew the world was expecting compositions. He, however, considered the cause of ethnomusicology more important than anything else, as he himself told me several times. He thought that only a few people had expertise in that field, and the treasures of folk music had to be recorded before they disappeared forever.

[The preceding recollections are from *Így láttuk Bartókot: Harminchat emlékezés* (Thus did we see Bartók: thirty-six recollections), ed. Ferenc Bónis (Budapest, 1981).]

From a Distant Land, to a Distant Land: On the Occasion of Béla Bartók's Sixtieth Birthday

BÉLA BALÁZS

TRANSLATED BY BALÁZS DIBUZ

Dear Béla,

I never thought I'd ever be writing to you so far away, from so far away, halfway around the world: from Moscow to America. From far this side, to far beyond, those Csongrád farms, where we gathered folk songs together thirty-three years ago. So you had to wait until your sixtieth birthday before you finally decided to resettle at Columbia as a gray-haired music professor, you most Hungarian of musicians, did you? So you became an emigrant, too, Béla Bartók, just when they're applauding you so loudly in Hungary?

Of course, those you despised could never win you over with their applause. I remember your first success, the premiere of *The Wooden Prince*. When the crowd cheered you wildly and chanted your name we had to drag you to get you onto the stage, where you probed the audience with a cold, stiff look. And you refused to go out to take a second bow. I know what it was that steeled your heart that night, and I'm going to recount that now; and I suspect what it is that's driven you to America with a head of gray hair. And yet, on your birthday, I certainly wish you good health until we meet again back home, because we'll live to see that day, Béla Bartók!

There was many a time that you thought about leaving the country whose peasants you knew and understood more deeply than anyone. You were such a patriot that you wore a corded Hungarian costume as an innocent youth and composed, as your first symphony, the *Kossuth Symphony*. You were ready to emigrate thirty-three years ago, right around the time we were scouring the Tiszahát for the last remnants of the folk song. "Before long," you said, "in order to chase them down, we'll have to follow the emigrants to America. *They* might still be singing, or singing again."

Well, you went after them, Béla Bartók. But thirty-three years ago you wanted to go to Bucharest, not America. The Romanian Music Academy in Bucharest, besides publishing the six Romanian folk songs you had gathered across Transylvania (only incidentally, at that time) and had sent to them, offered you a teaching position. In Romania. Whereas the Hungarian folk songs, of which you gathered not just six but six thousand, roaming the Nyírség, the Kunság, and the mountains of Transylvania on foot with Zoltán Kodály, summer and winter, for seven years; tramping through snow, from homestead to homestead, from sheepfold to pigpen, with a phonograph recorder on your back; sleeping on pub benches, haylofts, but most often under haystacks, so that you returned from each expedition deathly ill— those six thousand–plus folk songs, all but lost or forgotten, which you salvaged in the thirteenth hour with scientific precision, including all their variations, categorized according to their locality and migrations, relating their types and the correlations between them—this exemplary achievement of ethnomusicology and music philology, this vast monument to Hungarian folk culture and the spirit of the Hungarian people—no one in Hungary was interested in publishing this. It's not even worth talking about how no one backed your project financially, so that you, two dedicated paupers, had to finance it with the little money you had for your daily bread, since the Museum of Ethnography wouldn't donate the wax records needed for the undertaking. But even when the work was done, no one was willing to publish it. No one in Hungary would take it even for free. Neither the Academy, nor the Kisfaludy Society, nor the Ministry of Religion and Education, nor any other organization, publisher, or private citizen in all of Hungary was willing to give the Hungarian people this unique musical gem and, in its own right, impeccable collection of folk songs. It was finally published by the Viennese Universal Edition.

But you didn't emigrate to Bucharest at that time, Béla Bartók. It wasn't my pleading or my naive reassurances that kept you from leaving, and it wasn't because I encouraged you with the coming Hungarian cultural renaissance or the cultural mission of Hungary. You were not aware, after all, that there is no future for bourgeois culture and never will be. But, with your healthy skepticism, you saw the situation more clearly than I and thus you didn't believe in a "better tomorrow." Your battle seemed a somber ordeal, Béla Bartók, an arduous battle, without faith, without hope, endured out of duty. You didn't move to Romania, "because somebody has finally got to do this," you said plainly and dryly: "The Slovaks have had a superb, scholarly treasury of folk songs for a long time, as have the Serbs and the Swabians, and it's only we Hungarians who don't. And if we don't hurry, there won't be anything left to collect. Most old songs are becoming obsolete, and they're singing hit tunes from operettas in the villages, and silly contemporary songs—that is, where the peasants still even feel like singing. We have to hurry. No one else will undertake this task, so I'll have to do it."

This is what you said and did, Béla Bartók, though it was not just

the well-being of your fragile physique that you sacrificed to this difficult work. You sacrificed a great deal more, consciously conceding
seven years of creative endeavor. Because you were not a musical
scholar, after all, but one of Europe's most gifted composers. And you
set aside your personal artistic production, your own music, for the
sake of the Hungarian folk song, which the Hungarian gentry would
have nothing to do with and which therefore could not even be
released.

The reason you didn't have the time and energy for your own compositions during those seven years was that collecting those folk songs
did not consist only of your visiting homesteads, urging the silent,
joyless peasants to sing, and transcribing what they sang. With you,
Béla Bartók, it meant much more, because you set about learning
Slovak and Romanian with dictionaries and grammar books simply so
that you might study the migration and influence of Hungarian folk
songs in regions inhabited by Slovaks and Romanians, and the Slovak
and Romanian variations of these songs, so as to comprehend and
explore the deep folk internationalism by means of which folk music
and folk poetry flows across national, linguistic, and racial boundaries
and fuses all around the world. You developed into a philologist of
music and a music folklorist through a conscientious, strict sense of
duty.

Because—and here's the explanation for why the Hungarian aristocracy and bourgeoisie had no use for you and your folk song
collection—you, Béla Bartók were interested in folk music, the music
of all peoples, not just that of Hungarians. The Hungarian folk song
was dearest to you because you are Hungarian, but you loved all folk
music equally well, be it Slovak, Romanian, or Serbian, and hated
the popular songs of the gentry, the parasitic gypsy music of the cafés.
This is why your love of folk songs was not nationalistic but rather
internationalistic by nature. After all, you eventually spent more time
among Romanians than among Hungarians, and then you even had
some of your Romanians brought up to the Academy of Arts and
Sciences in order to sing, play, and dance before the Berzeviczys and
the Beöthys.[9] But the Albert Berzeviczys and the Zsolt Beöthys knew
what it was all about better than we did back then. With stronger instincts, they perceived that which we didn't know—that this kind of
propagation of folk music, generally without regard to nationality,
this kind of love of the people, is a class-based attitude, and dangerous
even if you yourself don't know this, Béla Bartók. Because for you, as
for Herder in his own time, it was not chauvinism but a deeply under-

stood internationalism that made it possible for you to hear and understand "die Stimme der Völker."[10]

Once, I discovered an Arabic grammar book on your desk.

"What, pray tell, is that?" I asked.

"I have to learn Arabic."

"You have to?"

"I have to, because I'm going to Africa."

"And why do you have to do that?"

"Because ten years ago, when I was still Ferenc Vecsey's piano accompanist, I traveled to Spain with him on tour, and I got to cross over to Africa for a day. There, in an Arab watering hole, I heard some Arabic songs that were very interesting. Since then I've been planning to look into this thing. But in order to understand folk songs, one has to understand the language of the lyrics."

You actually did travel to Africa that same year. You always were a stubborn little fellow.

You were very surprised, weren't you, when in 1920 during the regime[11] they accused you of being unpatriotic, almost of being a traitor, because an essay about the Hungarian folk song appeared in a German journal of musicology, in which you mentioned, among other things, that Hungarian folk songs can show signs of Romanian influence now and then. Jenő Hubay,[12] in particular, attacked you because of this. He defended the Hungarian folk song against you, who instituted it and first presented it in foreign journals. He was defending America against Columbus! Against you, the greatest Hungarian musician and the one closest to the people. Today, perhaps even you understand that Hubay was doing this not out of ignorance but out of a healthy class intuition, at the time of the most fervent white terror. No, the fact that not a single Hungarian vocalist was willing to perform these beautiful songs on the stage was not simply a matter of a lack of culture and taste. "These melodies are meant for the tavern" said Takács, the most famous baritone at the time. This was not conscious, intentional politics but rather an instinctual class position.

For a good while, you fared no better with your own compositions than with the folk songs. Why would you have? Yours was a music that grew from the soul of a true, peasants' folk music, not a gentrified casino csárdás, not tearjerking, woebegone, watered-down sentimentalism. It was not noble Hungarian music but music of the Hungarian folk, even in its most differentiated atonal manifestation. True, it wasn't always pleasant either—just as, let's say, Rembrandt's old woman is a fine expression of human qualities but not endowed with feminine charm. As I wrote:

> Your music is no sweet ecstasy.
> A relentless structure of steel.
> A throbbing subterranean rebellion.
> A savage pain, a shrieking pain.
> Who wounded you?
>
> Your violins cut, your horns stab.
> Hawk talons claw at your piano,
> And the sounds are strewn about,
> A ripped and bleeding flock of birds.
> What are you singing?[13]

It is not salon music. But then, *Macbeth*'s merit is not that it makes good vacation reading; and even Goethe was frightened by Beethoven's terrible savageness. He was frightened, but reverent. He didn't spit on him. You, on the other hand, Béla Bartók, were spat upon in Hungary.

The Philharmonic still played *Kossuth*, because its patriotic character made it acceptable, but it was composed under the influence of Richard Strauss and was a first work. It wasn't really Hungarian yet. Later, when you dug yourself ever deeper into the Hungarian humus, without compromise, to be sure, you hardly got a chance to be heard. You composed my *Bluebeard*. It was your first vocal piece. But you never submitted this, the melody scheme of a Transylvanian folk song blown up to a full-length opera. You were haughty, not a naive optimist like me. You despised futile experimentation. I smuggled a piano score to Count Miklós Bánffy, who was an intendant at that time (in fact, not the worst). I placed my hopes in Sándor Hevesy,[14] who was then temporary stage manager at the Opera. Mr. Hevesy said, "Too dark." He was promoting rococo at the time. You were right again, Béla Bartók.

You were far from happy in those days, and you became only more gloomy as time passed. You stopped working. "Why," you asked. "For whom? In Hungary?" You were sensitive, like an open wound. You might very well have starved to death, along with Zoltán Kodály, were it not for the attention of the one person who sympathized with you, the talented, spirited, and highly cultivated Emma Gruber[15] (clearly, she would now be prey to the anti-Jewish law herself); if Mrs. Emma, the Henriette Herz[16] of the Hungarian music world, had not been able to handle those two "incensed boors" with wise, heartfelt, delicate tact. . . . And if the Waldbauer-Kerpely Quartet had not been performing your String Quartet occasionally, not a single note of the genius of Béla Bartók would have been heard in Hungary. The result of the Waldbauer Quartet's Bartók-Kodály Evening was that the gutter papers of the Budapest tabloid press spat upon the geniuses of Hungarian music with the most cynical and obscene ridicule. Boorish musical illiterates, playing at being critics, joked about you. Believe me, Béla Bartók, it was not just a matter of frivolous crassness and cynicism, or of the envy of serious music demonstrated by operetta and music hall librettists; rather, it was class perspective, though unconsciously so. It is equally true of your class perspective and of theirs: "They don't know this, but they are doing it."[17] Because in those days, only the Buttykays, the Zerkovitzes, the Loránd Fráters, and the Jacobis were allowed to live in Hungary. That's according to the first-class complimentary press ticket.

You yourself saw back then, Béla Bartók, that living in Hungary was allotted only to them, and you lost your desire to live. We were good friends and talked openly about these things. "Let's try again," I encouraged you, "with a ballet this time." If the audience interprets your music through the effect of the dance and pantomime that enters through their eyes, and if movement and color also help, then perhaps it will work. That was how *The Wooden Prince* came about.

Nowadays, I often hear our ballet, and also our *Bluebeard*, on the radio. The world has changed a lot since then. When Toscanini and Mengelberg were directing your work abroad, at home they were so kind as to concede, though very coyly, that you are a musician and not an impostor, which is what Pál Kéri of *Az Est* (The evening) called you. A social situation that was becoming increasingly critical was forced to proclaim, among other demagogueries, the value of "folk art." You received your later successes with the same bitter suspicion as you did that first one, about which we can speak with a smile now, on the occasion of your sixtieth birthday.

So *The Wooden Prince* was printed in an issue of *Nyugat* (West). Count Miklós Bánffy stopped me outside the National Theater the following day.

"I read your ballet. Interesting . . . ," he said, rolling his *r*'s. "I like it. One could paint beautiful backdrops for it, in the style of the Hungarian folk story. Do tell, who are you going to commission to compose it?"

"The music is already finished," I lied. "Béla Bartók did it."

"Too bad, too bad," he said, as he tugged at his walrus moustache, "seeing as the public doesn't like him. Because I've conceived some very pretty scenery. I've even got sketches already. Come up and see me anyway, and we'll talk about it."

In a nutshell, the count became so enthusiastic about painting the scenery for the ballet that he agreed to do *The Wooden Prince*, along with its unheard, unwritten score by Bartók.

I ran to you. Let's have that music, quick! It must be done by fall. We traveled to some *Nachtkultur* sanitorium on a mountaintop near Zurich, with the Kodálys. (Kodály was a master at coming up with these hygienic whims.) But it wasn't a bad place. We would wear a swimsuit all day, only putting on pajamas or a nightgown out of habit when retiring in the evening. Then we'd button up the door. Because the wooden barracks had only canvas curtains for doors, which had to be buttoned to the doorjamb for greater security.

You worked with passionate energy, as always, and one day, which was dismal because of the pouring rain, you called us into the empty dining room, locked the glass doors and sat down at the upright piano in your soaking wet swimsuit in order to play *The Wooden Prince* for our small company of four, in bathing trunks and tops.

We were so engrossed that it took us a few minutes to notice that someone was banging loudly on the glass doors. A soaking wet, fat, old Böcklin monster stood outside the rain-streaked windows, staring fixedly at us with bulging eyes and pounding the door wildly. It was such a comical sight that we didn't really even grumble.

"Please," the jovial water monster wheezed asthmatically, in his merry Viennese German, "please don't be angry. But it's raining out. What can I do? Don't be angry," he pleaded with a whimper. "I know this is modern music, surely it is wonderful music, and if it weren't raining, I'd go for a walk in the forest. Please, go on, play modern music. It's just . . . it's raining, so I can't go into the forest. My barrack is right next door, and I'm an old man, and . . . I can't stand it!" he cried out suddenly. "Please, I can't stand it! I tried for a while. Please don't be angry . . . it must certainly be wonderful music, but it's raining, and I can't stand it, I can't stand it!"

He said all this so kindly, honestly, and respectfully, and with such good intentions, that we had to laugh. We closed the piano and made friends with the old merman. He was Rosenthal, the wonderful Austrian pianist. He considered you neither an impostor nor a lunatic.

Then, in the fall, the battle of *The Wooden Prince* began at the Opera. Because a count is an important man in Hungary, and if he feels a noble desire to paint the scenery for a pantomime, then nothing will daunt his intentions, not even the protestations of ten conductors, two stage managers, and a ballet master. But then came the counterattack. You didn't even know about that, Béla Bartók, because you had only one condition when you accepted the project: that you would not have to cross the threshold of the Opera before the premiere, and perhaps not even during it.

It was unimaginable that old Kerner should conduct. The ballet specialist, Szikla, said right out that he didn't understand the music. No one was willing to take it on but the little black-haired Egisto Tango,[18] the talented Italian they had just recently engaged, who understood and loved music and in whom you had more confidence than in the Hungarians of the Ábrányi sort. So is it by chance, would you say now, that at the sixtieth birthday celebration for you at the Opera an Italian guest conducted *The Wooden Prince* and *Bluebeard*?[19] Once again, the situation is that there isn't a Hungarian conductor for your music, to which you listened far away in America, just as I did far away in Moscow.

The stage manager at the Opera at that time, an animal named Bródy,[20] announced that neither the music nor the lyrics made any sense, and that he would have nothing to do with it. The ballet master, a Swedish rhythm-gymnastics teacher, ascertained that there was neither waltz nor polka in the music and that there was altogether nothing to dance to. So I approached the count: "Look at me, Sir Count." He stuck his monocle up to his eye. "As I stand here before you, I have never been on the stage before."

"I'm delighted."

"Let me direct *The Wooden Prince*. And let me direct the ballet, too, though I've never seen how it's done."

There was no other way to save your music, Béla Bartók. I had to take it in hand. That's how I became a director.

A count is a count so that he won't have to concern himself with trifles if he wants to paint scenery. He entrusted me with the direction of the stage and the dance. The events of the following two months might make an exciting chapter in a novel someday. It started with the copyists' sabotaging the transcription of the parts for voice, and Emília Nirschy's weekly resignations, immediately wanting to get an engagement somewhere else, because the count wanted her to dance in red riding boots, which are impossible to toe-dance in. The orchestra deliberately played out of tune. We could barely find a pianist for my rehearsals, and it was absolutely impossible to speak with the count during that time. He was never in his office, because he was up in the immense attic of the Opera, with his trousers and shirtsleeves rolled up, pouring buckets of paint onto enormous canvases spread out on the floor and painting scenery with a broom in each hand. His face glowed with ecstasy. He was a talented and intelligent man, and painted lovely scenery. As the date of the opening night battle approached, the newspaper critics were already circling the Opera, cawing, like crows awaiting death. They would have liked to write up the failure of the ballet before it happened. The audience of the boxes came to see a scandal. But the eager heartbeat of the youths in the gallery could virtually be heard through the suspenseful silence. And Tango's assertive whisper was audible on stage during the performance, because he conducted not with his hands alone but also with his voice. He sat above the intractable orchestra like a small, black, dangerous condottiere, an animal trainer, a hypnotist. He knew that the orchestra *wanted* to play out of tune.

After the curtain fell, a minute of dead silence. A gigantic, invisible, silent balance teetered. It hung between the honest feeling of an elementary effect and the recoil of a spiteful vulgarity. And then, like a sudden explosion, a thunderous applause began in the gallery and swept down to the stalls, the likes of which was last heard in the Hungarian Royal Opera at the premiere of *Madama Butterfly*, according to the ushers. Even the orchestra was cheered. The musicians looked at one another in amazement. They had played better than ever, against their will. (This was the Egisto Tango who was the first to conduct, beautifully, the *Internationale* in the Opera after the proclamation of the dictatorship of the proletariat.)

And then you stood there, Béla Bartók, stiff-necked, with an icy face, and watched the applauders. You wouldn't even come onstage to take a second bow, though your contempt was not wholly justified by then. The applause in the gallery was sincere. But it came too late. Something inside you had frozen up; and those whom you had disdained when they disdained you, you did not appreciate immediately when their taste turned and they began to applaud you. But the journalists of Pest were forced to write new reviews about you. They just ran me down. But it was your success that mattered then.

This all happened long ago. Since you've become renowned worldwide, though they might not love you they've been obliged to respect you in Hungary, too—especially since the bourgeois demagogy has come to require the slogan of "the folk" to take in the folk. But then, it costs less to propagate the peasants' art than to distribute the land. Your two works for the stage held the boards until the collapse of the dictatorship of the proletariat in Hungary. And then they set it aside, as the work of a member of the music directorate of the commune.

But even the regime needed your name, and they wanted to revive these two pieces—but without the name of the communist, emigrant librettist, of course. You protested against this, Béla Bartók, though doing so was not entirely safe. You preferred to prevent the performance of your pieces in this way and to surrender the royalties, of which you were nonetheless in dire need at the time. When I heard about this in Vienna, I let you know that I placed no significance in the appearance of my name on the program of the Hungarian Royal Opera, so they should just go ahead and perform your music. You've held the boards ever since. When you found out once that the Opera was withholding royalties from me (which it should have been paying through the Viennese Universal Edition, because these two masterpieces of Hungarian music could also be published only in Vienna), you sued the Opera for the sum it owed this communist. That's how stubborn you are, Béla Bartók.

We've only met once since then. I imagine it must have been in 1927, in Berlin, when you performed there. We talked briefly in the green room, but it was long enough for me to see that you are not a bit more cheerful than you were long ago. But you were an important figure in the world of music by then. You could never be won over by applause, though, Béla Bartók. You were always hardheaded. Clearly, it is this uncompromising implacability that has led you to emigrate to America now, when you are most celebrated at home. I believe I know why; it's not too difficult to guess. You, the most Hungarian of Hungarian artists, breathe more freely now in America. But don't grieve, Béla Bartók. There are many of us over here who greet you on your sixtieth birthday with love and wish that God may grant you strength and good health. Because we will meet again, back home. I already have opera lyrics for you. Something completely new and completely different from what I wrote for you long ago.

[The final text in this section is taken from the manuscript preserved in the Hungarian Academy of Arts and Sciences, MTA MS 5014/55. It was published in Hungarian in Béla Balázs, *Válogatott cikkek és tanulmányok* (Selected articles and essays) (Budapest, 1968).]

NOTES

1. The Csángós were a linguistically isolated Hungarian-speaking population in Moldova, Eastern Romania. [Ed.]

2. István Thomán (1862–1940), Bartók's renowned piano teacher at the Conservatory, a former pupil of Franz Liszt. [Ed.]

3. Sándor Veress's wife was English-born. [Ed.]

4. János Demény, ed., *Bartók Béla levelei* (Béla Bartók's letters) (Budapest, 1976), p. 626. [Ed.]

5. The first volume of Bartók's Hungarian folk song collection was finally published in 1991, as edited by Sándor Kovács. [Ed.]

6. In 1988, Bartók's remains were returned to Hungary. [Ed.]

7. Balogh is referring to the Norton Lecture Series at Harvard. More recently, Leonard Bernstein and John Cage were also invited to give Norton Lectures. [Ed.]

8. In English in the original. [Ed.]

9. Albert Berzeviczy (1853–1936), a conservative politician and aesthete, important leader in cultural life during the Horthy regime, and president of the Kisfaludy Society; and Zsolt Beöthy (1848–1922), literary historian and leading member of the Kisfaludy Society.

10. A reference to *The Voice of the Peoples*, J. G. Herder's collection of folk songs, which first appeared in 1778. It was at that time that Herder introduced the term *folk song*.

11. The regime of the 1920s was led by Count István Bethlen, who was appointed prime minister in 1921.

12. Jenö Hubay (Huber) (1858–1937), the director of the College of Music at the time, got involved with the debate that had been initiated by the 19 May 1920 issue of the *Nemzeti Ujság* (National journal). In that issue, one Dr. S. E. (Elemér Sereghy) attacked Bartók, pronouncing him unpatriotic. He wrote, among other things, that Bartók "proclaims Máramaros, Ugocsa, and Szatmár to be Romanian territory. . . . He wants to show that every one of our Transylvanian songs is of Romanian origin." The article made a stir in the political groves of the regime and in professional music circles.

A few days later, a correspondent for *Szózat* (The voice) looked Hubay up and asked him for a statement. Under the cloak of "bosom buddy" Hubay said the following: "I consider the publication of the article extremely ill timed, and what's more, unfortunate. . . . I am not surprised that Bartók's careless behavior may have seemed unpatriotic in very wide circles. As far as the contents of the article are concerned, I consider them highly debatable."

Bartók's article had actually appeared in 1914, in the Hungarian Ethnography Society's bulletin *Ethnography*. This time, it appeared in German translation, published in the March 1920 issue of the *Zeitschrift für Musikwissenschaft*, with the title "Musikdialekt der Rumänen von Hunyad."

13. Excerpt from Balázs's poem "Bartók Béla," in *Az én utam* (My path) (Budapest, 1958).

14. Sándor Hevesy (1873–1939), a writer and the stage manager of the National Theater from 1901 and its director from 1922 to 1932. He took part in the work of the progressive Thalia Society from 1904 and was stage manager of the Opera House from 1912 to 1916.

15. The best young artists met and discussed their work in the home of Mrs. Henrik Gruber, *née* Emma Sándor. It was here that Bartók met Kodály. Mrs.

Gruber became Kodály's wife in 1910. She herself composed, wrote verses, and was a fine translator.

16. The greatest of the German intelligentsia paid homage to Henriette Hertz (1764–1847), one of the most beautiful, accomplished, and intelligent women of her day, who resided in Berlin and was the daughter of de Lemos, a Jewish doctor of Spanish descent. Contemporary scholars of the arts and sciences gathered in her house, most notably the romantics Humboldt, Schlegel, Börne, Engel, Moritz, and others.

17. "Sie wissen nicht, aber sie tun es"; from Karl Marx's *Das Kapital*, vol. 1.

18. Egisto Tango (1873–1951), the outstanding Italian conductor, worked at the Budapest Opera House from 1913 until 1919. He conducted the premiere performances of Bartók's *The Wooden Prince* and *Bluebeard's Castle*.

19. A reference to Sergio Failoni (1890–1946), conductor of the Budapest Opera from 1928 until his death.

20. Miklós Bródy, who functioned, however, only as guest director at the Budapest Opera.

A Change in Style

EDWIN VON DER NÜLL

TRANSLATED BY SUSAN GILLESPIE

Until this point, Bartók relied on a single dominant melody in the tonal conception of his ideas, exploring it in a purely chordal manner. From the Bagatelles, Op. 6, to the Etudes, Op. 18, his works are wholly harmonically determined in their tonal structure, aside from the minimal contrapuntal episodes in his folk song settings—and these, by virtue of their accidental character, are not fit to provide a compelling stylistic criterion of even minimal significance. Contrapuntal elements that are deserving of critical stylistic attention appear for the first time in the Improvisations, where they announce the impending shift in the tonal form of Bartók's music. The 1926 Sonata also gives intermittent prominence to counterpoint—for example, in the first development section of the first movement; in the second movement, and in the second part of the third movement, in the elaboration of the second theme. Apart from this, however, the harmonic musician Bartók has the last word in the above works.

To refer, in this general framework, to Schoenberg and his piano music, with its primarily linear conception, is to point up another essential difference between Bartók and Schoenberg. This difference also distances Bartók's piano music from the stylistic ambitions of his era. In a period that tends toward linear polyphony without binding harmonies, the harmonic musician Bartók occupies a unique place. Bartók explains his individuality with a touch of humor:

> Why do I make so little use of counterpoint? I would like to respond like this: because that's just the way I am. But since that is no answer at all, I will attempt to explain: 1) In any case, a natural predisposition is involved. 2) In my youth my ideal of beauty was not so much the style of Bach or Mozart as that of Beethoven. Recently, this has changed somewhat; in the last few years I have

also been engrossed in music from the pre-Bach period, and I believe traces of this can be found, for example, in the Piano Concerto and in the Nine Little Piano Pieces.

The path by which Bartók arrives—late enough—at linear polyphony is remarkably circuitous, and is characteristic of this solitary man. It is not the direct influence of his own era that brings about his transformation from a purely harmonic to a contrapuntal composer; instead, the stylistic transformation in Bartók's piano music has a music-historical basis. First, his ideal of beauty is transferred from Beethoven to Bach. This is not without concrete consequences for his own compositional activity. In rapid succession, in the year 1926, there appear a series of small pieces that Bartók published as "Nine Little Piano Pieces" and "Out of Doors (Five Piano Pieces)." Here one can find the first broad influence of the contrapuntal movement, expressed in ways that range from strict linear duets (Four Dialogues) to free, occasional counterpoint (*Preludio all'Ungherese*). The Four Dialogues, which are the first four pieces of the Nine Little Piano Pieces, should be seen as an offshoot of the Inventions of J. S. Bach. The themes, especially in Nos. 1 and 13, describe a somewhat longer arc than those generally found in Bach's Two-Part Inventions. But the dependence on Bach remains so plainly evident that one can only describe the Four Dialogues as studies that Bartók made in order to unite the strict [contrapuntal] style with *his own* tonal method of composition.

[Source: Edwin von der Nüll, "Stilwende," in *Béla Bartók. Ein Beitrag zur Morphologie der neuen Musik* (Halle [Saale], 1930)]

Bartók's Third String Quartet

THEODOR ADORNO

TRANSLATED BY SUSAN GILLESPIE

To fully appreciate Bartók's Third String Quartet, unquestionably the best of the Hungarian's works to date, requires reflection on his development. However immediate the evidence of beauty that it contains, its extraordinary achievement can be measured only against the arc of development. The latter does not move forward, like Schoenberg's, with dialectical steadiness, does not advance by leaps around the un-constructable middle, like Stravinsky's; rather, it moves as a spiral in faithful repetition of the tasks of its origin, in a process that is at the same time continuous rejuvenation. The only danger that threatens it is aberration. But in this very development Bartók proves himself substantively. From the most perilous ventures he is able to draw strengths that concentrically strengthen his attack on what is uniquely suited to him. Nowhere does the notion of the experiment, to which perfidious reaction has given a bad name, make more sense than in his work. From the cruel precision of the tasks that his musical nature sets for him, wholly intensive and inimical to any expansion into the realm of qualitative possibilities, he leaps into the void; into a musical sphere that remains incomprehensibly alien to him—in contrast to composers whose intentions are comprehensive—in order to return from it to the slender flame of the work, which is rekindled by the wind from the alien, wide musical plain. Bartók's development is ori-ented exclusively toward three movements, movement models, as it were, which are never represented in typical purity yet at the same time are never quite allowed to dissolve. Their ideas have been ignited by the blast of European musical consciousness striking the still-glowing embers of Hungarian folklore, whose genuineness Bartók le-gitimizes once more by accepting the European attack rather than retreating into romantic security. The psalmodic, motivically loose rhapsody, as through-composed sonata; the sweeping, open monody, as adagio; the unresistingly agitated csárdás, driven even by its syncopation, as rondo—this is how these types appear in the context of the developed techniques of European composition. That Bartók unwrapped them from the genre of costumed foreignness and opened up their real strangeness, by confronting them with European musical consciousness, was his first achievement. After that, his struggle concentrated on the realization of the three movements. The decision came with the Second Quartet, where the sonata bumps crashing into the types and tames them. The First Violin Sonata is the first to reduce the types to their common denominator and construct the sonata, quite strictly, out of them. Implicitly, it raises the issue of the survival of the three types. For the sonata's reprise and the rondo's repetitions, which had succeeded so convincingly, had not been able to penetrate the motivic material completely, while the improvisational forms of folklore threatened to rigidify as soon as they came under the domination of the sonata forms that were meant to preserve them. This, and not some new inclination toward folklore, is why the sonata had to go; at the same time, this is why the Hungarian types also had to divest themselves of their form-creating rights, for they no longer withstood the force of music that had grown strong through the sonata and broken it apart. This is the situation of the Second Violin Sonata. Rhapsody and Lento merge into one; they emerge as a great introduction to a fresh overall situation, which bends the types together constructively and makes room for motivic details, not by dissolving them into the total form but by presenting them strophically. The csárdás becomes an irregular complex of musical phrases, a phrase village, with a middle part that is set improvisationally at its center, like a trio; the reprise, through radical change, is drawn into the unhesitating forward movement; the whole is given structure by the principal theme of the introduction, in a penetrating reminiscence through which the early single-movement nature of gypsy music is brought home.

To develop the composition of the three initial types further than this was not immediately possible. Bartók had both realized and broken their forms. His experiment could nowhere have been more appropriate than at this very juncture. He allowed himself to be seduced by the neoclassical Stravinsky, and by his own past, in the series of works that are grouped around the Piano Concerto. Bartók may be perceptible in their driving movement and motivic core, but their overall stance is an unceremonious negation of the inner compositional position he had previously achieved. Yet the strange gamble of the first leap is justified by the subsequent boldness of the second.

Seldom has a composer returned to his own zone more greatly enriched than Bartók in the Third Quartet. Once more, he takes up his position on the culmination point from which he had leapt, to forge ahead from there in a continuity that would not have been possible earlier. Now, the formal ideas of the Second Violin Sonata take on an extensive richness in *counterpoint*, which Bartók brings home from his classical adventure as booty into the tent camp of restless improvisation. Not that Bartók could not have written counterpoint earlier. In the development of the finale of the First Quartet, polyphony already unfolded supremely. But now counterpoint, which was previously a means of development, has become material, like motives, chords, and motion. Nothing [is] more instructive than the comparison of the fugato passage in the First Quartet with its analogue in the Third. The Lento at the beginning, as in the Second Violin Sonata, and, like it, layered in "intonations" rather than unfolded in sonatalike fashion, yet protected by its free, arching imitativeness from the dissolution of mere improvisation; then again and again *Allegro barbaro*, but interrupted today, in its mere forward movement, by the autonomy of the voices; where their homophonic calm is wanted, the sound also becomes extremely dense, thus sharply distinguishing itself from the polyphonic progression. The second part of the work is the reprise; first the very abbreviated one of the Lento, which in anticipation of the Allegro no longer finds time to establish itself; then a rapid coda, corresponding to the rondo reprise of the Second Violin Sonata, variational play with the Allegro motives. The themes from which the work has been formed, with stern economy, are more pliable than even before in Bartók, more strongly formed and more reliably heard; the harmonies are developed with a bold looseness out of lines and crossings of lines, their intervallic values nevertheless followed exactly. What is decisive is the *formative power* of the work; the iron concentration, the wholly original tectonics, so precisely suited to Bartók's actual position. Hungarian types and German sonata are fused together in the white heat of impatient compositional effort; from them truly contemporary form is created.

This brings us to the Quartet movement. The instrumentation of Bartók's chamber music has always been unusually concrete and appropriate to the material. The Third Quartet surpasses all earlier efforts in this regard. He has wrested from neoclassicism, which he has left behind, the thing one would least have expected: new color. Not only is the compact hardness of the Piano Quartet made use of in parts of the Quartet; the counterpoint has unloosed all its colors and injected the wealth of nuances into the tension between black and white that had otherwise dictated Bartók's sound. The remote possibilities of the instruments bend willingly to his hand, as do the broad spans of multivocal chords. In the Third Quartet, Bartók made his actual discovery of the productivity of color. It not only guarantees this masterwork but opens a perspective on what will follow.

[Source: "Béla Bartóks Drittes Streichquartett," in Theodor W. Adorno, *Gesammelte Schriften*, vol. 18 (Frankfurt am Main, 1978). The article first appeared in 1929.]

Bartók's Foreign Tour

ALADÁR TÓTH

TRANSLATED BY DAVID E. SCHNEIDER
AND KLÁRA MÓRICZ

Aladár Tóth (1898–1968) was the most important Hungarian music critic of the interwar period. From 1922 to 1939 he frequently contributed to the literary journal *Nyugat* (West), from 1923 to 1939 he was the head critic for the *Pesti Napló* (Pest journal), and in the years 1926–29 he served as senior editor of *Zenei Szemle* (Music review). Bartók's tour of Western Europe in March and April 1922 included his first concerts in England and France since 1904 and 1905 respectively. The following account of the trip is especially important for its record of Bartók's impressions of Stravinsky, whom he met at the home of Henry Prunières in Paris. Also noteworthy are Bartók's opinions regarding two mechanical instruments, the Pleyela and the Pianola (see "Mechanical Music," in Béla Bartók, *Essays*, ed. Benjamin Suchoff [New York, 1976], pp. 289–303), and the harpsichord, which was undergoing a renaissance in the 1920s (see "The Performance of Works Written for the Clavecin," in ibid., pp. 285–86). [Trans.]

[Source: Aladár Tóth, "Bartók külföldi útja" (Bartók's foreign tour), vol. 7 (*Bartók Béla művészi kibontakozásának évei II—Bartók megjelenése az európai zeneéletben [1914–1926]* [The years of Bartók's artistic evolution, part 2—Bartók's appearance in European musical life (1914–1926)], ed. János Demény) of *Zenetudományi tanulmányok*, ed. Bence Szabolcsi and Dénes Bartha (Budapest, 1959), pp. 219–22; originally published in *Nyugat* 15, no. 12 (1922): 830–33.]

It is most natural for every composer setting out on tour to want to cover large territories in order to see his art reflected in the temperaments of diverse peoples. It is natural for him to want to see whether he is known and understood, and finally be given the opportunity to provide a genuine picture of himself through his own performance.

Even more important for Béla Bartók on his trip to London, Paris, and Frankfurt[1] was whether he could find allies for his artistic goals— what would they be like? Would he be able to gather inspirational impressions; would he glimpse new areas that his genius would consider worthy of cultivation? This is the sacred egoism of great artists—it drives them to collect everything that might contribute to their work, and as they do so even revolutionary artists such as Bartók take their inspiration from many sources.

Bartók's expectations were entirely met in the course of his tour. True, Chopin was perhaps the only artist to return from England disappointed. Handel's second homeland, which rejoiced in the reception of every great artist from the time of Haydn and Beethoven onward, was only remaining faithful to its customs when it recognized the world-class value of two representatives of new Hungarian music, Bartók and Kodály, and invited one of them, the performing artist Bartók, to London. In anticipation of Bartók's arrival, the *Daily Telegraph* published an article several columns long about the Hungarian composer, and the *Daily Mail* greeted Bartók with the publication of his biographical data. Bartók first performed for a select audience consisting mainly of musicians in the salon of Hedry, the Hungarian chargé d'affaires. Already this private concert caused a great sensation. The *Times* reported on it twice; the second article was dedicated entirely to the Sonata for Violin and Piano. Additionally, six other daily newspapers contained articles citing Bartók as one of the greatest spirits of modern music.[2] His large public concert took place in Aeolian Hall and was reviewed in at least seventeen newspapers.[3] Even most of the conservative critics acknowledged Bartók's natural talent. Bartók's Parisian concert was covered by the *Figaro, Excelsior, Comœdia*, and *L'Eclair*. The closing sentence of the review in *L'Eclair* deserves quotation: "This sonata [the First Sonata for Violin and Piano] is truly a masterpiece: clear and hard, transparent as crystal." Bartók's successes were due in large part to his partner, the first-rate Hungarian violinist Jelly Arányi.[4] Not only did she receive the highest praise from the press but in the music salons of London and Paris she was compared to the greatest performing artists. Arányi unfortunately could not accompany Bartók to Frankfurt; there he had to make do with a lesser violinist.

It takes only a glance at the papers to see that Bartók achieved a number of his goals: he was known, understood, and acknowledged. His art was accepted as an eternal gift to humanity. But how did he profit from it? Did he find allies, sympathetic comrades, in his artistic endeavors? We ask Bartók himself. Some anecdotes from his tour, related through the jaggedness of everyday conversation, provide interesting answers characteristic of both the musical life of the countries visited and the narrator.

Bartók heard far too little music by the English modernists to be able to form much of an opinion about them. He could not perceive anything beyond skillful fluency in the music of Eugene Goossens;[5] nor did smaller piano pieces by other young English composers reveal to him stronger, more distinct personalities. Delius's great Requiem, which was performed while Bartók was in London, is decidedly a retrogression compared to the composer's earlier compositions, and Bartók was surprised by Delius's lack of imagination, which resulted for Bartók in a completely flat work.

In England, modern music has outstanding advocates in [Albert] Coates and Sir Henry Wood,[6] the conductors of the London Symphony Orchestra. In a concert conducted by Coates, Bartók heard a spineless piece of program music by the Italian Respighi,[7] Strauss's *Till Eulenspiegel*, and the last movement of Stravinsky's *Firebird Suite*, whose sparkling, lively rhythms and Eastern dynamism were quite refreshing, "especially after *Till Eulenspiegel*." So it seems that Bartók is increasingly turning away from Strauss.

Bartók spoke about the London Symphony Orchestra with great appreciation. He especially praised the unusually high quality of the strings. In his opinion, however, the winds are not at the level of our Philharmonic. Coates proved his ability as a first-rate conductor of the classical repertory by closing his program with the Fifth Symphony [by Beethoven].

In England Bartók was introduced to the cembalo and harpsichord through the offices of the pianist Gordon Woodhouse,[8] the English Wanda Landowska. Bartók heard [Gordon Woodhouse] play Bach's B♭-major Partita and pieces by Scarlatti and Couperin with stylistic perfection, yet freely and with exceptional individuality. Bartók the folklorist was especially intrigued by the unique structure of an Old English peasant dance in mixolydian mode. It sounded quite good in a skillful transcription for the cembalo. The instrument's rich and varied timbre even brought to life the composition's hidden colors. It was a pleasant surprise when Gordon Woodhouse played a few of Bartók's pieces for children on the harpsichord.

In London Bartók was also introduced to the cembalo's most recent descendant, the Pianola. Edwin Evans, the music critic of the *Pall Mall Gazette*, took Bartók to the Pianola Company's exhibition room. There is no need to mention that this mechanical piano did not win Bartók's sympathy as did its eighteenth-century ancestor. The operator of the instrument can control the pedaling, tempo, and dynamics, but the keyboard-percussion instrument's most secret magic, the art of refined touch, is replaced by a soulless percussion device. The prophets of modern "objective music," however, consider precisely this imperfection to hold great promise for the future of the Pianola. From now on the composer will not be subjected to the intrusion of the performing artist's emotions, to the falsification of the true image of the work. In comparison to the physical limits of the piano, the Pianola guarantees boundless technique, but it also demands a unique "Pianola-like" technique of composition. The compositions by Goossens and Casella[9] that Bartók heard were rather unsuited to the Pianola's mechanical "objectivity." The wooden and lifeless rhythm of the Pianola exposed the cheap superficiality of a harmonically twisted waltz by Casella. Bartók was more convinced by Stravinsky's composition for Pianola.[10] Although similar in style to Piano-Rag-Music, it is wittier and much more significant. The theoretical development of the composer of *Petrouchka* necessarily led him to compose with mechanical sounds; and nobody knows how to capture this style more effectively than Stravinsky. Nevertheless, according to Bartók, the work for Pianola would sound better on several pianos.

After Bartók's performance in Paris, Henry Prunières, editor-in-chief of *La Revue Musicale* and one of the most eminent French art historians and aestheticians of music, threw a party in Bartók's honor. Here Bartók met Stravinsky for the first time. That evening the following musicians inscribed their names in Prunières's guest book: Bartók, Stravinsky, Ravel, Szymanowski, Roussel, and the members of the group "Les Six." Thus the names of the greatest modern composers appeared on a single page of a guest book. Prunières rightly observed that only Schoenberg's name was missing. After dinner even more Parisian musicians appeared at the party, including "Les Six," the young reform club of French music, whose members are working with great enthusiasm on re-creating a French national music—so far with only mixed results. Bartók had to repeat his Sonata for Violin and Piano at Prunières's salon. Stravinsky liked the third movement best, naturally; its style is most similar to his own. Ravel, however, preferred the emotionally expressive second movement. Bartók describes Stravinsky as quite a remarkable personality—even his demeanor is sensational. His sharp, resolute gaze, somewhat brutal nose, and wide lips are what instantly strike one about his face. Stravinsky finds every opportunity to chide the Germans. He calls them *boche*[11] and noted sarcastically that it is obvious that they do everything "perfectly." Stravinsky gives the impression of being a person who is fully aware of his own worth. He speaks with pride about his works, but this pride is far from the German self-importance with which, for example, composers like Pfitzner[12] write about their own compositions. When Prunières asked [Stravinsky] how long one of his pieces was, Stravinsky answered, "Not long." Then he specified the length of the performance down to the second and added with a smile, "There is more in it, however—it's like a small suitcase that simply shocks you with its unexpected weight when you try to lift it."

Of course, Stravinsky explained to Bartók that his [Stravinsky's] music is the most objective absolute music; it does not paint, symbolize, or express anything and has nothing to do with emotion; it is simply line, harmony, and rhythm. This "objective" theory of music spreads dangerously, although its principles are not at all clear. This new theory manifests itself in a very strong opposition to Beethoven. In England, for example, an anti-Beethoven society was formed. "I don't know who founded it; it's possible that they are quite shady characters," Bartók notes. He in no way identifies himself, by the way, with Stravinsky's ideas. Nevertheless, he has faith in this great Russian musician's natural talent, which, as the opus for Pianola proves, cannot be spoiled by aesthetic theories. After all, Stravinsky's *Le Sacre du printemps* (his best work, in Bartók's opinion) is full of true poetry. In the midst of their conversation in Paris Bartók mentioned this to Stravinsky. Although Stravinsky did not renounce his earlier work, he assured Bartók that *Rossignol* was the last in this style; after that he turned to "completely objective" music.

Bartók was very surprised when Stravinsky said he developed his barbaric, folklike, primitivistic style completely independently from the influence of Russian peasant music.[13] Bartók met Stravinsky a second time at the Pleyel Company, where Stravinsky has two workrooms. Bartók had come to look at the Pianola's French sibling, the Pleyela. The Pleyela differs from the Pianola in that the composition is recorded by a pianist. This mechanical piano, which can handle dynamics delicately, repeats the rhythm with true fidelity. Most of Stravinsky's compositions have already been recorded. Bartók recorded a few of his pieces on the Pleyela, too.[14]

Stravinsky's workroom is full of all kinds of instruments. To Bartók's surprise, next to some exotic percussion instruments was a Hungarian gypsy cimbalom. This instrument, which came to Stravinsky's attention during his Hungarian travels,[15] is used in his *Renard*. It is a real headache for Stravinsky to find a suitable performer, and he is afraid that he may have to replace the cimbalom with the piano most of the time. Stravinsky is very interested in the development of instrumental technique and was captivated by Bartók's innovative writing for the violin, which was brought to life so splendidly by Jelly Arányi in the Sonata for Violin and Piano. He could hardly believe that Bartók did not play the violin at all. The greatest stumbling block in the performance of Stravinsky's works is the limits of the instruments' capabilities. Stravinsky has already experimented with placing mechanical instruments in the orchestra. But these "objective" instruments left him in the lurch, because it was impossible to start playing them precisely enough. In resignation, Stravinsky arranged the score [of *Les Noces*] for traditional orchestra. Bartók listened to a few sections from *Petrouchka* on the Pleyela. Unfortunately, Paris did not have any greater musical experiences in store for him. On first hearing Bartók could not get anything out of Darius Milhaud's Fifth String Quartet, and several other new works of this young composer are quite shallow. If we cannot speak of bright prospects for the future of French music, at least for the time being its present is ensured by the refined and distinguished composer Ravel. Ravel's newest Duo for Violin and Cello made a favorable impression on Bartók. True, after several hearings Ravel's works begin to wear a little thin. The Duo, however, one of whose movements was published in the issue of *Revue Musicale* dedicated to the memory of Debussy, is more attractive than his Piano Trio.

After the great, rich culture of Paris, Frankfurt could provide virtually nothing for Béla Bartók. The direction of his stage works was highly problematic, and the performances were considerably worse than in Hungary. The cast and orchestra were equally weak, and the efforts of the talented young conductor Jenő Szenkár[16] were in vain. The musical life of Frankfurt still suffers from the sentimentality of the metaphysics of Pfitznerism and Schrekerism.[17] Even excellent musicians like Alma Moodie and Erdmann[18] were incapable of saving Pfitzner's Sonata for Violin and Piano from deathly boredom. The Three Orchestral Pieces of the young Hindemith just barely rose above Pfitzner's *niveau*. Hyper-Wagner, hyper-Strauss, hyper-Reger. Who will stop the decline of the nation of Bach, Mozart, Beethoven? Schoenberg? He is still a puzzle.

NOTES

1. Bartók also performed in Aberystwyth and Liverpool. [Trans.]

2. The *Daily Mail, Daily Telegraph, Evening News, Glasgow Herald, Liverpool Courier*, and *New-Castle Daily Chronicle* [Tóth]. For a detailed discussion of Bar-

tók's reception in England see Malcolm Gillies, *Bartók in Britain* (Oxford, 1989), esp. pp. 30–49. [Trans.]

3. The *Glasgow Herald, Manchester Guardian, Ladies' Morning Post, Sunday Times, Evening Standard, Liverpool Courier, Star, Eastern Press, Daily Sketch, Evening News, Daily Telegraph, Westminster Gazette, Daily Express, Daily News, Daily Mail, Pall-Mall Gazette,* and *Observer.* [Tóth]

4. Jelly Arányi (1893–1966) was a Hungarian-born violinist who had emigrated to London. She was the grand-niece of Joseph Joachim. Bartók wrote both his Sonatas for Violin and Piano for Arányi, who was also the inspiration for Ravel's *Tzigane.* [Trans.]

5. Sir (Aynsley) Eugene Goossens (1893–1962), an English conductor and composer whose impressionistic compositions were considered to be on a par with William Walton and Arnold Bax in the time between the two World Wars. [Trans.]

6. Albert Coates (1882–1953), an English conductor who specialized in Russian works and Wagner; and Sir Henry Wood (1869–1944), the conductor of the Queen's Hall Promenade Concerts from 1895 to 1940. [Trans.]

7. *Ballad of the Gnomes.* Identified in Gillies, *Bartók in Britain,* p. 43. [Trans.]

8. Violet Gordon Woodhouse (1872–1948) was the first to make a gramophone recording of the harpsichord, and a pioneer in the English revival of interest in early keyboard instruments. [Trans.]

9. Alfredo Casella (1883–1947), a staunch supporter of musical modernism, was the most influential composer in interwar Italy. [Trans.]

10. "Study for Pianola," written in 1917 and later arranged for orchestra as "Madrid," the fourth of Stravinsky's Four Studies for Orchestra. [Trans.]

11. A derogatory French nickname for Germans. [Trans.]

12. Hans Pfitzner (1869–1949) wrote vicious pamphlets against modern ideas about music, such as the 1917 *Futuristengefahr* (The danger of futurism), a response to Ferruccio Busoni's *Sketch for a New Aesthetic of Music* (1906). [Trans.]

13. For a discussion of Stravinsky's use of Russian folk music and his efforts to suppress his debt to them, see Richard Taruskin, "Russian Folk Melodies in *The Rite of Spring,*" *Journal of the American Musicological Society* 33, no. 3 (1980): 501–43, and "Stravinsky and the Traditions: Why the Memory Hole?" *Opus,* no. 3 (1983): 10–17. [Trans.]

14. No trace of Bartók's Pleyela recordings remains. [Trans.]

15. In fact, Stravinsky became familiar with the cimbalom in Geneva, where Ernest Ansermet introduced him to the Hungarian cimbalom virtuoso Aladár Rácz (1886–1958). [Trans.]

16. Jenő Szenkár (1891–1977), Hungarian conductor who championed Bartók's stage works. These performances of *The Wooden Prince* and *Bluebeard's Castle* in Frankfurt were the first outside of Hungary. In 1926 Szenkár conducted the world premiere of *The Miraculous Mandarin* in Cologne. [Trans.]

17. Franz Schreker (1878–1934), Austrian composer who served as the director of the Hochschule für Musik in Berlin from 1920 to 1932. [Trans.]

18. Alma Moodie (1900–1943), an Australian-born violinist of high renown in Germany and a particular favorite of Hans Pfitzner, who wrote his Violin Concerto (1925) for her; and Eduard Erdmann (1896–1958), a Latvian pianist and composer active in Germany. [Trans.]

Two Bartók Obituaries

BENCE SZABOLCSI

TRANSLATED BY PETER LAKI

Bence Szabolcsi (1899–1973) was one of the founders of Hungarian musicology. He was born in Budapest, where his father, Miksa, was the longtime editor of an important Hungarian-Jewish weekly. Szabolcsi studied musicology in Leipzig under Hermann Abert and took his doctorate in 1923 with a thesis on the Italian monodists Benedetti and Saracini. In 1951 he co-founded the musicology program at the Ferenc Liszt Academy in Budapest, which to this day is the only department of its kind in Hungary; he taught there until his death. He was a revered scholar, teacher, and public figure and is the subject of a recent two-volume biography by György Kroó. [Ed.]

"It becomes more and more certain that the post-Debussy period in European music will be marked by the name of Béla Bartók," wrote a Flemish writer two years ago in his book on Bartók.[1]

The Hungarian composer, of whom these lines were written and who died at the age of sixty-four on the other side of the ocean, stood at the forefront of the aspirations of European music up to the last minute of his life—he was more youthful, even beyond his sixtieth year, than the whole era and the whole world around him.

But that's precisely why his entire career seems like a single impulse, a single unbroken line today, even though it proceeded to its final peak in zigzags and by many strange leaps. The romantic works of his youth continued Liszt's path, until, in his Suite No. 2, he came to a sudden halt and with an abrupt turn relinquished the entire tradition of orchestral romanticism; this gulf is marked by the two years (1905–7) separating the last movement of this work from the others. But the Four Orchestral Pieces, fifteen years later, raise the same questions on a different plane, with darker and more sparkling emotions.[2] The enthusiastic tone of the youthful Ideal Portrait will sound more mysterious, grown to extraordinary heights, in the first movement of the Music for Strings, Percussion, and Celesta thirty years later, and even the very idea of the Two Portraits, the principle of a central theme developed through a series of contrasting images, will recur in the Sixth String Quartet, written thirty-five years later. On the pages of the *Mikrokosmos*, the problems of earlier works such as the Bagatelles, Sketches, Dirges, *Out of Doors*, and the Nine Piano Pieces return all at once, more powerfully resolved.

In this *élan vital*, replete with unexpected turns and leaps lies the explanation of Bartók's unique situation in Hungary and particularly in Europe. He had learned and assimilated everything that contemporary Europe, even Eastern Europe, could teach him, but it was always he who took the decisive step; it was always he, more than any of his contemporaries East or West, who made the turn that resulted in a new situation. Three dates—three characteristic moments from our century's second decade—will show the best how the historical situation ripened until it reached this critical point. In 1910, the art of Debussy, Ravel, and Strauss, a novel and yet overripe, stunningly colorful orchestral idiom, is on its zenith in Europe. In Hungary, Bartók and Kodály are still disciples and novices. Around the mid-1910s, these disciples grow up to become colleagues. *Duke Bluebeard's Castle* and *The Wooden Prince*: the ballad opera and the fairy tale emerging from dance rhythms (1911–17) unwittingly grapple with common European questions, as does Kodály's great cello sonata. Then, 1920—European music is experimenting with two kinds of idioms: a polyphonic and polytonal "linear" style, and the extremely dynamic development of new East European dance rhythms. The most enduring results of this new, Janus-faced art, however, were born not in the works of Stravinsky, Schoenberg, Hindemith, de Falla, or Milhaud but in those of Bartók. For he got to the bottom of expressionistic experimenting in *The Miraculous Mandarin* as early as 1919, and a few years later, in his two piano concertos, exhausted the possibilities of the neoclassical direction as well: the vocabulary is complete, enough of that—and already he springs forward, soars on, ready to erupt anew and eager for new surprises.

Only a feverish temperament, filled with tensions and compulsions, is capable of such eruptions. In fact, the contrasts seen in Bartók's art and personality have never been encountered in the course of the centuries. Sheer extremes and antinomies everywhere—everything mundane has long since withered away and fallen off from under him. Boiling point and freezing point, minutest detail and broadest unity, the widest diatonicism and the narrowest chromaticism, the most triumphant artistic self-discipline and the most unbridled impulse to disintegrate, the most restless flittering and the most obstinate constancy, and above all, East and West: all these were part of Bartók's personality. An art that is completely introverted and, after the Fifth String Quartet, systematically suppresses the pomps and vanities of the outside world—but at the same time, an art obsessed with motion and movement, feeling most at home (next to the black mourning of night musics and dirges) in the frenzy of barbaric dances of triumph and revolutionary bacchanalia! An art that is anything but simple and naive, yet was regenerated through folk music. Music that is fundamentally averse to the singing voice, yet is able to tell the myth of *Cantata profana* only in the unsonglike song of solo voices and chorus, in a murmur and a screech! It is a constant duel between the depth of the unconscious and the height of the intellect, a battle fought and started again every moment, that can be won only by the form-creating will, strained to the extreme, ever alert and ready to bound. Willpower, even brute force, are therefore integral parts of such phenomena; they create something new by accomplishing the impossible. The Dance Suite, the Fourth String Quartet, the Second Piano Concerto (1923–33), as well as almost every Bartók work written since then, are filled with sonorities that no musician would have thought possible earlier, and, as a matter of fact, musicians still don't. He accomplished all this by brute force, in a way bordering on the miraculous; he forced the instruments to evoke unprecedented hallucinations. He did not care about their traditional laws and gave them new laws, like Beethoven.

No doubt it was Nature—the ceaseless wonders of life and death, becoming and dying, that had infused his entire being since his youth—that taught him this brute force and this loyalty that listens only to itself. The sensitive nerves of this artist from the big city felt the civilized human world to be so suffocating that he had to break out of all familiar settings: like the heroes of his *Cantata profana*, the magic stags, he was unable to go through the doors of human abodes and drank only from a pure source, never again from a glass. He himself wrote that the happiest days of his life were those spent in the countryside among peasants, precisely because his interest in the peasants was less motivated by concerns of nation, people, or race (these issues became less and less important to him) than by the image of primeval man. If this was an error, it was certainly one of the century's most fertile errors. But primeval man and nature, instincts and elemental phenomena: clearly, *they* taught him to listen only to his own internal laws. From compulsion and forceful clasping it is only a step to freedom in the broadest sense. This is what enabled him to burst into Western music with the folk music of Eastern Europe, as if leading an army of Huns; this is also how he was able (through his ceaseless and never-subsiding quest, through his grappling with questions of time and freedom, change and death) to guess the most secret thoughts of the musicians of Europe and to say them out loud before they had found the words themselves. Soon it seemed that was all folk music had taught him: like so many others, Bartók only learned what he knew already. The monophonic music of the peasants only appears to be simple. Those who have seen Bartók's transcriptions of Székely and Turkish melodies or his last Romanian folk music publication will suddenly notice how much this music is like an awesome labyrinth or jungle and understand why Bartók had to be the one to reveal this thousand-branched thicket to the world. Here one realizes that in a genius, the unreal imagination, exploding the material, functions together and is interwoven with an analytical passion that buries itself in the material and exalts it. The uninterrupted and fanatic work of four decades raised both Bartók the shaman of twentieth-century instrumental music and Bartók the natural historian of the most ancient world of melodies.

Thus in this giddy drive, in this mad rush, in this tension, this chase to the end of the world, he left behind his whole era caught in tensions. He left behind romantic nationalism, the impressionists, the expressionists, and neoclassical experiment; and he, the first proclaimer of Community, even left behind the Rule of Communities. The one thing he could never abandon, the one thing that held him captive like an eternal magic beckoning, was the Timeless Music of the peoples and of the great masters of old, in which he always recognized his kin. It has often been said that he had reached down to the roots, to the eternal foundations of race and ethnicity. If these roots had in the meantime been written on banners, if they had become a matter of fashion and politics, that didn't interest him in the least. The Europe that absorbed the slogans about "roots" and "communities" only to defile them was ready, in 1940, to be left behind by Bartók, like old schools that had proved to be impasses. He shed them like outgrown garments. Maybe he did so just in time to save the real soul of Europe, in time to be the representative of our perishing world's nobler, more immortal portions in a new world that will sweep aside the debris of the old. Has this saving of souls been successful? Just now, we don't know yet. But it might well be in his dazzlingly clean, relentless, and beautiful fight that postwar Europe, to which

Bartók may now return in his death, will awaken to its tasks, its thousand-year mission, which it has missed, delayed, or never even acknowledged.

[Revised version of an article first written in 1941 and published as "A hatvanéves Bartók Béla" (Béla Bartók at sixty) (*Nyugat* 34, no. 4 [April 1941]: 137–39). Reprinted in Bence Szabolcsi, *Kodályról és Bartókról* (Of Kodály and Bartók), ed. Ferenc Bónis (Budapest, 1987), pp. 163–66.]

He died far away, in a strange country, on the other side of the ocean; he, the poet of endless secrets, faraway vistas, and the remotest reaches, in his death proclaimed the deepest secret and the most painful remoteness—the one that separates the poet from his fatherland. Béla Bartók repudiated this visible fatherland when he saw that it had sunk into servitude and become unworthy of itself; he left in order to proclaim the invisible fatherland, the eternal one that cannot be humiliated and will not humiliate itself, the one that shone within him with a most glaring light. Oh, but can a poet ever separate from his own fatherland, whether it be in his proudest righteousness and deepest offense?

In this moment, in these first hours of our affliction, we cannot yet gauge all he has meant to us. All we know is that death has deprived us of one of the nation's greatest sons and maybe the greatest of this century's artistic personalities, our times' most shining focus of consciousness and willpower, which, now that it is extinguished, has left us all orphans. He was a poet and a genius, a revolutionary and a creator, a conjurer of demons and a soul-liberating sage, a shaman and a humanist, pioneer of a new world and innovator of the old; in addition, a faultless man who never backed down, in whose struggle the pure man's fight was united with that of the pure artist. With him, the voice of the peoples of Eastern Europe and the Carpathian basin entered the world's great music as art, as scholarship and human behavior. He was our most resonant voice in the wide world, our spokesman, our excuse and our justification, and the most important this small, tormented, and disgraced country could say before the world in its own defense.

He died in a strange country, like Rákóczi, Kossuth, and Széchenyi;[3] and, like them, Bartók died at a tragic moment when his fatherland needed his intercession more than anything. And in fact we feel and know that this nation has not been afflicted with such deep mourning since the deaths of Kossuth and Széchenyi, Vörösmarty, and Petőfi.[4]

Yet who knows: maybe it wasn't without reason that the invisible laws decided thus; and if there is consolation, we must find it in them. It seems as though Providence has sent its greatest sons, those who start new epochs and those who crown them, at the moment when they are needed according to the great clock of communities, and it has sealed their lips with the seal of eternal silence when they accomplish their mission. Maybe this was the case with the destinies of Bartók and Hungary as well: let us believe that the nation and society, which have for so long proven unworthy of their greatest sons, will rise to their height one day and become worthy of the work left behind by their prophets—prophets repudiated at first and later accepted in atonement—those pure and shining geniuses.

[First published in *Opera* (Fall 1945): 3–4. Reprinted in Bence Szabolcsi, *Kodályról és Bartókról* (Of Kodály and Bartók), ed. Ferenc Bónis (Budapest, 1987), pp. 167–68.]

NOTES

1. Denijs Dille, *Béla Bartók* (Antwerp, 1939). [Ed.]
2. The Four Orchestral Pieces, Op. 12 (1912), were orchestrated in 1921. [Ed.]
3. Ferenc Rákóczi II, prince of Transylvania, leader of an insurrection against the Habsburgs (1703–11), who died in Rodosto, Turkey; Lajos Kossuth (1802–94), leader of the revolution of 1848–49, who died in Turin, Italy; and Count István Széchenyi, leading Hungarian political reformer, who died at the Döbling asylum, near Vienna. [Ed.]
4. Mihály Vörösmarty (1800–55) and Sándor Petőfi (1823–49), both Hungarian poets. [Ed.]

A Selection of Poems

Inspired by Béla Bartók

Cantata profana

SÁNDOR CSOÓRI

TRANSLATED BY PETER LAKI

We didn't go home tonight either,
We boys didn't go home.
In vain did our mother scrub the knives;
In vain did she wash
The knotty table.
With its throat cut,
In the mud of its blood,
In vain did the goose cry out in pain.

We didn't send word,
We did not write,
As if a flood had carried off our hands.

Easter is no longer Easter;
The swept house
Is our house no more.

Who is that old man over there?
He sits in front of the white wall's incubus;
He sits in the cigarette smoke from the end of the world.

His face is a squashed wicker basket.

Maybe he is waiting for us,
Maybe he is looking for us,
Maybe he would like to see us,
In the street beyond the window,
In his myopic life.

Don't look for us,
Don't wait for us,
You old man reeking of tobacco,
You poor man, doghouse-chested.
We are no longer your sons.
If a door opens, it's as a knife.
If we speak,
We prevaricate like false witnesses.

We'd fall upon you like a bombshell;
We'd tremble beside you
Like a power station.
The plate and the wineglass
Would rend in half,
And our hair, shoulder-length hair
(The roots of continents),
Would weave through your stomach,
You'd turn into a hair basket,
A man made of body hair,
A cadaver reducible to ashes.

[Sándor Csoóri (b. 1930) is one of the foremost representatives of the "populist" trend
in postwar Hungarian poetry.]

With Thundering Steps: Listening to Bartók's Second Piano Concerto

GÁBOR DEVECSERI

TRANSLATED BY PETER LAKI

With thundering steps,
With thundering steps,
Comes Fate, tearing off buds and branches,
Slices us in fourteen hundred pieces,
He breaks us, smashes us, divides us,
Populates the world with us.
He doesn't feel like
Thinking of us,
He doesn't feel like
Being without us:

He winks down to us
While he is pounding us:
He needs us for his march,
He wades in us,
He gets ahead by taking us with him,
We have no rest,
He has no rest,
Between his teeth, crossways,
Like an Indian's knife,
Nothingness glistens.

[Gábor Devecseri (1917–71), a poet and classical scholar, translated the Homeric epics and many other Greek and Latin poetic works into Hungarian.]

Joy

AMY KÁROLYI

TRANSLATED BY PETER LAKI

Geometrical pleasure to hear his voice,
For I not only listen, I watch as well:
An abstract drawing on a map of stars.
The lines, forever parallel,
The lines intersect as with knives,
The angles now grow, now shrink,
The rhythmic circles drawn by compass,
The straight line lost in Infinity
Recoils, new Infinity appears,
A crystalline equation abiding by strict laws,
Fate, dissolving to the beat,
Distances, ringing to one another,
Their attraction holds the world together.
Through these sounds the blind will see:
An abstract heaven spread out above them.

[Amy Károlyi, a poet and translator, was the wife of the poet Sándor Weöres.]

A Selection of Poems

Béla Bartók

LAJOS KASSÁK

TRANSLATED BY PETER LAKI

Let us say something of the composer, too.
You can see him on stage, in tails
And in the street, with his hat off,
Walking in the morning sun.

He is as thin as a fish bone,
As white as a lily,
But if he sits down at the piano
He turns into a dragon,
Rattles, cries, and sometimes barks,
So that the sky becomes dark, and the walls of the
    houses crumble.

He was not at all cut out
To stand before the children and teach them
Manners and respect for their parents.
He turns his face toward us only in his sleep;
He plays music for us and never asks
If we are there at the moment of the Elevation.

He crosses the line between Good and Evil daily,
And sometimes he arrives, with a colorful bouquet of
    flowers in his hand,
From where the fire goes out,
The virgins disappear, and the soldiers die.
No one would believe that he is the odd man
Whom the angel chased out of Paradise with a flaming
    sword.

Yet there is no doubt that he is Satan,
Who walks with his hat off or sits at the piano,
Rattles, cries, and sometimes barks,
So that the sky becomes dark, and the walls of the
    houses crumble.

[Lajos Kassák (1887–1967), a poet and painter, was one of the leading figures of the Hungarian avant-garde beginning in the 1920s.]

Bartók's String Quartet No. 5

GÉZA KÉPES

TRANSLATED BY PETER LAKI

a bell, sunken in a mountain lake,
which suddenly begins to ring,
the pilgrim's staff began to bloom,
the flute that caused to sound
whole orchestras

four spirits four otherworldly figures apparitions—
violin in their hands and
they play—do you understand?
no! can you feel?
maybe: your cells,
your hair, and your entrails
understand
the glass shriek of
the violins' throttled throat,
the bloodless shadows of writhing willow trees,
the magnetic rustle of the earth's poles,
the light signals of distant planets.

on their looms of glass
four Fates spin
the thread of your destiny—
the sound stops.
your life falls headlong
like a soldier
killed on a snowy peak.
blood trickles
from his invisible wound . . .
the matterless matter
grows screeching, fluttering dully
it streams
it dissolves your muscles
your shinbones
your skull.
your obsessions
have been washed away by the waves—
only your primal memories
are still alive

glittering, creeping, living blossoms:
coral thickets sprouted
underwater, on the chest of rocks,
octopuses, squids,
medusas
and electric shock-giving
stingrays, smooth as glass.

[Géza Képes (1909–89) was a poet and translator.]

✦

Bartók's Farewell

GYÖRGY SOMLYÓ
TRANSLATED BY PETER LAKI

As he was leaving his *famous little* country,[1]
He bent his head, his never-bending head,
Watching the roaring forest of hands—
No, this was not an audience; it was a military camp

That suddenly received an inkling of its strength,
Inspired by the music and the shared sorrow,
And felt, with more sadness than ever,
That it is time to act—it's time to act.

Block the way of disaster while still possible,
Give rebellion a name we can all share,
Break open the gates of its prison, make its stiff lips
    speak.

But the wanderer was already leaving.
And we went too, each our own way,
Wherever our own homegrown loneliness awaited
    us.

Bartók's Homecoming

GYÖRGY SOMLYÓ
TRANSLATED BY PETER LAKI

The famous little country slowly expands—
The one you had left behind, narrow and dark;
Even though still oppressed by dwarfdom old and new,
It now desires you as its measure and model.

You, who have revealed the magic of the morning
Through every frightful night,
Come, break into our viscous gloom, and tear
Our throats out of their convulsive muteness.

You, who have expanded your voice to be the world,
Make us now grow to the size of your voice;
Stretch us, no matter how much the muscles may hurt!

For we can only call a place home
Where your homeless song, having wandered the globe,
Can return to find its pure home.

[György Somlyó (b. 1920), a poet and translator, is the son of the poet Zoltán Somlyó and one of the main representatives of the "urban" trend in postwar Hungarian poetry.]

Bartók

GYULA ILLYÉS
TRANSLATED BY CLAIRE LASHLEY

"Harsh discord?" Yes! They think it thus
Which brings us solace!
Yes! Let the violin strings,
Let singing throats
Learn curse-clatter of splintering grass
Crashing to the ground
The screech of rasp
Wedged in the teeth
Of buzzing saw; let there be no peace, no gaiety
In gilded, lofty far

And delicate, closed-off concert halls,
Until in woe-darkened hearts!

"Harsh discord?" Yes! They think it thus
Which brings us solace!
That the people live
And have still a soul
Their voice is heard! Variations on the curse
Of steel grating crashing against stone
Through on the tuned and taut
Piano and vocal cords
To stark existence their bleak truth,
For this same "harsh discord,"
This woeful battle cry disturbing hell's infernal din
Cries out
Harmony!
For this very anguish cries out—
Through how many falsely sweet songs—and shouts
To fate: Let there be Harmony,
Order, true order, or the world is lost,
The world is lost, if the people
Speak not again—in majesty!

O, stoic, stern musician, true Magyar
(Like many of your peers—"notorious"[2]),
Was it ordained by law that from the depth
Of the people's soul, whither you descended
Through the trumpet, the as yet mine-shaft throat
Of this pit, you should send up the cry
Into this frigid-rigid giant hall
Where the stars are the chandeliers?[3]

Frivolous, soothing melodies played in my ear
Insult my grief:
Let no light-tuned Zerkovitz[4] sing the dirge at this,
Our mother's funeral;
Homelands are lost—who dares to mourn them
With organ-grinder arpeggios?
Is there hope yet in our human race?
If this be our care and the reeling brain battles
Benumbed, speak, you
Fierce, wild, severe, aggressive great musician,
That—for all that!—we still have cause

To hope, to live,
And that we have the right—
For we are mortals and life-givers
To look all that in the eye
Which we may not avoid.
For troubles grow when they are covered.
It was possible, but no more,
To hide our eyes, to cover our ears
While storms wreak their havoc,
And later revile: you did not help!

You do us honor by revealing what
Is revealed to you,
The good, the bad, virtue and sin—
You raise our statute by
Speaking to us as equals.
This—this consoles!
What different words are these!
Human, not sham.
It gives us the right, and so the strength, to face
The harshest despair.

Our thanks for it,
For the strength to take victory
Even over hell.
Behold the end that carries us on.
Behold the guidon: by speaking out
The horror is dissolved.
Behold the answer to life's riddle
By a great mind, an artist's spirit: it was worth suffering
Through hell.

Because we have suffered such things that still
There are no verbs for them.
Picasso's two-nosed women,
Six-legged stallions
Alone could have keened abroad
Galloping, neighed out
What we have borne, we men,
What no one who has not lived it can grasp,
For which there are no words now, nor can be perhaps,
Only music, music, music, like your music
Twin lodestars in our sky of sound,[5]

Music alone, music alone, music,
Hot with ancient breath of mine-depths,
Dreaming "the people's future song,"
Nursing them to triumph,
Setting them free that the very walls
Of prisons are razed,
For bliss promised, here on earth
Praying with blasphemy,
Sacrificing with sacrilege,
Wounding to cure,
Music now lifting
Worthy listeners to a better world—

Work, a good healer, who lulls not to sleep;
Who, probing our soul
With your chord-fingers, touches
Where trouble lies,
And how strange, how wholesome, is the salve you give:
The plaintive call,
The lament which would spring from us
But cannot spring,
For we are born to dumb stillness of heart:
Your nerve strings sing for us.

[Gyula Illyés (1902–83), Hungary's unofficial poet laureate, was also a playwright and the author of an influential sociological study of the Hungarian countryside.]

NOTES

1. A reference to a well-known folk song collected by Bartók, "Elindultam szép hazámból, híres kis Magyarországból" (I left my beautiful homeland, famous little Hungary). [Ed.]

2. An allusion to a reference to Franz Liszt in a famous poem by Mihály Vörösmarty (1800–1855). [Ed.]

3. This line has been amended to correspond to the original, "Melynek csillárjai a csillagok." [Trans.]

4. Béla Zerkovitz was a Hungarian composer who wrote many sentimental popular songs. [Trans.]

5. I.e., Bartók and Kodály. [Trans.]

Index of Names and Compositions

Abert, Hermann, 290
Adorno, Theodor W., 3, 4, 7, 8, 9–10, 12, 52n.4
Ady, Endre, 22–23, 25, 34, 35, 37, 39, 48, 60n.101, 81–82, 138, 162, 166, 171n.70, 237
Alkan, Charles Valentin, 73
Ansermet, Ernest, 288n.15
Antal, Frigyes, 46
Antheil, George, 237, 238n.3
Antokoletz, Elliott, 54n.26, 120
Appia, Adolf, 122
Arányi, Jelly, 239n.6, 283, 287, 288n.4
Arma, Paul (formerly Imre Weisshaus), 210, 226n.20

Babits, Mihály, 139–40, 148n.45
Bach, Johann Sebastian, 81, 90, 91–92, 113, 180, 186, 196, 232, 249, 276; Partita in B♭ major, 284; Two-Part Inventions, 277; Well Tempered Clavier, 51
Backhaus, Wilhelm, 39
Balázs, Béla, 34, 36, 46, 47, 58n.71, 62n.123, 120–23, 124–43, 144nn. 2, 3, and 4, 144–45n.6, 145n.18, 145–46n.19, 146nn. 20 and 28, 147nn. 30, 33, 38, and 42, 148nn. 49, 51, and 52, 168n.35, 174, 264–73
Baller, Adolph, 116
Balogh, Ernő, 103, 257–63
Bánffy, Miklós, 268, 269–72
Bartók, Béla: Allegro barbaro, 25, 69, 72–77, 93, 107, 235, 250, 263, 280; Bagatelle No. 14, 86–87; Bear Dance, 73, 78nn. 5, 6, and 7, 235, 263; "A Bit Drunk," 73, 235; Bluebeard's Castle, 25, 50, 58n.71, 84–85, 119–20, 125, 127, 143, 144n.4, 160, 161–62, 169n.45, 178, 180, 246, 268, 269, 271, 272–73, 287, 288n.16; Cantata profana, 12, 51, 88–90, 93, 96, 98–99n.11, 99n.16,

248, 292, 296–97; For Children, 46, 249; Concerto for Orchestra, 7, 10, 112, 113, 114, 261; Contrasts, 11, 104, 105; Dance Suite, 14, 93, 111, 237, 245, 248, 292; Divertimento, 93, 111, 112, 114; Etudes, Op. 18, 276; "Evening in the Country" ("Evening in Transylvania"), 73, 78nn. 5, 6, and 7, 235, 251; Fifteen Hungarian Peasant Songs, 78n.7, 235; Five Slovak Songs for voice and piano, 42; Four Dialogues, 277; Four Dirges, 34, 78nn. 5 and 6, 235, 246, 291; Four Hungarian Folk Songs for piano and voice, 39; Four Orchestral Pieces, Op. 12, 290–91, 295n.2; Fourteen Bagatelles (Fourteen Piano Pieces), Op. 6, 25, 37, 82, 83–84, 86–87, 230, 276, 291; Improvisations, Op. 20, 68, 276; Kossuth, 22, 24, 25, 31, 37–38, 39, 52, 61n.106, 197n.9, 230, 264, 268; Mikrokosmos, 46, 51, 104, 107, 108, 109, 249, 291; The Miraculous Mandarin, 5, 6, 36, 50, 51, 88, 93, 94, 149, 154, 156, 158–66, 168–69n.35, 171n.69, 173, 248, 288n.16, 291; Music for Strings, Percussion, and Celesta, 11, 103, 108, 112, 291; Nine Little Piano Pieces, 186, 277, 291; Old Dance Tunes, 235; Old Hungarian Dances, 107, 277; "Out of Doors" (Five Piano Pieces), 107, 291; Petite Suite, 107; Piano Concerto No. 1, 173–74, 181, 185, 186–93, 248, 257, 258, 277, 291; Piano Concerto No. 2, 88, 90, 96, 106, 111, 173–74, 178, 185, 192–95, 291, 292, 297–98; Piano Concerto No. 3, 52, 113, 261, 262; Piano Quintet, 38, 40, 78n.6; Rhapsodies for Violin and Piano, 248, 251; Rhapsody for Piano, Op. 1, 186, 197n.9; Rhapsody for Pi-

INDEX OF NAMES AND COMPOSITIONS

Bartók (*cont.*)
ano and Orchestra, 73, 111, 258;
Rondo No. 1, 107; Scherzo (1903)
from "Four Piano Pieces," 78;
Scherzo, Op. 2, 41, 78n.5; Sketches,
291; Sonata for Piano, 116, 173, 276;
Sonata for Two Pianos and Percussion, 11, 106, 107, 247, 248; Sonata
for Unaccompanied Violin, 116, 261;
Sonata for Violin and Piano No. 1,
115, 116, 118n.45, 238, 239n.6, 245–
46, 283, 285, 287, 288n.4; Sonata for
Violin and Piano No. 2, 238, 239n.6,
288n.4; Sonatina, 235, 263; String
Quartet No. 1, 25, 37, 62n.123, 82–
83, 84, 111, 230, 280; String Quartet
No. 2, 111, 120, 279; String Quartet
No. 3, 9, 10, 111, 227n.31, 278–81;
String Quartet No. 4, 10, 11, 90, 111,
292; String Quartet No. 5, 11, 96,
111, 292, 300–301; String Quartet
No. 6, 114, 291; Study for the Left
Hand, 78n.5; Suite for Orchestra No.
1, 37, 38–39, 40, 41, 88, 111, 113,
197n.9; Suite for Orchestra No. 2, 41,
87, 107, 197n.9, 290; Suite Op. 14,
107, 263; Ten Bagatelles, 73, 82; *Ten
Hungarian Folk Songs*, 42; Three Burlesques, Op. 8/c, Nos. 1 and 2, 73,
78n.5; Two Elegies, Op. 8/b, No. 2,
78n.5; Concerto for Two Pianos and
Orchestra, 111; Two Portraits, 80–81,
291; Two Romanian Dances, 64–65,
73, 76, 78n.7, 80, 82, 235, 246–47,
263; Variations on a Hungarian Peasant Song, 235; Village Scenes, 173,
185; Viola Concerto, 261–62; Violin
Concerto No. 2, 93, 111, 112, 113,
114, 248; Violin Sonata No. 1, 279;
Violin Sonata No. 2, 279, 280; *The
Wooden Prince*, 46, 50, 58n.71, 86, 93,
120, 123, 159, 160, 168n.35, 173,
174–78, 180, 184, 187, 191, 230, 264,
269–73, 287, 288n.16, 291
Bartók, Béla, Jr., 19, 66, 69, 117, 203,
217, 244, 245
Bartók, Ditta. *See* Pásztory, Ditta
Bartók, Erzsébet, 243, 244, 258–59
Bartók, Marta. *See* Ziegler, Marta

Bartók, Peter, 66, 67, 74, 203, 217, 235,
243, 245
Bauer, Marion, 114
Beethoven, Ludwig van, 17, 82, 180,
181, 182, 185, 186, 191, 232, 249–50,
268, 276, 283, 286, 292; *Creatures of
Prometheus*, 184; Fifth Symphony, 284;
"Kreutzer" Sonata, 250; Ninth Sym-
phony, 17, 82, 180, 181, 182, 185,
186, 187; Sonata in E♭ major, Op. 31,
No. 3, 235; Third Symphony (*Eroica*),
232
Béldi, Izor, 82–83, 94
Beöthy, Zsolt, 266, 274n.9
Berény, Róbert, 34
Berg, Alban, 4, 6, 21, 66, 114
Bernstein, Leonard, 274n.7
Berzeviczy, Albert, 266, 274n.9
Bethlen, István, 274n.11
Bónis, Ferenc, 168n.41
Boulanger, Nadia, 9
Boulez, Pierre, 4, 6, 10
Brahms, Johannes, 13, 23, 39, 181, 249
Breuer, János, 94
Broch, Hermann, 24
Bródy, Miklós, 271, 275n.20
Bródy, Sándor, 160, 162, 163, 170nn. 46
and 58
Broughton, Simon, 128
Bukofzer, Manfred, 108
Bull, Storm, 111

Cage, John, 115, 116, 274n.7
Casella, Alfredo, 285, 288n.9
Cézanne, Paul, 33, 34
Chopin, Frédéric, 249, 283; Nocturne in
C♯ minor, 235
Coates, Albert, 284, 288n.6
Coolidge, Elizabeth Sprague, 103
Copland, Aaron, 11, 54n.28, 260
Couperin, François, 284
Csáth, Géza, 83–84
Csók, István, 31, 59n.83
Csontváry, Tivadar Kosztka, 36
Csoóri, Sándor, 96, 296–97
Czóbel, Béla, 34

d'Annunzio, Gabriele, 131
Davies, John Lloyd, 148n.51

Debussy, Claude, 13, 14, 15, 24, 120, 181, 232, 249, 291; *Pelléas et Mélisande*, 120, 132; *Pour le piano*, 235
Demény, János, 69, 101–2
Devecseri, Gábor, 96, 297–98
Dietl, Fedor, 88–90, 91
Dietl, Lajos, 40
Dille, Denijs, 61n.113, 68, 73
Dohnányi, Ernő, 78nn. 5 and 6, 159–61, 169nn. 41 and 43, 258; Symphony in D minor, 39–40
Doráti, Antal, 21
Dósa, Lidi, 42
Downes, Olin, 107, 116

Eagleton, Terry, 4
Egressy, Béni, 84, 98n.5
Eisler, Hanns, 3, 5, 11, 54nn. 22 and 29
Engel, Ivan, 245–46
Erdmann, Eduard, 287, 289n.18
Erkel, Ferenc: *Bánk Bán*, 175; *Hunyadi László*, 227n.29
Evans, Edwin, 284

Failoni, Sergio, 275n.19
Farkas, Ferenc, 251
Farkasinszky, Maca, 244
Fényes, Adolf, 209, 226n.17
Ferenczi, Sándor, 151
Ferenczy, Károly, 25, 28, 30, 36
Flaubert, Gustave, 134
Fodor, András, 92–93, 99n.11
Fodor, Gyula, 86–88
Fokine, Michel, 158
Foldes, Andor, 115–16
Forgács, Éva, 34, 59–60n.89
Forte, Allen, 11, 54n.26
Frankenstein, Alfred, 106–7
Freksa, Friedrich, 158
Freud, Sigmund, 151
Frid, Géza, 247–51
Frigyesi, Judit, 16, 17
Fülep, Lajos, 46
Furtwängler, Wilhelm, 257

Gál, Susan, 6
Galafrés, Elza, 159–60, 161, 168n.33, 169n.42
Garzó, Péter, 243

Gerő, Lidia, 170n.61
Geyer, Stefi, 57n.58, 61n.110, 62n.123
Giergl, Kálmán, 31
Gillies, Malcolm, vii, 5, 14, 203
Gleiman, Wanda, 209, 226n.15
Gluck, Mary, 138, 147n.38
Goethe, Johann Wolfgang von, 137, 139, 268
Gombocz, Adrienne, 203
Gombosi, Otto, 110–11
Goodman, Benny, 104, 105, 106
Goossens, Sir Eugene, 284, 285, 288n.5
Gordon Woodhouse, Violet, 284, 288n.8
Gorky, Maksim, 41–42, 43
Gretchaninov, Alexander, 110
Grey, David, 76–77
Gruber, Mrs. Henrik (*née* Emma Sándor), 17, 45, 46, 268, 274–75n.15

Hába, Alois, 247
Halls, W. D., 146n.22
Haluska, Hermina, 244
Hammerschlag, János, 178
Handel, George Frideric, 187, 196, 283
Hannover, György, 254
Haraszti, Emil, 91, 128, 192
Hatvany, Lajos, 156
Hausegger, Siegmund von, 8
Hauser, Arnold, 6, 46
Haydn, Joseph, 182, 283
Hebbel, Friedrich, 121, 122, 136–43, 148n.49, 149
Hegyi, Emánuel, 251
Heinsheimer, Hans Walter, 225, 227n.37
Helm, Everett, 3, 7, 11
Herder, J. G., 274n.10
Hertz, Henriette, 268, 275n.16
Heseltine, Philip, 158, 178–79
Hevesy, Sándor, 150, 268, 274n.14
Hindemith, Paul, 3, 11, 21, 66, 110, 111, 232, 260, 287
Hirschfeld, Robert, 38–39, 41
Hitler, Adolf, 7, 259
Hofmannsthal, Hugo von, 149
Hollósy, Simon, 25
Honegger, Arthur, 239n.6
Hornbostel, Erich Moritz von, 216
Hubay (Huber), Jenő, 267, 274n.12
Huszár, Klára, 97

Ibsen, Henrik, 121, 149–50, 157
Illyés, Gyula, 94–95, 302–5

Jászi, Oszkár, 219, 227n.28
Jemnitz, Sándor, 88
József, Attila, 91–92
Juhász, Gyula, 86
Jurkovics, Irma, 39, 43, 45, 244
Jurkovics, Othmar, 18

Kadarkay, Arpad, 148n.49
Kadosa, Pál, 251, 254
Kálmán, Imre, 21
Károlyi, Amy, 96, 298
Kárpáti, János, vii
Kassák, Lajos, 86, 95, 237, 238n.5, 299
Kaufmann, László, 253
Kentner, Louis, 88, 90
Kenton, Egon (formerly Egon Korn-
stein), 209, 226n.17
Képes, Géza, 96, 300–301
Kéri, Pál, 269
Kern, Aurél, 80
Kernstok, Károly, 33–34, 35, 47
Klemperer, Otto, 90
Klose, Friedrich, 8
Kocsis, Róza, 243
Kodály, Zoltán, 13, 25, 31, 34, 45–46,
48, 50–51, 73, 84, 90, 91, 92, 108,
123, 124, 172, 182, 183, 236, 238,
249, 251, 252, 256, 265, 268, 270,
274–75n.15, 283, 291; Psalmus hun-
garicus, 238, 245; Ten Hungarian Folk
Songs, 42
Kodály, Mrs. Zoltan. See Gruber, Mrs.
Henrik
Koessler, Hans, 13, 23
Kohner, Kató, 209, 226n.16
Kolisch, Rudolf, 11, 112, 114
Kolodin, Irving, 103, 105
Korb, Flóris, 31
Korngold, Erich Wolfgang, 53n.8
Kornstein, Egon. See Kenton, Egon
Körösfői, Aladár Kriesch, 30, 31–33, 38,
40
Kós, Károly, 28, 30
Kósá, György, 209, 226n.14, 238
Kosztolányi, Dezső, 180, 228
Koussevitzky, Serge, 103, 113
Kovács, Sándor, 80–83, 91, 274n.5

Křenek, Ernst, 21, 109, 232; Concerto
Grosso, 232
Kriesch, Aladár Körösfői, 30, 31–33, 38,
40
Kroó, György, 148n.52, 290
Kun, Béla, 36, 51
Kún, László, 80

Laban, Rudolf von, 158
Lajta, Béla, 59n.86
Lajtha, László, 251, 255
Laki, Peter, 55n.33
Lechner, Ödön, 25, 27–28, 29, 31, 37,
40, 41
Ledermann, Minna, 108
Lehár, Franz, The Merry Widow, 21
Leibowitz, René, 10
Lendvai, Ernő, 54n.27, 120
Lengyel, Melchior (Menyhért), 6, 53n.8,
144n.6, 149–71
Lesznai, Anna, 33, 46, 47, 49
Liszt, Franz, 45, 61–62n.118, 120, 249,
273n.2, 290; Totentanz, 250
Loos, Adolf, 36
Lowell, Amy, 99n.12
Lukács, György, 6, 12, 46–47, 49, 138–
40, 147nn. 38 and 42, 148n.49, 149

Madarász, Viktor, 27
Maeterlinck, Maurice, 121, 122, 124–
25, 128–31, 132–35, 136–37, 138,
143, 145n.18, 146nn. 20 and 22,
147n.30
Magyari, Imre, 109
Mahler, Gustav: First Symphony, 187
Mann, Thomas, 3, 8, 11, 55n.31, 99n.15
Mannheim, Karl, 6, 46–47, 48–49, 62–
63n.131
Maróti, Géza, 31
Marteau, Henri, 250
Martinů, Bohuslav, 109, 110
Medgyaszay, István, 28
Menasce, Jacques de, 114
Mengelberg, Willem, 269
Menuhin, Yehudi, 114, 116
Mihalovich, Odön von, 13
Mihály, András, 94
Milhaud, Darius, 21, 110, 111, 239n.6;
String Quartet No. 4, 287
Miloss, Aurel, 166

Molnár, Antal, 84–85, 94, 181–83, 185, 191, 192
Moodie, Alma, 287, 289n.18
Móricz, Zsigmond, 19–20, 22, 57nn. 53, 55, and 58
Morris, William, 30
Mozart, Wolfgang Amadeus, 182, 186, 232, 249, 276
Munkácsy, Mihály, 26, 27
Murillo, Bartolomé Esteban, 43–45, 61n.116
Murray, William, 257–58

Nagy, Sándor, 31
Nietzsche, Friedrich, 122
Nirschy, Emília, 271

Oláh, Gusztáv, 171n.69
Oláh Tóth, Elza, 209, 226n.19
Oláh Tóth, Emil, 243
Oláh Tóth, Éva, 243–45
Olbrich, Joseph Maria, 8, 27

Palotai, Vili, 254
Pártos, Ödön, 254
Pásztory, Ditta (Mrs. Béla Bartók), 66, 184–85, 186, 195, 203, 235, 243, 244, 245, 248, 260, 261, 262, 263
Péntek, Mrs. Janos, 255
Perger, Richard von, 41
Perle, George, 54n.26
Perrault, Charles, 134, 146n.28
Pethő, Bertalan, 80
Pfitzner, Hans, 7, 38, 286, 287, 288n.12, 289n.18; Sonata for Violin and Piano, 287; Violin Concerto, 289n.18
Picasso, Pablo, 237
Pleasants, Henry, 110
Popper, David, 17
Popper, Leo, 46
Pósa, Lajos, 38
Poulenc, Francis, 239n.6
Prévost, Arthur, 76
Primrose, William, 261
Prokofiev, Sergey, 94, 111
Prunières, Henry, 173, 239n.6, 285–86

Rácz, Aladár, 288n.15
Ravel, Maurice, 239n.6, 249, 285, 291; Duo for Violin and Cello, 287; Piano Trio, 287; Scarbo, 73; Tzigane, 288n.4

Reger, Max, 14, 15, 24
Reiner, Fritz, 106, 203, 220–25, 227n.31, 258
Reinhardt, Max, 122, 150, 158, 163, 165
Reinitz, Béla, 162, 170n.54
Rembrandt, 237
Respighi, Ottorino, Ballad of the Gnomes, 284, 288n.7
Révai, József, 94
Révész, Géza, 163, 164–65
Revueltas, Silvestre, 110
Richter, Hans, 41
Rimsky-Korsakov, Nikolay Andreyevich, 175, 176, 177
Rippl-Rónai, József, 27
Rosenwald, Hans, 102
Roussel, Albert, 239n.6, 285
Ruskin, John, 30

Sanders, Ivan, 130, 134, 139
Sándor, Emma. See Gruber, Mrs. Henrik
Sándor, László, 233
Scarlatti, Alessandro, 235, 284
Schillings, Max von, 8
Schoenberg, Arnold, 3, 4, 6, 7, 8–9, 11, 12, 14, 15, 21, 24, 51, 52n.4, 53nn. 13 and 17, 55n.35, 61n.118, 66, 79, 80, 108, 110, 116, 182, 232, 237, 249, 276, 278, 285, 287
Schreker, Franz, 287, 289n.17
Schulhof, Andrew, 104, 221, 227n.33, 259
Schumann, Robert, 141, 249
Scriabin, Alexander, 131–32
Sereghy, Elemér, 274n.12
Serly, Tibor, 110
Shostakovich, Dmitry, 94, 109, 110, 111–12, 113; Seventh Symphony, 7, 55n.33, 112
Sibelius, Jean, 109, 110, 111
Simmel, Georg, 48
Simonffy, Kálmán, 84, 98n.5
Slonimsky, Nicolas, 83
Somlyó, György, 96, 301, 302
Spivakovsky, Tossy, 114
Steindl, Imre, 27
Stevens, Halsey, vii, 134–35
Strauss, Richard, 7, 8, 13, 14, 15, 23, 24, 38, 39, 40, 41, 120, 180, 232, 268, 291; Also sprach Zarathustra, 37, 43;

Strauss *(cont.)*
 Aus Italien, 39; *Ein Heldenleben,* 37;
 Sinfonia domestica, 61n.106; *Till Eulen-*
 spiegels lustige Streiche, 284
Stravinsky, Igor, vii, 3, 4, 6, 8, 9, 11, 14,
 15, 21, 24, 52n.3, 66, 79, 92, 108, 110,
 111, 172–97, 232, 235, 237, 238,
 239n.6, 249, 260, 278, 279, 285–87,
 288n.15; *Concerto en Ré* for violin and
 orchestra, 196; Concerto for Piano and
 Winds, 173–74, 183, 185, 186–87,
 188–91, 192, 193; Concerto for Two
 Solo Pianos, 195, 196; Etude for piano,
 196; *The Firebird,* 173, 174–75, 177,
 191, 193, 284; Four Russian Songs,
 179; Four Studies for Orchestra,
 288n.10; *L'histoire du soldat,* 196,
 199n.43; *Les Noces,* 173, 196, 287; *Pe-*
 trouchka, 173, 174, 183, 193, 194, 196,
 285, 287; Piano-Rag-Music, 179, 285;
 Pribaoutky, 179; *Renard,* 196, 286; *The*
 Rite of Spring (Le Sacre du printemps),
 173, 178, 180, 191, 286; *Le Rossignol,*
 173, 174, 178, 180, 183, 286; Sonata
 for Piano, 173; "Study for Pianola"
 ("Madrid," Study for Orchestra No. 4),
 285, 286, 288n.10; *Suite de Pulcinella,*
 196; *Symphonies d'instruments à vent,*
 196; Three Tales for Children, 179
Strindberg, August, 121, 131, 145–
 46n.19, 149
Suchoff, Benjamin, 64, 102–3
Sullivan, Louis, 36
Szabó, Ferenc, 251–52
Szabolcsi, Bence, 57n.53, 61n.118, 155–
 56, 290
Szabolcsi, Miklós, 134, 143
Szabolcsi, Miksa, 290
Szántó, Tivadar, 18, 57n.52
Székely, Júlia, viii
Székely, Zoltán, 238, 239nn. 6 and 7,
 248, 250
Szélenyi, István, 253
Szenkár, Jenő, 287, 288n.16
Szigeti, Joseph, 18, 103, 104, 105, 106,
 250
Szinyei, Pál Merse, 27
Szőllősy, András, 68
Szymanowski, Karol, 13–14, 55n.35,
 239n.6, 285

Takács, Jenő, 214–15, 226n.22, 267
Tallián, Tibor, vii, 69
Tango, Egisto, 271, 272, 275n.18
Taruskin, Richard, 173
Thomán, István, 17, 31, 161, 163, 246,
 253, 273n.2
Thomson, Virgil, 115
Tolnay, Charles de, 46
Toscanini, Arturo, 269
Tóth, Aladár, 24, 88, 90–91, 99n.19,
 180, 183–84, 185, 187, 191–92, 282

Ujfalussy, József, vii

Vas, István, 92
Vecsey, Ferenc, 267
Veress, Sándor, 251–57, 274n.3; Piano
 Sonata No. 1, 254; Solo Violin Sonata,
 254
Vinkó, József, 153, 167n.10
Voit, Éva, 243–45
Voit, Pál, 245
Vollmoeller, Karl, 158

Wagner, Otto, 27
Wagner, Richard, 13, 18, 23, 40, 82,
 139, 140, 180, 232; *Der fliegende Hol-*
 länder, 140; *Lohengrin,* 140; *Parsifal,*
 134; *Das Rheingold,* 187; *Tristan und*
 Isolde, 43
Wagner, Siegfried, 38
Waldbauer, Imre, 80, 238, 239n.6, 245–
 46, 269
Waldbauer, Iván, 68
Wangenheim, Annette von, 154
Webern, Anton, 4, 6, 11, 21, 66
Wedekind, Frank, 131
Weicher, John, 114
Weisshaus, Imre. *See* Arma, Paul
Weissmann, Adolf, 14, 50–51, 52
Wilson, Paul, 54n.26
Wood, Sir Henry, 284, 288n.6
Wormser, André, 159

Ybl, Miklós, 27

Zichy, Mihály, 27
Ziegler, Márta (Mrs. Béla Bartók), 73,
 178, 203, 226n.11

List of Contributors

Leon Botstein is President of Bard College, where he is also Leon Levy Professor in the Arts and Humanities. He is the author of *Judentum und Modernität* (Vienna, 1991) and *Music and Its Public: Habits of Listening and the Crisis of Modernism in Vienna, 1870–1914* (Chicago, forthcoming) as well as Music Director of the American Symphony Orchestra and Editor of *Musical Quarterly*.

Balázs Dibuz, a scholar of Hungarian language and culture, is a doctoral student of comparative literature at Indiana University in Bloomington. He is currently completing a dissertation on twentieth-century Eastern European literature.

Susan Gillespie is Vice President for Public Affairs at Bard College. She has contributed translations of music-historical essays, reviews, letters, and memoirs to each of the previous volumes published in conjunction with the Bard Music Festival. Her translations of essays by Theodor W. Adorno have appeared in *Grand Street*, *Raritan*, and *Musical Quarterly*.

Peter Laki, a musicologist and native of Budapest, has served as Program Annotator for the Cleveland Orchestra since 1990. He has lectured on Bartók at conferences in Hungary, France, and the United States.

Vera Lampert, a musicologist, served for many years on the staff of the Bartók Archives in Budapest. She has published a catalog of folk songs used in Bartók's folk music and is the editor of the essays on folk music in the forthcoming collected edition of Bartók's writings. She is currently a music librarian at Brandeis University in Waltham, Massachusetts.

Carl Leafstedt is Assistant Professor of Music at Southwestern University in Georgetown, Texas. He recently completed a doctoral dissertation on *Bluebeard's Castle* at Harvard University and published an article on *Bluebeard* in *College Music Symposium*.

Klára Móricz is a musicologist and former staff member of the Bartók Archives in Budapest. She has published articles on Bartók and Schubert and is currently completing a doctoral dissertation on Bartók's Concerto for Orchestra at the University of California, Berkeley.

David E. Schneider, a musicologist and clarinetist, is currently completing a doctoral dissertation on Bartók and neoclassicism at the University of California, Berkeley.

László Somfai is head of the Bartók Archives in Budapest and Professor of Musicology at the Liszt Academy of Music. He has been a visiting professor at several American universities and is a frequent contributor to international scholarly music journals as well as Editor-in-Chief of the Béla Bartók Critical Edition. His latest book on Bartók is soon to be published in English by the University of California Press.

Tibor Tallián is Professor of Musicology at the Liszt Academy of Music and a former associate at the Bartók Archives in Budapest. He is the author of *Béla Bartók: The Man and His Work* (Budapest: Corvina, 1981), published in English, as well as works on the *Cantata profana* and on Bartók's American reception.